Canada's Missing Dimension

Science and History in the Canadian Arctic Islands
Volume II

Edited by C.R. Harington

Published by: Canadian Museum of Nature

 Shell Canada Limited

 Petro-Canada Inc.

Polar Continental Shelf Project

Published by the:

Canadian Museum of Nature
Ottawa, Canada K1P 6P4

Catalogue No. NM98-13/2-1990E

Publié par le :

Musée canadien de la nature
Ottawa, Canada K1P 6P4

No de catalogue NM98-13/2-1990E

Available by mail order from:

Canadian Museum of Nature
Direct Mail Section
P.O. Box 3443, Station "D"
Ottawa, Canada K1P 6P4

L'editeur remplit les commandes postales
adressées au :

Musée canadien de la nature
Section des commandes postales
C.P. 3443, Succursale D
Ottawa, Canada K1P 6P4

Printed in Canada

Imprimé au Canada

ISBN: 0-660-13054-8

ISBN: 0-660-13054-8

Cover: Cape Clarence, Somerset Island
Painting by Brenda Carter, Merrickville, Ontario

Brenda Carter sketches: title page, pages 21, 40, 53,
54, 90, 104, 130, 152, 160, 186, 254, 258, 271, 272,
293, 326, 404, 420, 441, 442, 470, 510, 513, 543, 567,
589, 607, 632, 664, 676, 694, 742, 767, 792, 805, 834

Peinture de la couverture : Cap Clarence, Île
Somerset, de Brenda Carter (Merrickville, Ontario)

Esquisses de Brenda Carter : page titre, p. 21, 40,
53, 54, 90, 104, 130, 152, 160, 186, 254, 258, 271, 272,
293, 326, 404, 420, 441, 442, 470, 510, 513, 543, 567,
589, 607, 632, 664, 676, 694, 742, 767, 792, 805, 834

CONTENTS

Volume I

FRESHWATER, SEA AND ICE

THE ATMOSPHERE

THE PLANTS

Volume II

HUMAN PREHISTORY

HISTORY AND RECENT EXPEDITIONS

INDEX   835

INSECTS

ARCTIC INSECTS: INSTRUCTIVE DIVERSITY

H.V. Danks[1]

Abstract: Although the terrestrial arthropod fauna of the Arctic is much less diverse than that of temperate areas, about 860 species in 150 families have been reported from the Canadian Arctic Islands. Many others await discovery or description. More than 550 species occur even in the Queen Elizabeth Islands. Many characteristics of these arctic insects have evident adaptive advantages in environments with short, cool, unpredictable summers and long cold winters. The composition of the fauna, and its habitat and trophic characteristics are closely related to the availability of resources. Most northern arthropods are saprophages, predators, or ectoparasites of vertebrates. Most species are confined to superficial soil and shallow waters warmed by the sun, or to the skin of warm-blooded hosts. Although arctic habitat-structure and food supply for insects therefore are limited relative to temperate situations, the diversity of insects and of their adaptations is very instructive. There are many interactions between arthropods and vertebrates, other invertebrates and plants; and resources are transferred between different habitats. Therefore, the biotic communities of the Canadian Arctic Islands are surprisingly complex.

Résumé: Malgré une diversité nettement plus restreinte par rapport à ce qui est observé dans les régions tempérées, les arthropodes terrestres de l'Arctique canadien comptent près de 860 espèces regroupées en 150 familles. Il en reste beaucoup d'autres à découvrir ou décrire. Plus de 550 espèces sont trouvées même dans les îles Reine-Elisabeth. Ces insectes ont nombre de caractéristiques offrant des avantages sur le plan de l'adaptation à un milieu aux étés courts, frais et imprévisibles ainsi qu'aux longs hivers froids. La composition faunique, l'habitat et les caractéristiques trophiques sont liés de près à la disponibilité des ressources. La plupart des arthropodes septentrionaux sont des saprophages, des prédateurs ou des ectoparasites de vertébrés. La plupart des espèces sont confinées à la couche superficielle du sol et aux eaux peu profondes réchauffées par le soleil ou encore à la peau d'hôtes à sang chaud. Bien que la structure des habitats arctiques et que les sources alimentaires imposent des contraintes additionnelles par rapport à la situation en zone tempérée, la diversité des insectes et leurs adaptations sont fort révélatrices. Il existe beaucoup d'interactions entre les arthropodes et les vertébrés, les autres invertébrés et le monde végétal, et les ressources sont transférées d'un habitat à l'autre. Les communautés d'êtres vivants de l'archipel arctique ont donc une complexité étonnante.

INTRODUCTION

Terrestrial arthropods, the spiders, mites, springtails, etc., and especially the insects, are the most diverse macroscopic organisms in non-marine ecosystems everywhere. More than 2,000 species of terrestrial arthropods are known from regions beyond the northern limit of trees in North America, and as many more are anticipated to await discovery or description (Danks 1981). Although much more limited than in temperate regions, such diversity provides unrivalled opportunities to investigate how and why the composition of northern faunas is modified relative to more southern regions, how the successful arctic species are adapted, and how northern ecosystems function.

The Arctic Islands contain a more limited arthropod fauna than the North American Arctic as a whole because they lack many mainland elements and those that just enter

---

[1] Biological Survey of Canada (Terrestrial Arthropods), Zoology Division, National Museum of Natural Sciences, Ottawa, Ontario K1P 6P4

tundra habitats. The characteristically arctic species found in the islands provide especially instructive insights into Arctic ecological communities.

FAUNAL COMPOSITION AND DISTRIBUTION

About 860 species of terrestrial arthropods have been reported from the Arctic Islands, 660 of them named to species (Table 1). Based on knowledge of such faunas in Canada as a whole (Danks 1979), nearly 2,000 species might eventually be expected there. Final figures cannot currently be obtained, except in a few well-known groups such as mosquitoes, because specialized collecting has been sporadic, and difficult taxonomic problems remain in many groups (especially among the mites and parasitic Hymenoptera). Nearly three-quarters of the reported species are insects. The Queen Elizabeth Islands contain only 553 reported species of arthropods. By contrast, a well-known temperate area (Great Britain) of about the same size contains over 22,000 species of insects alone (Stubbs 1982).

The diversity of arthropods in the Arctic, therefore, is greatly reduced. Certain groups are much better represented than others (Table 2). Compared with tropical or temperate regions, for example, beetles (Coleoptera) are much less well-represented in the Arctic, whereas flies (Diptera) are very well-represented there (Table 3). A small number of families is characteristic: well over half the species of arthropods of the Arctic Islands belong to only about 25 of the 155 families present (Table 4); more than 910 families of terrestrial arthropods occur in Canada (Danks 1979). Such selective arctic representation occurs at all taxonomic levels, including the genus. It suggests generalizations, developed in later sections, about the habitats and ecology of species that are successful.

Well over half of the individual species of the Arctic Islands are Holarctic, occupying large expanses of similar terrain that characterize the northern high latitudes (Danks 1981). Both tundra specialists (e.g. Figure 1) and more widely distributed forms (e.g. Figure 2) occur there. Specific collecting has not been sufficiently systematic to discover if there are detailed patterns of occurrence or absence from one island to another. Such patterns would, in any case, depend on island size and other features. Moreover, most arctic insects are concentrated in "oases" (Babb and Bliss 1974) where topography and other factors ameliorate

TABLE 1: NUMBER OF NAMED SPECIES OF MAJOR GROUPS OF TERRESTRIAL ARTHROPODS REPORTED FROM CANADA AND ARCTIC REGIONS.

GROUP	NUMBER OF NAMED SPECIES			
	CANADA[1]	ARCTIC CANADA AND ALASKA[2]	CANADIAN ARCTIC ISLANDS[2]	QUEEN ELIZABETH ISLANDS[2]
Arachnida (spiders)	1,256	112	30	18
Acari (mites)	1,915	261	120	77
Collembola (springtails)	295?	97	49	44
Insecta (insects)	29,976	1,468	462	242
Total named species[3]	33,672	1,943	661	381
Minimum species present[4]	------	2,237	858	553

[1] Based on Danks (1979).
[2] Based on Danks (1981), with additions published through 1986, and this paper.
[3] Including minor groups not listed.
[4] Including additional reported, unnamed taxa.

TABLE 2: *DIVERSITY OF TERRESTRIAL ARTHROPODS IN ARCTIC NORTH AMERICA.*

GROUP	ARCTIC NORTH AMERICA		CANADIAN ARCTIC ISLANDS		QUEEN ELIZABETH ISLANDS	
	no. of genera	min. no of spp.[1]	no. of genera	min. no of spp.[1]	no. of genera	min. no of spp.[1]
Arachnida	233	474	119	213	83	137
Araneae	54	117	19	30	13	18
Opiliones	1	1	0	0	0	0
Acari	178	354	99	179	69	117
Mesostigmata	34	76	20	45	13	29
Prostigmata	65	125	45	76	36	56
Acaridiae	7	7	3	3	3	3
Oribatei	72	146	31	55	17	29
Chilopoda	3	3	0	0	0	0
Protura	2	2	0	0	0	0
Collembola	49	110	29	61	27	55
Insecta	691	1,650	313	588	202	363
Ephemeroptera	11	22	1	3	0	0
Odonata	3	6	0	0	0	0
Plecoptera	13	20	3	3	0	0
Orthoptera[2]	4	6	1[4]	1[4]	1[4]	1[4]
Phthiraptera[3]	32	52	25	44	18	32
Hemiptera	43	66	17	18	6	6
Thysanoptera	5	5	3	3	3	3
Neuroptera	2	2	0	0	0	0
Coleoptera	86	203	21	30	9	13
Diptera	246	787	131	307	93	199
Siphonaptera	13	20	4	6	4	4
Lepidoptera	87	162	39	62	19	23
Trichoptera	20	25	3	3	1	1
Hymenoptera	124	272	63	106	47	80
Others[4]	2	2	2	2	1	1

[1] Minimum species includes named species, plus those reported as taxonomically distinct from named species within a genus, and species in genera without named species.
[2] Including Grylloptera.
[3] Based partly on host-ranges.
[4] Adventitious.

Sources as in Table 1.

TABLE 3: COMPOSITION OF THE INSECT FAUNA IN DIFFERENT REGIONS, TO SHOW CHANGES IN THE REPRESENTATION OF SELECTED ORDERS (BASED ON NAMED SPECIES REPORTED).

ORDER	PERCENTAGE OF REGIONAL FAUNA				
	WORLD[1]	NORTH AMERICA[1]	ARCTIC NORTH AMERICA[2]	CANADIAN ARCTIC ISLANDS[2]	QUEEN ELIZABETH ISLANDS[2]
(Total No. of Insect spp.)	(762,659)	(93,728)	(1,468)	(462)	(242)
Orthoptera	4	1	0.4	0.2[3]	0.4[3]
Phthiraptera	0.4	0.4	4[4]	9[4]	14[4]
Hemiptera	7	12	4	4	3
Coleoptera	39	32	13	6	3
Diptera	16	19	50	53	61
Lepidoptera	15	12	11	12	10
Hymenoptera	14	19	13	11	10

[1] Borror *et al.* (1981).
[2] Danks (1981) with additions through 1986, and this paper.
[3] Adventitious.
[4] Based partly on host-ranges.

448

TABLE 4: *FAMILIES OF TERRESTRIAL ARTHROPODS CHARACTERIS-TIC OF THE CANADIAN ARCTIC ISLANDS*[1].

TAXA	MINIMUM NUMBER OF SPECIES		
	ARCTIC NORTH AMERICA	CANADIAN ARCTIC ISLANDS	QUEEN ELIZABETH ISLANDS
Arachnida			
Erigonidae	39	15	13
Acari			
Ascidae	25	16	13
Rhagidiidae	14	11	6
Ceratozetidae[2]	26	11	5
Collembola			
Hypogastruridae	18	12	11
Isotomidae	45	27	26
Mallophaga			
Philopteridae	32	28	22
Hemiptera			
Aphididae	21	13	3
Diptera			
Tipulidae[2]	50	16	6
Chironomidae	157	108	94
Simuliidae	26	10	0
Mycetophilidae	15	10	9
Sciaridae	14	11	11
Anthomyiidae	139	28	6
Muscidae	162	48	21
Lepidoptera			
Papilionoidea (5 fams.)	54	21	7
Geometridae	22	9	2
Noctuidae	35	12	6
Hymenoptera			
Tenthredinidae	34	21	14
Braconidae	22	11	6
Ichneumonidae	162	60	49
Total (families listed)	1,112 (26)	498 (26)	330 (26)
Total (all families)	2,237 (341)	858 (155)	553 (118)

[1] Characteristic families are any that include more than 1% of the fauna of the islands.

[2] Figures revised from unpublished information assembled for the Ceratozetidae by V.M. Behan-Pelletier (personal communication) and for Tipulidae by F. Brodo (personal communication).

Sources as in Table 1.

local temperatures and moisture supply (Corbet 1972). These oases support rich sedge-moss meadows and associated faunas even in the High Arctic.

Some broad distributional patterns can be recognized within the islands. Faunas are especially impoverished in the northwestern archipelago,

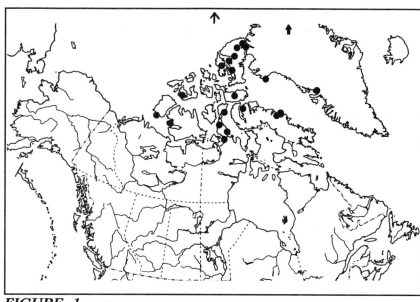

FIGURE 1:   Distribution of the lycosid spider <u>Alopecosa exasperans</u>, a species confined to the northern Arctic (Danks 1981).

where low summer temperatures are associated with smaller island size and greater cloud-cover (Danks 1980; see Figures 1, 2). Southern Banks and Victoria islands in the west and southern Baffin Island in the east have richer vegetation (including shrubs that are absent farther north), and a number of island species have been collected only in this southern "low arctic" zone (e.g. Figure 3). The southern richness and northwestern impoverishment of the fauna suggest that ecological, chiefly climatic, factors control its predominantly north-south zonation in the Canadian Arctic Islands. On the mainland, on the other hand, the influence of historical

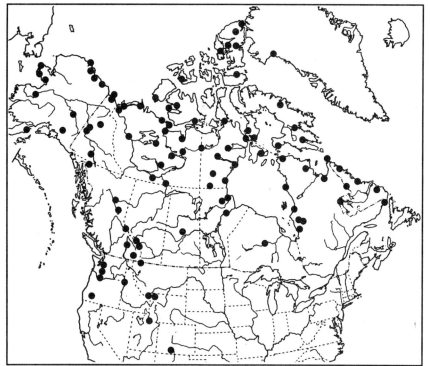

FIGURE 2:   North American distribution of the mosquito <u>Aedes</u> <u>impiger</u>, a species found in arctic, alpine and boreal habitats (Danks 1981).

450

factors is easier to see because many east-west range limits coincide with the Mackenzie River and Hudson Bay (e.g. Figure 3), which are major dispersal-barriers for tundra forms. Some western forms extend to Banks Island.

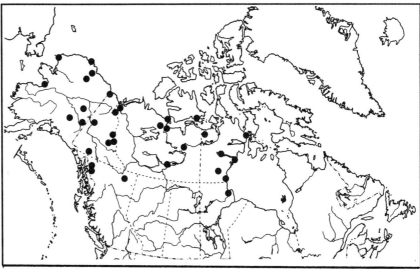

FIGURE 3: North American distribution of the stonefly <u>Nemoura arctica</u>, a species just entering the southern Canadian Arctic Islands, and confined to the west of Hudson Bay (Danks 1981).

ADAPTATIONS

Most northern species are clearly adapted to arctic conditions. The adaptations conform to the short, cool growing-season, to the limited diversity of habitats, and to other features of northern environments. Characteristic adaptations of arctic arthropods are listed in Table 5. However, some cosmopolitan arthropod species appear to occupy microsites in the surface soil that are relatively warm and moist - even in polar deserts (Addison 1975).

Colour and Structure

Arctic species commonly are darker than temperate relatives (Danks 1981, p. 266), usually because they contain the black pigment melanin. Such dark colours facilitate the absorption of solar heat. Therefore, arthropods tend to be darker northward, unlike vertebrates in which white (air-filled) pelage enhances insulation and white plumage or pelage provides camouflage in snow-covered terrain.

Some larger species such as bumble bees and some flies and caterpillars are especially hairy. The hairs allow solar radiation to warm the body, but prevent convective heat loss (Kevan *et al.* 1982).

Structures in several arctic species are reduced, usually because their functions are curtailed by the harsh conditions. For example, especially on the mainland some northern species of fungus gnats, midges, crane flies and moths are brachypterous (wings reduced) or

451

TABLE 5: SUMMARY OF ADAPTATIONS OF ARCTIC ARTHROPODS[1].

ADAPTATION	SUPPOSED ADVANTAGE	EXAMPLES
Colour and Structure		
Melanism	Solar heat gain in cool environments	Many insects
Hairiness	Conserves heat gained, in larger insects	Many insects
Robustness	Moisture conservation	Some ichneumonids
Reduced wings	Energy saved (flight limited by cool conditions)	Several flies, moths
Reduced eyes	Normally nocturnal forms are active in light in Arctic	Some noctuid moths
Reduced antennae of males	Detection of females during swarming flights is not necessary when flight is limited	Some chironomid midges
Small size	Species can use limited resources	Many species
Activity and Behaviour		
Selection of warm habitats for activity or progeny production	Activity allowed in cool environments in locally favourable sites	Most species
Selection of protected sites for overwintering (e.g. plant clumps)	Protection against cold or wind-driven snow	Many species (but some species overwinter fully-exposed)
Low temperature thresholds for activity	Activity allowed in cool environments	Several species
Opportunistic activity	Activity whenever temperatures are permissive	Bumble bees, midges, etc.
Basking	Heat-gain in sunshine	Many butterflies, etc.
Physiology and Metabolism		
Adjustment of metabolic-rate	Life-processes continue in cool environments	Some species of various groups
Resistance to cold	Survival during cold winters	All species
Resistance to starvation	Survival when food supplies are unpredictable	Some moth larvae, some springtails

- - - - - - - - - -

TABLE 5: (cont'd)

ADAPTATION	SUPPOSED ADVANTAGE	EXAMPLES
Life-Cycles and Phenology		
Multi-year life-cycles	Life-cycle completed although resources are limited	Moth larvae, midge larvae, etc.
Rapid development	Life-cycle completed before winter supervenes	Mosquitoes, etc.
Abbreviation of normally complex life-cycles	Life-cycle completed before winter supervenes	Aphids, etc.
Earliest possible emergence in spring	Life-cycle completed before winter supervenes	Midges, etc.
Brief and synchronized reproductive activity	Life-cycle completed before winter supervenes	Many moths, etc.
Dormancy	Activity stops before damaging winter cold; individuals held dormant through summer to emerge as early as possible the next spring	Chironomid midges, etc.
Prolonged dormancy for more than one season	"Insurance" against a summer unsuitable for reproduction	Various species of flies, moths, sawflies, etc.
Food Range		
Autogeny (development of eggs without a blood-meal in biting flies)	Offsets shortage of hosts; or short season	Mosquitoes
Different foodplants	Survive although a particular foodplant is absent	Few species
Polyphagy	Survival despite low density of foods	Many species, especially saprophages/detritivores and predators
Genetic Adaptations		
Parthenogenesis	Reduced mating activity in harsh conditions; well-adapted genotypes buffered against change	Midges, black flies, caddisflies, mayflies, scale insects, etc.

[1] See references in text and Danks (1981).

apterous (wings absent) - generally in the females (Downes 1962; Vockeroth 1972). The dynamics of dispersal or the need to move in sand and litter habitats can select for aptery, but in arctic forms the reduction of wings appears to be correlated chiefly with temperatures that often are below the threshold for flight activity. In some groups of nematocerous Diptera, forms with reduced antennae are found in the Arctic. Those groups normally mate in male swarms (Downes 1969), and females are detected in flight by the antennal sense organs of the males. In the Arctic, swarming of many species of chironomids is curtailed or eliminated, and some species have reduced antennae (Downes 1969; Oliver 1984).

Activity and Behaviour

Behavioural traits often are correlated with structural adaptations that must be interpreted through observations of living animals. For example, many arctic butterflies (Kevan and Shorthouse 1970; Kingsolver 1985), flies (Kevan 1973), bugs (Böcher 1972) and other arctic insects bask in sunshine especially on flowers, raising the body-temperature for activity (e.g. Roland 1982), and accelerating growth or the development of eggs (Corbet 1965, for mosquitoes). This type of basking behaviour is closely tied to the location of dark pigments. For example, some butterflies bask laterally to the sun's rays with their wings closed; the wings have melanic undersides. Some species open the wings and expose the dark uppersurfaces to the sun. Other butterflies expose the body, or settle on dark, warm substrates. Optimum temperatures for activity sometimes are high and narrowly limited, so that thermal regulation by behavioural means such as basking is surprisingly precise and effective (Sherman and Watt 1973). In other insects, however, activity can continue even when temperatures are low - down to 0°C in some midges and stoneflies.

Whether or not they have specialized basking behaviour, nearly all arctic arthropods, even those confined to widespread soil microsites, actively select the most favourable habitats. Moist, vegetated patches contain much higher populations of mites and springtails than the intervening barrens. High Arctic butterflies are active chiefly in a small number of sheltered, insolated depressions (Kevan and Shorthouse 1970). The finely-tuned responses of High Arctic mosquitoes result in the deposition of eggs only in the warmest sheltered south-facing sites, and only during the warmest part of the day (Corbet and Danks 1975). These sites first become free of snow the following spring, when the eggs hatch.

454

Most High Arctic insects show opportunistic daily activity whenever it is warm enough (Danks and Oliver 1972B), unlike their temperate relatives with temporally-fixed activities. Such behaviour allows the insects to take advantage of warm, calm periods at any time, although normally activity is greatest near midday when incoming solar radiation is highest (Fox and Stroud 1986).

Physiology and Metabolism

Some arctic species continue development at temperatures that would prevent development of typical temperate species. For example, threshold temperatures for development are only about 1°C in tundra mosquito larvae (Haufe and Burgess 1956); metabolic-rates at a given temperature apparently are higher in some arctic aquatic (but not terrestrial) forms compared to southern forms (Scholander et al. 1953). However, many arctic species have no such lower thresholds or higher rates of development, and they grow only during periods with relatively favourable conditions.

Particularly interesting physiological adaptations have been reported in some High Arctic caterpillars (*Gynaephora* species: Ryan and Hergert 1977; Kukal, this volume) and springtails (*Hypogastrura "tullbergi"*: Addison 1977 - actually *H. concolor* : Fjellberg 1986). Individuals of these species can survive for a whole summer virtually without feeding, allowing them to overcome temporary shortages of scattered food resources.

All arctic species resist cold. Many polar mites and springtails supercool, remaining unfrozen even at very low temperatures (Block and Sømme 1982; Sømme 1981). Most High Arctic insects are freezing-tolerant, surviving extracellular ice formation in the tissues. Many can survive low temperatures during spring and fall activity, as well as during prolonged winter dormancy. Nevertheless, survival while frozen is temperature- and time-dependent (Danks 1978). Arthropod cold-hardiness depends on the build-up of cryoprotectants, usually polyhydric alcohols such as glycerol, but also in some species macromolecules such as peptides. However, the cold-hardiness of relatively few arctic species has been investigated in detail (Ring 1981, 1983). Different species have different mechanisms of cold-hardiness. Cold-hardiness also tends to give resistance to anoxia and desiccation.

Life Cycles and Phenology

In markedly seasonal environments, development coincides with suitable conditions through various linked adaptations that control: (1) the time taken to complete a generation; (2) the seasonal position of active, especially reproductive, stages; and (3) the onset and completion of dormancy.

Some species develop very slowly in the Arctic where heat and food are limited. Few High Arctic species complete a generation in a single year. For example, up to 14 years are required in the moth *Gynaephora groenlandica* (Kukal and Kevan 1987), 7 years in two *Chironomus* species (Butler 1982), 6-8 years in the crane fly *Tipula carinifrons* (Lantsov 1982), 6-7 years in spiders (Leech 1966), and perhaps many years in some species of mites (Ryan 1977). Such long-lived species pass the winter in early stages, continuing to feed the following year.

Other species, especially those from warm shallow ponds or other warm insolated microsites, develop rapidly, and even in the Arctic are univoltine - completing a generation each year. Arctic mosquitoes develop from egg to egg (Corbet and Danks 1973); arctic aphids (W.R. Richards 1963), bumble bees (K.W. Richards 1973), and other species (e.g. MacLean 1983) also are univoltine.

Because the arctic summer is so short, most arctic insects emerge at the earliest opportunity in spring, and reproduce rapidly before winter returns. Although different species appear at somewhat different intervals (depending largely on the overwintering stage), and the same species may experience different conditions and hence emerge at different times in different habitats, most life-cycles end in early, synchronized adult emergence.

Such a pattern of "spring" emergence in some species depends on dormancies that prevent development from being completed during the summer. All individuals, except those that can proceed to emergence immediately after the thaw without further feeding, defer emergence until the following year (Danks and Oliver 1972A, for chironomid midges). Also, many species, emerging with well-developed ovaries, deposit eggs almost at once (Oliver 1968, for *Gynaephora*).

In several kinds of arctic insects, dormancy keeps a fraction of individuals inactive for more than one winter (and the intervening summer(s)) (e.g. Chernov 1978). Such a strategy buffers the population against occasional summers that are unsuitable for development or reproduction, an unpredictability well-known in the Arctic Islands (cf. Danks 1983).

456

Food Range

Many arctic species are detritivores or predators - trophic groups that tend to contain generalists eating widely available foods. Many arctic herbivores are polyphagous. Such broad food-ranges might be expected where food supplies are limited. However, this generalization is not easy to establish, since many other species (especially herbivores and parasitoids) are specialists, taking into the Arctic the specialist habits typical of their temperate relatives (Danks 1981, 1987). The caterpillar of the butterfly *Rumicia phlaeas* eats *Oxyria* in the Arctic Islands, but elsewhere feeds on *Rumex*, a plant that is absent from the High Arctic. Very few such switches of existing foodplants (correlated with floral changes in the Arctic) are known.

Genetic Adaptations

Parthenogenetic insects are commoner in the Arctic (Table 5) than farther south. Such parthenogenesis has been correlated with the difficulty of mating in harsh conditions. In particular, it has been considered as an adaptation to buffer well-adapted genotypes by minimizing genetic responses to change (Danks 1979; Downes 1965). In unpredictable environments like the Arctic, the rapid elimination of temporarily "unsuitable" genes would usually prove to be disadvantageous.

General Considerations

The characteristic adaptations of arctic insects demonstrate that many species survive in these harsh habitats by avoiding, rather than confronting, the worst conditions. For example, they seek out the most favourable habitats or microsites. The various adaptations of arctic insects, though characteristic, are known also from certain temperate species. They are merely more frequent (e.g. parthenogenesis), more conspicuous (e.g. basking) or better-developed (e.g. hairiness) in the Arctic. Moreover, adaptations may be assembled into complementary sets, such as simultaneous adaptations for overwintering, cold-hardiness and seasonal control of the life-cycle.

One especially interesting discovery, possible only because arthropods are so diverse, is that the ecological pressures of arctic life can be overcome in markedly different ways. Even though long life-cycles, generalist feeding and small size appear to be prevalent in High Arctic arthropods, species with annual life-cycles, specialist herbivores and large insects also occur there. Apparently, such adaptive types depend chiefly on the previous evolutionary history of a given group that may allow appropriate adaptations to be developed. The selective taxonomic composition of the arctic fauna accords with this view.

Many linked or alternative adaptations therefore can meet particular arctic conditions. Studies of adaptation are very difficult, and may lead to spurious conclusions because the adaptive value of a given trait often cannot be directly tested but may be determined only by correlation and the apparent "reasonableness" of the supposed adaptation. Paradoxically, in a few groups, intensive studies in a small area have been carried out in the Arctic in more detail than for comparable temperate situations (e.g. Corbet and Danks 1973). Typically, however, detailed biological information on many more arctic species is required to refine existing generalizations about the range of foods eaten, the prevalence of metabolic adaptations, and the control of emergence and activity by ambient conditions.

ECOLOGICAL RELATIONSHIPS

Habitats

The habits of most arthropods are relatively consistent at the generic and even the family level, so that general habitats can be inferred from the taxonomic composition of the fauna as well as from collecting data. Aquatic habitats contain more arthropods in the Arctic than elsewhere (Figure 4). Indeed, most of the production in arctic terrain comes from fresh waters (Ryan 1977; Welch 1973). Terrestrial forms therefore comprise a smaller fraction of arctic than of other faunas. Terrestrial species that

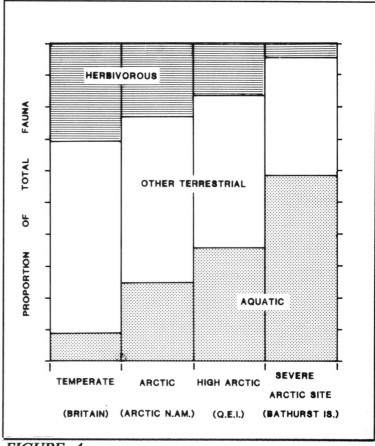

FIGURE 4: Relative representation of herbivorous, non-herbivorous terrestrial, and aquatic species of insects in a temperate area and in arctic areas of different severity (based on named species; data from Danks 1987).

458

live in or near the soil are relatively well represented, however, especially in moist sites, whereas the number of herbivores is markedly reduced - to a much greater degree than the plants on which they could feed (Danks 1987). Ectoparasites living on vertebrate hosts also are well represented in the Arctic (cf. Phthiraptera, Table 3).

Most of the arctic fauna therefore comes from three types of habitat: (1) shallow waters; and (2) surface soils - both of which are warmed by the sun; and (3) the skin of warm-blooded animals. In the Canadian Arctic Islands, these are the most hospitable habitats available to arthropods.

Trophic Groups

Like ecosystems everywhere, arctic systems are decomposition-based, and saprophagous arthropods (those feeding on decaying matter) are especially significant in the Arctic. Poor drainage above permafrost conserves terrestrial nutrients; locally rich sites are associated with vertebrates (see below); substantial allochthonous ("foreign") detritus enters aquatic habitats. Members of several characteristic families from the Arctic Islands (Table 4) are primarily saprophagous in the broad sense. They eat detritus, algae, bacteria or fungal hyphae in decaying material, for example. Saprophages include the larvae of flies such as tipulids, chironomids, mycetophilids, sciarids and anthomyiids, as well as many springtails and oribatid mites. These groups are the dominant arctic arthropods in soils and fresh waters.

Nevertheless, arthropods belonging to all of the other trophic groups occur in the Arctic. Arthropod predators of other small arthropods are common, especially in the nutrient-rich sites where prey is most abundant. Predators are found in the characteristic families Erigonidae (spiders), Rhagidiidae (mites) and Muscidae (flies), especially in the genus *Spilogona*. Parasitoids of other arthropods are well represented in the Arctic Islands (ichneumonid wasps, other parasitic wasps and tachinid flies). Parasitoids act in many ways like predators because they grow in or on a single host, which eventually is killed and consumed. Arctic parasitoids attack butterflies and moths, sawflies, flower flies, fungus gnats, muscoid flies, and other groups. Reported or potential parasitoids are known from the Arctic Islands for all kinds of insects that commonly occur there.

Ectoparasites of vertebrates are characteristic arctic arthropods. They feed on blood, tissue fluids, or hair. Most species of birds and mammals have at least one or two species each of more or less host-specific lice and fleas, as well as several kinds of mites (Emerson 1972; Holland 1985; Lindquist *et al* 1979). There are also some less specific ectoparasites.

Phytophagous (plant-eating) forms are present in the Arctic, although rather poorly represented (see above). Their poor representation seems to be due chiefly to general climatic constraints that eliminate species living in less favourable microhabitats, rather than to the absence of food plants or to other particular insect-plant interactions (Danks 1987).

Although the trophic status of many arctic arthropods is known generally, we lack detailed biological information for most species. Whether some saprophages are detritivores or fungivores, for example, is not known. Some crane fly larvae eat living as well as dead plant tissues (Striganova 1982). Moreover, some species commonly associated with sites of decay and assumed to be saprophages may even be predators exploiting locally high populations of other species. By the same token, detailed taxonomic and ecological work is required to understand the ecological significance (as opposed to the basic habits) of most species.

Ecosystem Function

All of the trophic groups known from temperate areas are found in arctic systems; the total fauna, including arthropods, is ecologically as well as taxonomically diverse. Therefore, arctic ecosystems are not the "simple" systems sometimes claimed.

Trophic interactions demonstrate the many interdependencies in arctic ecosystems (Table 6). Various arthropods depend on vertebrates directly as hosts, on their dung or carrion, or live in nests or burrows of vertebrates. Populations of saprophages such as blow flies can depend on the lemming cycle, for example (Chernov 1973). A few species, such as the winter gnat (*Trichocera columbiana*) and perhaps some anthomyiid flies, appear to be obligate lemming associates, since adults have been collected only in or near burrow entrances. Grazing and trampling by vertebrates may alter the suitability of habitats for arthropods. In turn, vertebrates, especially arctic migratory birds, depend heavily on supplies of arthropod food to rear their young.

Some arthropods depend on plants. A characteristic fauna of butterflies and moths, sawflies, aphids, and several other insects consumes plant tissues. A much larger number of insects visits flowers for nectar or pollen. Bumble bees use pollen to rear their brood; large flies such as the muscid (*Pogonomyioides segnis*) eat pollen (McAlpine 1965B). At

460

TABLE 6 : SUMMARY OF SOME TROPHIC INTERACTIONS BETWEEN ARTHROPODS AND OTHER ORGANISMS[1].

INTERACTION BETWEEN AND	NOTES	EXAMPLES
Arthropods / Vertebrates	Many saprophages depend on dung or carrion	Blow flies, some crane flies, midges, etc.
	Some saprophages scavenge in vertebrate nests or burrows	Some mites, etc.
	Ectoparasites attack birds and mammals	Characteristic biting flies, many ectoparasitic mites, fleas, lice, etc.
Arthropods / Plants	Several arthropod herbivores eat arctic plants	Butterflies, moths, sawflies, aphids, etc.
	Many arctic arthropods visit flowers, for nectar or pollen (and for basking or other activities)	Bumble bees, various flies; mosquitoes, butterflies, etc.
Arthropods / Arthropods	Parasitoids of insects such as sawflies and moths are numerous	Chiefly ichneumonids, but also chalcidoids, braconids, etc.
	Some mites are ectoparasitic on arthropods	Water mites
	A few nest parasites steal nest-provisions or parasitize established nests of related species	The bumble bee (<u>Bombus hyperboreus</u>)
	Many predators attack other arthropods	Diving beetles, several kinds of flies, and other insects. Small predatory mites and spiders are especially numerous
Arthropods / Microflora	Arthropods stimulate decomposition	Many mites, springtails
Vertebrates / Arthropods	Many arctic birds prey on arthropods, especially to feed the young; non-insectivorous adults also supplement their diet with insects	Large or abundant prey are most used (e.g. crane flies, some midges), but also Collembola and other small arthropods
	Mammals and fishes eat insects	
Invertebrates/Arthropods	Invertebrate parasites of arthropods are widely distributed in the Arctic	Microsporidians, mermithids, etc.

[1] See references in text and Danks (1981).

Lake Hazen on Ellesmere Island, more than a hundred species of insects are known to visit flowers for nectar (Kevan 1970, 1973). In turn, insects pollinate flowers. Although relatively few arctic plants rely exclusively on insect-pollination, seed set of many species is enhanced thus, and several of the most abundant High Arctic plants (e.g. *Salix arctica*, *Dryas integrifolia* and *Saxifraga oppositifolia*) are chiefly insect-pollinated (Danks 1987; Kevan 1972).

Parasitism and predation among arthropods generate further cross-links in arctic systems. Some predators consume arthropods from different trophic levels, leading to complex food-chains. Moreover, both short food-chains (e.g. plant detritus, to tipulid larvae, to insectivorous birds) and long food-chains (e.g. dead plant material, to fungi, to springtails, to small spiders, to large spiders, to shore birds, to egg predators such as arctic foxes) occur.

Arthropods also interact with the soil microflora in helping to cycle nutrients. Decomposition by the microflora is much faster in the presence of arthropods than in their absence (Douce and Crossley 1982; Whittaker 1974). Preliminary evidence suggests that arthropods stimulate decomposition by comminuting litter into smaller fragments that can be invaded by microflora, inoculating the fragments with microflora, and by grazing microfloral populations to levels of exponential growth (Douce and Webb 1978).

Cross-links in arctic systems also transfer resources from one habitat to another (Table 7). Some of the trophic links that do this, enhanced by the polyphagy of many species, have already been discussed. Larvae from aquatic habitats are transported to terrestrial habitats when they are eaten by birds, or when they move there after emerging as adults. Conversely, some terrestrial insects, especially weakly-flying forms, are washed into aquatic habitats along with terrestrial detritus. Terrestrial groups from lower ground are transported to nest sites by foraging birds. Many soil-dwelling larvae emerge as aerial adults.

Climatic fluctuations, and other factors influenced by them, lead to great variation from year to year in the supply of resources and in the abundance of particular insect species (e.g. Danks 1981, p. 119). Repeated sampling in one place over long intervals to assess such changes would be worthwhile (McAlpine 1965A).

Various processes therefore act together to generate complexity within arctic systems. A partial food-web emphasizing arthropod components (Figure 5) illustrates this complexity.

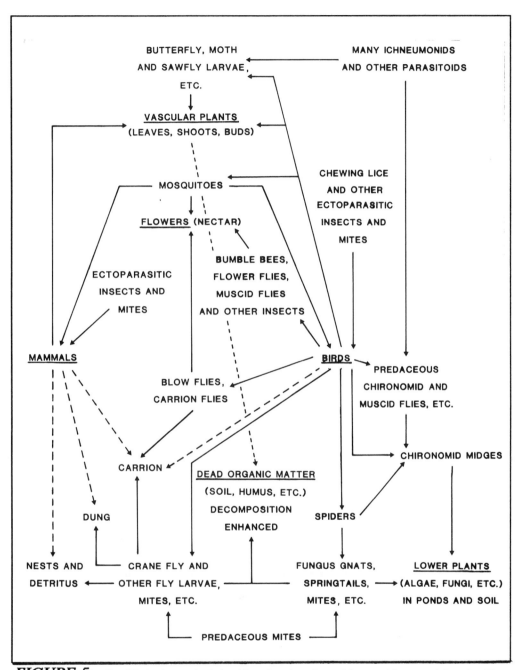

FIGURE 5: Simplified scheme of relationships of arctic arthropod faunas with some of the other biota (interaction except with arthropods, and some links in decomposer food-chains, are omitted for clarity). Solid arrows show trophic dependencies; broken arrows show products of organisms.

TABLE 7: GROUPS THAT TRANSFER RESOURCES BETWEEN HABITATS.

SAMPLE GROUPS	RESOURCES TRANSFERRED FROM	RESOURCES TRANSFERRED TO
Various aquatic groups eaten by birds	Aquatic (and marine and littoral) habitats	Terrestrial habitats
Chironomid midges and other aquatic groups	Aquatic larvae	Terrestrial adults
Predatory fly-larvae (e.g. _Spilogona_)	Chironomids in aquatic and semi-aquatic substrates	Aerial habitat of _Spilogona_ adults
Many groups	Dead arthropods in terrestrial habitats	Detritus in aquatic habitats, especially at snow-melt
Many groups	Terrestrial habitats	Aquatic habitats (by accident)
Crane flies	Larvae in soil-layers	Adults in aerial zone
Various terrestrial groups eaten, especially by young birds	Arthropod habitats in valleys	Nest sites on ridges
Some vertebrate ectoparasites	Vertebrate blood and tissues	Excrement or eggs in soil and aquatic substrates
Blow flies, etc.	Vertebrate carrion and dung on surface	Aerial adults after development of decomposer larvae
Larvae of butterflies, moths, etc.	Plant leaves, etc.	Leaf fragments and excrement in litter
Many groups	Nectar of flowers	Used for flight by aerial adults
Bumble bees, some other groups	Pollen of flowers	Aerial adults

CONCLUSIONS

Hundreds of arthropod species live in the Canadian Arctic Islands. They are involved in northern ecosystems in the majority of the many ways known for temperate zones. Their general numerical importance makes them significant as decomposers, pollinators, food for birds, etc.

The fauna is much poorer than farther south, but considerable diversity remains. Species that survive on the Arctic Islands do so by means of coincident advantages for life in harsh environments, such as particular habitats, foods, and life-cycles, most of which stem from pre-existing habits of given taxonomic groups. Species that live in surface soil or shallow freshwaters warmed by the sun, or on the skin of warm-blooded animals, are most common. Species that rely on generally available food such as detritus are prevalent. Diverse adaptations to cold and unpredictable climates are best developed in the arctic species, even though they occur in insects from other life zones.

Interactions among arthropods and other arctic organisms are especially noteworthy. The arctic ecosystem is not simple. Diversity is high enough to retain considerable complexity, but complexity that can perhaps be more easily studied because diversity is not overwhelming. However, studies must be based on careful taxonomic and biological work. Most of the conclusions presented in this paper stem from basic collecting and identification of the fauna, because the major clues about habitats and trophic structure were derived from an analysis of faunal composition. Further basic taxonomic work, especially concerning inadequately known groups like the mites and parasitic Hymenoptera, therefore is necessary.

More ecological data on arctic species are also required. For example, generalist feeders appear to be especially common, presumably correlated with shortage of resources. So are denizens of generalized soil microsites. However, such generalists may not be as prevalent as present data suggest, since the detailed habits of many species of the decomposer-complex are unknown. In gathering such data, studies of arctic systems are likely to prove of wide ecological interest.

ACKNOWLEDGEMENTS

I thank Dr. V.M. Behan-Pelletier and Dr. R.A. Ring for helpful comments on the manuscript.

REFERENCES

Addison, J.A. 1975. Ecology of Collembola at a High Arctic site, Devon Island, N.W.T. Ph.D. thesis, University of Calgary, Calgary, Alberta. 212 pp.

_____. 1977. Population dynamics and biology of Collembola on Truelove Lowland. In: Truelove Lowland, Devon Island, Canada: A High Arctic Ecosystem. Edited by: L.C. Bliss. University of Alberta Press, Edmonton. pp. 363-382.

Babb, T.A. and L.C. Bliss. 1974. Susceptibility to environmental impact in the Queen Elizabeth Islands. Arctic 27(3):234-237 and map.

Block, W. and L. Sømme. 1982. Cold hardiness of terrestrial mites at Signy Island, Maritime Antarctic. Oikos 38(2):157-167.

Böcher, J. 1972. Feeding biology of *Nysius groenlandicus* (Zett.) (Heteroptera:Lygaeidae) in Greenland. Meddelelser om Grønland 191(4):1-41.

Borror, D.J., D.M. DeLong, and C.A. Triplehorn. 1981. An introduction to the study of insects. Fifth Edition. Saunders, Philadelphia, Toronto, etc. 827 pp.

Butler, M.G. 1982. A 7-year life cycle for two *Chironomus* species in arctic Alaskan tundra ponds (Diptera:Chironomidae). Canadian Journal of Zoology 60(1):58-70.

Chernov, Yu. I. 1973. [A review of the trophic groups of invertebrates in typical tundra subzone of western Taimyr.] In: [Biogeocenoses of Taimyr Tundra and Their Productivity, Volume II]. Edited by: B.A. Tikhomirov and N.V. Matveyeva. (In Russian - English translation in International Tundra Biome Translation 12:18-29).

_____. 1978. [Adaptive features of the life cycles of tundra zone insects.] Zhurnal Obshchei Biologii 39(3):394-402. (In Russian, English summary).

Corbet, P.S. 1965. Reproduction in mosquitoes of the High Arctic. Proceedings of the 12th International Congress of Entomology (London, 1964):817-818.

_____. 1972. The microclimate of arctic plants and animals, on land and in fresh water. Acta Arctica 18:1-43.

Corbet, P.S. and H.V. Danks. 1973. Seasonal emergence and activity of mosquitoes in a High Arctic locality. Canadian Entomologist 105(6):837-872.

_____. 1975. Egg-laying habits of mosquitoes in the High Arctic. Mosquito News 35(1):8-14.

Danks, H.V. 1978. Modes of seasonal adaptation in the insects. I. Winter survival. Canadian Entomologist 110(11):1167-1205.

_____. (Editor). 1979. Canada and its insect fauna. Memoirs of the Entomological Society of Canada 108:1-573.

_____. 1980. Arthropods of Polar Bear Pass, Bathurst Island, Arctic Canada. Syllogeus 25:1-68.

_____. 1981. Arctic arthropods. A review of systematics and ecology with particular reference to the North American fauna. Entomological Society of Canada, Ottawa. 608 pp.

_____. 1983. Extreme individuals in natural populations. Bulletin of the Entomological Society of America 29(1):41-46.

_____. 1987. Insect-plant interactions in arctic regions. Revue d'entomologie du Québec 31(1-2)[1986]:52-75.

Danks, H.V. and D.R. Oliver. 1972A. Seasonal emergence of some High Arctic Chironomidae (Diptera). Canadian Entomologist 104(5):661-686.

_____. 1972B. Diel periodicities of emergence of some High Arctic Chironomidae (Diptera). Canadian Entomologist 104(6):903-916.

Douce, G.K. and D.A. Crossley, Jr. 1982. The effect of soil fauna on litter mass loss and nutrient loss dynamics in arctic tundra at Barrow, Alaska. Ecology 63(2):523-537.

Douce, G.K. and D.P. Webb. 1978. Indirect effects of soil invertebrates on litter decomposition: elaboration via analysis of a tundra model. Ecological Modeling 4(4):339-359.

Downes, J.A. 1962. What is an arctic insect? Canadian Entomologist 94(2):143-162.

_____. 1965. Adaptations of insects in the Arctic. Annual Review of Entomology 10:257-274.

_____. 1969. The swarming and mating flight of Diptera. Annual Review of Entomology 14:271-298.

Emerson, K.C. 1972. Checklist of the Mallophaga of North America (North of Mexico). Desert Test Center, Dugway, Utah; Part I. Suborder Ischnocera. 200 pp.; Part II. Suborder Amblycera, 118 pp.; Part III. Mammal host list, 28 pp.; Part IV. Bird host list, 216 pp.

Fjellberg, A. 1986. Collembola of the Canadian High Arctic. Review and additional records. Canadian Journal of Zoology 64(10):2386-2390.

Fox, A.D. and D.A. Stroud. 1986. Diurnal rhythms in a snow-surface springtail (*Isotoma violacea*, Collembola) and its predators in Equalungmuit Nunaat, West Greenland. Pedobiologia 29(6):405-412.

Haufe, W.O. and L. Burgess. 1956. Development of *Aedes* (Diptera:Culicidae) at Fort Churchill, Manitoba, and prediction of dates of emergence. Ecology 37(3):500-519.

Holland, G.P. 1985. The fleas of Canada, Alaska and Greenland (Siphonaptera). Memoirs of the Entomological Society of Canada 130:1-631.

Kevan, P.G. 1970. High Arctic insect-flower relations; the interrelationships of Arthropoda and flowers at Lake Hazen, Ellesmere Island, N.W.T., Canada. Ph.D. thesis, University of Alberta, Edmonton, Alberta. 399 pp.

_____. 1972. Insect pollination of High Arctic flowers. Journal of Ecology 60(3):831-847.

_____. 1973. Flowers, insects, and pollination ecology in the Canadian High Arctic. Polar Record 16(104):667-674.

Kevan, P.G., T.S. Jensen, and J.D. Shorthouse. 1982. Body temperatures and behavioral thermoregulation of High Arctic woolly-bear caterpillars and pupae (*Gynaephora rossii*, Lymantriidae:Lepidoptera) and the importance of sunshine. Arctic and Alpine Research 14(2):125-136.

Kevan, P.G. and J.D. Shorthouse. 1970. Behavioural thermoregulation by High Arctic butterflies. Arctic 23(4):268-279.

Kingsolver, J.G. 1985. Butterfly thermoregulation: organismic mechanisms and population consequences. Journal of Research on the Lepidoptera 24(1):1-20.

Kukal, O. and P.G. Kevan. 1987. The influence of parasitism on the life history of a High Arctic insect, *Gynaephora groenlandica* (Wocke) (Lepidoptera:Lymantriidae). Canadian Journal of Zoology 65(1):156-163.

Lantsov, V.I. 1982. [Adaptive characteristics of the life cycle of the arctic crane fly *Tipula carinifrons* (Diptera:Tipulidae).] Ekologiya 13(1):71-76. (Translation in Soviet Journal of Ecology 13(1):67-71).

Leech, R.E. 1966. The spiders (Araneida) of Hazen Camp 81°49'N, 71°18'W. Quaestiones Entomologicae 2(2):153-212.

Lindquist, E.E., B.D. Ainscough, F.V. Clulow, R.C. Funk, V.G. Marshall, H.H.J. Nesbitt, B.M. O'Connor, I.M. Smith, and P.R. Wilkinson. 1979. Acari. In: Canada and Its Insect Fauna. Edited by: H.V.Danks. Memoirs of the Entomological Society of Canada 108:252-290.

MacLean, S.F., Jr. 1983. Life cycles and the distribution of psyllids (Homoptera) in arctic and subarctic Alaska. Oikos 40(3):445-451.

McAlpine, J.F. 1965A. Insects and related terrestrial invertebrates of Ellef Ringnes Island. Arctic 18(2):73-103.

_____. 1965B. Observations on anthophilous Diptera at Lake Hazen, Ellesmere Island. Canadian Field-Naturalist 79(4):247-252.

Oliver, D.R. 1968. Insects. In: Science, History and Hudson Bay, Volume I. Edited by: C.S. Beals and D.A. Shenstone. Energy, Mines and Resources Canada, Ottawa. pp. 416-436.

_____. 1984. Male dimorphism in an arctic chironomid. Memoirs of the American Entomological Society 34:235-240.

Richards, K.W. 1973. Biology of *Bombus polaris* Curtis and *B. hyperboreus* Schonherr at Lake Hazen, Northwest Territories (Hymenoptera:Bombini). Quaestiones Entomologicae 9(2):115-157.

Richards, W.R. 1963. The Aphididae of the Canadian Arctic (Homoptera). Canadian Entomologist 95(5):449-464.

Ring, R.A. 1981. The physiology and biochemistry of cold tolerance in arctic insects. Journal of Thermal Biology 6:219-229.

_____. 1983. Cold tolerance in Canadian arctic insects. In: Plant, Animal and Microbial Adaptations to Terrestrial Environments. Edited by: N.S. Margaris, M. Arianoutsou-Faraggitaki, and R.J. Reiter. Plenum Press, New York. pp. 17-29.

Roland, J. 1982. Melanism and diel activity of alpine *Colias* (Lepidoptera, Pieridae). Oecologia (Berlin) 53(2):214-221.

Ryan, J.K. 1977. Synthesis of energy flows and population dynamics of Truelove Lowland invertebrates. In: Truelove Lowland, Devon Island, Canada: A High Arctic Ecosystem. Edited by: L.C. Bliss. University of Alberta Press, Edmonton. pp. 325-346.

Ryan, J.K. and C.R. Hergert. 1977. Energy budget for *Gynaephora groenlandica* (Homeyer) and *G. rossii* (Curtis) (Lepidoptera:Lymantriidae) on Truelove Lowland. In: Truelove Lowland, Devon Island, Canada: A High Arctic Ecosystem. Edited by: L.C. Bliss. University of Alberta Press, Edmonton. pp. 395-409.

Scholander, P.F., W. Flagg, V. Walters, and L. Irving. 1953. Climatic adaptation in arctic and tropical poikilotherms. Physiological Zoology 26(1):67-92.

Sherman, P.W. and W.B. Watt. 1973. The thermal ecology of some *Colias* butterfly larvae. Journal of Comparative Physiology 83(1):25-40.

Sømme, L. 1981. Cold tolerance of alpine, arctic, and antarctic Collembola and mites. Cryobiology 18:212-220.

Striganova, B.R. 1982. [Food relationships of soil larvae of crane flies (Diptera, Tipulidae) in the arctic tundra.] Zoologicheskii Zhurnal 61(4):535-542. (In Russian, English summary).

Stubbs, A.E. 1982. Conservation and the future for the field entomologist. Proceedings and Transactions of the British Entomological and Natural History Society 15(3-4):55-67.

Vockeroth, J.R. 1972. A new nearctic genus of Mycetophilidae (Diptera) with a stenopterous female. Canadian Entomologist 104(10):1529-1533.

Welch, H.E. 1973. Emergence of Chironomidae (Diptera) from Char Lake, Resolute, Northwest Territories. Canadian Journal of Zoology 51(11):1113-1123.

Whittaker, J.B. 1974. Interactions between fauna and microflora at tundra sites. In: Soil Organisms and Decomposition in Tundra. Edited by: A.J. Holding, O.W. Heal, S.F. MacLean, Jr, and P.W. Flanagan. Tundra Biome Steering Committee, Stockholm. pp. 183-196.

Eureka Aug 17

470

Illustrated by Brenda Carter

CRANE FLIES (DIPTERA:TIPULIDAE) OF THE ARCTIC ISLANDS

Fenja Brodo[1]

Abstract: Sixteen species of Tipulidae occur on the Canadian Arctic Islands. They are a distinct Arctic element; their combined, known distributions are restricted to Arctic, Boreal and Alpine regions in North America. The largest populations and greatest concentration of species is in the Low Arctic. Seven species are known from the High Arctic, and the distributions of six of these extend to Ellesmere Island. The High Arctic species tend to be more common with the broadest distributions. At least four of the High Arctic species are circumpolar.

As with most other insects, there is an inverse correlation with species richness and latitude. However, the proportion of Tipulidae with respect to the entire insect fauna remains roughly the same.

Arctic Island Tipulidae may have evolved during the Pleistocene and possibly in high-altitude wetlands south of the ice sheets, as well as in several of various refugia postulated.

Résumé: On trouve seize espèces de Tipulidés sur les îles de l'Arctique canadien. Elles constituent un élément distinct de l'Arctique, et leurs distributions connues combinées sont limitées aux régions arctique, boréale et alpine de l'Amérique du Nord. Les plus vastes populations et les plus grandes concentrations d'espèces se retrouvent dans le Bas-Arctique. On en connaît sept espèces dans le Haut-Arctique et la distribution de six d'entre elles s'étend jusqu'à l'île Ellesmere. Les espèces du Haut-Arctique tendent à être plus connues, et avoir les plus larges distributions. Au moins quatre espèces du Haut-Arctique sont présentes tout le tour du pôle.

Comme dans le cas de la plupart des insectes, il y a une relation inverse entre la richesse en espèces et la latitude. Cependant, la proportion de Tipulidés dans toute la faune entomologique reste sensiblement la même.

Les Tipulidés des îles de l'Arctique peuvent avoir évolué pendant le Pléistocène et, peut-être, dans les terres humides en altitude au sud des nappes de glace, de même que dans plusieurs des divers refuges naturels envisagés.

INTRODUCTION

Crane flies are a more important and more conspicuous faunal element as one goes northward. The number of crane fly species, indeed of most insects, declines rapidly with increasing latitude, but this phenomenon is offset in the crane flies by the enormous populations attained by several species. The sudden appearance of large numbers of tipulids is a characteristic of the Arctic (Chernov 1985; Holmes 1966; MacLean 1975). Yet possibly because these flies are not particularly beautiful and pose no threat to humanity, their biology, species-composition and distribution are poorly known (Teskey 1979, p. 396).

An interest in the Tipulidae and the presence of over 2,000 unsorted Arctic Tipulidae in the Canadian National Collection (CNC) prompted this study. My purpose was to determine which species of crane flies occur in the Canadian Arctic Islands, and to assess their distributions and morphological and geographical affinities. I was also interested in

---

[1] Research Associate, National Museum of Natural Sciences, Ottawa, Ontario K1P 6P4

determining the thoroughness and extent of the collecting records with a view to suggesting where further collecting might be profitable.

SPECIES COMPOSITION AND DISTRIBUTION

Sixteen species of Tipulidae are listed from the Canadian Arctic Islands (Table 1). Although this represents an addition of only two species, we now have a far better understanding of the distributions of these species. Previous to this study and that of *Prionocera* (Brodo 1987), collections from only seven Arctic Island localities had been recorded: Clyde, Baffin Island (Alexander 1947); Nettilling Lake, Baffin Island (McDunnough 1929); Cornwallis Island (Bruggemann 1958); Ellesmere Island (Lake Hazen) (Bruggemann 1958; Oliver 1963); Melville Island (Winter Harbour) (Kirby 1824); Prince Patrick Island (Mould Bay) (Bruggemann 1958); and Southampton Island (Alexander 1934). By contrast, information from over 40 Arctic Island localities is included in this study, as well as additional collection data and literature records from mainland northern Canada, Alaska and Greenland.

The combined, known distributions of the 16 species of the Arctic Archipelago are shown in Figure 1. These species form a distinctly northern element. They are almost exclusively restricted to the Arctic and Boreal regions, except for one species discussed below. None of these species can be considered rare, and many are common and widespread in the Arctic. By contrast, I have recorded several species on the basis

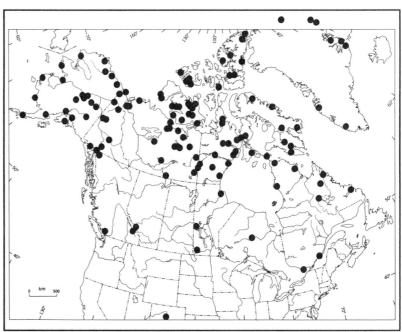

FIGURE 1: Combined distribution records of the 16 Tipulidae species recorded from the Canadian Arctic Archipelago.

TABLE 1: KNOWN RANGES OF CRANE FLIES OF THE CANADIAN ARCTIC ISLANDS.

SPECIES	ECOSYSTEMS							NEARCTIC			PALEARCTIC	
	Temperate	Alpine	Boreal Forest	Boreal Forest-Tundra	Low Arctic	Mid Arctic	High Arctic	West of Hudson Bay	East	Greenland	West of Urals	East
Erioptera (Symplecta) hybrida complex	x		x	x	x		x	x	x	x	x	
Erioptera (Symplecta) sp.					x			x				
Dactylolabis rhicnoptiloides (Alexander)				x	x	x	x	x	x		x	x
Nephrotoma lundbecki (Nielsen)			x	x	x	x	x	x	x	x	x	x
Prionocera ominosa (Alexander)				x	x	x		x	x		x	x
Prionocera recta Tjeder			x	x	x	x		x	x		x	x
Prionocera ringdahli Tjeder			x		x	x		x	x		x	x
Tipula (Angarotipula) parrioides (Alexander)[1,2]			x	x	x	x		x	x		x?	x?
Tipula (Arctotipula) besselsi Osten Sacken			x	x	x	x	x	x		x	x	x
Tipula (Arctotipula) suttoni Alexander					x	x		x	x			
Tipula (Arctotipula) thulensis Alexander			x		x	x	x	x	x			
Tipula (Arctotipula) tribulator Alexander					x	x		x	x			
Tipula (Pterelachisus) diflava Alexander			x		x	x		x	x			
Tipula (Pterelachisus) hewitti Alexander[3]			x	x	x	x	x	x	x			
Tipula (Pterelachisus) hollandi Alexander			x	x	x	x		x	x			
Tipula (Vestiplex) arctica Curtis			x	x	x	x	x	x	x	x	x	x

1 New records for the Canadian Arctic Islands.
2 May include the Palearctic species tumidicornis Lundström.
3 Includes Tipula macleani Alexander.

473

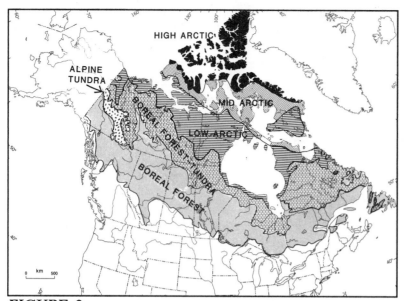

FIGURE 2: Major ecosystems in northern Canada (after Edlund 1984).

of only one or two specimens and from only one locality in the western Alpine Tundra and Boreal Forest-Tundra Regions. The larger collections and localities exhibiting greatest species diversity are in the Mid and Low Arctic (Figure 2). Indeed, all 16 species occur in the Low Arctic, and species diversity drops off rapidly northward. About 50 Tipulidae occur in Boreal and Arctic North America (Danks 1981), but my data indicate that most of these do not extend into the Arctic Islands.

Chernov (1985) suggests that circumboreal species tend to lack close relatives. Probably eight of the Arctic Island species are circumboreal (Table 1). The taxonomic status of two species is still in doubt. Circumboreal *Tipula (Arctotipula) besselsi* has close relatives (see below). The three *Prionocera* species have sister species (Brodo 1987). *Nephrotoma lundbecki*, although placed in the *lundbecki* subgroup, does not seem to have a sister species (Oosterbroek 1980, 1984). The taxonomic relationships of the other species have yet to be decided.

Circumpolarity may be a consequence of out-competing sister species. The presence of circumpolar arctic species having closely related sister species may reflect the youthfulness

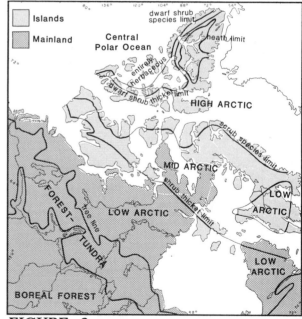

FIGURE 3: Major vegetative zones in the Arctic (modified from Edlund 1986).

of the ecosystem. Little is known of competition and resource partitioning among these species.

The distributional pattern of crane flies on the Arctic Islands is not immediately evident. These flies occur near the northernmost limits of land (Alert, Ellesmere Island), and seem to have invaded most of the islands. However, comparison of Figure 1 with Figure 3 reveals that the "dwarf-shrub species limit" is also a crane fly limit. No tipulids have been found in the entirely herbaceous zone (McAlpine 1964, 1965). As Edlund and Alt (1989) point out, this region experiences the harshest climate in the North. Minimum summer temperatures, heavy cloud-cover and shortest melt-season occur here. Thus the sharply reduced growing season, the scarcity of available water and poorly-developed soils apparently preclude crane fly development. Absence of crane flies is probably not a collecting omission, nor does it reflect lack of time available for invasion of this region.

Similarly, crane flies have not been reported from Bathurst Island despite entomological investigations (Danks and Byers 1972; Bissett 1977; Danks 1980). I have seen no tipulid records from Devon, Prince of Wales and Somerset islands or the long southwestern flank of Baffin Island. Lack of adequate collecting may be the problem. The scattered distributions of suitable habitats (Bruggemann 1958; Danks 1981; Edlund 1983A,B), very short periods of adult emergence and dramatic annual climatic differences (Danks 1981) suggest that many visits over several years are necessary to establish adequate faunal records in the High Arctic. This means that no Arctic Island locality can be considered to have been adequately collected with respect to its crane fly fauna.

ELLESMERE AND AXEL HEIBERG ISLANDS

Six species are known from Ellesmere and Axel Heiberg islands: *Erioptera (Symplecta) hybrida cana* complex, *Erioptera (Symplecta) sp.*, *Dactylolabis rhicnoptiloides*, *Nephrotoma lundbecki*, *Tipula (Arctotipula) besselsi* and *Tipula (Vestiplex) arctica*. A seventh species, *Tipula hewitti*, occurs on northern Baffin Island, and Melville Island in the High Arctic. *Ormosia sp.* was recorded from Lake Hazen, Ellesmere Island (Oliver 1963). I could not locate the specimen and this genus is otherwise not known to occur in the islands.

The climate where these flies were collected is not so severe as the latitude would indicate. Collection sites were in a valley sheltered by an ice-capped mountain chain from the brunt of cold winds off the Central Arctic Ocean to the west. These mountains also act as a barrier to heavy cloud cover from the ocean, thus adding to the "Chinook" or "Foehn"-effect, which lowers the water-vapour content of the air on the leeward side of the mountains. The winter accumulation of snow provides a ready reservoir of water, enhanced by early snow-melt. The albedo effect (reflected solar radiation) is thus minimized (Edlund and Alt 1989). This region has one of the richest floras in the Queen Elizabeth Islands, including diverse wetlands, the domain of several crane flies.

Two species of *Erioptera (Symplecta)* occur on Ellesmere Island. One is apparently a new species and is known only from this locality. The other belongs to a widespread circumpolar complex. The distinctions between the largely Palearctic *hybrida hybrida* complex and the mainly temperate Nearctic *hybrida cana* Walker (Alexander 1955; Theowald 1971) are not clear in the Arctic Island specimens.

ORIGIN AND GEOGRAPHIC AFFINITIES

Most of the Canadian Arctic Islands have been subject to Pleistocene glaciations (Danks 1981), and colonization by plants and animals is relatively recent. The origin and geographic affinities of the Arctic Island species is, therefore, of great interest. As noted above, 15 of the Arctic Island Tipulidae are restricted to the Arctic and Boreal zones, and presumably to the wetter soils therein. Most of these species probably originated before the terrain they now inhabit became available. Presumably they survived the glaciations in one or more of the Arctic Refugia postulated (Danks 1981).

The parallels between Alpine and Arctic tundra forms have long been recognized (Danks 1981). A significant proportion of present arctic taxa may have evolved in alpine conditions (Chernov 1985). Seven of the Arctic Island Tipulidae also occur in Alpine zones (Table 1). *Tipula (V.) arctica* Curtis has been collected in the southern Rocky Mountains, Colorado. *Tipula sacra* Alexander (which I suggest is the sister species to the *besselsi* group discussed below) is known only from the Canadian Rocky Mountains and their foothills.

When the sister-group relationships of the other components of the Arctic Island fauna have been worked out, it is predicted that several other species will show an alpine connection.

TIPULA (ARCTOTIPULA) BESSELSI SPECIES-GROUP

A striking feature of Arctic Tipulidae is the remarkable morphological similarity and broadly overlapping ranges among certain species-groups, making identification difficult. Examples are within the genus *Prionocera* (Brodo 1987), the *Erioptera (Symplecta) hybrida* group, and the *Tipula (Arctotipula) besselsi* group. This contradicts Chernov's (1985) finding that the more closely related the species the more distinct and better differentiated are their ranges.

The *Tipula besselsi* group in North America comprises *besselsi* Osten Sacken, *suttoni* Alexander and *tribulator* Alexander. Apparently only *besselsi* is Holarctic; it seems to be just as closely related to at least two species restricted to the Palearctic (Savchenko 1961). *Tipula besselsi* is also the most widespread of the three species in the Nearctic (Figure 4).

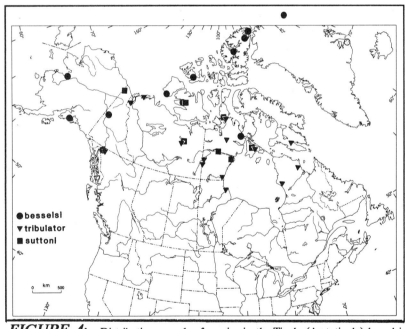

FIGURE 4: Distribution records of species in the <u>Tipula</u> (<u>Arctotipula</u>) <u>besselsi</u> group in North America. Each symbol represents one or more records at that locality.

Usually male crane flies are easier to identify to species than are females. In the *besselsi* group the reverse is true. Females can be distinguished by the shape of a lateral lobe on the terminalia which is usually visible in pinned specimens. On the other hand, the characters that separate the males are often obscured on pinned specimens, making literature references to these species suspect.

477

The distributions of the three species in North America, based on identifications of several hundred specimens in the CNC, are presented (Figure 4). The range-overlaps suggest that these are indeed well-defined species. Furthermore, the striking morphological similarities noted in the *besselsi* group, in the species of the genus *Prionocera*, and in the species in the *Erioptera (Symplecta) hybrida* complex, suggests that within all these species-groups, evolution has occurred relatively recently. Recent differentiation within these species-groups is also suggested by the extraordinary (for Tipulidae, Byers 1961) record of presumably mismatched attempted matings and the hybrid specimen noted in *Prionocera* (Brodo 1987).

The present overlapping ranges of the species within each group probably reflects the shifting ice fronts of the past. Earlier ranges must have been disrupted several times, and possibly some species were eliminated. To what extent current distributional patterns reflect the climate and each species' ability to recolonize ice-free areas is unknown.

Edlund (1984) shows "... that most [High Arctic] vegetation and plant communities are regionally replicated wherever climatic, soil and moisture conditions are the same, ..." and that these communities are not "... merely heterogeneous groups of pioneer species". The distribution of arctic crane flies may be similarly firmly established, but it is also possible that some of these tipulids may be actively extending or reducing their ranges. There is probably a time-lag between the establishment of the plant community and that of the potential fauna.

PROPORTION OF INSECT FAUNA

Table 2 shows the numbers of species of Tipulidae as a percentage of the entire insect fauna of the region in question. Unlike many other families of insects, the proportionate number of species of Tipulidae increases very slightly with latitude. Tipulids comprise a slightly larger percentage of the estimated insect fauna in the Arctic and on the Arctic Islands than in the temperate zone.

In the North, the Tipulidae make up in quantity for their decrease in variety. Where crane flies occur on the Arctic Islands, they usually hatch abruptly and in very large

FAUNAS	CANADA	ARCTIC	CANADIAN ARCTIC ISLANDS	QUEEN ELIZABETH ISLANDS
Total Insect Fauna	66,498[1]	1,805[2]	588[3]	363[3]
Tipulidae	670[1]	50[2]	16	7
Tipulidae/Insect Fauna x 100	1.01%	2.77%	2.72%	1.93%

[1] Danks (1979).
[2] Danks (1981).
[3] Danks (personal communication).

numbers. The shorter, sparser arctic vegetation and the dearth of several other insect groups contribute to their conspicuousness.

ARCTIC ADAPTATIONS

Probably the most important arctic adaptation is the ability of larvae to prolong their life-cycle and develop over several years (MacLean 1973). Thus, they are not decimated by lack of sufficient growing-days in any one year. However, they are vulnerable to predators over a longer period of time. The shortness of summer rather than low temperatures is probably the limiting factor (Pritchard 1983).

Arctic Island Tipulidae tend to be darker and hairier than temperate species. In agreement with Allen's Rule in mammals, the most northern *Prionocera* and *Tipula* (*Arctotipula*) species have the nasus (small snout at the end of the rostrum; Figure 5) much reduced or absent, and relatively shorter, stouter legs.

Several northern tipulids are noted for wing reduction either in both sexes or only in the female (Downes 1965; Byers 1969). None of the species found on the Arctic Islands has this characteristic. Byers (1969) shows that wing reduction is correlated with adult emergence in a cold environment. One would expect, then, to find brachypterous tipulids on the Arctic Islands: their absence is surprising.

479

FIGURE 5: A crane fly (<u>Prionocera</u> <u>recta</u> Tjeder, left side view of anterior parts) found in Canadian Arctic Islands, showing the position of the nasus.

Brachypterous crane flies are probably older than the Pleistocene and, I suggest, evolved at high altitudes, not necessarily at high latitudes. Only the more mobile-winged species have been able to colonize the Arctic Islands.

BIOLOGY AND ECOLOGY

Very little is known of the biological or ecological adaptations of Arctic Island Tipulidae. Studies in Alaska and in Siberia give some clues. These northern tipulids seem to be restricted to wet or moist regions , and the larva is the overwintering stage (Chernov 1985). Most northern crane fly larvae are presumed to be herbivores or saprovores, eating living and decaying plants, mostly sedges, grasses and mosses and the rich algal slime surrounding these plants and covering inorganic substrates (Chernov 1985). Preliminary study of the larvae of *Prionocera* (Brodo 1987) indicates that they have a typical vegetarian-type of caeca, although they have been known to eat tabanid larvae (personal communication , H . J . Teskey). The occasional small worm or other invertebrate probably gets eaten , but apparently accidentally. No truly predatory crane flies have been recorded from the Arctic

Islands, although one such species, *Pedicia hannai antennata* occurs at Point Barrow, Alaska (MacLean 1975). Cold-hardiness in Arctic crane flies has not been studied (Pritchard 1983).

PREDATORS

Fourth-instar tipulid larvae are among the larger invertebrates in the Arctic, and several generations of larvae may coexist because of the prolonged life-cycle. Thus populations of several hundred larvae per square metre have been recorded in the tundra of Alaska and Siberia (MacLean 1975; Lantzov 1984; Chernov 1985). The nesting success of shore birds (e.g. sandpipers, plovers, phalaropes) seems to be linked to this crane fly population. Adult birds eat both crane fly larvae and adults (Holmes and Pitelka 1968; personal communication, G.W. Byers). Egg-laying by these birds is abruptly terminated in early summer just when the availability of adult crane flies is rapidly increasing. The hatching of young chicks is apparently timed to correspond to the maximum abundance of adult insects (Holmes 1966).

Adult crane flies are also eaten by Long-tailed Jaegers, several of the smaller arctic gulls, as well as arctic foxes (Chernov 1985).

The highly synchronous adult hatch noted by many workers in the North is apparently correlated with a minimum threshold temperature of 5°C (Clement in Pritchard 1983). Ironically, this results in a higher biomass in harsher climates because last-instar larvae and pupae of several generations accumulate in the substrate until the favourable temperature is reached. This probably has a predator-swamping effect (MacLean and Pitelka 1971).

CONCLUSIONS

The sixteen tipulid species occurring on the Arctic Islands have broad distributions that probably parallel the development of appropriate soils on the islands. Other than tending to be darker and possibly stouter than their more southern relatives, these species do not have striking morphological adaptations. Their ability to survive in the North is more probably related to a flexible life-cycle, which allows for several years of interrupted larval development, and relatively unspecialized feeding requirements.

Little is known of the biology, ecology and competitive interactions among these species.

ACKNOWLEDGEMENTS

This study was greatly facilitated by the generosity of Dr. George W. Byers, University of Kansas, who provided me with his drawings of several important types. I thank Drs. H.J. Teskey and Jeffrey Cumming, Agriculture Canada, for access to the Canadian National Collection, and the National Museum of Natural Sciences for ample work space.

REFERENCES

Alexander, C.P. 1934. II. Diptera collected on Southampton Island by G.M. Sutton. Trichoceridae and Tipulidae. In: G.M. Sutton. The Exploration of Southampton Island, Hudson Bay. Memoirs of the Carnegie Museum 12, Pt 2, Sect. 4:3-10.

_____. 1947. Undescribed species of crane-flies from the eastern United States and Canada (Diptera:Tipulidae), Part X (1946). Entomological News 58:245-252.

_____. 1955. The crane flies of Alaska and the Canadian Northwest (Tipulidae, Diptera). The genus *Erioptera* Meigen. University of Michigan, Museum of Zoology, Miscellaneous Publications 90:1-33.

Bissett, J. 1977. Preliminary observations on the vascular plants, fungi and insects of Polar Bear Pass, Bathurst Island, N.W.T. 39 pp. (Unpublished report submitted to National Museum of Natural Sciences, Ottawa).

Brodo, F. 1987. A revision of the genus *Prionocera* (Diptera:Tipulidae). Evolutionary Monographs 8:1-93.

Bruggemann, P.F. 1958. Insects and environments of the High Arctic. Proceedings 10th International Congress of Entomology (Montreal, 1956) 1:695-702.

Byers, G.W. 1961. The crane fly genus *Dolichopeza* in North America. University of Kansas Science Bulletin 42(6):665-924.

Byers, G.W. 1969. Evolution of wing reduction in crane flies (Diptera:Tipulidae). Evolution 23(2):346-354.

Chernov, Y.I. 1985. The living tundra. Cambridge University Press, Cambridge. 213 pp. (Translated from Russian by D. Löve).

Danks, H.V. 1980. Arthropods of Polar Bear Pass, Bathurst Island, Arctic Canada. Syllogeus 25:1-69.

_____. 1981. Arctic arthropods. A review of systematics and ecology with particular reference to the North American fauna. Entomological Society of Canada, Ottawa. 608 pp.

Danks, H.V. and J.R. Byers. 1972. Insects and arachnids of Bathurst Island, Canadian Arctic Archipelago. Canadian Entomologist 104:81-88.

Downes, J.A. 1965. Adaptations of insects in the Arctic. Annual Review of Entomology 10:257-274.

Edlund, S.A. 1983A. Bioclimatic zonation in a High Arctic region: central Queen Elizabeth Islands. Geological Survey of Canada, Paper 83-1A:381-390.

_____. 1983B. Reconnaissance vegetation studies on western Victoria Island, Canadian Arctic Archipelago. Geological Survey of Canada, Paper 83-1B:75-81.

_____. 1984. High Arctic plants: new limits emerge. Geos 13(1):10-13.

_____. 1986. Vegetation-geology-climate relationships of western Melville Island, District of Franklin. Geological Survey of Canada, Paper 86-1A:719-726.

Edlund, S.A. and B.T. Alt. 1989. Regional congruence of vegetation and summer climate patterns in the Queen Elizabeth Islands, Northwest Territories, Canada. Arctic 42(1):3-23.

Holmes, R.T. 1966. Feeding ecology of the Red-backed Sandpiper (*Calidris alpina*) in Arctic Alaska. Ecology 47:32-45.

Holmes, R.G. and F.A. Pitelka. 1968. Food overlap among coexisting sandpipers on northern Alaskan tundra. Systematic Zoology 17:305-318.

Kirby, W. 1824. Land invertebrate animals. In: Supplement to the Appendix of Captain Parry's Voyage for the Discovery of a North-West Passage, in the years 1819-1820, Containing an Account of the Subjects of Natural History. Appendix X. Natural History. Murray, London. pp. ccxiv-ccxix.

Lantsov, V.I. 1984. Ecology, morphology and taxonomy of arctic crane-flies of the genus *Prionocera* (Diptera:Tipulidae). Zoologischeskii Zhurnal 43(8):1196-1204. (In Russian).

MacLean, S.F., Jr. 1973. Life cycle and growth energetics of the arctic crane fly *Pedicia hannai antenata*. Oikos 24:436-443.

MacLean, S.F., Jr. 1975. Ecology of tundra invertebrates at Prudhoe Bay, Alaska. In: Ecological Investigations of the Tundra Biome in the Prudhoe Bay Region, Alaska. Edited by: J. Brown. Biological Papers, University of Alaska, Special Report No. 2:115-123.

MacLean, S.F., Jr. and F.A. Pitelka. 1971. Seasonal patterns of abundance of tundra arthropods near Barrow. Arctic 24:19-40.

McAlpine, J.F. 1964. Arthropods of the bleakest barren lands: composition and distribution of the arthropod fauna of the northwestern Queen Elizabeth Islands. Canadian Entomologist 96(1-2):127-129.

_____. 1965. Insects and related terrestrial invertebrates of Ellef Ringnes Island. Arctic 18(2):73-103.

McDunnough, J.H. 1929. Insects from Baffin Island. In: J.D. Soper - A faunal investigation of Southern Baffin Island. National Museum of Canada, Bulletin 53:118-119.

Oliver, D.R. 1963. Entomological studies in the Lake Hazen area, Ellesmere Island, including lists of species of Arachnida, Collembola, and Insecta. Arctic 16:175-180.

Oosterbroek, P. 1979. The western Palaearctic species of *Nephrotoma* Meigen, 1803 (Diptera, Tipulidae). Part 5, Phylogeny and biogeography. Beaufortia 29:311-393.

_____. 1984. A revision of the crane-fly genus *Nephrotoma* Meigen, 1803, in North America (Diptera, Tipulidae). Part II: The non-*dorsalis* species-groups. Beaufortia 34:117-180.

Pritchard, G. 1983. Biology of Tipulidae. Annual Review of Entomology 28:1-22.

Savchenko, E.N. 1961. [Family Tipulidae, Subfamily Tipulinae, Genus *Tipula* L. (Part 1)]. Fauna SSSR No. 79:1-487. (In Russian).

Teskey, H.J. 1979. 42. Diptera. In: Canada and Its Insects Fauna. Edited by: H.V. Danks. Memoirs Entomological Society of Canada No. 108:389-424.

Theowald, Br. 1971. Drei holarktische *Symplecta*-arten (Diptera, Limoniidae). Beaufortia No. 247(19):47-54.

ENERGY BUDGET FOR ACTIVITY AND GROWTH OF A HIGH-ARCTIC INSECT, Gynaephora groenlandica (WOCKE) (LEPIDOPTERA: LYMANTRIIDAE)

Olga Kukal[1]

Abstract: Growth and development of the woolly-bear caterpillar (Gynaephora groenlandica) are confined to a brief period of activity interrupted before each mid-summer of its 14 year life-cycle. Consequently, I investigated the physiological consequences of thermoregulatory and feeding behaviour. Basking is pivotal to larval thermoregulation since it raises body temperature by as much as 25°C above the ambient temperature (T_a ~5°C), which is often below the larval developmental threshold. Larval growth-rate and assimilation efficiency is optimized at T_b ~15°C, whereas at high basking T_b of ~30°C, the assimilation efficiency decreases with increased maintenance metabolism and ingestion-rate. Conversely, at low T_b of ~5°C, the growth-rate is lower as is the rate of ingestion. Changes in metabolic state influence the metabolic-rate; highest in feeding larvae and decreasing progressively for digesting, moving, starved, cold-acclimated and inactive larvae. Influence of temperature on digestion-rate and maintenance metabolism is the likely cause of the feeding behaviour pattern in G. groenlandica. The larvae maximize their assimilation efficiency by selective and seasonal feeding and also by raising their digestion-rate while basking. The larvae undergo "voluntary hypothermia" in order to avoid an energy deficit resulting from high maintenance metabolism during mid-season, when the energy content and food quality of Salix arctica declines. Since behaviours other than basking cause larval T_b to drop, basking plays a central role in the diel and sequential organization of larval behaviour. Movement, other than in search of new feeding sites is minimized, basking time is maximized and feeding is followed by basking. At low ambient temperatures basking prevails. Basking under optimal conditions leads to maximal rates of oxygen consumption at T_b >30°C, whereas below 5°C, oxidative metabolism is depressed. The larvae of G. groenlandica are thermoregulators, able to alter their developmental rate by changes in behaviour and feeding strategy.

Résumé: La croissance et le développement de la Gynaephora groenlandica se limitent à une courte période d'activité qui cesse avant le milieu de l'été, chaque année de son cycle biologique de 14 ans. J'ai donc étudié les conséquences physiologiques des comportements thermo-régulatoires et des comportements alimentaires chez l'espèce. L'exposition au soleil est un élément crucial pour la thermorégulation larvaire, étant donné qu'elle amène une hausse de la température du corps (T_b) qui peut atteindre 25°C au-dessus de la température ambiante (T_a) de ~5°C, ce qui est souvent inférieur au seuil de développement larvaire. Le taux de croissance de la larve et l'efficacité d'assimilation sont optimisés à une T_b de ~15°C, alors qu'à une T_b de ~30°C, l'efficacité d'assimilation diminue et le métabolisme de maintien et le taux d'ingestion sont à la hausse. À l'inverse, si la T_b est de ~5°C, le taux de croissance comme le taux d'ingestion sont plus bas. Des changements de l'état métabolique ont une influence sur le rythme du métabolisme, qui est plus élevé pour les larves qui se nourrissent et baisse graduellement pour celles qui digèrent, celles qui bougent, celles qui sont affamées, celles qui sont acclimatées au froid et celles qui sont inactives. L'influence de la température sur le taux de digestion et le métabolisme de maintien est la cause probable du modèle de comportement alimentaire de la G. groenlandica. Les larves portent au maximum leur efficacité d'assimilation par le biais d'une alimentation saisonnière et sélective et aussi en augmentant leur taux de digestion lors de l'exposition au soleil. Les larves se livrent à une "hypothermie volontaire" afin d'éviter un déficit d'énergie qui serait le résultat d'un métabolisme de maintien élevé en milieu de saison, quand l'apport d'énergie et la qualité de la nourriture du Salix arctica sont moindres. Étant donné qu'il existe des comportements autres que l'exposition au soleil qui amènent une baisse de la T_b, l'exposition au soleil occupe un rôle important dans l'organisation nycthémérale et séquentielle du comportement de la larve. Le mouvement, à part celui effectué lors de la recherche de sites alimentaires, est minimisé, la durée de l'exposition au soleil est maximisé et l'alimentation est suivie de l'exposition au soleil. À des températures ambiantes basses, l'exposition au soleil est l'activité dominante. L'exposition au soleil dans des conditions optimales conduit à des taux maximaux de consommation d'oxygène à une T_b de >30°C, tandis qu'en-dessous de 5°C, le métabolisme d'oxydation est diminué. Les larves de la G. groenlandica sont thermorégulatrices et ont la capacité de modifier leur taux de développement en changeant leurs stratégies d'alimentation et de comportement.

INTRODUCTION

Insects inhabiting polar and temperate regions show varying degrees of cold-adaptation in their active and inactive states. During the summer, active insects may modulate their

---

[1] Department of Biological Sciences, University of Notre Dame, Notre Dame, Indiana 46556, U.S.A.

FIGURE 1: Woolly bear caterpillar (<u>Gynaephora groenlandica</u>).

metabolism by behaviourial thermoregulation (May 1979; Heinrich 1981), and few species show fixed metabolic compensation for cold (Scholander *et al.* 1953). Higher metabolic-rates at low temperatures may stem from increased enzyme concentrations, lowered activation energies, or from the synthesis of seasonal isozymes (Storey and Storey 1983; Hochachka and Somero 1985). During the winter most insects remain inactive, either in diapausing or quiescent state (Tauber *et al.* 1986). The diapause state, together with cold hardening, is usually linked to environmental cues such as temperature, photoperiod, thermoperiod or nutrition (Beck 1983). A few insect species avoid the cold periods by extensive migration to warmer regions (Danks 1978, 1981). Summer hiatus of activity (aestivation) is comparatively rare in insect life histories, but occurs in the High Arctic larvae of *G. groenlandica* (Kukal 1988; Kukal *et al.* 1988A).

486

The arctic woolly-bear caterpillar *Gynaephora groenlandica* (Wocke) (Figure 1) is endemic to the northernmost Arctic Islands and Greenland, and is one of the most northerly occurring representatives of the order Lepidoptera (Ferguson 1978). Consequently, it is exposed to an extreme environment characterized by wide climatic fluctuations, short summer seasons, low temperatures, xeric conditions, continuous daylight in summer, and continuous darkness in winter. At Alexandra Fiord lowland, growth and development of *G. groenlandica* are confined to a brief period of activity within each summer of its 14 year life-cycle (Kukal and Kevan 1987). The adult and early larval stages last less than 6% of the entire life-cycle, and are entirely dependent on the energy stored by later instar larvae - the only overwintering phase. During the summer, more than two-thirds of the larval stages are killed by insect parasitoids (Kukal and Kevan 1987). In comparison, the winter mortality is at most 13% of the population, which suggests biotic as opposed to abiotic population regulation (Kukal and Kevan 1987). The insect is well adapted to cold, especially in its larval stage which overwinters in frozen state and resumes feeding for a short period during the summer.

Solar radiation is a scarce and often limiting resource in the High Arctic (Bliss 1977; Danks 1981; Svoboda and Freedman 1988). The heat budget is limited seasonally by the number of sunny days, and also daily by changes in intensity of sunshine with angle of the sun above the horizon. The development of *G. groenlandica* larvae at Alexandra Fiord lowland is therefore probably enhanced by their behavioural use of sunshine. The larvae of *G. groenlandica* (Kukal *et al.* 1988A) and *G. rossii* (Kevan *et al.* 1982), as well as some other High Arctic insects (Bertram 1935; Krog 1955; Kevan and Shorthouse 1970; Kevan 1975), raise their body temperatures by basking. Although elevation of body temperature enhances development (May 1979; Scriber and Slansky 1981), *G. groenlandica* requires 14 years to complete its life-cycle. Basking may enhance the rate of larval development but probably also interferes with other maintenance activities, such as feeding.

Evolution of insect life-cycles has been ascribed to variation in consumption and use of food (Slansky and Scriber 1985). In spite of the difficulties associated with construction of nutritional energy budgets (Wightman 1981; McEvoy 1985), many insect species have been examined (cf. Slansky and Scriber 1985). The focus, however, has been on insects inhabiting regions other than the physically-limiting arctic environment. Consequently, I investigated the nutritional energy budget of *G. groenlandica*. Despite the short summer characteristic of the species' habitat, the larvae cease foraging prior to mid-summer (Kukal and Kevan 1987). This interrupted summer feeding may contribute to the long life-cycle of the moth.

The preferred, although not entirely exclusive, food for arctic woolly-bear caterpillars is the arctic willow (*Salix arctica*) (Kukal and Kevan 1987). *Salix arctica* is a deciduous species. It synthesizes new, nutrient-rich tissues as a food source, compared with other arctic plant species (primarily evergreens and wintergreens), which are more depauperate - particularly in their reserves of tissue nitrogen and total non-structural carbohydrates (TNC) (Chapin *et al.* 1980, 1986; Dawson 1987). Together with purple saxifrage (*Saxifraga oppositifolia*), the arctic willow has the earliest new growth available at the onset of summer (Bliss 1977; Svoboda and Freedman 1988). The young buds and shoots contain very high levels of nutrients and carbohydrates, which decline and are translocated to other plant parts by mid-season (Dawson 1987). Depletion of nutrients and carbohydrates from *S. arctica* is accompanied by a mid-summer buildup of secondary metabolites (Dawson 1987). Could this change in food quality influence the feeding behaviour and metabolic state of *G. groenlandica* larvae?

The general aim of this study was to investigate the thermoregulatory behaviour of larvae in relation to their daily activity pattern and feeding energy budget. The sequential and temporal organization of different types of behaviour was analyzed and related to changes in body temperatures and metabolic rate. The feeding activity of *G. groenlandica* larvae was related to growth-rate and assimilation efficiency as a function of temperature and food quality. Specifically investigated were: (1) seasonal phenology and comparmentation of nutrients, carbohydrates, caloric content and secondary metabolites of *Salix arctica*; (2) seasonal changes in feeding behaviour and metabolic state of *G. groenlandica* larvae; (3) the effect of temperature, feeding activity and digestion on the larval metabolic-rate; and (4) influence of temperature on the growth-rate and assimilation efficiency of the larvae. The ultimate aim is to provide a scheme for food utilization in a High Arctic insect limited by low temperatures and variations in food quality.

MATERIALS AND METHODS

Study Site

Investigations were conducted during 1982-1987 at two sites: Truelove Lowland, Devon Island and Alexandra Fiord Lowland, Ellesmere Island. Insect feeding-behaviour was examined mostly at Alexandra Fiord. Climate and microclimate were monitored at both sites using Campbell CR-5 and CR-21 data acquisition stations (Campbell Scientific, Logan, Utah) equipped with fine wire copper-constantan thermocouples, quantum and pyranometer sensors (LiCor Inc., Lincoln, Nebraska) for measuring solar and photosynthetically active radiation respectively (Dawson 1987; Henry 1987).

Behaviour

Larvae of *Gyanephora groenlandica* were observed during June 1983 and 1985 at Alexandra Fiord Lowland (Kukal *et al.* 1988A,B). Behavioural observations were made for larvae encountered on the open tundra and in a circular area of tundra (diameter ~6 m), containing approximately 40% *Dryas integrifolia*, 10% *Cassiope tetragona*, 10% *Saxifraga oppositifilia* and 10% *Luzula confusa*, that was surrounded by snow.

The diel pattern of behaviour was determined by hourly recordings of the proportion of enclosed larvae (N=500) engaged in particular types of behaviour (i.e., basking, feeding, moving) over 24 hours. Sequential organization of behaviour was recorded for 10 larvae observed continuously from 13:00-17:00 hours on a sunny, calm day (ambient temperature: T_a = 8°C). Duration of different behaviours was scored by minutes for each larva, and frequencies of transitions between behaviours were analyzed in a transition matrix of preceding vs following behaviours, with the diagonal held to logical zeroes (assuming a behaviour cannot follow itself, Fagen and Young 1978). A kinematic graph of behavioural states and sequences was constructed from the transition matrix by showing average durations of different behaviours and frequencies of transitions among different behavioural states (Sustare 1978). Transitions from one behaviour to another were tested for significance with the X^2-statistic by collapsing the table about the cell of interest to form a 2 x 2 contingency table (Leonard and Ringo 1978; Nelson and Fraser 1984).

Physiological Effects of Behaviour

Effects of different types of behaviour on larval body temperatures (T_b) were recorded in the enclosure at constant ambient conditions. Larval T_b was obtained in 2-4 secs by indenting the dorsal cuticle with the tip of a copper-constantan thermocouple (Bailey Bat-12; Type MT-29/1, time constant = 0.25 sec, diameter = .33 mm) read to the nearest 0.1°C. Air and substrate temperatures (T_a recorded ~1 m above larvae; T_s within 1 cm from larvae) were always measured with the same thermocouple as T_b. The changes in T_b of eight larvae were followed in the field; records of T_b, T_a and T_s were made every 0.5-2 hours over a 38-hour period beginning at 10:00 hours. The mean T_b for larvae basking, moving, feeding, molting, spinning or for parasitized larvae were compared by t-tests. Coefficients of variation were computed as indicators of variance within each behavioural state. Effects of different ambient conditions on T_b were compared for larvae basking and spinning cocoons. The effect of sun, cloud cover, wind, and time of day on larval T_b was tested by measuring T_b of basking and spinning larvae while only one of the ambient conditions varied. The degree of cloud cover was estimated by a measurement of the relative light intensity with a "super-sensitive darkroom meter" (S & M Model A-3, Science and Mechanics, New York), and wind velocity was recorded with an anemometer at 0.25 m height above ground. T_b of larvae basking at noon without cloud cover were compared to those of larvae basking at midnight, at noon with cloud cover, and in sun with wind from the direction of insolation.

Oxygen Consumption at Different Body Temperatures

Oxygen-consumption rates were measured with an Amotek S-3A Applied Electrochemistry oxygen-analyzer capable of measuring to 0.001% O_2-concentration using a flow-through system of 30 ml volume. The excurrent air was desiccated and depleted of CO_2 by passing it through a water and CO_2 absorbent before being pumped to a Model N-37M sensor. Readings were taken every 30 minutes over 3 hours for three groups of larvae: (1) actively feeding prior to measurements; (2) active but starved; and (3) "inactive" (i.e., immobile and spinning hibernacula, therefore presumably aestivating; see Kukal and Kevan 1987). Ten larvae from each of the three groups were enclosed in a chamber with a thermocouple and their rate of oxygen consumption was recorded over a range of temperatures from 0-50°C. The larvae were allowed to equilibrate for 30 minutes at each temperature recorded.

Larval Feeding Behaviour on the Tundra

Host plant preference was determined by observation of larvae feeding on the tundra over a period of three days at the onset and three days at the end of their feeding season in June 1987 (cf. Kukal and Dawson 1988). The species and plant part eaten was recorded for 200 larvae observed at each of the two periods. Preference for certain parts of *Salix* was estimated as the feeding periods allocated to leaves, buds, or catkins for 30 different larvae. Feeding larvae (N=10) were brought back into the laboratory, their guts were dissected out and examined for microbial symbionts.

Seasonal Trends in Food Quality and Availability

Six, entire plants were carefully excavated each week over the growing-season. Each plant was washed of all soil, blotted dry and sorted into leaves, reproductive structures, above- and below-ground shoots, fine roots and taproots. These tissues were weighed fresh and subsequently dried at 80°C in a force-draft oven to a constant weight. Dried samples were diced, thoroughly mixed, ground to 1 mm (20 mesh screen) in a Wiley Mill and analyzed for macro-nutrients (N,P,K,) and caloric content as outlined by Dawson (1987). Total non-structural carbohydrates (TNC) analyses followed a modified version of the methods outlined by Allen *et al.* (1974). Six individuals of *S. arctica*, harvested at three times during the 1985 growing-season, were used for the carbohydrate analyses. Plants were harvested and prepared as above, fixed immediately in boiling 80% EtOH (plus ~1 g of sodium bicarbonate) and sealed in a glass jar for transport to the laboratory. Tissue samples from the 1984 and 1985 samples were also prepared and analyzed for secondary plant metabolites following the methods of Bryant *et al.* (1983).

Temperature Influence on Growth-Rate and Assimilation Efficiency

Larvae collected at Alexandra Fiord throughout their feeding period in June 1987 were maintained in the laboratory at 5°, 15°, and 30°C under constant light for one month (July). *Salix arctica* was collected at Alexandra Fiord between 15-29 June, and kept near 0°C in the dark. Thirty larvae (instar IV, V) at each of the three incubation temperatures were kept in separate containers in groups of 10 and fed ample arctic willow. Each week the larvae and their dried frass (excreta) were weighed, old food removed, dried and weighed and ~50 g of fresh food replenished. Because the leaves were removed (preventing translocation) and kept in the dark (preventing photosynthesis and other light reactions), it can be assumed that food quality did not change significantly over the experimental period. The low-temperature larvae required only bi-weekly feeding. Dry weight of larvae was estimated from a standard proportion of fresh to dry weight. Amount ingested was determined from a standard relationship between fresh and dry weight of willow which precluded an error introduced by desiccation of food over the feeding period. Rates of growth and efficiencies of food consumption at different temperatures were computed as in Slansky and Scriber (1985). The nitrogen levels in frass excreted by larvae incubated in the laboratory at 15° vs 30°C was compared with frass collected from larvae in nature. Two hundred larvae were held in a wooden box exposed to daily temperature and light changes. They were fed ample willow throughout June and then their frass was collected, dessicated and analyzed for nitrogen content as described above.

The Effect of Feeding and Digestion on Larval Metabolism

Metabolic-rates of late instars were measured with an oxygen analyzer as described previously. Individual larvae (N=10) were placed in a 10 ml flask with or without *Salix* leaves and their oxygen uptake was detected by a Model N-37M sensor in a flow-through system where the intake and outlet-air was filtered through water and carbon dioxide absorbent. The flow rate of air was maintained at 12.5 ml O_2/hr by a pump, and the oxygen inside the flask was continuously compared to the ambient O_2 concentration.

Comparisons were made between oxygen update at 25°C by feeding larvae, digesting, moving, cold-acclimated and inactive larvae in hibernacula. From these data the length of the digestion period was estimated. Standard metabolic-rate was assigned from the comparison of larvae after digestion with larvae in hibernacula.

RESULTS

Behaviour

Larvae spent 95% of their time basking, moving or feeding and 5% immobile in shaded crevices ("hiding") or grooming. More than half of the total time was spent basking, followed by feeding (20%) and moving (15%) (Figure 2). In behavioural sequences, basking most often followed feeding ($X^2 = 50.22$, p <.005). In order of decreasing frequency were the behavioural transitions from feeding to basking ($X^2 = 14.93$), then moving to basking ($X^2 = 13.11$), feeding to moving ($X^2 = 8.53$), hiding to moving ($X^2 = 6.74$), and finally, moving to hiding ($X^2 = 5.18$). All other behavioural transitions were not significant. The transitions between basking and feeding and bet-

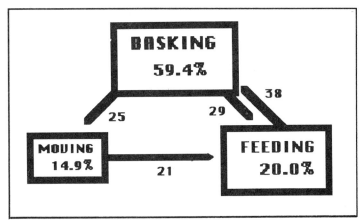

FIGURE 2: Frequency and sequential organization of major behaviours in eight G. groenlandica larvae. Relative sizes of squares and arrows indicate the frequency of occurrence by percentage of time spent in particular behaviour (within squares), and the number of times one behaviour followed another (arrows) (see text for details). Infrequent behaviours, such as grooming and hiding among vegetation clumps, are excluded from the kinematic graph.

ween basking and feeding and between moving and hiding were reversible, however, the transitions from basking to moving to feeding were rare and consequently not statistically significant. Over the course of 24 hours, the larvae moved or fed primarily around mid-day, but most basked near midnight (Figure 3).

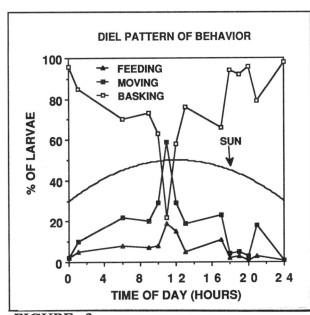

FIGURE 3: Diel changes in the pattern of major behaviours (basking, feeding and moving) in G. groenlandica larvae (N = ~500) in a natural enclosure of the tundra under sunny, calm conditions (T_a at 1 m = 2.0-6.3°C). Change in the height of sun above the horizon is indicated; minimum at 10° and maximum at 33° above the horizon.

Physiological Effects of Behaviour

Behavioural changes significantly affected larval body temperatures (Table 1). Larvae attained a maximal T_b of 30.5°C by basking. Moving caused the mean T_b to drop by approximately 4°C, and a further significant drop occurred when feeding commenced. The body temperatures of moulting and spinning larvae were similar to those observed in feeding and parasitized larvae. All of the mean T_b at different behaviours were significantly different by t-test (p <.001) from basking T_b, and the T_b of moving larvae were statistically different from the feeding larvae (p <.01). Body

TABLE 1: MEAN BODY TEMPERATURES OF G. groenlandica LARVAE IN DIFFERENT BEHAVIOURS OBSERVED BETWEEN 12:00-13:00 HOURS, 25 JUNE, ON THE TUNDRA (SUNNY, CALM, T_a = 7°C, T_s = 16.5°C).

BEHAVIOUR	N	MEAN[1]	STANDARD DEVIATION	COEFFICIENT OF VARIATION
Basking	20	30.5[a]	2.2	7.2%
Feeding	14	23.9[b]	2.2	9.2
Moving	15	26.7[b]	2.6	9.7
Spinning	22	24.1[b]	4.3	17.8
Molting	5	25.5[b]	4.0	15.7
Parasitized	18	24.3[b]	3.1	12.8

[1] Sample means followed by a different letter are significantly different by t-test (p <.001) from the mean T_b of basking larvae. Mean T_b of feeding vs moving larvae are also significantly different by t-test (p <.01).

TABLE 2: CHANGES IN MEAN BODY TEMPERATURE OF BASKING LARVAE OF G. groenlandica (N=20-30) UNDER DIFFERENT WEATHER CONDITIONS AND DURING DIFFERENT TIMES OF DAY (T_a at 1m = 2-6.5°C).

CONDITIONS	MEAN BODY TEMPERATURE ±S.D.[1]
Noon/sunny/calm	30.5 ± 2.2[a]
Noon/sunny/windy	14.2 ± 1.8[b]
Noon/cloudy/calm	12.4 ± 1.9[b]
Midnight/sunny/calm	13.2 ± 2.8[b]

[1] Sample means followed by a different letter are significantly different by t-test (p<.001).

494

temperatures of basking and spinning larvae were lowered by 16-18°C in cloud cover, wind and midnight sun (Table 2). All of the mean T_b at different ambient conditions showed significant differences by t-test (p <.001). Figure 4 shows the mean T_b of eight larvae followed in the field over 38 hours. Maximum T_b was reached at mid-day and minimum T_b at midnight; a trend also shown by T_a and T_s. Lower T_b was attained at mid-day on the first day under a partial cloud cover than on the second day which was sunny. Variation between body temperatures of individual larvae are reflected in the large standard deviation (± ~5°C) from the mean T_b.

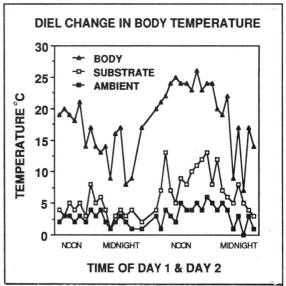

FIGURE 4: Diel changes in mean body temperature (± S.D. ≤5) of eight G. groenlandica larvae relative to ambient and substrate temperatures recorded nearly bi-hourly over two days (overcast day followed by a sunny one) on the open tundra.

Oxygen Consumption at Different Body Temperatures

The relationship between body temperature and oxygen consumption was exponential to sigmoidal in the three groups of larvae (Figure 5). The Q_{10} was lowest between 0-10°C for all groups of larvae. The highest Q_{10} for active larvae was between 10-20°C, whereas for starved larvae between 20-30°C. However, no significant difference was found between oxygen uptake in the three groups of larvae. Hence the "inactive" larvae were unlikely in aestivation, since their metabolic-rate was the same as in the active larvae. Similarly, starvation did not alter the larval metabolic-rate.

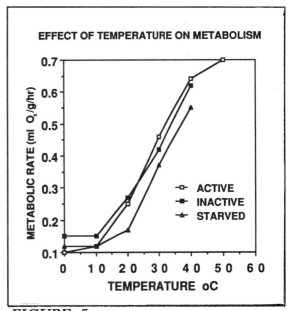

FIGURE 5: Metabolic-rate as a function of body temperature (range from 0-50°C) recorded for 10 actively feeding, active but starved and inactive larvae of G. groenlandica.

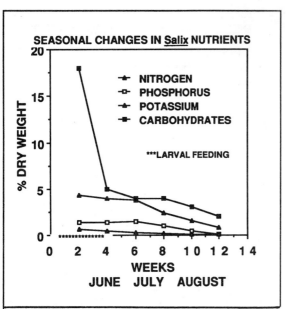

FIGURE 6: Seasonal variation in nutrient and carbohydrate (TNC) content of <u>Salix arctica</u> leaves in the High Arctic (N=17; mean values ± S.E. ≤1 for TNC; S.E. ≤0.1 for macro-nutrients). The period of <u>G. groenlandica</u> feeding activity is indicated.

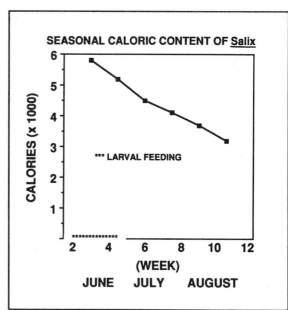

FIGURE 7: Seasonal variation in the caloric content of <u>Salix arctica</u> leaves in the High Arctic (N=5; mean values ± S.E. ≤3x10^3). The period of <u>G. groenlandica</u> feeding activity is indicated.

496

Feeding Behaviour on the Tundra

Ninety-seven percent of larvae (N=200) fed primarily on new leaf-buds of arctic willow (*Salix arctica*) at the onset of their feeding season. However, at the end of June, just prior to cessation of feeding, only 9% of larvae fed on new leaf-growth. At the onset of summer <3% of larvae fed on the flowers of purple saxifrage (*Saxifraga oppositifolia*) and on senescent leaves of arctic avens (*Dryas integrifolia*). As the frequency of feeding decreased there was no switch to a different food source or to a different plant part. The length of larval feeding period was only about 30% of the degree-days available for growth as indicated by the microclimatic measurements (Henry 1987). Feeding was usually followed by basking while digesting for approximately five hours. Feeding larvae (N=10) contained no bacterial symbionts in their guts.

Seasonal Trends in Resource Availability and Insect Feeding

Nutrient, carbohydrate and caloric-content of *S. arctica* leaves declines steadily over the course of the summer (Figures 6, 7). A particularly sharp decrease at the end of June is evident in the carbohydrate-content of leaves (Figure 6). Secondary plant metabolites, on the other hand, increase in concentration over the summer season (Figure 8).

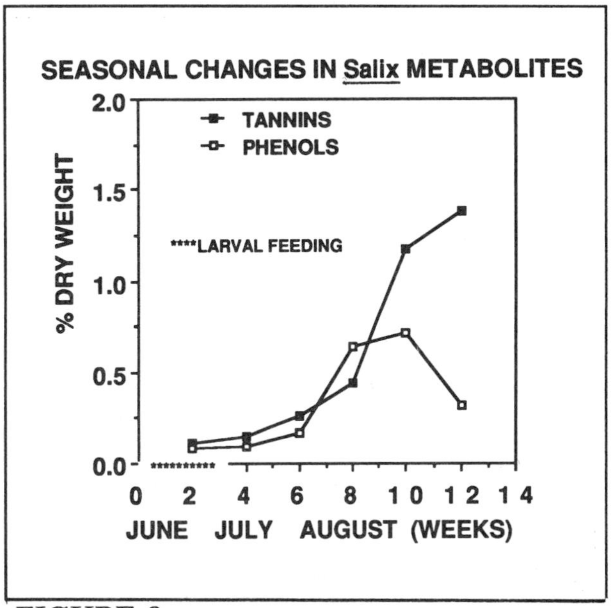

FIGURE 8: Seasonal variation in the secondary metabolites of Salix arctica leaves in the High Arctic (N=5; mean values ± S.E. ≤0.1). The feeding activity of G. groenlandica is indicated.

Temperature Influence on Growth Rate and Assimilation Efficiency

Larval growth rates and assimilation efficiencies are shown in Table 3. Growth rates were similar at 15° and 30°C (approximately double the rate at 5°C). However, the amount of *Salix* ingested and frass excreted varied between the three incubation temperatures, as did assimilation efficiencies. At the lowest temperature the amount ingested and egested was very low compared to the amounts of food processed at higher temperatures (Table 3). The amount ingested at 30°C was about four times the amount consumed at 15°C, and the

497

TABLE 3: *TEMPERATURE INFLUENCE ON GROWTH RATE AND ASSIMILATION EFFICIENCY OF G. groenlandica LARVAE FEEDING ON Salix arctica*[1].

INCUBATION TEMP.	LARVAL GROWTH RATE	FOOD INGESTED	FRASS EXCRETED	METABOLIC -RATE	ASSMILATION EFFICIENCY
	mg dry wt/larva/day (mg dry wt/mg larva/day)				
5°C	2.33 ± .33 (.008)	3.67 ± .67 (.012)	0.33 ± .13 (.001)	1.0 .033	70%[2]
15°C	4.67 ± 2.00 (.016)	16.67 ± 4.00 (.056)	5.00 ± 2.67 (0.17)	7.0 .023	40%
30°C	5.00 ± 2.00 (.017)	68.33 ± 5.00 (.227)	16.00 ± 2.33 (0.53)	47 .157	9.5%

[1] Each incubation temperature contained three groups of 10 larvae. Assimilation efficiency = % mass gain per mass ingested; metabolic-rate = (food ingested - excreted) - mass gain (Values = mean - ±1 S.E.) (mean dry wt of larva = .30 ± .05 g).

[2] Value overestimated due to the extended residence time of food in the gut at low temperatures.

TABLE 4: *OXYGEN CONSUMPTION AT 25°C BY LARVAE IN DIFFERENT METABOLIC STATES; FEEDING, DIGESTING, STARVED, IN HIBERNACULA AND FOLLOWING COLD ACCLIMATION*[1]

METABOLIC STATE	OXYGEN CONSUMPTION (ml/g/hr)[2]
Standard metabolism	0.06 ± .02 a
Starved larvae	0.06 ± .02 a
Moving larvae	0.11 ± .03 b
Feeding larvae	0.29 ± .03 c
Digesting larvae	0.17 ± .02 d
Larvae in hibernacula	0.07 ± .02 a
Low-temperature acclimation[3]	0.07 ± .02 a

[1] (N=10; Values = mean ± S.E.).

[2] Means followed by a different letter are significantly different by t-test (p>0.005).

[3] Larvae held at 5°C and in the dark for three months.

498

amount excreted was approximately three times more at the higher temperature. The corresponding assimilation efficiencies were 9.5% at 30°C, 40% at 15°C and 70% at 5°C. Dissections of guts indicate food retention in the guts of larvae incubated at 5°C.

The Effect of Feeding and Digestion on Larval Metabolism

The effect of metabolic state on respiration-rate is shown in Table 4. The starved larvae, cold-acclimated and inactive larvae within hibernacula, maintained basal metabolic-rates. This rate increased during movement, and further increase was evident when feeding ensued. Following feeding, approximately five hours of elevated metabolic-rate indicated a digestion period. The oxygen-consumption rate by digesting larvae was greater than in actively moving larvae.

DISCUSSION

Behavioural Thermoregulation

Sunshine-dependent behavioural thermoregulation is crucial for the survival of *G. groenlandica* at Alexandra Fiord, where low ambient (<5°C) and ground temperatures (usually <10°C) prevail during their brief activity in June (Kukal 1984, 1988C). Although the ambient and substrate temperatures gradually increase and peak in July, the intensity of incoming solar radiation declines after the summer solstice (Svoboda and Freedman 1988). The activity (i.e., feeding and basking on the tundra surface) of *G. groenlandica* larvae coincides with the period of most intense solar radiation during June.

The energy cost of different types of activities is best seen from the effect of different behaviours on body temperature, which can in turn be related to metabolic-rate. Maximal T_b in excess of the ambient temperature, which is attained by basking at mid-day, decreases by about 20% (-4°C) when behaviour changes to moving, feeding, molting or spinning. Fifty percent heat-loss (-17°C) occurs in basking larvae at midnight, under cloud cover at midday, or in strong wind. However, if the larvae stop basking at midnight and start moving they suffer a further 20% heat-loss, a total of 70% of body temperature attained by larvae basking at midday. Evidently, energy balance of larvae is influenced by the different behaviours, which are in turn affected by larval food status and habitat temperature. Raising body temperature in fed larvae likely enhances digestion rate by stimulating activity of gut enzymes since no bacterial flora is present to aid digestion. Thus body temperature and energy status of larvae is probably pivotal in controlling the type of behaviour. At higher T_b more energy can be obtained in a limited time from the food ingested, however, when energy from food is depleted, then feeding commences at the expense of energy lost as heat. On the other hand, at higher T_b the "maintenance metabolism" is probably increased, hastening use of energy reserves obtained from food, as noted in other thermoregulating ectotherms (Brett 1971).

The precarious energy balance is reflected in the daily behavioural pattern of larval *G. groenlandica* and in the sequential organization of different behaviours. Larvae spend most (60%) of their time basking (even during pupation the basking position is assumed), which increases their body temperature and metabolic-rate, and may lead to an increased rate of digestion. Feeding activity provides the source of energy and ranks in its frequency second to basking, while movement, in search of food or new basking sites, ranks last. These three most prominent behaviours follow a definite sequence; most often from feeding to basking, less often from basking to feeding or from basking to moving and then feeding. Interestingly, the reverse sequence of behaviours from feeding to moving and then basking rarely occurs. This suggests an intimate reciprocity between basking and feeding, with movement restricted to finding new food sites or changing their basking position. During the course of a day the relative importance of the three behaviours changes; more larvae feed and move at midday, and relatively more larvae bask at night. This temporal partitioning of activity may be caused by lower ambient temperatures at night which lower larval T_b. During daytime, greater incoming solar radiation raises larval T_b enabling feeding and mobility. In contrast to *G. groenlandica*, the "thermally independent" gypsy moth (*Lymantria dispar*) larvae feed mostly in early mornings and evenings and are immobile at midday (Knapp and Casey 1986) - an adaptation attributed to the avoidance of predation and parasitism (Campbell 1981). Although more than two-thirds of *Gynaephora* are killed by parasitoids (Kukal and Kevan 1987), these "thermally dependent" larvae probably cannot sacrifice their basking time to hiding from parasitoids. The larvae probably "compromise" by maximizing development during the period of lowest parasitoid activity (Kukal and Kevan 1987).

Larval metabolic-rate increases exponentially with body temperature, even during starvation or apparent inactivity, and approaches zero below 10°C as in the majority of insects that also lack metabolic compensation to cold (Scholander et al. 1953). Consequently, without the aid of 24-hour sunlight to raise their T_b by as much as 20°C, the larvae would likely remain at most times below their developmental threshold temperature. Similar excess body temperatures have been recorded in basking larvae of the nearctic-alpine conspecific of G. groenlandica, G. rossii (Kevan et al. 1982). In contrast to the strict dependence of the arctic larvae on solar radiation, gypsy-moth larvae are "thermoconformers". Thermoregulation is apparently unnecessary for gypsy-moth larvae since the ambient temperature is well above their developmental threshold (Knapp and Casey 1986).

Conservation of heat by larvae is best viewed from an anatomical perspective. As the wind-tunnel experiments with G. groenlandica showed, the cooling rate is minimized by the dense, dark setae combined with radiant energy input (Kukal et al. 1988A). Larval setae create a boundary-layer of undisturbed air which, nevertheless, can be disrupted by high winds. The insulative quality of larval setae has also been demonstrated in the gypsy moth (Casey and Hegel 1981), and as shown by our results, this insulation can be greatly enhanced by insolation. Similarly, in the field, heat was best conserved as excess T_b at mid-day under sunny conditions, and further enhanced by the albedo effect of surrounding snow. Noteworthy is the decreased ability of larvae to warm up in the midnight sun (Kukal et al. 1988A).

The albedo effect may be involved in the disappearance of larvae from the tundra surface early in the arctic summer. Melting of snow from the larval habitat and surrounding ice-fields is the main cause of the sharp decrease in incoming radiation (Svoboda and Freedman 1988). In light of the strict dependence of these larvae on the sun's heat, it may be energetically more viable for them to cease feeding than to maintain activity at lower body temperature. This brief period available for feeding likely extends the developmental time of G. groenlandica to 14 years. The evolutionary strategy of G. groenlandica appears to involve a brief period of "maxithermy" (cf. Hamilton 1973) followed by a "voluntary hypothermia" (cf. Regal 1967) in mid-summer.

INFLUENCE OF TEMPERATURE ON GROWTH RATE AND ASSIMILATION EFFICIENCY

The larvae of *Gynaephora groenlandica* are energetically limited by the quantity and quality of their main food source, the buds and young leaves of *Salix arctica*. Larval feeding behaviour and assimilation efficiency is therefore expected to vary with seasonal changes in nutrient, carbohydrate and caloric content of *Salix* tissues (cf. Ayres and MacLean 1987; Chapin *et al.* 1986; MacLean and Jensen 1985). This variation in food quality is reflected in the restriction of larval feeding behaviour to June, when both the nutrient and carbohydrate content of the host plant is maximal. At this time the bud and new leaves contain the greatest concentrations of nutrients and carbohydrates, which in July are translocated to the reproductive parts. The willow catkins, however, are rarely consumed by the larvae. The observed larval response (i.e. cessation of feeding) to changing quality of their host plant is compensatory rather than inductory (cf. Slansky and Scriber 1985), where a behavioural change in the seasonal feeding pattern leads to physiological modification of assimilation efficiency and growth rate. These physiological changes are a direct consequence of larval "voluntary hypothermia" (Kukal *et al.* 1988A) caused by their hiding in vegetation or cracks near the permafrost. There is no evidence, however, of an inductory-type of response resulting in genetically programmed summer aestivation since the larval metabolic-rate does not decrease and, if provided with fresh willow, the larvae continue feeding beyond June.

Further support for the decreased quality of food before mid-season in July, and its possible link to the cessation of larval feeding, may be the increased concentrations of secondary metabolites in the older leaves of *Salix*. Although not directly correlated, the buildup of tannins and phenols may also function as a feeding deterrent to the larvae of *G. groenlandica* (Feeney 1970; Rosenthal and Janzen 1979; Haukioja *et al.* 1985).

The shortened feeding period extends the developmental life-cycle of *G. groenlandica* and consequently has an effect of reducing its fitness by reduced reproductive potential (Price *et al.* 1980). On the other hand, if larvae remain active throughout July they will be more susceptible to parasitoid attack (Kukal and Kevan 1987). It appears that the larvae do not use their physiological potential for growth during July because of the heavy mortality caused by parasitoids. Moreover, decreased energy available from the host plant in the form

502

of starch results in decreased physiological potential for larval-growth during July. Similarly, the decreased July levels of plant nutrients, nitrogen in particular, may affect larval feeding behaviour. Molting may represent as much as 27% of the nitrogen or caloric content of a gypsy-moth larva (Montgomery 1982). These comparable losses may be minimized in *G. groenlandica* by its feeding strategy; maximizing energy intake from food by selectivity (both spatially and temporally) and minimizing energy expenditure in activities (i.e. feeding, mobility, molting) while food quality is relatively poor. Natural selection in tundra environments is abrupt and evolution slow. This type of feeding strategy would be selectively favoured.

Superimposed on the decreased quality of food influencing larval feeding behaviour is the effect of temperature. Being ectothermic, the larvae depend on sunshine to raise their body temperature. By preferential orientation toward the sun the larvae can reach a body temperature of ~20°C above the ambient temperature (Kukal *et al.* 1988A). Consequently, by basking, the larvae may regulate their metabolic and digestion-rates; however, at very high body temperatures (e.g. ~30°C), the maximal energy gain from digestion is counter-balanced by simultaneous increase in maintenance metabolism. Larval body temperature drops but the metabolic-rate increases as soon as feeding or moving commences. Consequently, the time spent feeding compared to basking is an essential determinant of larval energy balance. Under sunny conditions, larvae tend to feed during the highest temperatures at mid-day and bask at night when they cannot attain the higher temperatures required for activity (>5-10°C) due to reduced incoming radiation. The larvae spend more than 60% of their time basking, and move primarily to feed. Since digestion requires approximately five hours, it is probably necessary for the larvae to maintain elevated body temperature by basking in order to activate digestive enzymes. The lack of bacterial symbionts underscores the importance of raised body temperature to aid digestion in *G. groenlandica*. The lack of symbionts may influence the length of ingestive vs digestive phase. The feeding periods in *G. groenlandica* larvae are interspaced with relatively long periods of digestion while basking. McEvoy (1984) estimated a median feeding period for the cinnabar moth to be 40 minutes - much longer than in the arctic larvae. Feeding cinnabar-moth larvae also increase their respiratory-rate, however, contrary to *G. groenlandica* no significant increase was shown in digesting larvae (McEvoy 1984).

Laboratory experiments indicate that larvae assimilate food and nitrogen (Kukal and Dawson 1988) most efficiently at 15°C as opposed to 5° or 30°C; taking into account that the assimilation rate obtained for 5° is an overestimate resulting from the increased residence time of food in the gut. Assimilation efficiency decreases with increasing temperature (30°C) despite the similar larval growth rate. This decrease is undoubtedly caused by increased maintenance metabolism through increased activity, ingestion and egestion rates. Assimilation of nitrogen at the lower temperature of 15° is greater than at 30°C. In contrast to other Lepidoptera inhabiting warmer regions, assimilation efficiency of *G. groenlandica* decreases rather than increases with a temperature rise to 30°C (Slansky and Scriber 1985). Despite the relatively low rates of food consumption and growth, the efficiency of conversion of ingested food in *G. groenlandica* larvae exceeds the mean value for other species of Lepidoptera (Table 5).

TABLE 5: FOOD UTILIZATION BY Gynaephora groenlandica COMPARED TO: (A) 29 SPECIES OF LEPIDOPTERA; (B) DATA FROM SLANSKY AND SCRIBER (1985).

	RGR[1]	RCR[2]	AD[3] %	ECD[4] %	ECI[5] %
	(mg dry wt/day/mg)				
A: *Gynaephora* at 5, 15, 30°C					
5°	.008	.012	91.7	72.7	66.7
15°	.016	.056	69.6	41.0	28.5
30°	.017	.227	76.7	9.8	7.5
B: Other Lepidoptera (Values = x/range; N=444-629)					
	0.38/.03-1.50	2.03/.27-6.90	53/16-97	40/2-87	20/1-78

[1] Relative growth rate.
[2] Relative consumption-rate.
[3] (Approximate digestibliity)=(food ingested-frass)/food ingested.
[4] (Efficiency of conversion)=biomass gained/(food ingested-frass).
[5] (Efficiency of conversion of ingested food) = AD x ECD.

On the tundra, larvae spent most of their time basking at "night" when the ambient temperature is about 5°C (cf. Kukal *et al.* 1988A). This behaviour correlates with the comparatively low metabolic and digestion-rates measured in the laboratory. At high temperatures approaching ~30°C the larvae start feeding. This may stem from the high energy requirements for maintenance metabolism reflected in high food consumption in the feeding experiment at 30°C. The intermediate incubation temperature of 15°C simulates the average body temperature of larvae in nature during their activity period in June.

Although the larval growth rate at 15°C is similar to the rate at 30°C, the assimilation efficiency is better because the energy loss in metabolism is much lower at the lower temperature. Supportive of the optimal intermediate temperature is the relatively high nitrogen content of larval frass following incubation at 30° vs 15°C (Kukal and Dawson 1988). An analogous study of growth rate by optimization of food assimilation and maintenance metabolism was performed on sockeye salmon (Brett 1971). Although the organisms studied are not closely related, they show similar energy budgeting in terms of feeding strategy and thermoregulation characteristic of ectotherms (May 1979). The salmon feed only at dawn and dusk, descending to lower depths where lower temperatures reduce their energy expenditure in maintenance metabolism while digestion takes place. The fishes' final perferrendum temperature is 15°C (Brett 1971).

In his review of insect-plant relationships in the Arctic, Danks (1986) addresses the relative importance of physical vs biological constraints on the interdependence between herbivores and their plant hosts. He suggests that the decreasing ratio of herbivores to host plant species indicates an increasing influence of physical constraints over herbivores at high latitudes. The prevailing physical constraints may result in decreased specialization of arctic plant feeders i.e., more frequent polyphagy or oligophagy and lack of synchrony with plant phenology and resource allocation (Danks 1986). Chemical plant defenses, although common in temperate and tropical regions, have been rarely documented in the Arctic. An extreme case is exemplified by an Alaskan species of *Salix sitchensis* showing a defensive response to damage that can be pheromonally-communicated to neighbouring plants (Rhodes 1985). This study indicates a possible correlation between a buildup of tannins and phenols in *Salix arctica* and the feeding hiatus in *G. groenlandica* larvae. However, it is difficult to determine a single cause for the cessation in feeding prior to mid-season. Another likely cause may be the abrupt decline in the level of starch in the buds and young willow leaves that provide the primary source of energy for the larvae. If the larvae already exists "at the edge" in terms of their energy budget for growth and development, this decline in energy stores of their host plant may be crucial to maintenance of larval activity. Furthermore, the increased July ambient temperatures (Svoboda and Freedman 1988) probably raise the maintenance metabolism, which may exceed the energy demands for growth, especially in light of the declining food quality. Consequently, it may be advantageous for the larvae to undergo "voluntary hypothermia"; stop feeding and hide among vegetation and crevices, where close to the permafrost layer the larval body temperatures range between 0-5°C. The result is a lowered metabolic-rate and maintenance metabolism which enables storage of energy compounds, such as glycogen, for the synthesis of winter cryoprotectants (Kukal *et al.* 1988B). The metabolic-rate of larvae (presumably readying themselves for winter) in hibernacula is equivalent to the basal metabolic-rate of "inactive" larvae. This suppression of metabolic-rate may be adaptive in conserving the energy stores of larvae, and appears to be mainly temperature-regulated.

The insect-plant interaction between *G. groenlandica* larvae and *Salix arctica* reveals the importance of both, physical and biotic factors in influencing the insect's life-cycle and development. Temperature plays a crucial role in optimizing growth rate offset by maintenance metabolism. Host plant phenology and resource allocation influences the feeding pattern of *G. groenlandica* larvae. Concurrent increase in temperature and decrease in food quality probably confines the larval feeding activity to June, thereby extending the moth's life-cycle to 14 years at the Alexandra Fiord Lowland.

ACKNOWLEDGEMENTS

My research was supported by grants from the Polar Continental Shelf Project, Arctic Institute of North America, the Indiana Academy of Science, the IBM Women in Science Fund (University of Notre Dame), the Zahm Travel Grant (University of Notre Dame) and by a National Science Foundation grant to J.G. Duman. B. Heinrich (University of Vermont, Burlington) collaborated in investigating behavioural thermoregulation, and T.E. Dawson (University of Utah, Salt Lake City) provided the plant data for the study of growth rate and assimilation efficiency of *Gynaephora*. M. Kaufman (Kellogg Biological Station, Michigan State University) examined the guts of larval *G. groenlandica* for potential symbionts. J.G. Duman, P.G. Kevan and E.D. Walker are acknowledged for their ideas and comments on the manuscript. J.G. Duman, B. Heinrich, A.S. Serianni and Kerry Temple were great research and survival companions in the Arctic. We are also much indebted to the Polar Continental Shelf Project personnel for logistic support in the field.

REFERENCES

Allen, S.E., H.M. Grimshaw, J.A. Parkinson, and C. Quanrmby. 1974. Chemical analysis of ecological materials. John Wiley and Sons, New York.

Ayres, M.P. and S.F. MacLean. 1987. Development of birch leaves and the growth energetics of *Epirrita autumnata* (Geometridae). Ecology 68(3):468-558.

Beck, S.D. 1983. Insect thermoperiodism. Annual Review of Entomology 28:91-108.

Bertram, G.C.L. 1935. The low temperature limit of activity of arctic insects. Journal of Animal Ecology 4:35-42.

Bliss, L.C. (Editor). 1977. Truelove Lowland,Devon Island, Canada: A High Arctic ecosystem. University of Alberta Press, Edmonton. 714 pp.

Brett, J.R. 1971. Energetic responses of salmon to temperature. A study of some thermal relations in the physiology and freshwater ecology of sockeye salmon (*Oncorhynchus nerka*). American Zoologist 11:99-113.

Bryant, J.P., F.S. Chapin, and D.R. Klein. 1983. Carbon/nutrient balance of boreal plants in relation to vertebrate herbivory. Oikos 40:357-368.

Campbell, R.W. 1981. Population dynamics. In: The Gypsy Moth: Research toward Integrated Pest Management. Edited by: C.C. Doane and M.L. McManus. United States Department of Agriculture, Washington, D.C. pp. 65-214.

Casey, T.M. and J.R. Hegel. 1981. Caterpillar setae: insulation for an ectotherm. Science 214:1131-1133.

Chapin, F.S., D.A. Johnson, and J.D. McKendrick. 1980. Seasonal movement of nutrients in plants of differing growth form in an Alaskan tundra ecosystem: implications for herbivory. Journal of Ecology 68:189-209.

Chapin, F.S., J.D. McKendrick, and D.A. Johnson. 1986. Seasonal changes in carbon fractions in Alaskan tundra plants of differing growth form: implications for herbivory. Journal of Ecology 74:707-731.

Danks, H.V. 1978. Modes of seasonal adaptations in the insects. I. Winter survival. Canadian Entomologist 110:1167-1205.

_____. 1981. Arctic arthropods. A review of systematics and ecology with particular reference to the North American fauna. Entomological Society of Canada, Ottawa. 608 pp.

_____. 1986. Insect/plant interactions in arctic regions. Revue d'Entomologie du Québec 31(1,2):52-75.

Dawson, T.E. 1987. Comparative ecophysiological adaptations in arctic and alpine populations of a dioecious shrub, *Salix arctica* Pall. Ph.D. thesis, University of Washington, Seattle.

Fagen, R.M. and D.Y. Young. 1978. Temporal patterns of behaviour: durations, intervals, latencies and sequences. In: Quantitative Ethology. Edited by: P.W. Colgan. Wiley and Sons, New York. pp. 79-114.

Feeny, P. 1970. Seasonal changes in oak leaf tannins and nutrients as a cause of spring feeding by winter moth caterpillars. Ecology 51:565-581.

Ferguson, D.C. 1978. Noctuoidea, Lymantriidae. In: The Moths of North America North of Mexico, Fasc. 22.2. Edited by: R.B. Dominick *et al.* E.W. Classey Ltd. and The Wedge Entomological Research Foundation. London. pp. 17-21.

Hamilton, W.J. 1973. Life's color code. New York, McGraw-Hill.

Haukioja, E., P. Hiemela, and S. Siren. 1985. Foliage phenols and nitrogens in relation to growth, insect damage, and ability to recover after defoliation in the mountain birch *Betula pubescens* spp *tortuosa*. Oecologia 65:214-222.

Heinrich, B. (editor). 1981. Insect thermoregulation. John Wiley and Sons, New York. 328 pp.

Henry, G.H.R. 1987. Ecology of sedge meadow communities of a polar desert oasis: Alexandra Fiord, Ellesmere Island, Canada. Ph.D. thesis, University of Toronto, Toronto, Ontario. 272 pp.

Hochachka, P.W. and G.N. Somero. 1985. Biochemical adaptation. Princeton University Press, Princeton. 537 pp.

Kevan, P.G. 1975. Sun tracking solar furnaces in High Arctic flowers: significance for pollination and insects. Science 189:723-726.

Kevan, P.G., T.J. Jensen, and J.D. Shorthouse. 1982. Body temperatures and behavioural thermoregulation of High Arctic woolly-bear caterpillars and pupae (*Gynaephora rossii*, Lymantriidae: Lepidoptera) and the importance of sunshine. Arctic and Alpine Research 14:125-136.

Kevan, P.G. and J.D. Shorthouse. 1970. Behavioural thermoregulation by High Arctic butterflies. Arctic 23:268-279.

Knapp, R. and T.M. Casey. 1986. Thermal ecology, behavior, and growth of gypsy moth and eastern tent caterpillars. Ecology 67(3):598-608.

Krog, J. 1955. Notes on temperature measurements indicative of spacial organization in arctic and subarctic plants for utilization of radiated heat from the sun. Physiologia Plantarum 8:836-839.

508

Kukal, O. 1984. Life history and adaptations of a High Arctic insect, *Gynaephora groenlandica*) (Wocke) (Lepidoptera: Lymantriidae). M.Sc. thesis, University of Guelph, Guelph, Ontario. 108 pp.

_____. 1988. Behavioral and physiological adaptations to cold in a freeze tolerant High Arctic insect, *Gynaephora groenlandica* (Wocke) (Lepidoptera: Lymnatriidae). Ph.D. thesis, University of Notre Dame, Notre Dame, Indiana.

Kukal, O. and T.E. Dawson. (in press). Feeding "on the edge": temperature and food quality influences on feeding behavior, assimilation efficiency and growth rate of arctic woolly-bear caterpillars. Oecologia.

Kukal, O. and P.G. Kevan. 1987. The influence of parasitism on the life history of a high arctic insect, *Gynaephora groenlandica* (Wocke) (Lepidoptera: Lymantriidae). Canadian Journal of Zoology 65:156-163.

Kukal, O., B. Heinrich, and J.G. Duman. 1988A. Behavioral thermoregulation in the freeze tolerant arctic caterpillar, *Gynaephora groenlandica*. Journal of Experimental Biology 138:181-193.

Kukal, O., A.S. Serianni, and J.G. Duman. 1988B. Glycerol metabolism in a freeze-tolerant arctic insect: An in vivo 13-C NMR study. Journal of Comparative Physiology, B158:175-183.

Leonard, S. and J.M. Ringo. 1978. Analysis of male courtship patterns and mating behavior of *Brachymeria intermedia*. Annals of the Entomologcal Society of America 71:817-826.

MacLean, S.F. and T.S. Jensen. 1985. Food plant selection by insect herbivores in Alaskan arctic tundra: the role of plant life form. Oikos 44:211-221.

May, L.M. 1979. Insect thermoregulation. Annual Review of Entomology 24:313-349.

McEvoy, P.B. 1984. Increase in respiratory rate during feeding in larvae of the cinnabar moth *Tyria jacobaeae*. Physiological Entomology 9:191-195.

_____. 1985. Balancing insect energy budgets. Oecologia 66:154-156.

Montgomery, M.E. 1982. Life-cycle nitrogen budget for the gypsy moth, *Lymantria dispar*, reared on artificial diet. Journal of Insect Physiology 28:437-442.

Nelson, M.C. and J. Fraser. 1984. Communication in the courtship of a Madagascan hissing cockroach. I. Normal courtship. Animal Behaviour 32:194-203.

Price, P.W., C.E. Bouton, P. Gross, B.A. McPherson, J.N. Thompson, and A.E. Weiss. 1980. Interactions among three trophic levels: influence of plants on interactions between insect herbivores and natural enemies. Annual Review of Ecological Systematics 11:41-65.

Regal, P.J. 1967. Voluntary hypothermia in reptiles. Science 155:1551-1553.

Rhoades, D.F. 1985. Pheromonal communication between plants. In: Chemically Mediated Interactions between Plants and Other Organisms. Edited by: G.A. Cooper-Driver, T. Swain and E.E. Conn. Plenum Publishing Corp., New York. pp. 195-218.

Rosenthal, G.A. and D.H. Janzen. 1979. Herbivores: their interaction with secondary plant metabolites. Academic Press, New York.

Scholander, P.F., W. Flagg, R.J. Hoch, and L. Irving. 1953. Climatic adaptation in arctic and tropical pokilotherms. Physiological Zoology 26:67-92.

Scriber, J.M. and F. Slansky, Jr. 1981. The nutritional ecology of immature insects. Annual Review of Entomology 26:183-211.

Slansky, F. Jr. and J.M. Scriber. 1985. Food consumption and utilization. In: Comprehensive Insect Physiology, Volume 4, Chapter 3. Edited by: G.A. Kerkut and L.I. Gilbert. Pergamon Press, Oxford. pp. 87-163.

Storey, K.B. and J.M. Storey. 1983. Biochemistry of freeze tolerance in terrestrial insects. Trends in Biochemical Sciences 8:242-245.

Sustare, B.D. 1978. Systems diagrams. In: Quantitative Ethology. Edited by: P.W. Colgan. Wiley and Sons, New York. pp. 275-311.

Svoboda, J. and B. Freedman (Editors). 1988. Ecology of a High Arctic lowland oasis, Alexandra Fiord (78°53'N, 75°55'W), Ellesmere Island, N.W.T., Canada. University of Toronto Press, Toronto.

Tauber, M.J., C.A. Tauber, and S. Musaki. 1986. Seasonal adaptations of insects. Oxford University Press, New York. 411 pp.

Wightman, J.A. 1981. Why insect energy budgets do not balance. Oecologia 50:166-169.

Illustrated by Brenda Carter

FISHES, BIRDS AND MAMMALS

PRIORITIES FOR ICHTHYOLOGICAL RESEARCH IN THE CANADIAN ARCTIC ARCHIPELAGO

Don E. McAllister[1]

Abstract: Although much information is already available on fishes of the Canadian Arctic Islands, improved sampling is required involving collection of: (1) species not already represented in national collections; (2) deepwater fishes; (3) midwater fishes; (4) fishes in the south-central islands; (5) fishes in the Queen Elizabeth Islands; (6) fishes in winter. A book on the fishes of Arctic Canada is needed.

Résumé: Quoi que l'on connaisse déjà bien les poissons des îles de l'Arctique canadien, il faudrait améliorer l'échantillonnage par le prélèvement de: (1) certaines espèces qui ne figureraient pas déjà dans les collections de musées nationaux; (2) poissons d'eau profonde; (3) poissons vivant entre deux eaux; (4) poissons des îles du centre-sud; (5) poissons des îles Reine-Élisabeth; (6) poissons en hiver. Un manuel sur les poissons du Canada Arctique est nécessaire.

The ichthyological collections in the National Museum of Natural Sciences (NMNS) provide an important resource for ichthyological, fisheries, and environmental studies. Over 1,737 stations and 58,336 specimens of 95 of the 137 known fish species are represented in these Arctic Canadian collections, many from the Canadian Arctic Islands. Information on these specimens (including ecological and geographical data) can be selected, sorted, listed, summarized and mapped from our computer database. Study of these data and literature sources (McAllister and Steigerwald 1986) show deficiencies as far as the Canadian Arctic Islands are concerned.

Parts of the Arctic Archipelago ichthyofauna are poorly sampled, and the following should be given high priority in field work: (1) collect specimens of the 42 species not represented in the national collections; (2) collect deepwater fish fauna, especially in the Canadian sector between the North Pole and the Arctic Archipelago; (3) collect midwater fishes; (4) collect in the south-central Arctic Archipelago; (5) collect in the Queen Elizabeth Islands; (6) make winter collections. The improved sampling would yield reliable distribution maps useful for a number of purposes, and would provide the samples needed for research to produce a book on Arctic fishes. In addition, field research (Figure 1) is one means of demonstrating sovereignty.

---

[1] Zoology Division, National Museum of National Sciences, Ottawa, Ontario K1P 6P4

A volume on the fishes of Arctic Canada is urgently needed. The groundwork for such a book has been laid by publication of maps of existing species records (Hunter *et al.* 1984) (Figures 2-4); a list of Inuktitut, French, English and scientific names (McAllister *et al.* 1987; McAllister, in press); and a bibliography on Arctic fishes (McAllister and Steigerwald 1986). Now the NMNS needs resources to complete this project. The book would serve in the development and management of commercial, sustenance and sport fisheries, serve the needs of environmental-impact studies, and provide data for ecologists and biogeographers. Adequate life history studies are available for only 10% of Arctic marine fish species; behaviour is almost unknown. This research should involve Arctic native people. The Arctic coast of Canada is our longest,yet least known, coastline and deserves the highest priority.

REFERENCES

Hunter, J.G., S.T. Leach, D.E. McAllister, and M.B. Steigerwald. 1984. A distributional atlas of records of the marine fishes of Arctic Canada in the National Museums of Canada and Arctic Biological Station. Syllogeus 52:1-35.

McAllister, D.E. (in press). List of fishes of Canada. Syllogeus 63:1-300.

McAllister, D.E., V. Legendre, and J.C. Hunter. 1987. Liste des noms inuktitut (equimaux), français, anglais et scientifiques des poissons marins du Canada arctique/List of Inuktitut (Eskimo), French, English and scientific names of marine fishes of Arctic Canada. Report manuscrit canadien des sciences halieutiques et aquatiques No. 1932:1-106.

McAllister, D.E. and M.B. Steigerwald. 1986. Bibliography of the marine fishes of Arctic Canada, 1771-1985. Canadian Manuscript Report of Fisheries of Aquatic Sciences No. 1909:1-108.

Illustrated by Brenda Carter

FIGURE 1: Don McAllister preparing for underwater fish studies involving diving in shore-leads. Intrepid Inlet, Prince Patrick Island, 1972.

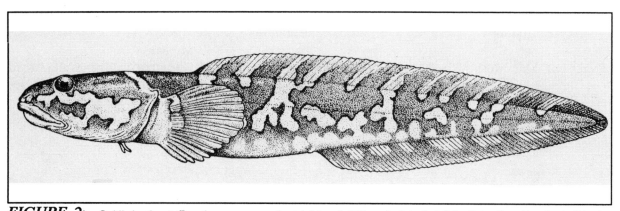

FIGURE 2: Saddled eelpout (Lycodes mucosus; male, total length 210 mm). A typical fish of the Canadian Arctic Islands.

514

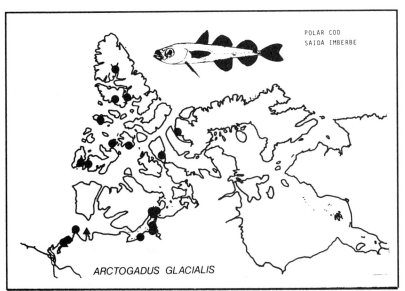

FIGURE 3: Recorded distribution of the polar cod (<u>Arctogadus glacialis</u>), a species common in the Arctic Islands. Dots represent specimens in the National Museum of Natural Science fish collection; triangles represent specimens in the Arctic Biological Station (Fisheries and Oceans Canada) collection (Hunter <u>et al.</u> 1984).

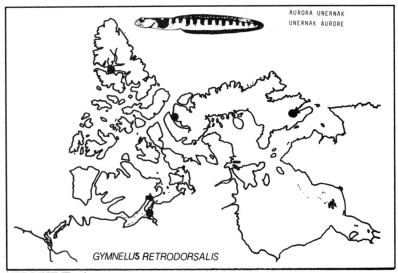

FIGURE 4: Recorded distribution of another widespread fish in the Arctic Islands, the aurora unernak (<u>Gymnelus retrodorsalis</u>). See Figure 3 for explanation of symbols.

AVIAN ZOOGEOGRAPHY IN THE CANADIAN ARCTIC ISLANDS

Henri Ouellet[1]

Abstract: The current knowledge of bird distribution in the Canadian Arctic Islands is based on more than 200 years of exploration and field studies. This vast database available mainly, but not exclusively, from the literature, constitutes a solid but incomplete source of information upon which general distribution patterns can be generated for a number of species. However, many islands have not been surveyed yet by ornithologists. Consequently little is known about the precise distribution of many species, particularly among the small passerines and the shorebirds. Similarly, specimens are insufficient to allow the delimitation of breeding ranges of several species with populations originating in the Palearctic Region. So it is difficult to make significant progress in the analysis of geographic variation and of the origins and evolution of the bird fauna. These areas, and the species which require special attention from ornithologists and naturalists, are identified. New information is essential for comprehensive studies on the evolution and zoogeography of the bird fauna of the Canadian Arctic.

Résumé: L'état des connaissances actuelles de la répartition des oiseaux dans les îles de l'Arctique canadien est fondé sur plus de deux cents ans d'exploration et d'études de terrain. Cette vaste accumulation de données, disponible surtout dans la littérature, forme une source d'information fiable, mais souvent incomplète lorsqu'il s'agit de déterminer les aires de répartition de plusieurs espèces. En effet, plusieurs îles n'ont pas encore été inventoriées par des ornithologistes. Conséquemment, la répartition de plusieurs espèces, notamment des petits passereaux et des limicoles, n'est connue que d'une façon fragmentaire. De même, il existe dans les collections peu ou pas de spécimens provenant des certaines îles qui pourraient permettre de délimiter l'aire de nidification des espèces originaires de la Région Paléarctique. Ces lacunes ralentissent considérablement les progrès dans les études de la variation géographique ou encore de l'origine et de l'évolution de la faune aviaire des régions arctiques. Les régions qui requièrent une attention particulière de la part des ornithologistes et des naturalistes sont identifiées. Il est donc primordial de combler ces lacunes afin d'entreprendre des études plus détaillées sur l'évolution et la zoogéographie des oiseaux de l'Arctique canadien.

INTRODUCTION

Bird distribution in the Canadian Arctic has remained poorly known for a long time - as indicated by the ornithological and natural history works published during the eighteenth (Hearn 1795; Latham 1781-1785; Pennant 1785) and nineteenth centuries (Chamberlain 1887; Forster 1882; Fielden 1877; Fox and James 1894; Kumlien 1879; MacFarlane 1891; Payne 1887; Rae 1888; Richardson 1829-1837; Swainson 1836-1837; Swainson and Richardson 1831; Turner 1885, 1886; Vieillot 1807; Wilson 1808-1814). In the early part of the twentieth century the situation improved when John and James Macoun published their "Catalogue of Canadian Birds" (1909). They summarized and incorporated most of the known information about Canadian birds, including the little that was available about the avifauna of the Arctic. However, the knowledge of distribution of arctic birds in Canada was at that time very fragmentary. Bird species occurring in the vast regions north of treeline had not been surveyed in any detail. The breeding ranges remained very approximate and were restricted

---

[1] Zoology Division, National Museum of Natural Sciences, Ottawa, Ontario K1P 6P4

mainly to those areas that had been visited by the early explorers and naturalists. No systematic and comprehensive survey of the birds had yet been undertaken anywhere in that vast area of Canada.

Exploratory surveys were undertaken at the turn of the twentieth century by E.A. Preble (1902, 1908) and others, which provided much needed new information. In the following, years plans for the Canadian Arctic Expedition (1913-1918) led one to expect exciting results about bird distribution from the immense unknown areas to be surveyed. Information on bird distribution and specimens gathered by the Arctic Expedition did not meet expectations primarily because the results were not generally available and were not published for many years after the return of the expedition (Anderson 1937). Following the Canadian Arctic Expedition other expeditions took place until the late 1930s, contributing to a more precise but still preliminary knowledge of bird distribution in the Canadian Arctic (Bray 1943; Gross 1937; Horring *et al.* 1937; Low 1906; Sutton 1929, 1931, 1932; Soper 1946A; Schaanning 1933; for other sources see References). Little ornithological activity took place during the Second World War, but many arctic areas were systematically explored soon after, and new data on avian distribution and ecology were obtained, contributing at least to a general overview of distribution patterns for most of the species known to occur in Canada.

Recently, particularly since the mid-1950s, many articles and papers have been published (see References), and the distribution information has been summarized in both editions of "The Birds of Canada" (Godfrey 1966, 1986). At present, the bird fauna of the Canadian Arctic, including that of most of the islands, is known at least in its broad distributional features.

PHYSIOGRAPHY

The Canadian Arctic, including the Arctic Islands, extends north of treeline to the northern extremity of Ellesmere Island (Anonymous 1985). The total area of the Canadian Arctic Islands, including Boothia and Melville peninsulas, covers 20% of Canada's territory (Table 1). Relief of the entire region is relatively gentle and remains generally under 2,000 m except for small areas on Ellesmere, Devon and Baffin islands which nevertheless lie below 2,500 m (Anonymous 1985). The entire area is included in a continuous

TABLE 1: RELATIVE AREA OF VARIOUS TERRITORIES AND ISLANDS NORTH OF TREELINE CONSIDERED TO BE IN THE ARCTIC ZONE.

REGION	AREA (km^2)
District of Franklin (including Melville and Boothia peninsulas)	1,403,134
Melville Peninsula	40,000
Boothia Peninsula	32,000
Queen Elizabeth Islands	425,000
Southampton Island	16,114
Coats Island	5,499
Mansel Island	5,375
Ottawa Islands	3,200
Belcher Islands	13,000
District of Keewatin	565,809
District of Mackenzie	1,277,447
Total area of Canadian Arctic Islands including Melville and Boothia peninsulas	1,446,322

permafrost zone with restricted ice caps and glaciers on Axel Heiberg, Ellesmere, and Baffin islands (Anonymous 1985). All the islands were glaciated and deglaciation started generally some 13,000 years ago on the western islands, but only about 10,000 years ago, or more recently, on most of the other islands (Anonymous; 1985).

The vegetation of this region is of three main types: (1) arctic tundra with low shrub; (2) rocky arctic tundra with lichens; (3) barren rocky arctic tundra (Anonymous 1985; see Bliss, and Edlund, this volume). The mean precipitation in June and July is low - under 5.1 cm (Anonymous 1985, see Mackay, this volume).

The Arctic Islands are part of the Arctic Biome (Aldrich 1967) with its characteristic climate, plants, and animals. With Greenland they belong to the Nearctic Zoogeographical Region (Wallace 1876) - an important part of the Holarctic Region.

THE BIRD FAUNA OF THE ARCTIC BIOME OF CANADA

A total of 103 bird species is given for the Arctic Zone as recognized by Salomonsen (1972), whereas Johansen (1960) lists only 80 species for approximately the same area. The definition of the "Arctic Zone" of these two authors is different because Salomonsen included several elements that could be classified as "subarctic". Considering these conflicting views in qualifying the Arctic Zone of Canada, it seems best to define it for the purposes of this work as the tundra area north of treeline. This zone thus corresponds to Aldrich's (1967) "Arctic Biome".

Using these limits and confining the species count to the Arctic Islands (Table 1), but including the Hudson Bay islands as well as Melville and Boothia peninsulas, I arrive at a total of 64 species, counting only those species known to breed or have bred within the area. Vagrants, accidentals, and irregular visitors have been excluded. Table 2 summarizes the 18 families and 64 species known to breed in the Canadian Arctic Islands. To have a clear understanding of the situation in each group, it seems appropriate to review critically each family separately in the light of the information currently available.

Gaviidae

Of the five species of this panboreal family (Mayr 1946, 1976), four are known to breed in the Arctic Islands. Among these, only one can be considered an authentic arctic species, the Red-throated Loon (*Gavia stellata*) - primarily on the basis that its breeding range extends mainly from treeline to the northern extremity of Ellesmere Island (Godfrey 1986; Figure 1A)). The others have a more southern range and their breeding distribution extends barely to the southern part of the Arctic Islands.

Procellariidae

This large family, which has a world-wide oceanic distribution, is represented in the Arctic Islands by a single species, the circumpolar Northern Fulmar (*Fulmarus glacialis*). It breeds in a number of large colonies primarily in the northeastern Arctic Islands, although it has recently extended its breeding range southward in Newfoundland and on the Labrador coast (Godfrey 1986; Brown *et al.* 1975). The Canadian breeding population is

TABLE 2: *FAMILIES AND SPECIES OF BREEDING BIRDS RECORDED ON THE CANADIAN ARCTIC ISLANDS. FOR COMPARATIVE PURPOSES THE NUMBER OF SPECIES ARE GIVEN FOR THE ARCTIC ISLANDS AND THE PALEARCTIC REGION, AS WELL AS THE REGIONS OF ORIGIN OF THE TAXA.*

FAMILY	NUMBER OF SPECIES IN HOLARCTIC REGION[1]	NUMBER OF SPECIES ON ARCTIC ISLANDS[2]	REGION[3]	SPECIES
1. Gaviidae	5	4	H	1. *Gavia stellata*
			N-H	2. *Gavia pacifica*
			N-H	3. *Gavia immer*
			N	4. *Gavia adamsii*
2. Procellariidae	1	1	H	1. *Fulmarus glacialis*
3. Anatidae	22	12	N	1. *Cygnus columbianus*
			N	2. *Anser albifrons*
			N-H	3. *Chen caerulescens*
			N	4. *Chen rossii*
			H	5. *Branta bernicla*
			N	6. *Branta canadensis*
			H	7. *Anas acuta*
			H	8. *Somateria mollissima*
			H	9. *Somateria spectabilis*
			H	10. *Histrionicus histrionicus*
			H	11. *Clangula hyemalis*
			H	12. *Mergus serrator*
4. Accipitridae	2	1	H	1. *Buteo lagopus*
5. Falconidae	2	2	H	1. *Falco peregrinus*
			H	2. *Falco rusticolus*
6. Phasianidae	2	2	H	1. *Lagopus lagopus*
			H	2. *Lagopus rusticolus*
7. Gruidae	1	1	N-H	1. *Grus canadensis*
8. Charadriidae	5	4	H	1. *Pluvialis squatarola*
			N	2. *Pluvialis dominica*
			P	3. *Charadrius hiaticula*
			N	4. *Charadrius semipalmatus*
9. Scolopacidae	27	14	H	1. *Arenaria interpres*
			H	2. *Calidris canutus*
			H	3. *Calidris alba*
			N	4. *Calidris pusilla*
			N	5. *Calidris minutilla*
			N	6. *Calidris fuscicollis*
			N	7. *Calidris bairdii*
			N	8. *Calidris melanotos*

TABLE 2: *(cont'd)*

FAMILY	NUMBER OF SPECIES IN HOLARCTIC REGION[1]	NUMBER OF SPECIES ON ARCTIC ISLANDS[2]	REGION[3]	SPECIES
9. Scolopacidae (cont'd)			H	9. *Calidris maritima*
			H	10. *Calidris alpina*
			N	11. *Calidris himantopus*
			N	12. *Tryngites subruficollis*
			H	13. *Phalaropus lobatus*
			H	14. *Phalaropus fulicaria*
10. Laridae	12	11	H	1. *Stercorarius pomarinus*
			H	2. *Stercorarius parasiticus*
			H	3. *Stercorarius longicaudus*
			H	4. *Larus argentatus*
			H	5. *Larus glaucoides (thayeri)*
			H	6. *Larus hyperboreus*
			H	7. *Rissa tridactyla*
			H	8. *Rhodostethia rosea*
			H	9. *Xema sabini*
			H	10. *Pagophila eburnea*
			H	11. *Sterna paradisaea*
11. Alcidae	11	3	P	1. *Alle alle*
			H	2. *Uria lomvia*
			H	3. *Cepphus grylle*
12. Strigidae	2	1	H	1. *Nyctea scandiaca*
PASSERIFORMES				
13. Alaudidae	1	1	H	1. *Eremophila alpestris*
14. Corvidae	1	1	H	1. *Corvus corax*
15. Muscicapidae	1	1	P	1. *Oenanthe oenanthe*
16. Motacillidae	3	1	H	1. *Anthus spinoletta*
17. Emberizidae	3	2	H	1. *Calcarius lapponicus*
			H	2. *Plectrophenax nivalis*
18. Fringillidae	2	2	H	1. *Carduelis flammea*
			H	2. *Carduelis hornemanni*
TOTAL	103	64		

[1] Based on Salomonsen (1972).
[2] Based on various published and unpublished records, and on Godfrey (1986).
[3] N = Nearctic, H = Holarctic, P = Palearctic.

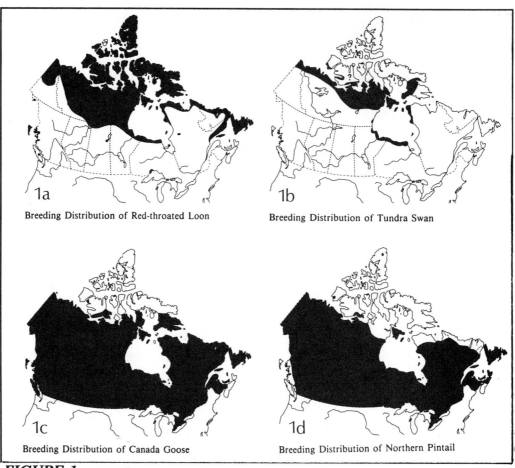

FIGURE 1: Breeding distribution in Canada of selected bird species. Originals from Godfrey (1986) have sometimes been modified in the light of more recent information.

subspecifically different (*F. g. minor*) from the populations of the eastern and western Palaearctic (*F. g. glacialis, F. g. rodgersii*).

Anatidae

This large cosmopolitan family of 147 species (Bock and Farrand 1980) is represented by only 12 species in the Arctic Islands. Most of them, like the Tundra Swan (*Cygnus columbianus*) (Figure 1B), Greater White-fronted Goose (*Anser albifrons*), Ross's Goose (*Chen rossii*), Canada Goose (*Branta canadensis*) (Figure 1C), Northern Pintail (*Anas acuta*) (Figure 1D), Harlequin Duck (*Histrionicus histrionicus*), and Red-breasted Merganser (*Mergus serrator*), occur only on the southern Arctic Islands. Other species are more widespread and are found almost throughout the islands, namely: Snow Goose (*Chen caerulescens*) (Figure 2A), Brant (*Branta bernicla*) (Figure 2B), Common Eider (*Somateria mollissima*), King Eider (*Somateria spectabilis*) (Figure 2C), and Oldsquaw (*Clangula hyemalis*) (Figure 2D).

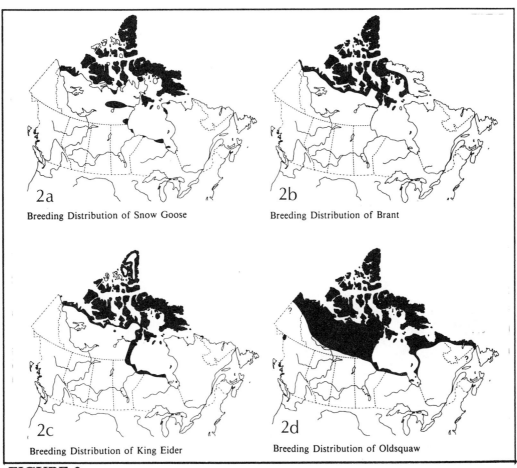

FIGURE 2: Breeding distribution in Canada of selected bird species. Originals from Godfrey (1986) have sometimes been modified in the light of more recent information.

Accipitridae

The cyclic Rough-legged Hawk (*Buteo lagopus*) is the sole representative of this large family with a nearly world-wide distribution. Another northern member of the family, the White-tailed Eagle (*Haliaetus albicilla*) breeds from southern Greenland to eastern Siberia but has not entered North America, although its range is expanding in Greenland (Salomonsen 1979).

Falconidae

Only two species of this world-wide family occur in the Arctic Islands: the Peregrine Falcon (*Falco peregrinus*) restricted to the southern islands (Figure 3A) and the Gyrfalcon (*Falco rusticolus*) from treeline to northern Ellesmere Island (Figure 3B). Both birds have

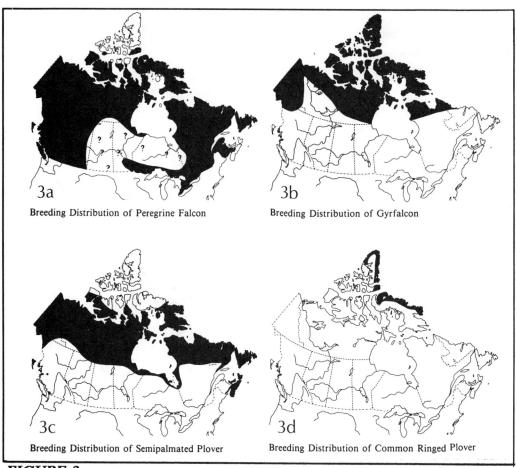

FIGURE 3: Breeding distribution in Canada of selected bird species. Originals from Godfrey (1986) have sometimes been modified in the light of more recent information.

diverged from the Palearctic populations to some extent, and subspecies can be recognized in the Arctic Zone of Canada (Todd and Friedmann 1947; White 1968).

Phasianidae

The subfamily Tetraoninae is widespread in Europe, Asia, and North America, but has only two representatives in the Arctic Islands. The Willow Ptarmigan (*Lagopus lagopus*) has a more southerly distribution than its congener the Rock Ptarmigan (*Lagopus mutus*), which ranges from treeline and Newfoundland to northern Ellesmere Island. Several subspecies, different from the Palearctic forms, have been recognized throughout their breeding ranges in Canada.

524

Gruidae

The Sandhill Crane (*Grus canadensis*) occurs in the southern part of the Arctic Archipelago (Banks, Victoria, and Baffin islands) and in the extreme southeastern part of Devon Island. The Arctic Islands population is subspecifically different from other southern populations.

Charadriidae

This small world-wide family, with five species in the circumpolar regions, is represented by four species in the Arctic Islands. The Black-bellied Plover (*Pluvialis squatarola*), Lesser Golden Plover (*Pluvialis dominica*), and Semipalmated Plover (*Charadrius semipalmatus*) (Figure 3C), occupy the southern islands, whereas the Common Ringed Plover (*Charadrius hiaticula*) (Figure 3D), apparently a recent immigrant from the Old World, breeds on the eastern fringe of the northernmost eastern islands. Its range overlaps that of its North American congener on Baffin Island (Smith 1969), but the area of sympatry in the two species has yet to be defined precisely.

Scolopacidae

This highly diverse world-wide family has 14 representatives in the Arctic Zone of North America, some of which occur only in the Canadian Arctic Islands and in Alaska. But some species, such as the Least Sandpiper (*Calidris minutilla*) and Dunlin (*Calidris alpina*), have a breeding range restricted to the southern islands, whereas others reach eastern Siberia. The other species breed virtually on all the islands to the northern tip of Ellesmere Island, although their distribution can be very patchy in parts of their ranges. Species such as the Ruddy Turnstone (*Arenaria interpres*) (Figure 4A) and Red Knot (*Calidris canutus*) (Figure 4B), are composed of two distinct populations. The northernmost belongs to the Old World subspecies and migrates to and from the Old World (see Morrison and Davidson, this volume), whereas the more southern one migrates to and from South America during the non-breeding season. The ranges of these subspecies can only be approximated in the light of the data currently available. It is important to obtain additional material to determine the extent to which the ranges of these subspecies overlap in the Arctic Islands.

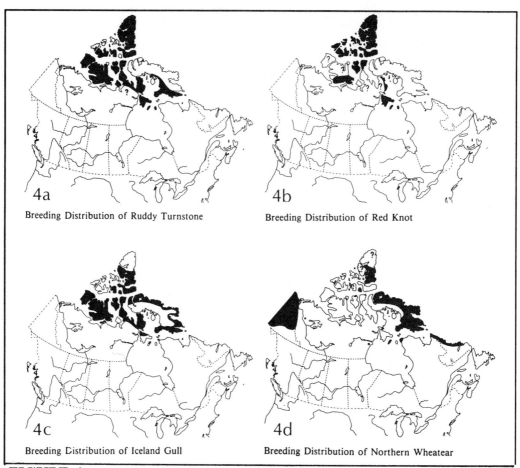

FIGURE 4: Breeding distribution in Canada of selected bird species. Originals from Godfrey (1986) have sometimes been modified in the light of more recent information.

Laridae

This cosmopolitan family is represented in the Arctic Islands by 11 species, which occur also in the other circumpolar regions although their distribution can form a complex mosaic. Of the three jaeger (*Stercorarius*) species, only one reaches the northern extremity of Ellesmere Island. The others occur in the central portion of the Arctic Zone. The Herring Gull (*Larus argentatus*) reaches only the southern islands and appears to be replaced farther north by the Iceland Gull (*Larus glaucoides*) (Figure 4C) and the Glaucous Gull (*Larus hyperboreus*). The distribution of *Larus glaucoides* is complex and only known in a cursory manner - at least as far as its various populations are concerned. The Black-legged Kittiwake (*Rissa tridactyla*), although not confined to the Arctic Zone, maintains large colonies on some of the eastern Arctic Islands, and is expending in the southern part of its range. The rare Ross's Gull (*Rodostethia rosea*) and Ivory Gull (*Pagophila eburnea*) (Thomas and

MacDonald 1987; Frisch 1983; Reed and Dupuis 1983; Renaud and McLaren 1982) have a patchy distribution, and their precise ranges are still incompletely known.

Alcidae

Of the 11 species recorded in the Arctic Zone of the Holarctic Region, only two breed regularly in the Arctic Islands of Canada, the Thick-billed Murre (*Uria aalge*) and Black Guillemot (*Cepphus grylle*). Neither species reaches the northern extremity of Ellesmere Island; they are found mainly along the eastern periphery of the archipelago. A third species, the Dovekie (*Alle alle*) has recently been reported on Baffin Island (Finley and Evans 1984) and may represent a recent range extension from Greenland.

Strigidae

Only the circumpolar Snowy Owl (*Nyctea scandiaca*) is known to occur on all the Arctic Islands. The Short-eared Owl (*Asio flammeus*) may breed on the southern islands but this requires confirmation.

Alaudidae

The cosmopolitan Horned Lark (*Eremophila alpestris*), with one recognized subspecies, is known to breed on all the islands south of Ellesmere Island.

Corvidae

In this cosmopolitan and resourceful family, only the Common Raven (*Corvus corax*) occupies the Arctic Islands to the latitude of central Ellesmere Island. It seems absent from Coats and Mansel islands as a breeding bird but detailed field observations are still required for those islands, although nesting sites may be very rare on Mansel Island.

Muscicapidae

This very large Old World family (1,427 species; Bock and Farrand 1980) is poorly represented in the Arctic Zone by a single circumpolar species, the Northern Wheatear (*Oenanthe oenanthe*). In Canada, there are two distinct subspecies (Figure 4D) (Godfrey 1986; Boothroyd 1984; Sutton and Parmelee 1954). This bird is probably a recent immigrant to North America.

Motacillidae

A single representative of this small cosmopolitan family can be found on the southern islands of the archipelago: the Water Pipit (*Anthus spinoletta*). It is generally widespread where it occurs.

Emberizidae

This large family of Nearctic origin (Mayr 1946, 1976) is represented in the Arctic Islands by two members of the subfamily Emberizinae: the Lapland Longspur (*Calcarius lapponicus*) (Figure 5A) and Snow Bunting (*Plectrophenax nivalis*) (Figure 5B). They are found on all the islands, although they have a patchy distribution in certain sectors of the archipelago.

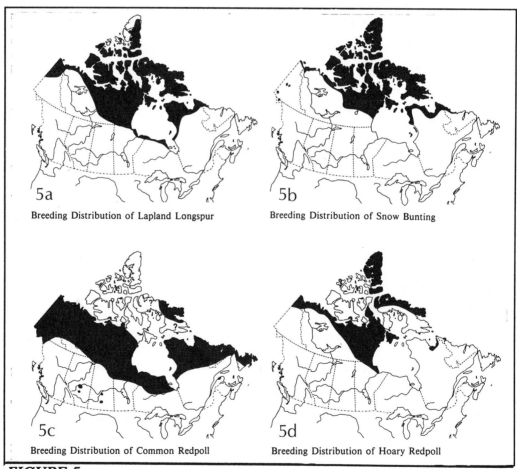

5a
Breeding Distribution of Lapland Longspur

5b
Breeding Distribution of Snow Bunting

5c
Breeding Distribution of Common Redpoll

5d
Breeding Distribution of Hoary Redpoll

FIGURE 5: Breeding distribution in Canada of selected bird species. Originals from Godfrey (1986) have sometimes been modified in the light of more recent information.

Fringillidae

Two members of the subfamily Carduelinae represent this family of Palearctic origin: the Common Redpoll (*Carduelis flammea*) (Figure 5C) and Hoary Redpoll (*Carduelis hornemanni*) (Figure 5D). Both species display considerable geographic variation, and their relationships within the entire Holarctic Region are unclear. The status of these two species is currently under review and requires additional study.

Summary

This cursory taxonomic review provides basic information about the diversity and origin of the bird fauna of the Canadian Arctic Islands. It also indicates the need for detailed distribution studies for many species in northern Canada to determine their origin, precise taxonomic status, and range alterations relative to historical events, climatic fluctuations, and ecological variations.

SPECIES DIVERSITY

Latitudinal gradients in species diversity have been discussed at some length (Pianka 1966), but no study has been undertaken concerning this aspect of bird distribution in the Canadian Arctic. An analysis of species densities in North American birds (Cook 1969) presented interesting data about breeding birds on the continent, but the information given for the Canadian Arctic is incomplete, or inadequate in some cases. A thorough analysis is warranted, even if the information on hand is still incomplete. As an example, I have plotted for six arctic and subarctic localities the number of known breeding species. The results (Figure 6) indicate a statistically-significant correlation between latitude and the number of breeding species ($r = -0.9531$). As expected, the number of breeding species diminishes significantly northward. Although more data are required, a preliminary analysis of species diversity in the Arctic Islands is possible when all currently available data have been compiled. This would reveal interesting, if not spectacular, facts about avian distribution patterns in Arctic Canada.

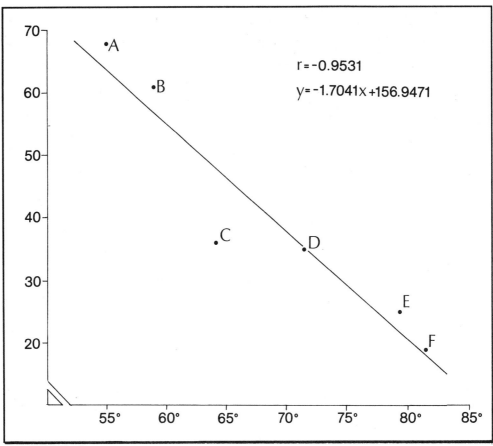

FIGURE 6: Linear regression between the total number of breeding species against latitude for selected localities, as follows: (A) Schefferville, (B) Kuujjuak (Fort Chimo), (C) Iqaluit (Frobisher Bay), (D) Pond Inlet, (E) Alexandra Fiord, and (F) Alert.

THE ORIGIN OF THE BIRD FAUNA

My review of the bird fauna of the Arctic Islands shows that not one of the families considered to be of Neotropical origin (Mayr 1946, 1976) has reached the Arctic Zone or the southernmost islands of the archipelago. This is not surprising considering that most members of those families or subfamilies (e.g. Trochilidae, Tyrannidae, Vireonidae, Parulinae, and Thraupinae) are forest or woodland species. However, most species of two other subfamilies (Cardinalinae and Icterinae), birds of open or semi-open areas, are also absent from the Arctic Zone.

The immigrants from the Palearctic Region are numerous, and are still colonizing the archipelago. As an example, the Northern Wheatear (*Oenanthe oenanthe*) is probably a recent immigrant on both sides of the North American continent (Figure 4D). The western Palearctic subspecies *O. o. leucorhoa* is colonizing the eastern Arctic Islands and continues to expand, as indicated by data collected since the turn of the century. On the western side of the continent, the more eastern nominal Palearctic subspecies *O. o. oenanthe* is colonizing North America via Alaska, the Yukon, and the northwestern part of the District of Mackenzie. Although it has not yet reached the western Arctic Islands, it is only a question of time before it becomes established on some of them. In a less spectacular fashion, subspecies from the western Palearctic have colonized at least the eastern Arctic Islands, and appear to be still expanding (e.g. the Ruddy Turnstone (*Arenaria interpres interpres*) (Figure 4A) and Red Knot (*Calidris canutus canutus*) (Figure 4B). Similarly, although little information is available at present, it is predictable that an eastern Palearctic population, possibly originating in Siberia may colonize the western islands of the Archipelago, if present climatic conditions remain relatively stable.

DISCUSSION AND CONCLUSIONS

Information currently available indicates that the bird fauna of the Canadian Arctic Islands originates mainly from two centres outside North America: (1) the western European Arctic; and (2) the eastern Palaearctic boreal region, particularly Siberia. This agrees with the results of earlier studies (Mayr 1946, 1976), and shows a small diversity and much movement among populations, which have given rise to colonization by certain members of the Pan-boreal Element (Mayr 1946, 1976) within the Gaviidae, Phalaropinae, and Alcidae. On the other hand, the Gruidae, Strigidae, Corvidae, Muscicapidae, Motacillidae, and Carduelinae constitute the Old World Element (Mayr 1946, 1976) of the northern Nearctic avifauna. The North American Element is more restricted and comprises the Phasianidae (Tetraoninae) and the Emberizidae (Emberizinae) (Mayr 1946, 1976). No species considered to belong to the Pan-American Element or the South American Element (Mayr 1946, 1976) have reached and colonized the Arctic Islands. Range shifts related to climatic fluctuations have undoubtedly occurred in the Arctic Islands, but little information is available at present. Data collected regularly for taxonomic, systematic, distribution, and ecological studies over wide areas in the Arctic Zone would permit a better understanding of colonizing populations - particularly such aspects as genetics, ecology, and variation at the intra and interspecific levels (Parsons 1982). Furthermore, such data would provide insight into the mechanisms of invasions (Mooney and Drake 1986) and possibly extinctions as well (Martin and Klein 1984).

ACKNOWLEDGEMENTS

I wish to extend my sincere thanks to Michel Gosselin for assistance and for preparing the figures.

REFERENCES (SELECTED BIOGRAPHY)

Abraham, D.M. and C.D. Ankney. 1984. Partitioning of foraging habitat by Sabine's Gulls and Arctic Terns. Wilson Bulletin 96(2):161-172.

Abraham, K.F. and C.D. Ankney. 1986. Summer birds of East Bay, Southampton Island, Northwest Territories. Canadian Field-Naturalist 100(2):180-185.

Abraham, K.F., C.D. Ankney, and H. Boyd. 1983. Assortative mating by Brant. Auk 100(1):201-203.

Aldrich, J.W. 1967. Taxonomy, distribution and present status. Chapter 2. In: The Wild Turkey and Its Management. Edited by: O.H. Hewitt. Wildlife Society, Washington, D.C. pp. 1-589.

Allen, E.G. 1951. The history of American ornithology before Audubon. Transactions of the American Philosophical Society 41:386-591.

Allen, J.A. 1908. Pennant's 'Indian zoology'. Bulletin of the American Museum of Natural History 24:111-116.

Anderson, R.M. 1913. Report on the natural history collections of the expedition. Birds. In: V. Stefansson - My Life with the Eskimo. The Macmillan Company, New York. pp. 456-494.

_____. 1937. Mammals and birds of the western Arctic district, North-west Territories, Canada. In: Canada's Western Northland. Lands, Parks and Forests Branch. Ottawa. pp. 97-122.

Anonymous. 1985. The national atlas of Canada; 5th Edition. Energy, Mines and Resources Canada, Ottawa.

Austin, O.L., Jr. 1932. The birds of Newfoundland and Labrador. Memoirs of the Nuttall Ornithology Club 7:1-229.

Barry, T.W. and J.N. Eisenhart. 1958. Ross' Geese nesting at Southampton Island, N.W.T., Canada. Auk 75(1):89-90.

Bee, J.W. 1958. Birds found on the Arctic Slope of northern Alaska. University of Kansas, Publication of the Museum of Natural History 10(5):163-211.

Birkhead, T.R., E. Greene, J.D. Biggins, and D.N. Nettleship. 1985. Breeding site characteristics and breeding success in Thick-billed Murres. Canadian Journal of Zoology 63(8):1880-1884.

Birkhead, T.R. and D.N. Nettleship. 1981. Reproductive biology of Thick-billed Murres (*Uria lomvia*): an inter-colony comparison. Auk 98(2):258-269.

_____. 1982. The adaptative significance of egg size and laying date in Thick-billed Murres *Uria lomvia*. Ecology 63(2):300-306.

Bliss, L.C., O.W. Heal, and J.J. Moore (Editors). 1981. Tundra ecosystems: a comparative analysis. Cambridge University Press, Cambridge. pp. 1-813.

Blomqvist, S. and M. Elander. 1981. Sabine's Gull (*Xema sabini*), Ross's Gull (*Rhodostethia rosea*) and Ivory Gull (*Pagophila eburnea*). Gulls in the Arctic: a review. Arctic 34(1):122-132.

Blondel, J. 1979. Biogéographie et évolution. Collection d'écologie, no. 15. Masson, Paris. 173 pp.

_____. 1986. Biogéographie évolutive. Collection d'écologie, no. 20. Masson, Paris. pp. 1-221.

Bock, W.J. and J. Farrand, Jr. 1980. The number of species and genera of recent birds: a contribution to comparative systematics. American Museum Novitates 2703:1-29.

Boothroyd, P.N. 1984. Northern Wheatears, *Oenanthe oenanthe* on Axel Heiberg and Ellesmere Islands, Northwest Territories. Canadian Field-Naturalist 98(1):48-49.

Boyd, H. and L.S. Maltby. 1979. The brant of the western Queen Elizabeth Islands, N.W.T. In: Management and Biology of Pacific Flyway Geese. Edited by: R.J. Jarvis and J.C. Bartonek. Oregon State University, Corvallis. pp. 5-21.

Boyd, H., G.E.J. Smith, and F.G. Cooch. 1982. The Lesser Snow Geese of the eastern Canadian Arctic. Canadian Wildlife Service, Occasional Paper 46:1-25.

Bray, R. 1943. Notes on the birds of Southampton Island, Baffin Island, and Melville Peninsula. Auk 60(4):504-536.

Brooks, W.S. 1915. Notes on birds from east Siberia and Arctic Alaska. Bulletin of the Museum of Comparative Zoology 59(5):361-413.

Brown, R.G.B., D.N. Nettleship, P. Germain, C.E. Tull, and T. Davis. 1975. Atlas of eastern Canadian seabirds. Canadian Wildlife Service, Ottawa. 220 pp..

Cairns, D.K. 1985. Ermine visitation to Black Guillemot colonies in northeastern Hudson Bay. Condor 87(1):144-145.

Chamberlain, M. 1887. A catalogue of Canadian birds, with notes on the distribution of the species. J.&A. McMillan. Saint John. 143 pp..

Chernov, Y.I. 1985. The living tundra. Cambridge University Press, Cambridge. 213 pp.

Cheylan, G. 1984. Les mammifères des îles de Provence et de Méditerranée occidentale: un exemple de peuplement insulaire non-équilibré? Terre et Vie 39(1):37-54.

Cook, R.E. 1969. Variation in species density of North American birds. Systematic Zoology 18(1):63-84.

Cooke, A. and C. Holland. 1978. The exploration of northern Canada: 500 to 1920, a chronology. The Arctic History Press, Toronto. 549 pp.

Coulter, R. 1981. The Joint Services Expedition to Princess Marie Bay, Ellesmere Island, 1980. Part 2 - Brief impressions. Sea Swallow 30:21-22.

Eifrig, C.W.G. 1905. Ornithological results of the Canadian "Neptune" expedition to Hudson Bay and northward, 1903-1904. Auk 22(3):232-241.

Ellis, D.V. and J. Evans. 1960. Comments on the distribution and migration of birds in Foxe Basin, Northwest Territories. Canadian Field-Naturalist 74(1):59-70.

Fielden, H.W. 1877. List of birds observed in Smith Sound and in Polar Basin during the Arctic Expedition of 1875-76. Ibis, 4th series, 1(4):401-412.

Finley, K.J. and C.R. Evans. 1984. First Canadian breeding record of the Dovekie (*Alle alle*). Arctic 37(3):288-289.

Forster, J.R. 1882. XXIX. An account of the birds sent from Hudson's Bay; with observations relative to their natural history and Latin descriptions of some of the most uncommon. Read June 18-25, 1772. Willughby Society, London. pp. 382-433.

Fox, L. and T. James, 1894. Voyages of Foxe and James. Hakluyt Society Publication 2:88-89.

Freedman, B. and J. Svoboda. 1982. Populations of breeding birds at Alexandra Fjord, Ellesmere Island, Northwest Territories, compared with other Arctic localities. Canadian Field-Naturalist 96(1):56-60.

Frisch, T. 1983. Ivory Gull colonies on the Devon Island Ice Cap, Arctic Canada. Arctic 36(4):370-371.

Gabrielson, I.N. and F.C. Lincoln. 1959. The birds of Alaska. Wildlife Management Institute. Stackpole Co., Harrisburg. 922 pp.

Gaston, A.J. 1980. Populations, movements and wintering areas of Thick-billed Murres *Uria lomvia* in eastern Canada. Canadian Wildlife Service, Progress Notes 110:1-10.

_____. 1982A. Migration of juvenile Thick-billed Murres through Hudson Strait in 1980. Canadian Field-Naturalist 96(1):30-34.

_____. 1982B. On the seabirds of northern Hudson Bay. Naturaliste Canadien 109:895-903.

_____. 1985. The diet of Thick-billed Murre chicks in the eastern Canadian Arctic. Auk 102(4):727-734.

Gaston, A.J., G. Chapdelaine, and D.G. Noble. 1984. Phenotypic variation among Thick-billed Murres from colonies in Hudson Strait. Arctic 37(3):284-287.

Gaston, A.J. and R. Decker. 1985. Interbreeding of Thayer's Gull, *Larus thayeri*, and Kumlien's Gull, *Larus glaucoides kumlieni*, on Southampton Island, Northwest Territories. Canadian Field-Naturalist 99(2):257-259.

Gaston, A.J., R. Decker, F.G. Cooch, and A. Reed. 1986. The distribution of larger species of birds breeding on the coasts of Foxe Basin and northern Hudson Bay, Canada. Arctic 39(4):285-296.

Gaston, A.J. and D.N. Nettleship. 1981. The Thick-billed Murres of Prince Leopold Island. Canadian Wildlife Service, Monograph Series 6:1-350.

Giroux, J.F., Y. Bédard, and J. Bédard. 1984. Habitat use by the Greater Snow Geese during the brood-rearing period. Arctic 37(2):155-160.

Godfrey, W.E. 1953. Notes of Ellesmere Island birds. Canadian Field-Naturalist 67(2):89-93.

_____. 1966. The birds of Canada. National Museums of Canada, Biological Series 73, Bulletin 203:1-428.

_____. 1986. The birds of Canada. Revised Edition. National Museum of Natural Sciences, Ottawa. 595 pp.

Gross, A.O. 1937. Birds of the Bowdoin-MacMillan Arctic Expedition 1934. Auk 54(1):12-42.

Hearne, S. 1795. A journey from Prince of Wales Fort in Hudson's Bay to the Northern Ocean. J.W. Davis, London. 458 pp.

Holyoak, D.T. 1983. Notes on the birds of southwestern Banks Island, Northwest Territories, Canada. Bulletin of the British Ornithological Club 103(2):37-39.

Horring, R., J.R. Pfoff, K.L. Henriksen, and K. Stephenson. 1937. Report on the Fifth Thule Expedition, 1921-24. Part 2, Zoology. In: The Danish Expedition to Arctic North America in Charge of Knud Rasmussen. Copenhagen. 133 pp.

Houston, C.S. 1983. Birds first described from Hudson Bay. Canadian Field-Naturalist 97(1):95-98.

_____. 1984A. Arctic ordeal. The journal of John Richardson, surgeon-naturalist with Franklin, 1820-1822. McGill-Queen's University Press, Kingston and Montreal. 348 pp.

_____. 1984B. John Richardson - first naturalist in the Northwest. Beaver, autumn:10-15.

Hussell, D.J.T. and G.L. Holroyd. 1974. Birds of the Truelove Lowland and adjacent areas of northeastern Devon Island. Canadian Field-Naturalist 88(2):197-212.

Johansen, H. 1960. Die Entstehung der arktischen Vogelfauna. In: Proceedings of the XII International Ornithological Congress, 1958. Helsinki. pp. 358-362.

Johnson, S.R. and J.G. Ward. 1985. Observations of Thick-billed Murres (Uria lomvia) and other seabirds at Cape Parry, Amundsen Gulf, N.W.T. Arctic 38(2):112-115.

Kennedy, A.J. 1981. Snowy Owl prey on Prince of Wales Island, Northwest Territories. Naturaliste Canadien 108(2):195-197.

Kerbes, R.H. 1983. Lesser Snow Goose colonies in the western Canadian Arctic. Journal of Wildlife Management 47(2):523-526.

Kerbes, R.H., M.R. McLandress, G.E.J. Smith, G.W. Beyersbergen, and B. Godwin. 1983. Ross' Goose and Lesser Snow Goose colonies in the central Canadian Arctic. Canadian Journal of Zoology 61(1):168-173.

Kessel, B. and D.D. Gibson. 1978. Status and distribution of Alaska birds. Studies in Avian Biology 1:1-100.

Kishchinskii, A.A. 1979. Birds and the problem of the Bering land bridge between the continents. Bulletin of the Moscow Society of Naturalists 84(1):5-12.

Kumlien, L. 1879. Contribution to the natural history of Arctic America. United States National Museum, Bulletin 15:1-179.

Latham, J. 1781-1785. A general synopsis of birds. Volume I. Parts 1, 2; Volume II. Parts 1, 2: Volume III. Parts 1, 2. Leigh and Sotheby, London.

Longcore, J.R., J.D. Heyland, A. Reed, and P. Laporte. 1983. Contaminants in Greater Snow Geese and their eggs. Journal of Wildlife Management 47(4):1105-1109.

Low, A.P. 1906. Report on the Dominion Government Expedition to Hudson Bay and the Arctic Islands on board the D.G.S. *Neptune*, 1903-1904. Government of Canada, Ottawa. pp. 314-319.

MacDonald, S.D. 1954. Report on biological investigations at Mould Bay, Prince Patrick Island, N.W.T. Annual Report, National Museum of Canada 1952-53, 132:214-238.

_____. 1960. Biological investigations at Isachsen, Ellef Ringnes Island, N.W.T. National Museum of Canada, Bulletin 172:90-97.

MacFarlane, R. 1891. Notes on and list of birds and eggs collected in Arctic America, 1861-1866. Proceedings of the United States National Museum 14:413-446.

Macoun, J. and J.M. Macoun. 1909. Catalogue of Canadian birds. Geological Survey of Canada, Publication 973:1-761.

Macpherson, A.J. and T.H. Manning. 1959. The birds and mammals of Adelaide Peninsula, N.W.T. National Museum of Canada, Biological Series 59, Bulletin 161:1-63.

Macpherson, A.H. and I.A. McLaren. 1959. Notes on the birds of southern Foxe Peninsula, Baffin Island, Northwest Territories. Canadian Field-Naturalist 73(1):63-81.

Maher, W.J. and D.N. Nettleship. 1968. The pintail (*Anas acuta*) breeding at latitude 82°N on Ellesmere Island, N.W.T., Canada. Auk 85(3):320-321.

Maltby, L.S. 1978. Birds of the coastal zone of Melville Island, 1973-1975. Canadian Field-Naturalist 92(1):24-29.

Manning, T.H. 1952. Birds of west James Bay coast between Long Point and Cape Jones. Canadian Field-Naturalist 66(1):1-35.

_____. 1981. Birds of Twin Islands, James Bay, N.W.T., Canada. Syllogeus 30:1-50.

Manning, T.H., E.O. Hohn, and A.H. Macpherson. 1956. The birds of Banks Island. National Museum of Canada, Biological Series 48, Bulletin 143:1-144.

Manning, T.H. and A.H. Macpherson. 1961. A biological investigation of Prince of Wales Island, N.W.T. Transactions of the Royal Canadian Institute 33(2):116-239.

Martin, P.S. and R.G. Klein. (Editors). 1984. Quaternary extinctions: a prehistoric revolution. University of Arizona Press, Tucson. 892 pp.

Mayfield, H.F. 1983. Densities of breeding birds at Polar Bear Pass, Bathurst Island, Northwest Territories. Canadian Field-Naturalist 97(4):371-376.

Mayr, E. 1946. History of the North American bird fauna. Wilson Bulletin 58(1):1-68.

_____. 1976. History of the North America bird fauna. In: Evolution and the Diversity of Life, Selected Essays. Edited by: E. Mayr. The Belknap Press, Cambridge, Massachusetts. pp. 565-588.

Mayr. E. and R.J. O'Hara. 1986. The biogeographic evidence supporting the Pleistocene forest refuge hypothesis. Evolution 40(1):55-67.

Mayr, E. and L.L. Short. 1970. Species taxa of North American birds, a contribution to comparative systematics. Nuttall Ornithological Club, Publication 9:1-127.

McLaren, M.A. and W.G. Alliston. 1985. Effects of snow and ice on waterfowl distribution in the central Canadian Arctic Islands. Arctic 38(1):43-52.

McLaren, M.A. and P.L. McLaren. 1984. Tundra Swans in northeastern Keewatin District, N.W.T. Wilson Bulletin 96(1):6-11.

McLaren, P.L. 1982. Spring migration and habitat use by seabirds in eastern Lancaster Sound and western Baffin Bay. Arctic 35(1):88-111.

McLaren, P.L. and M.A. McLaren. 1982. Waterfowl population in eastern Lancaster Sound and western Baffin Bay. Arctic 35(1):149-157.

McLaren, P.L. and W.E. Renaud. 1982. Seabird concentrations in late summer along the coasts of Devon and Ellesmere islands. Arctic 35:112-117.

Molau, U. 1985. Grasiskkomplexet i Sverige. Vår Fågelvärld 44:5-20.

Montgomerie, R.D., R.V. Cartar, R.L. McLaughlin, and B. Lyon. 1983. Birds of Sarcpa Lake, Melville Peninsula, Northwest Territories: breeding phenologies, densities and biogeography. Arctic 36(1):65-75.

Mooney, H.A. and J.A. Drake. (Editors). 1986. Ecology of biological invasions of North America and Hawaii. Springer-Verlag, New York, Berlin. 321 pp.

Muir, D. and D.M. Bird. 1984. Food of Gyrfalcons at a nest on Ellesmere Island. Wilson Bulletin 96(3):464-467.

Nettleship, D.N. and T.R. Birkhead. (Editors). 1985. The Atlantic Alcidae. Academic Press, New York. 574 pp.

Nystrom, B. and H. Nystrom. 1987. Biotopval och hackning hos grasiskor *Carduelis flammea* och snosiskor *C. hornemanni* i Ammarnasomradet, sodra Lappland. Vår Fågelvärld 87(3):119-128.

Orr, C.D., R.M.P. Ward, N.A. Williams, and R.G.B. Brown. 1982. Migration patterns of Red and Northern Phalaropes in southwest Davis Strait and in the northern Labrador Sea. Wilson Bulletin 94(3):303-312.

Osborne, D. 1983. Brent Geese in the Arctic. Irish Birds 2(3):303-308.

Parker, G.R. and R.K. Ross. 1973. Notes on the birds of Southampton Island, Northwest Territories. Arctic 26(2):123-129.

Parmelee, D.F. and S.D. MacDonald. 1960. The birds of west-central Ellesmere Island and adjacent areas. National Museum of Canada, Biological Series 63, Bulletin 169:1-103.

Parmelee, D.F., H.A. Stephens, and R.H. Schmidt. 1967. The birds of southeastern Victoria Island and adjacent small islands. National Museum of Canada, Bulletin 222:1-229.

Parsons, P.A. 1982. Adaptive strategies of colonizing animal species. Biological Review 57(1):117-148.

Paulson, D.R. and W.J. Erckmann. 1985. Buff-breasted Sandpipers nesting in association with Black-bellied Plovers. Condor 87(3):429-430.

Payne, F.F. 1887. Mammals and birds of Prince of Wales Sound, Hudson's Strait. Proceedings of the Canadian Institute, 3rd series 1:119-123.

Pennant, T. 1785. Arctic zoology. Volume II. Class II, Birds. Henry Hughs, London. pp. 188-586.

Pianka, E.R. 1966. Latitudinal gradients in species diversity: a review of concepts. American Naturalist 100(910):33-46.

Ploeger, P.L. 1968. Geographical differentiation in Arctic Anatidae as a result of isolation during the last glacial. Ardea 56(1):1-159.

Porsild, A.E. 1951. Bird notes from Banks and Victoria islands. Canadian Field-Naturalist 65(1):40-42.

Prach, R.W., H. Boyd, and F.G. Cooch. 1981. Polynyas and seaducks. In: Polynyas in the Canadian Arctic. Edited by: I. Stirling and H. Cleator. Canadian Wildlife Service, Occasional Paper No. 45:67-70.

Preble, E.A. 1902. A biological investigation of the Hudson Bay region. North American Fauna 22:75-131.

_____. 1908. A biological investigation of the Athabasca-Mackenzie region. North American Fauna 27:1-574.

Rae, J. 1888. Notes on some of the birds and mammals of the Hudson's Bay Co's. Territories and the Arctic Coast. Canadian Record of Science 3(3):125-136.

Reed, A. and P. Dupuis. 1983. Ivory Gulls, *Pagophila eburnea*, nesting on the Brodeur Peninsula, N.W.T. Canadian Field-Naturalist 97(3):332.

Renaud, W.E., W.G. Johnston, and K.J. Finley. 1981. The avifauna of the Pond Inlet region, N.W.T. American Birds 35(2):119-129.

Renaud, W.E. and P.L. McLaren. 1982. Ivory gull (*Pagophila eburnea*) distribution in late summer and autumn in eastern Lancaster Sound and western Baffin Bay. Arctic 35:141-148.

Richardson, J. 1829-1837. Fauna boreali-americana, or the zoology of the northern parts of British America. (4 volumes). J. Murray, London.

Salomonsen, F. 1950. The birds of Greenland. Ejnar Munksgaard, Copenhagen. 607 pp.

_____. 1972. Zoogeographical and ecological problems in arctic birds. In: Proceedings of the XV International Ornithological Congress, 1970. Edited by: K.H. Voous. E.J. Brill, Leiden. pp. 25-77.

_____. 1979. Ornithological and ecological studies in S.W. Greenland (59° 46'-62°27'N. Lat.). Meddelelser om Grønland 204(6):1-214.

Savile, D.B.O. 1950. Bird observations at Chesterfield Inlet, Keewatin 1950. Canadian Field-Naturalist 65(4):145-157.

_____. 1961. Bird and mammal observations on Ellef Ringnes Island in 1960. National Museum of Canada, Natural History Papers 9:1-6.

Schaanning, H.T.L. 1933. Birds from Arctic North America. Ornithological results of the Fram-expedition 1898-1902 and the Gjoa-expedition 1903-1907. Meddeleleser fra det Zoologiske Museum, Oslo 33:137-165.

Smith, N.G. 1969. Polymorphism in Ringed Plovers. Ibis 111(1):177-188.

Smith, T.G. 1973. The birds of the Holman region, western Victoria Island. Canadian Field-Naturalist 87(1):35-42.

_____. 1981. Sharp-shinned Hawk, *Accipiter striatus* (Accipitriformes: Accipitridae), on Victoria Island, Northwest Territories. Canadian Field-Naturalist 95(3):366.

Snyder, L.L. 1957. Arctic birds of Canada. University of Toronto Press, Toronto. 310 pp.

Soper, J.D. 1928. A faunal investigation of southern Baffin Island. National Museum of Canada, Biological Series 15, Bulletin 53:1-143.

Soper, J.D. 1940. Local distribution of eastern Canadian arctic birds. Auk 57(1):13-21.

_____. 1946A. Ornithological results of the Baffin Island Expeditions of 1928-1929 and 1930-1931, together with more recent records. Auk 63(1-3): 1-24, 223-239, 418-427.

_____. 1946B. Supplementary data concerning the Blue Goose. Canadian Field-Naturalist 60(5):110-113.

Steadman, D.W. and P.S. Martin. 1984. Extinction of birds in the late Pleistocene of North America. Chapter 21. In: Quaternary Extinctions: A Prehistoric Revolution. Edited by: P.S. Martin and R.G. Klein. University of Arizona Press, Tucson. pp. 466-477.

Stevens, O.A. 1936. The first descriptions of North American birds. Wilson Bulletin 47(3):203-215.

Stresemann, E. 1975. Ornithology from Aristotle to the present. Harvard University Press, Cambridge, Massachusetts. 432 pp.

Sutton, G.M. 1929. Notes on a collection of birds from Mansel Island, Hudson Bay, Condor 34(1):41-43.

_____. 1931. Notes on birds observed along the west coast of Hudson Bay. Condor 33(4):154-159.

_____. 1932. The birds of Southampton Island. Memoir of the Carnegie Museum, Part 2, Section 2, 12:1-275.

Sutton, G.M. and D.F. Parmelee. 1954. Nesting of the Greenland Wheatear on Baffin Island. Condor 56(5):295-305.

Swainson, W. 1836-1837. On the natural history and classification of birds. Volumes 1, 2. Lardner's Cabinet Encyclopedia, London. pp. 1-365; 1-398.

Swainson, W. and J. Richardson. 1831. Fauna boreali-americana; or the zoology of the northern parts of British America. Part second, the birds. John Murray, London.

Taverner, P.A. 1916. List of specimens collected by Capt. Jos. Bernard on the Arctic Coast, N.W.T., Canada. Geological Survey of Canada, Summary Report for 1915:158-260.

_____. 1919. Birds of eastern Canada. Geological Survey of Canada, Biological Series 1563, Memoir 104(3):1-297.

_____. 1922. Birds of eastern Canada. Second Edition. Geological Survey of Canada, Biological Series 1564, Memoir 104(3):1-308.

Taverner, P.A. 1926. Birds of western Canada. Geological Survey of Canada, Museum Bulletin, Biological Series 10(41):1-380.

_____. 1940. The nesting of Ross's Goose, *Chen rossi*. Canadian Field-Naturalist 54(9):127-130.

_____. 1942. The distribution and migration of the Hudsonian Curlew. Wilson Bulletin 54(1):3-11.

_____. 1953. Birds of Canada. Musson Book Company Ltd., Toronto. 446 pp.

Thomas, V.G. and S.D. MacDonald. 1987. The breeding distribution and current population status of the Ivory Gull in Canada. Arctic 40(3):211-218.

Todd, W.E.C. 1963. Birds of the Labrador Peninsula and adjacent areas. University of Toronto Press, Toronto. 819 pp.

Todd, W.E.C. and H. Friedmann. 1947. A study of the Gyrfalcon with particular reference to North America. Wilson Bulletin 59(3):139-150.

Townsend, C.W. and G.M. Allen. 1907. Birds of Labrador. Proceedings of the Boston Society of Natural History 23(7):277-428.

Tuck, L.M. and L. Lemieux. 1959. The avifauna of Bylot Island. Dansk Ornithlogisk Forenings Tidskrift, 53(3):137-154.

Turner, L.M. 1885. List of the birds of Labrador, including Ungava, East Main, Moose, and Gulf districts of the Hudson Bay Company, together with the island of Anticosti. Proceedings of the United States National Museum 8:233-254.

_____. 1886. Contributions to the natural history of Alaska. Arctic Series, Publication of the Signal Service, United States Army 2:1-226.

Udvardy, M.D.F. 1969. Dynamic zoogeography with special reference to land animals. Van Nostrand Reinhold Co., New York. 445 pp.

Vieillot, L.J.P. 1807. Histoire naturelle des oiseaux de l'Amérique septentrionale, contenant un grand nombre d'espèces décrites ou figurées pour la première fois. (Tomes 1 et 2). Desray, Libraire, Paris.

Wallace, A.R. 1876. The geographical distribution of animals. (2 volumes). Reprinted in 1962. Hafner, New York. 503 pp.; 553 pp.

White, C.M. 1968. Diagnosis and relationships of the North American tundra-inhabiting Peregrine Falcons. Auk 85(2):179-191.

Wilson, A. 1808-1814. American ornithology or the natural history of birds of the United States. (9 volumes). Bradford and Inskeep, Philadelphia.

Witts, B. 1981. The Joint Services Expedition to Princess Marie Bay, Ellesmere Island, 1980. Part 1 - Initial report. Sea Swallow 30:15-21.

Wynne-Edwards, V.C. 1952. Zoology of the Baird Expedition (1950). The birds of central and south-east Baffin Island. Auk 69(4):353-391.

Yeatman, L.J. 1971. Histoire des oiseaux d'Europe. Bordas, Paris-Montreal. 363 pp.

Illustrated by Brenda Carter

MIGRATION, BODY CONDITION AND BEHAVIOUR OF SHOREBIRDS DURING SPRING MIGRATION AT ALERT, ELLESMERE ISLAND, N.W.T.

R.I.G. Morrison[1] and N.C. Davidson[2]

Abstract: Banding studies were carried out at Alert, N.W.T., during the period of arrival of shorebirds on their High Arctic breeding grounds in late May and early June in 1986 and 1987. Band recoveries and morphometric analysis have confirmed and extended earlier work showing that Ellesmere Island populations of Red Knots (Calidris canutus) and Ruddy Turnstones (Arenaria interpres) migrate to wintering areas on the northern European seaboard. Ellesmere Island knots are indistinguishable morphometrically from European wintering populations and from knots caught on migration in Iceland and northern Norway, the two major routes used by the birds to reach Nearctic breeding grounds.

Weights of banded birds and preliminary data from biochemical analysis of specimens obtained during the arrival period indicate that knots reach Alert with substantial reserves of both muscle protein and fat, though the amounts retained after migration may vary between years. In 1986 and 1987, weights of knots declined after arrival, reflecting a loss of both protein and fat. Time/activity budgets in 1987 showed that early migrants spent much time resting, and that little feeding occurred during severe weather and high winds in early June. Feeding and display activities both increased as snow-melt proceeded and habitat became available. Early season food was scarce, consisting mostly of plant material; the garbage dump was also used for foraging - particularly in 1986. Body reserves thus appear important for early season survival in High Arctic shorebirds. The contribution of such reserves to the physiological requirements of breeding requires investigation.

Résumé: Des études par bagage ont été effectuées à Alert, T.N.-O., pendant la période d'arrivée d'oiseaux de rivage sur leur lieu de nidification dans le Haut-Arctique à la fin de mai et au début de juin en 1986 et 1987. La récupération des bagues et l'analyse morphométrique ont confirmé et prolongé les premiers travaux qui montraient que les populations de bécasseaux à poitrine rousse (Calidris canutus) et de tourne-pierres (Arenaria interpres) de l'Île Ellesmere migrent dans des gîtes d'hivernage sur le littoral de l'Europe du nord. On ne peut distinguer morphométriquement les bécasseaux à poitrine rousse de l'Île Ellesmere des populations hivernant en Europe, ni des bécasseaux à poitrine rousse capturés lors de la migration en Islande, et dans le nord de la Norvège, sur les deux principales voies empruntées par les oiseaux en directions des lieux de nidification du Néarctique.

Le poids des oiseaux bagués et les données préliminaires provenant de l'analyse biochimique d'individus recueillis pendant la période d'arrivée indiquent que les bécasseaux à poitrine rousse atteignent Alert avec de bonnes réserves de protéines musculaires et de graisse, bien que les quantités restant après les migrations puissent varier d'une année à l'autre. En 1986 et 1987, le poids des bécasseaux à poitrine rousse a baissé après l'arrivée, ce qui reflète une perte de protéines et de graisse. Les bilans temps/activité de 1987 ont démontré que les premiers migrateurs passaient beaucoup de temps à se reposer et qu'ils se nourrissaient peu lors des périodes de mauvais temps et de grands vents du début de juin. L'alimentation et les parades augmentaient toutes deux à mesure que la neige fondait et que des habitats étaient disponibles. En début de saison, la nourriture était rare et se composait principalement de plantes. Les oiseaux se nourrissaient aussi à la décharge, en 1986 surtout. Les réserves de l'organisme semblent donc importantes pour la survie des oiseaux de rivage du Haut-Arctique en début de saison. Le rôle de ces réserves dans les besoins physiologiques de la reproduction demande une étude plus approfondie.

INTRODUCTION

Red Knots (*Calidris canutus*) and Ruddy Turnstones (*Arenaria interpres*) breeding on Ellesmere Island (Figures 1A,B), N.W.T. and in northwest Greenland migrate to wintering areas on the European seaboard (Salomonsen 1950-1951; Godfrey 1953; Morrison 1975, 1984). Until recently, most birds were thought to migrate via staging grounds in Iceland, where they spend two to three weeks putting on fat to fuel the last stage of the flight

---

[1] Canadian Wildlife Service, 1725 Woodward Drive, Ottawa, Ontario K1A 0H3
[2] Nature Conservancy Council, Northminster House, Peterborough PE1 1UA, U.K.

FIGURE 1A: Red Knot (<u>Calidris</u> <u>canutus</u>).

FIGURE 1B: Ruddy Turnstone (<u>Arenaria</u> <u>interpres</u>). Note camouflage of plumage.

across Greenland (Morrison 1977). Radar studies and band recoveries have suggested that after leaving Iceland, the birds reach their breeding grounds in northwestern Greenland and northeastern Canada by flying across the southern part of the ice cap and up the west coast of Greenland (Alerstam *et al.* 1986). Research in Norway, however, has now shown that a significant part of the population (estimated as 25-35%) may reach Nearctic breeding grounds via fiords in northern Norway: migrants passing through such areas in spring were previously thought to have been en route to breeding grounds in Siberia (Davidson *et al.* 1986; Uttley *et al.* 1987; Wood *et al.* 1988).

Staging grounds assume critical importance in the life-cycles of shorebirds, since the birds must accumulate adequate reserves of fat and protein to enable them to complete the next stage of their journey, which often involves a long-distance, non-stop flight over an 'ecological barrier', where they are unable to rest or feed. For shorebirds breeding in the High Arctic, late spring stopover areas assume particular importance, since the level of reserves the birds are able to accumulate will not only determine their ability to complete the journey successfully, but will influence the physiological condition of the birds on their arrival on the breeding grounds at a time when weather conditions are often difficult and food scarce. Reserves remaining after migration may be important for early season survival and/or may affect the subsequent capability of the birds to breed successfully. For instance, severe weather in June 1974 on Ellesmere Island led to widespread mortality from starvation among shorebirds (Morrison 1975). It is now widely accepted that arctic-breeding ducks and geese carry reserves of fat and protein to their breeding grounds, and that the size of these reserves affects the ability of the birds to breed successfully. Little is known about whether this phenomenon may occur in shorebirds, and these studies of the physiological condition of shorebirds immediately after arrival at Alert form part of a research program investigating the accumulation and use of fat and protein reserves during spring migration by arctic-breeding shorebirds. Accumulation of fat and protein reserves of knots at their late spring staging area in northern Norway is reported in Davidson and Evans (1986, in press). Based on studies of flight performance calculations, Davidson and Evans (in press) predicted that knots would arrive on their breeding grounds with substantial protein reserves remaining.

Our work at Alert, N.W.T., was undertaken as part of an internationally coordinated investigation to clarify the spring migration routes of Red Knots (Piersma 1984) and Ruddy Turnstones breeding in the northern Canadian Arctic on Ellesmere Island, and to investigate

546

the physiological condition of the birds and their behaviour during the immediate post-migration period.

METHODS

Birds were captured at the garbage dump near Alert (82°30'N 62°20'W) for banding and for studies of weights and measurements, using mist-nets (1974-1976) and cannon-nets (1986-

FIGURE 2: Guy Morrison bird banding at the garbage dump near Alert, Ellesmere Island in June 1986.

1987) (Figure 2). Wing lengths were measured to the nearest mm (maximum length of stretched and flattened wing) using a metal ruler, bill lengths to the nearest 0.1 mm using dial-calipers and weights to the nearest 1 g using a spring balance. Weather records were from the nearby weather station. In 1986 and 1987, tissue samples were collected for biochemical analysis (carried out using techniques described by Piersma *et al.* (1984)). In 1987, observations were made of the behaviour and activity of shorebird flocks in the vicinity of Alert at regular intervals on most days between 27 May and 9 June, whenever a bird

547

or birds were in view and undisturbed by humans. The activity of each bird was allocated to one of five categories: (1) roosting, when the bird had eyes closed and bill tucked into scapulars; (2) resting, with eyes open and bill pointing forwards; (3) feeding; (4) flying; and (5) displaying, including both aerial and ground courtship displays, and aggressive and territorial displays.

RESULTS

Migration

Arrival

Arrival dates of knots and turnstones on High Arctic breeding grounds in Canada and northwest Greenland are generally in the last few days of May or first days of June (e.g. Salomonsen 1950-1951, 1967; Parmelee and MacDonald 1960). At Alert, recorded arrival dates of knots included 29 May 1975 and 30 May 1987 and of turnstones 26 May 1976; both species were present by 31 May 1986 and turnstones by 27 May 1987. Numbers build up in the week following the first sightings and quite large flocks may occur. At Alert, knot counts reached 56 and 118 on 6 and 9 June 1974, respectively, 34 on 1 June 1975, 89 on 2 June 1976, 43 on 3 June 1986 and approximately 50 on 4-5 June 1987. Counts of turnstones have included 150 on 9 June 1976, 73 on 4 June 1986 and approximately 30 in the first few days of June 1987.

Banding

Banding in 1974-1976 resulted in the capture of 28 knots and 61 turnstones, and in the years 1986-1987 of 41 knots and 76 turnstones. A summary of international and local band recoveries and sightings is shown in Figure 3.

International Movements

Recoveries and controls of banded birds have significantly extended evidence establishing that knots and turnstones from northern Ellesmere Island migrate to European wintering grounds.

548

Records of banded knots at Alert have included a bird from England in 1974, a bird from Scotland recorded in both 1986 and 1987, and a bird carrying bands from Norway and England first captured at Alert in 1974 and seen again in 1976 (Figure 3). The double-banded bird was originally captured as a juvenile in 1971 in southwestern Norway during its first autumn migration and was caught again after having spent its first (subadult) summer on the east coast of Britain in July 1972, before being captured at Alert in 1974 (Morrison 1975). One bird banded at Alert in 1974 was controlled in England. Other records between Ellesmere Island and European wintering grounds were obtained during work on the east coast at Princess Marie Bay in 1980, and included the recovery of a knot banded in England and movements of three birds banded at Princess Marie Bay to England, Scotland and Denmark (unpublished results, Joint Services Expedition to Princess Marie Bay, 1980).

Records of banded turnstones in the mid-1970s included the first double-journey record between Ellesmere Island and Europe. This bird was banded on The Wash on the east coast of England in August 1972, was captured at Alert in early June 1975 and was caught again on The Wash in January 1976. A British banded bird was caught at Alert in 1976, and another banded during spring migration in Iceland in May 1972 was recovered on its breeding grounds at Lake Hazen in June 1975 (see Morrison 1976). A further indication that Iceland may be used as a stopover by turnstones from northeastern Canadian High Arctic breeding grounds comes from the recovery of two birds in northwest Greenland in the summer of 1974. They had been captured during migration at the same locality in Iceland in 1971 and 1972 (unpublished results). Records of movements to Ellesmere Island were significantly extended in the 1980s, with three birds from England and one from Scotland at Alert in 1986, and a second double-journey record of an English turnstone banded on the west coast of England in May 1985, captured at Alert in June 1987 and subsequently caught in the same wintering area in England in August 1987.

Return Data

Recaptures and resightings of marked knots and turnstones from year to year have established that the same birds used the Alert area year after year. Records of sightings of marked birds and of captures of banded birds are summarized in Figure 3, and include records between adjacent years (e.g. 1974 to 1975) as well as over two years (e.g. 1974 to

1976). For knots, four such sightings and one band recapture were made between years, in addition to the resighting of the double-banded (Norway/England) bird between 1974 and 1976 and the recapture of the Scottish-banded knot between 1986 and 1987 (see above, Figure 3A). For turnstones, a total of 16 resightings and three band recaptures were made between years (Figure 3B).

Local Movements

While counts indicate that some birds move through the Alert area en route to breeding-grounds in other areas, at least some birds that use the garbage dump for early-season foraging breed near Alert. In 1975, one pair of banded turnstones (both of which had been colour-marked at the garbage dump) was located by a nest with four eggs some 3 km east of Alert on the slopes overlooking Ravine Bay. Another marked bird was sighted about 11 km west of Alert near the mouth of Wood Creek.

MORPHOMETRICS

Bill-measurements of mixed-sex samples of adult knots and turnstones obtained at Alert and other locations, including breeding, migration and wintering-areas, are shown in Table 1. In both species, measurements show that birds using the Alert area may be identified with populations wintering in Europe, and are distinguishable from populations breeding and wintering in other areas.

Mean bill-lengths of knots from the breeding-grounds at Alert and from Greenland, from migration-areas in Iceland and in Norway, and from wintering-areas in the United Kingdom, all fell in the range 32.0-33.0 mm (Table 1A), and were generally not statistically significantly different from one another. This group (*Calidris canutus islandica*) was clearly smaller than knots of the nominate race (*C. c. canutus*) breeding in Russia and wintering in Africa, whose measurements on migration-areas in Europe averaged 35.1-33.7 mm (Piersma *et al.* 1987). The *islandica* group may also be distinguished from the North American race (*C. c. rufa*), where bill-measurements of birds on southward migration in James Bay averaged 35.2 mm. Differences in bill-measurements between *islandica* and the other two races were

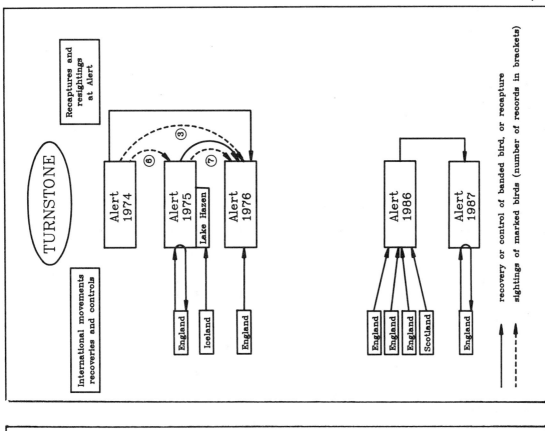

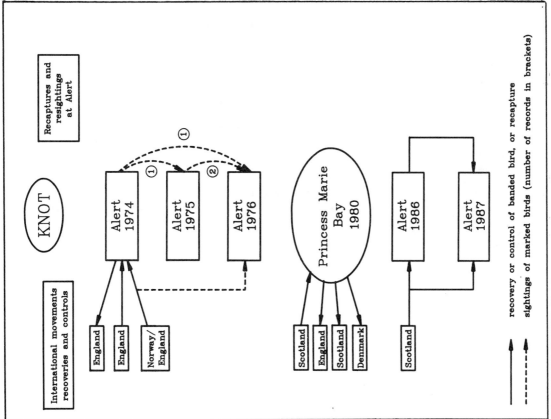

FIGURE 3: A summary of banding records involving: (A) knots and (B) turnstones on northern Ellesmere Island, 1974-1987. International movements of birds are shown on the left of the figures, with arrows indicating direction of movement from banding location to place of control (recapture) or recovery. (Between-year records of birds returning to Alert are shown on the right of the figures. Solid lines represent records involving a capture or recovery of a banded bird, whereas broken lines indicate sight records of marked birds (numbers indicate the number of sightings recorded).

551

TABLE 1: BILL MEASUREMENTS OF KNOTS AND TURNSTONES FROM ALERT AND OTHER LOCATIONS.

LOCATION	N	MEAN (MM)	S.D.	RANGE	REFERENCE[1]
(A) KNOT					
Calidris canutus islandica					
Alert (banding 1986)	40	33.0	2.07	28.7-38.1	
Alert (banding 1974)	23	32.0	1.47	30-35	(1)
Alert (specimens 1986-87)	32	32.5	2.13	28.3-35.7	
Iceland (W. Coast) (2 May 1972)	156	32.3	3.19	-----	(1)
Norway (Balsfjord) (May 1985)	96	33.0	1.81	28-38	(2)
Greenland	25	32.2	----	30.3-34.9	(3)
U.K. (Teesmouth)	59	32.5	1.72	29-38	(2)
Calidris canutus canutus					
Mauritania	280	35.1	1.78	-----	(4)
W-Central France	583	35.7	1.85	-----	(4)
Germany	291	35.1	1.86	-----	(4)
Calidris canutus rufa					
James Bay (July/August 1979)	43	35.2	1.76	32.5-39.0	(5)
(B) TURNSTONE					
Arenaria interpres interpres					
Alert (banding 1986)	53	22.3	1.24	20.6-24.9	
Alert (banding 1974)	35	21.9	1.17	20.0-24.2	(1)
Alert (specimens 1986-87)	28	22.1	0.91	20.1-24.1	
Iceland (3 May 1972)	33	22.9	0.98	-----	(1)
(23 May 1972)	44	21.5	1.06	-----	(1)
Netherlands	73	22.6	0.96	21-24	(3)
Siberia/Asia	24	21.9	0.79	21-23	(3)
Arenaria interpres morinella					
James Bay (July/August 1979)	49	23.0	1.15	20.6-25.5	(5)
South America	33	23.5	0.70	22-25	(3)

[1] Morrison (1975).
[2] Davidson and Evans (1986).
[3] Cramp and Simmons (1983).
[4] Piersma et al. (1987).
[5] R.I.G. Morrison (unpublished data).

552

statistically significant (t, d tests); differences within the *islandica* population, possibly resulting from a cline in size within the breeding-range (Morrison 1975), will be examined elsewhere.

Mean bill lengths of turnstones from Alert were again similar to birds of the nominate race (*Arenaria interpres interpres*) wintering in Europe: means from this group fell in the range 21.5-22.9 mm (Table 1B) - generally smaller than those of turnstones of the North American race *A. i. morinella* (23.0-23.5 mm). Statistical differences within the group will be explored more fully elsewhere.

FEEDING AND ACTIVITY PATTERNS

Weather

Maximum temperatures at Alert in late May/early June 1987 remained below freezing until 6 June, and had reached approximately 5°C when work finished on 9 June: minimum temperatures had still not reached 0°C by this date (Figure 4). Winds were generally northwesterly to northeasterly up to 3 June, with speed varying between 0 and 8 knots - apart from 27 May, when they rose to nearly 25 knots. Between 4-5 June, there was a period of relatively cold and bad weather, marked by strong, persistent northerly winds and a consistently high windchill factor (Figure 4). The weather became warmer and winds lighter and more variable from 6-9 June.

Behaviour

During much of the period 27 May to 9 June 1987, there was extensive snowcover around Alert, with snow melting rapidly only from 5 June onwards. In some previous years, including 1986, many birds of both species fed (with Long-tailed Jaegers *Stercorarius longicaudis*, Glaucous Gulls *Larus hyperboreus* and Ivory Gulls *Pagophila eburnea*) on the snow-free areas of the garbage dump. In contrast, very few knots and turnstones visited the garbage dump in 1987. Instead, the birds mostly frequented the snow-free patches on the slopes and around the sewage outfall pipe, between Alert, the airstrip and the frozen shoreline of Parr Inlet (an area approximately 3 km long and 0.5 km wide). Birds were mostly in small flocks throughout the period, but in the first week of June, turnstones were increasingly seen in pairs.

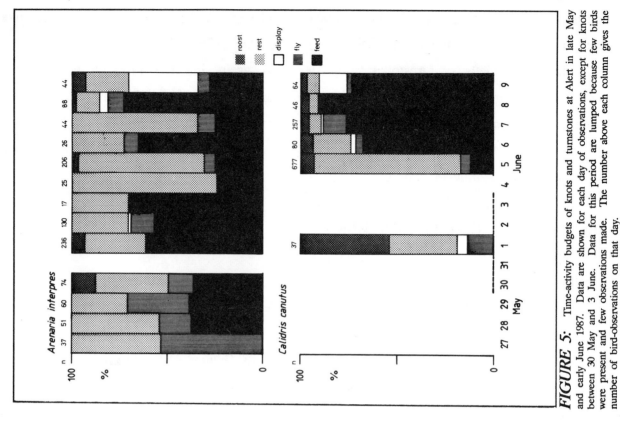

FIGURE 5: Time-activity budgets of knots and turnstones at Alert in late May and early June 1987. Data are shown for each day of observations, except for knots between 30 May and 3 June. Data for this period are lumped because few birds were present and few observations made. The number above each column gives the number of bird-observations on that day.

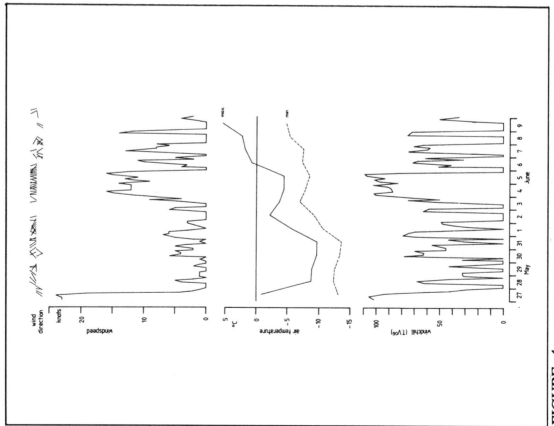

FIGURE 4: Weather at Alert in late May and early June 1987. Temperature, windspeed and wind direction are from hourly records at the Alert Meteorological Station. Windchill is calculated as $T.V^2$, where V is windspeed in knots, and T is the temperature deficit below 20°C (Davidson 1981B).

Both knots and turnstones spent much of their time resting or roosting immediately after their arrival at Alert (Figure 5). Between 28 May and 3 June, the time spent feeding by turnstones gradually increased from 35-40% to 70%. During the period of bad weather on 4-5 June 1987, both species spent most of their time resting, crouched and sheltering from the wind on the lee slopes of hills and hummocks. At this time, turnstones spent only 25% of their time feeding, and knots less than 15%. Before the bad weather, we did not see the few knots that were present in the area feeding. With improved weather from 6 June onwards, both species spent much more of their time feeding: knots 67-90% and turnstones 25-73%. Courtship activities became prominent in both species for the first time on 9 June. Although most observations were made between 0700 and 2300 local time, birds were seen feeding on occasion at all times of the day and "night". Arrival timings and behaviour suggests that, in 1987, turnstones were a few days more advanced in their activities than knots, which arrived at Alert mostly during and after the bad weather of 4-5 June. By 6 May, many of the turnstones appeared to be taking up breeding territories, and some birds were seen to fly from feeding areas around Alert more than 2 km across Parr Inlet, presumably to breeding sites on other slopes, such as those discovered in 1975 (see above).

Examination of gizzard contents revealed that birds were feeding on small seeds of various plants (unpublished observations). Feeding on seeds in the arrival period before insects emerge has been widely reported in arctic-breeding shorebirds, including knots and turnstones elsewhere on Ellesmere Island (Parmelee and Macdonald 1960; Nettleship 1973, 1974). The seed-bearing plants were scattered sparsely over the ground surface. During the two days of bad weather on 4-5 June, fine drifted snow covered most of the plants, which grew mostly in shallow depressions. When foraging, knots appeared to feed in a rather desultory manner for much of the time, in contrast to the rapid and active searching when feeding on mudflats just before departure in late May from their spring staging areas in northern Norway (Davidson and Evans 1986). Birds on the garbage dump took a wide variety of cooked and raw kitchen waste.

Many authors have reported that shorebirds spend much of their time soon after arrival at High Arctic breeding grounds loafing on snow-free patches of ground (e.g. Parmelee and MacDonald 1960), and have attributed this to birds waiting for the snow to melt sufficiently to expose feeding and nesting areas (Meltofte 1985). The considerable periods of the day spent not feeding by shorebirds at Alert during the two weeks after their arrival could either be because the birds did not need to feed for longer to satisfy their energy and nutrient demands, or because feeding was not profitable in the conditions that they faced. Both knots and turnstones became progressively more inactive as the windchill factor increased (Figure 6). High windchills mean high energy expenditure for thermoregulation. Hence shorebirds appear to be conserving energy by becoming inactive and seeking shelter when weather is poor. In turnstones, the trend of increased inactivity appears to begin when windchills are still quite low, so feeding on seeds may be worthwhile in the period soon after arrival only when the weather is fair and thermoregulatory demands are low. Birds were particularly inactive during periods of very high windchill during the bad weather of 4-5 June. Then, not only were energy demands high, but food was also barely available because drifted snow had covered the seed heads of most food plants.

BODY CONDITION

Detailed laboratory analysis of the physiological condition, including fat and protein content and muscle ultrastructure, of both knots and turnstones collected in 1986 and 1987 is in progress. Here we report preliminary results from this work.

Total Mass and Fat Load

Much of the variation in the total mass of shorebirds during the course of the year is a consequence of changes in fat load, although the lean mass can also vary substantially at times. Any variation in lean mass would modify the apparent fat load, but total body mass in spring usually reflects trends in fat loads (e.g. Davidson *et al.* 1986). Total body masses of knots and turnstones during the two weeks after their arrival at Alert are shown in Figure 7. For 1986 and 1987, mass was measured over periods of a week or more. Mass measurements collected over shorter periods in 1974 and 1975 are also shown in Figure 5 for further year-to-year comparisons. Total mass varies partly with the body size of the birds; however, the same trends as in Figure 7 remained after the effects of body size were allowed for by dividing total mass by wing-length. Data in Figure 7 come both from birds weighed during banding and from those collected for analysis of body condition.

556

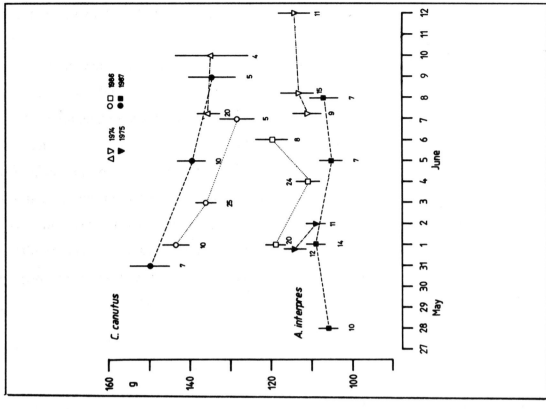

FIGURE 7: Total body mass of knots and turnstones at Alert in late May and early June in 1974, 1975, 1986 and 1987. Each point shows the mean ± 1 standard error; numbers give sample sizes. Each sample is from a period of 1-3 days, and is plotted on the median date of sampling.

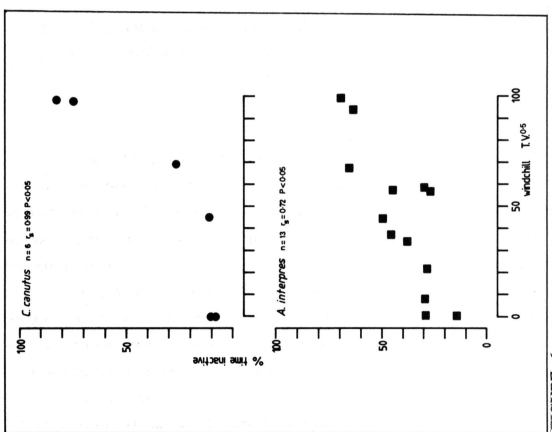

FIGURE 6: The relationship between the percentage of time spent inactive (roosting and resting) and windchill. Each data point is the mean activity during a bout of observations of up to three hours, with a minimum of 10 bird-observations, and the mean windchill during that period.

Birds weighed in 1987 were almost all feeding on snow-patches on the slopes around Alert, whereas birds weighed in other years had also fed on the garbage dump.

Body mass of knots decreased significantly between late May and mid-June in both 1986 ($r = -0.33$, $n = 40$, $p < 0.05$) and 1987 ($r = -0.57$, $n = 22$, $p < 0.01$). When mass was corrected for differences in body size (by dividing mass by wing length) the trend remained, and the correlations improved: 1986, $r = -0.40$, $n = 40$, $p < 0.02$; 1987, $r = -0.68$, $n = 22$, $p < 0.001$. Mean mass decreased by 15 g in nine days in 1987, and by 15 g in six days in 1986. Mean mass in 1986 was consistently 5-10 g less than for the same date in 1987. Between 7-12 June 1974 (i.e. approximately a week after the date of first arrivals), mass was similar to that in 1987. In 1987, the decrease continued both immediately after the first arrivals, and during the period of bad weather when the birds fed very little (Figure 5).

The mean mass of the first sample of knots in 1987 was 150 g, and was obtained within a few hours of the first observed arrival of the species at Alert. In comparison, knots of the same breeding population arrive on staging areas in Iceland in early May averaging approximately 135 g, with mean masses rising to some 200 g before departure near the end of the month (Morrison 1977, 1984). In northern Norway, knots arriving at their final spring staging site at Balsfjord weighed an average of 151 g, with a fat load of 11% of total body mass (Davidson and Evans 1986). However, the fat loads of knots arriving at Alert in late May and early June may be substantially higher than this, since preliminary results of laboratory analysis of samples collected in early June 1986 suggest that fat loads averaged 16% with an average body mass of only 143 g. This also implies that lean masses were lower in birds arriving at Alert than at Balsfjord. Whatever the precise amounts of fat carried on arrival, it is clear that knots arrive at their breeding grounds after a migratory flight of about 3,000 km (Davidson and Evans 1986) with substantial amounts of fat remaining. This confirms Davidson and Evans's (in press) prediction of arrival condition, made from the storage and use of reserves during earlier parts of their spring migration. Knots leave Balsfjord in late May with fat loads averaging 30% of total body mass (Davidson and Evans, in press), so appear to use only about half this fat load by the time they arrive in Ellesmere Island after one of the longest non-stop migratory flights known. Fat loads of knots on arrival at Alert are comparable with those in midwinter in northeastern England, and would be sufficient for survival for several days of severe weather without food (Davidson 1981A,B).

The steady decrease in mean total mass of knots during early June could arise in two ways: (1) individual birds lose mass by using up their fat reserves after their arrival at Alert; or (2) later arrivals reach Alert with lower masses than earlier birds, perhaps because fat reserves useful for survival in severe weather would be needed for a shorter period than faced by the early-arriving birds.

It was not possible to mark knots individually in 1986 or 1987, so it is not clear if the first arrivals remained at Alert during the following two weeks. Nor can the two alternative reasons for mass decline yet be distinguished. Only a few knots have been caught and recaptured at Alert. One bird caught on 8 June 1974 had gained 13 g when it was recaptured two days later, at a time when the mean total mass changed little. Two knots were weighed in both 1986 and 1987. One weighed 141 g on a 4 June 1985 and 140 g on 6 June 1987. The other weighed 127 g on 3 June 1986, but was 11 g heavier on the same date in 1987. This suggests that the difference in the mean mass between 1986 and 1987 is a consequence of poorer arrival condition of the same individual knots in 1986 compared to 1987.

The pattern of mass change in turnstones differs from that in knots. Mean total mass in 1987 changed little between late May and early June (Figure 7). Mass was lowest during the bad weather of 4-5 June, but at this time averaged only 4 g less than in the previous three days. Nineteen turnstones were individually colour-marked in 1987. Many of these remained around Alert throughout early June, and probably comprised the local breeding population. Two turnstones were recaptured during 1987. One had gained 11 g between 3 and 8 June, even though it had a damaged foot. The other weighed 114 g on 1 June, but had lost 9 g when reweighed on 5 June, during the bad weather. These results imply that in 1987 turnstones were able to maintain their body condition after arrival at Alert, with at most only slight use of reserves during the bad weather.

In contrast to knots, in which mass was lower in 1986 than 1987, the mass of turnstones was consistently higher in 1986 than 1987 (Figure 7). Total mass also fluctuated with time; the decline in mean mass of almost 8 g between 1-2 June and 3-4 June is significant (Student's t = 2.30, n = 42, p <0.01). In between-year comparisons, mean masses were significantly higher in 1986 in the samples weighed on 1-3 June, and 5-7 June

(Student's t test, both p <0.01). Only one turnstone was weighed in both years. This bird was of similar mass in both years: 115 g on 1 June 1986 and 114 g on 28 May 1987. Data from 1974 and 1975 suggest that condition in these years was intermediate between 1986 and 1987 (Figure 7). Masses in mid-June 1974 suggest that there may be a gradual increase in most years after about 5 June. Two birds recaptured in early June 1974 suggest that the decrease in mass between late May and early June of that year may reflect some use of reserves by individuals: one bird lost 6 g between 1 and 2 June, the other lost 1 g between 31 May and 2 June.

Preliminary results from 1986 suggest that turnstones, like knots, carry substantial fat reserves soon after arrival on the breeding grounds. Birds in early June 1986 averaged 19% fat. If lean masses were similar in 1986 and 1987, then even the much lower total mass in late May 1987 (mean 106 g) would still represent a fat load of approximately 10%.

Pectoral Muscle Size

Pectoral muscle size is a good measure of the protein reserves of shorebirds (Davidson et al. 1986). Davidson and Evans (in press) showed that knots accumulate protein reserves in their pectoral muscles on spring staging areas, and predicted that much of this reserve would be retained during the flight to the breeding grounds. Full laboratory analysis of pectoral muscle size is in progress. This will allow calculation of a Standard Muscle Index (SMI) (the lean dry mass of the pectoral muscles corrected for body size by dividing by a Standard Muscle Volume (SMV) based on skeletal measures) (Piersma et al. 1984; Davidson and Evans, in press). An initial indication of changes in pectoral muscle size is given by the fresh mass of the muscle, corrected by "f", the diagonal measurement from the posterior point of the sternum to the distal point of the coracoid bone. This is shown for pectoralis major (the main flight muscle) size in Figure 8. In knots, muscle size was similar in late May and early June in 1986 and 1987. Immediately before their departure from Balsfjord, this measure of muscle size in knots averaged 0.254 (unpublished data). Arrival condition of the first knots in 1987 averaged 0.230, so that pectoral muscle size appeared to have decreased by only about 9% during a flight from Norway to Ellesmere Island. This decrease is a maximum, since part is likely to be a decrease in the fat content of the muscles. The decrease is very close to 10% predicted by Davidson and Evans (in press).

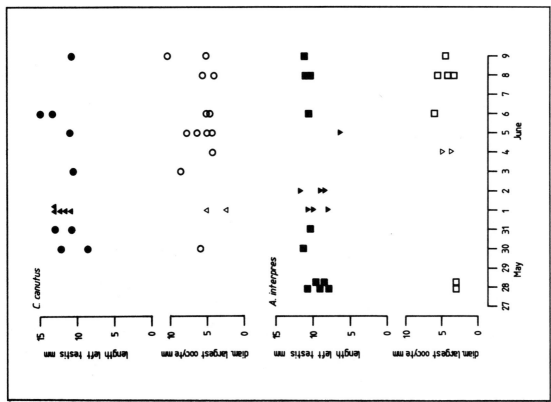

FIGURE 9. Reproductive condition of male (left testis) and female (largest oocyte) of knots and turnstones in late May and early June 1986 (triangles) and 1987 (circles knots, squares turnstones).

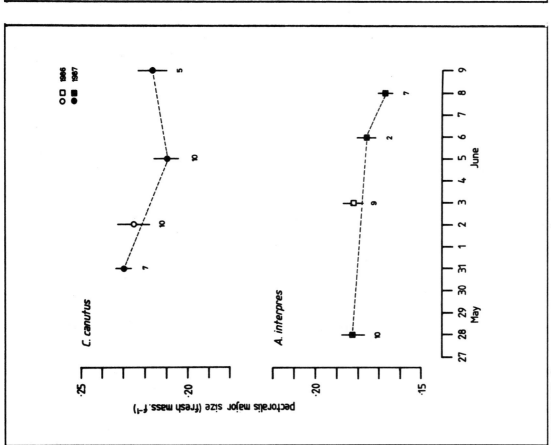

FIGURE 8. Pectoralis major muscle size of knots and turnstones in late May and early June 1986 and 1987. Pectoralis-major size is shown as the fresh mass of the muscle (g), corrected for body size by dividing by f (mm), the measurement from the posterior point of the keel to the distal point of the coracoid bone. Each point shows the mean ± 1 standard error; numbers give sample sizes. Each sample is from a period of 1-3 days, and is plotted on the median date of sampling.

This provides first confirmation that knots arrive on their breeding grounds with substantial protein reserves.

The muscle size of knots decreased significantly during early June 1987 (Student's t = 3.02, n = 17, p <0.05), but increased slightly after the bad weather on 4-5 June. The decrease in total mass could result either from use of protein reserves by birds during the cold spell when they fed little, or from the later arrival of birds with smaller pectoral muscles.

Pectoral muscle size in turnstones was the same in late May 1987 as in early June 1986 (Figure 8). Between late May and 8-9 June 1987, muscle size decreased by 8%, although the difference was not significant. This measure of muscle size is probably not directly comparable between species, as the form of the sternum may differ interspecifically. However, initial analyses of turnstone muscles from 1986 suggest that the Standard Muscle Index of the pectoralis major is about 0.28, which is similar to the muscle size in Britain in midwinter (Davidson 1981A). As pectoral muscles in midwinter are known to contain a substantial amount of protein reserve, so turnstones, like knots, must arrive on their arctic breeding grounds with substantial protein reserves.

REPRODUCTIVE CONDITION

The testes of males and the oocytes of females of both species appear not to be fully formed when the birds arrive at Alert, since the gonads increased in size between late May and early June (Figure 9). By mid-June, the testes of both species and the oocytes of turnstones had reached sizes similar to those of the respective peak sizes recorded by Nettleship (1973, 1974) on the Lake Hazen breeding grounds, about 80 km to the south in mid-June. In Nettleship's study, egg laying began at Lake Hazen on 10 June in turnstones and 15 June in knots. By analogy, the gonad size of knots and turnstones at Alert suggests that egg laying would begin within a few days after our work finished on 9 June.

562

DISCUSSION

Davidson and Evans (in press) predicted that shorebirds arrive on their arctic breeding-grounds with substantial reserves of fat and protein. They suggested that these reserves were needed for birds to survive through periods of severe weather soon after their arrival on the breeding grounds, when little food is available. Even when they carry such reserves, knots and turnstones are known to suffer occasional heavy mortality during prolonged severe weather, as reported for Ellesmere Island in the early 1970s (Morrison 1975). Davidson and Evans (in press) suggested that any reserves remaining at the start of the breeding attempt could then be used in breeding, perhaps by contributing a substantial proportion of the protein needed by females for egg formation. Reserves carried by males might allow more time for territorial and courtship activities by reducing feeding time.

Some previous evidence has suggested that shorebirds arrive on their arctic breeding grounds with fat reserves (Meltofte 1985). Our results from Alert provide the first confirmation that knots and turnstones carry substantial reserves of both fat and protein to arctic breeding grounds. Preliminary results indicate that part of these reserves are used to supply nutrient and energy demands in the two weeks after arrival, during even short spells of bad weather. This is not surprising, since we have shown that foraging was reduced as the windchill factor (and so the energetic costs of thermoregulation) increased. This is likely to arise because of the low availability of food shortly after the snow melts: in the two days of bad weather in early June 1987, snow covered most of what little food was available, and both knots and turnstones almost ceased feeding. Nevertheless, the relatively steady average total masses of turnstones through late May/early June 1987 suggest that these birds were mostly able to balance their energy requirements from the available food. This was achieved largely by feeding on natural vegetation on snow-free patches of tundra, rather than the artificial food source at the garbage dump.

The differences in the total masses of both knots and turnstones between 1986 and 1987 suggest that birds may arrive at Alert with different amounts of fat, and possibly protein, reserves in different years. This could arise through year-to-year differences in body condition when the birds depart from their late spring staging areas. It could also arise if birds faced varying weather conditions (e.g. head winds, during their flight to the breeding grounds), or from a combination of both factors.

563

We have found no evidence that knots or turnstones are able to increase their reserves appreciably after they arrive on the breeding grounds. However total masses from several years show that shorebirds retain substantial reserves of fat shortly before egg-laying begins. Similarly, pectoral-muscle size in 1987 indicates that both knots and turnstones usually enter the egg laying period with a protein reserve in their muscles. Shorebirds thus appear to prepare for an arctic breeding attempt in a similar manner to arctic-breeding geese, which carry fat and protein reserves to the breeding grounds for use in the breeding attempt (Ankney 1984; Mainguy and Thomas 1985).

Earlier studies have shown that knots and other shorebirds begin to accumulate fat and protein reserves on their late winter feeding grounds, before accumulating further reserves on spring staging areas. Our results suggest that arrival on the breeding grounds with sufficient fat and protein reserves is vital for the survival and breeding of these populations. Hence, the continued presence of wintering and of staging sites with an abundant food supply, which will enable the birds to accumulate energy reserves as well as meet their daily requirements, is also vital for the continued survival of these species. Many of the estuaries used by shorebirds in western Europe, the New World, and elsewhere, are threatened by land-claims and a wide variety of other human influences (e.g. Morrison 1984; Senner and Howe 1984; Smit et al. 1987). Even in the remote fiords used by knots in northern Norway in spring, intertidal feeding grounds are being lost through road improvements on the upper parts of the shore, so reducing the period of the tidal cycle available for the birds to feed.

Most studies of arctic birds have focused on their migrations or on the breeding attempt itself. Our recent studies of shorebirds at Alert have produced information on a short but critical part of the annual cycle about which very little was previously known. However, many questions remain unanswered. For instance, we do not know yet precisely which late spring staging areas are used by the knots and turnstones that reach Alert. Knots may come from either of the two main areas used in late spring: northern Norway and western Iceland. Detailed information on the departure condition of knots exists only for Norway (Davidson and Evans 1986, in press). However, total mass measurements from Iceland in the early 1970s (Morrison 1977, 1984) suggest a similar departure condition from the two areas. The distances from Iceland and Norway to Ellesmere Island are similar, so we could expect arrival condition at Alert to be similar in birds arriving from the two staging areas. In any case, recent evidence suggests that individual knots use different staging areas in different years (Uttley *et al.* 1987). Much less is known about the spring migration of turnstones, but most are thought to pass through Iceland (Cramp and Simmons 1983), as indicated by the band recovery between Iceland and Ellesmere Island (Morrison 1976).

Further investigations are planned to clarify the relationship between activity and weather conditions, how this affects the use of fat and protein reserves in the pre-breeding period, and how any reserves retained during this period are then used in breeding.

ACKNOWLEDGEMENTS

This work was supported logistically and financially by the Canadian Wildlife Service as part of its Shorebird Project. We are most grateful for financial support through a grant from the North Atlantic Treaty Organization enabling international collaboration to take place. We thank John Uttley and Professor Peter Evans (University of Durham, England) for information on body condition of shorebirds in 1986.

We particularly thank the Canadian Armed Forces for permission to work at Alert, and for their thoroughly professional and enthusiastic support in all aspects of the project, with special thanks to the Commanding Officer and staff at Alert. We also acknowledge with thanks the assistance of Atmospheric Environment Service staff at the Alert Weather Station, and Polar Continental Shelf Project staff for their support of the work in the 1970s.

REFERENCES

Alerstam, T., C. Hjort, G. Hogstedt, P.E. Jonsson, J. Karlsson, and B. Larsson. 1986. Spring migration of birds across the Greenland Inlandice. Meddelelser om Grønland, Bioscience 21:1-38.

Ankney, C.D. 1984. Nutrient reserve dynamics of breeding and molting Brant. Auk 101:361-370.

Cramp, S. and K.E.L. Simmons. (Editors). 1983. The birds of the western Palearctic. Volume 3. Oxford University Press, Oxford. 913 pp.

Davidson, N.C.   1981A.   Seasonal changes in the nutritional condition of shorebirds (Charadrii) during the non-breeding seasons.   Ph.D. thesis, University of Durham, U.K.

_____.   1981B.   Survival of shorebirds (Charadrii) during severe weather: the role of nutritional reserves.   In: Feeding and Survival Strategies in Estuarine Organisms.   Edited by: N.V. Jones and W.J. Wolff.   Plenum Press, New York and London.   pp. 231-249.

Davidson, N.C. and P.R. Evans. (Editors).   1986.   The ecology of migrant knots in north Norway during May 1985.   Department of Zoology, University of Durham, U.K. Report SRG86/1.

_____.   (in press).   Prebreeding accumulation of fat and muscle protein by Arctic-breeding shorebirds.   Proceedings of the XIX International Ornithological Congress, Ottawa. Canada.

Davidson, N.C., P.R. Evans, and J.D. Uttley.   1986.   Geographical variation of protein reserves in birds: the pectoral muscle mass of Dunlins *Calidris alpina* in winter.   Journal of Zoology (London) 208:125-133.

Davidson, N.C., K.-B. Strann, N.J. Crockford, P.R. Evans, J. Richardson, L.J. Standen, D.J. Townshend, J.D. Uttley, J.R. Wilson, and A.G. Wood.   1986.   The origins of Knots *Calidris canutus* in arctic Norway in spring.   Ornis Scandinavica 17:175-179.

Davison, N.C., J.D. Uttley, and P.R. Evans.   1986.   Geographic variation in the lean mass of Dunlins wintering in Britain.   Ardea 74:191-198.

Godfrey, W.E.   1953.   Notes on Ellesmere Island birds.   Canadian Field-Naturalist 67:89-93.

Mainguy, S.D. and V.G. Thomas.   1985.   Comparison of body reserve buildup and use in several groups of Canada Geese.   Canadian Journal of Zoology 63:1765-1772.

Meltofte, H.   1985.   Populations and breeding schedules of waders, Charadrii, in High Arctic Greenland.   Meddelelser om Grøland, Bioscience 16:1-43.

Morrison, R.I.G.   1975.   Migration and morphometrics of European Knot and Turnstone on Ellesmere Island, Canada.   Bird-Banding 46:290-301.

_____.   1976.   Further records, including the first double-journey recovery, of European-banded Ruddy Turnstones on Ellesmere Island, N.W.T.   Bird-Banding 47:274.

_____.   1977.   Migration of arctic waders wintering in Europe.   Polar Record 18:475-486.

_____.   1984.   Migration systems of some New World shorebirds.   In: Shorebirds: Migration and Foraging Behavior.   Edited by: J. Burger and B.L. Olla.   Plenum Press, New York and London.   Behavior of Marine Animals 6:125-202.

Nettleship, D.N. 1973. Breeding ecology of Turnstones *Arenaria interpres* at Hazen Camp, Ellesmere Island, N.W.T. Ibis 115:202-217.

_____. 1974. The breeding of the Knot *Calidris canutus* at Hazen Camp, Ellesmere Island, N.W.T. Polarforschung 44:8-26.

Parmelee, D.F. and S.D. MacDonald. 1960. The birds of west-central Ellesmere Island and adjacent areas. National Museum of Canada, Bulletin 169:1-103.

Piersma, T. 1984. International wader migration studies along the East Atlantic Flyway during spring 1985. Wader Study Group, Bulletin 42:5-9.

Piersma, T., N.C. Davidson, and P.R. Evans. 1984. Estimation of the protein reserve of waders: the use and misuse of Standard Muscle Volume. Wader Study Group, Bulletin 42:19-22.

Piersma, T.O., D. Bredin, and P. Prokosch. 1987. Continuing mysteries of the spring migration of Siberian Knots: a progress note. Wader Study Group, Bulletin 49:9-10.

Salomonsen, F. 1950-1951. Grønlands Fugle/The Birds of Greenland. (3 volumes). Ejnar Munksgaard, København. 609 pp.

_____. 1967. Fuglene pa Grønland. Rhodes, København. 341 pp.

Senner, S.E. and M.A. Howe. 1984. Conservation of Nearctic shorebirds. In: Shorebirds: Breeding Behavior and Populations. Edited by: J. Burger and B.L. Olla. Plenum Press, New York and London. Behavior of Marine Animals 5:379-421.

Smit, C., R.H.D. Lambeck, and W.J. Wolff. 1987. Threats to coastal wintering and staging areas of waders. Wader Study Group, Bulletin 49 (Supplement):105-113.

Uttley, J.D., C.J. Thomas, N.C. Davidson, K.B. Strann, and P.R. Evans. 1987. The spring migration of Nearctic Knots *Calidris canutus islandica*: a re-appraisal. Wader Study Group, Bulletin 49 (Supplement):80-84.

Wood, A.G., K.-B. Strann, F.L. Symonds, and S. Nilsen. 1988. Knot research at Porsangerfjord. University of Durham, U.K. (Unpublished report).

Illustrated by Brenda Carter

WINTER STUDIES OF BIRDS AND MAMMALS IN THE CANADIAN ARCTIC ISLANDS

David R. Gray[1]

Abstract: Despite the recent increase in biological research in the High Arctic, our knowledge of the life history of arctic birds and mammals throughout the entire year is still rudimentary. In many cases, observations made by the personnel of early arctic exploring expeditions are still the basis of our knowledge of certain species in winter. This lack of recent information on the winter period means that much largely anecdotal information, still unconfirmed by modern studies, is being published in current general texts on the Arctic. The establishment of biological research stations at several High Arctic localities, and the logistical support of the Polar Continental Shelf Project facilitated overwintering studies of muskoxen and other projects. Further cooperation with weather-station personnel, Inuit hunters and others will augment future biological research. New studies of terrestrial and marine mammals and migrating birds at both ends of the winter period are only slowly moving us closer to an acceptable level of knowledge of the High Arctic fauna.

Résumé: Malgré la récente augmentation de la recherche biologique dans le Haut-Arctique, nos connaissances sur la vie des oiseaux et des mammifères arctiques durant l'année complète sont encore rudimentaires. Dans bien des cas, les observations faites par les membres des toutes premières expéditions dans l'Arctique constituent encore la base de nos connaissances sur certaines espèces en hiver. Ce manque d'information récente sur la période hivernale signifie que beaucoup d'informations, largement anecdotiques, toujours pas confirmées par des études modernes, sont actuellement publiées dans des textes généraux sur l'Arctique. L'établissement de stations de recherche biologique au sein de plusieurs localités du Haut-Arctique et le soutien logistique de l'Étude du plateau continental polaire ont facilité les études sur l'hivernage des boeufs musqués, ainsi que d'autres projets. Une coopération plus poussée avec le personnel de stations météorologiques, les chasseurs inuit et d'autres personnes aura pour effet d'améliorer les futures recherches biologiques. De nouvelles études sur la animaux marins et terrestres et sur les oiseaux migrateurs au début et à la fin de la période hivernale ne nous rapprochent que très lentement d'un niveau de connaissances acceptable sur la faune du Haut-Arctique.

INTRODUCTION

If the Canadian Arctic Islands are "Canada's Missing Dimension", then it could be said on another level that the winter season is the missing dimension of the Arctic Islands. Despite a recent increase in biological research in the islands, our knowledge of birds and mammals in winter is still rudimentary. For purposes of this paper, I define winter as the period from September to April; roughly the time when the mean temperature in the central Arctic Islands is below 0°C and the sun is below the horizon for at least part of the day.

In some cases, the observations recorded in explorers' journals from the 1800s are still the basis of information presented in schools, as well as scientific and popular books. A definite lack of new information on the Arctic winter, plus the time-lag of getting what little

---

[1] Zoology Division, National Museum of Natural Sciences, Ottawa, Ontario K1P 6P4.

568

information there is to the public, means that the same old material continues to permeate the modern popular literature.

In magazines, children's books, and television films, we find two disturbing extremes. The first is the old, yet continuing notion of the Arctic as a land of year-round ice, snow, darkness, and howling winds. Summer is forgotten or dismissed for its brevity. The second is a newer misconception resulting from the increased accessibility of the Arctic to tourists and professional photographers - mainly in summer. So the public are overexposed to the other extreme, with misleading masses of flowering plants and breeding birds. One example is Hummel's (1984) book " Arctic Wildlife" containing 150 photographs, not one of which was taken in winter.

Apart from the general problem of satisfactorily communicating scientific results to the public, I am particularly concerned that little biological work has been done during the arctic winter in recent years. Many useful observations have been made, but some (not part of a specific study) are unlikely to be published, whereas others are parts of long-term studies awaiting completion.

OVERWINTERING STUDIES

Historical

Most early information on birds and mammals in winter comes from the journals of many expeditions in search of the North-West Passage or the North Pole. Because of the nature of such expeditions the information is usually not extensive (Figure 1). The records from those expeditions accompanied by an official naturalist are, of course, the most valuable. Fielden's (1877A,B) accounts are of particular interest. Of the many expeditions which overwintered in the Arctic Islands, perhaps one of the most biologically significant was that of William Parry, who spent the winter of 1819-1820 on Melville Island. The overwintering party observed muskoxen and caribou, recorded observations of Ravens in mid-winter, and ptarmigan in February (Fisher 1821). Observations made by Parry's group were used extensively by early writers on northern wildlife, and some are still useful.

The First International Polar Year (1882-1883) produced more information on High Arctic birds and mammals through the observations made during the American Expedition

FIGURE 1: Sledges of the British naval Franklin search expedition under Sir Edward Belcher passing Cape Lady Franklin, Bathurst Island. Drawing by W.W. May, 1854. Public Archives of Canada.

to Lady Franklin Bay led by Greely in 1881-1883 (Greely 1886).

In 1908-1909, members of J.E. Bernier's expedition aboard the *Arctic*, like Parry's crew before them, spent the winter at Melville Island. Although their observations of wildlife were not extensive, they confirmed earlier speculations that the larger mammals did not leave the islands in winter. Further they found that three species of birds remained there year-round (Bernier 1910).

The International Geophysical Year, 1957-1958

One of the first purely scientific winter studies in the High Arctic was the I.G.Y. party led by C.R. Harington, which conducted studies of weather, lake-ice, and snow conditions at Lake Hazen on northern Ellesmere Island in 1957-1958 (Hattersley-Smith 1974). During the winter, as well as performing other duties, Harington collected information on muskoxen - the basis for the first attempt to synthesize muskox behaviour (Harington 1961).

570

Recent Overwintering Studies

As part of my long-term study of muskox behaviour, Donald Cockerton and I spent the winter of 1970-1971 at the National Museum of Natural Sciences (NMNS) High Arctic Research Station at Polar Bear Pass on Bathurst Island (Figure 2). Our objectives were to determine what special adaptations to winter conditions were present in the muskox behavioural repertoire, and to assess the accuracy of previous published observations. We also collected weather data and made observations on other wildlife (Gray 1971, 1987).

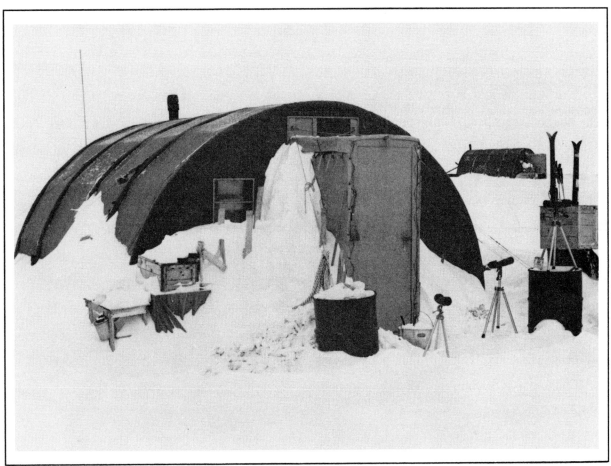

FIGURE 2: Parcoll huts at the NMNS High Arctic Research Station, Bathurst Island, during the winter of 1970-1971. The hut on the left was in use for 12 years.

A third study of muskoxen in winter was carried out in 1972 at the Arctic Institute of North America camp at Truelove Inlet on Devon Island by B.A. Hubert and four companions. Their main goal was to determine productivity of muskoxen. Again, they recorded weather and observations of other species (Hubert 1974, 1977).

Apart from the overwintering at Bathurst Island in 1970-1971, NMNS ethologists have observed the behaviour of arctic animals for a total of 15 months in early and late winter. Recently, Northwest Territories regional biologists stationed in northern communities, have collected more information on winter biology (personal communications, R. Popko, A. Gunn). Thus more data are being recorded on a long-term basis, and there are increased opportunities for conducting winter research.

PRESENT KNOWLEDGE AND GAPS

Birds

Our knowledge of the behaviour and even the presence of the main species of birds that might be expected to spend at least a part of the winter in the Canadian Arctic Islands is limited. From observations made at Bathurst Island (1970-1977), we know that at least 12 of the 30 species which breed in Polar Bear Pass can be seen in September - the start of the winter season. By October, the number is reduced to two species; Rock Ptarmigan, and Snowy Owl. Of the four species expected to spend the winter in the Arctic Islands (Raven, Rock Ptarmigan, Snowy Owl, and Gyrfalcon), we can say that all may winter within their breeding range, but probably in the southern part of that range (Godfrey 1986; Ouellet, this volume). In the 20-year gap between the two editions of "The Birds of Canada" (Godfrey 1966, 1986), so little new information was published on winter behaviour and range that the entries dealing with wintering of these species remain unchanged.

Following is a summary of our knowledge concerning winter survival of the four species in the Arctic Islands.

Raven

This species, which frequents human habitations and their associated refuse dumps, is an obvious possibility for overwintering around arctic settlements. One regularly visited HMS *Hecla* and HMS *Griper* during Parry's stay at Melville Island in the winter of 1819-1820 (Osborn 1856), and Cook (1913) reported Ravens on Devon Island in November and February. Ravens are said to remain on Banks Island year-round (Manning *et al.* 1956).

Rock Ptarmigan

Parry's observations of ptarmigan on Melville Island in February 1820 and Bernier's for 1908-1909 are still the northernmost records of wintering for this species (Godfrey 1986). Greely (1886) saw ptarmigan on northeastern Ellesmere Island in mid-October and in Newman Bay (Greenland) in early March. Our records from Bathurst Island indicate that ptarmigan leave about mid-October, returning in late April or early May. Records of the 1986 Christmas Bird-Count show this species present at Cambridge Bay on Victoria Island in December (personal communication, A. Gunn).

FIGURE 3:   Young Snowy Owl at Polar Bear Pass, Bathurst Island, September 30, 1977.

Snowy Owl

Bernier (1910) recorded Snowy Owls throughout the winter on Melville Island. On Victoria Island, they are reported to be present throughout the year, though the highest numbers are seen during the fall migration in October (Smith 1973). On Bathurst Island

573

Snowy Owls, particularly the young birds, remain throughout September (Figure 3). They are the first species to return in the new year. In 1971, we saw Snowy Owls in late February.

Gyrfalcon

Observations in the fall at several High Arctic localities indicate that Gyrfalcons remain in the Arctic Islands until at least mid-September - in some years well into November. Transient Gyrfalcons were seen near Eureka on Ellesmere Island until mid-September 1955 (Parmelee and MacDonald 1960). MacDonald (personal communication) saw a group of 13 perched on antenna masts at Resolute Bay on 10 November 1954. Indirect evidence (remains of several arctic hares) collected in April 1987 suggests that one or more Gyrfalcons killed hares in Sverdrup Pass, Ellesmere Island after our departure on 9 September 1986 (D.R. Gray, unpublished data). The only mid-winter record for the islands is a white Gyrfalcon collected on Taylor Island (just west of Victoria Island) in January 1918 (Parmelee *et al.* 1967).

Mammals

Arctic Fox

During the winter of 1970-1971 at Polar Bear Pass, foxes were rare, but some (one in particular) were seen frequently throughout September, October, and part of November. Occasionally fresh tracks were observed from December through February. Sightings of at least two individuals increased again in March (Figure 4). The decrease in mid-winter observations supports the idea that foxes spend much time on the sea ice then in search of food left by hunting polar bears (Macpherson 1969; Riewe 1977). Feeding and hunting strategies of individuals in winter will remain unknown until we can follow tagged and radio-collared foxes.

Late winter (mid-February to the end of April) is the arctic fox breeding season (Banfield 1974). We have observed courting pairs on Bathurst and Axel Heiberg islands in late March, and on Ellesmere Island from early to mid-April. The relationship between the timing of the breeding season and available food and weather affecting physical condition is not clear. There is still much to be learned about courtship behaviour - particularly the role of vocalizations.

FIGURE 4: Arctic Fox scavenging from wolf-killed muskox carcass.

Arctic Hare

The arctic hare is perhaps one of the poorest known of High Arctic mammals. Greely's observations of hares, their tracks and snow-burrows in December and February were offered as "strong, if not convincing, proof that the animal does not hibernate". Our recent long-range studies have only begun to build on some intriguing observations made by early arctic explorers (Gray and Hamilton 1982; Aniśkowicz *et al.*, this volume). Parker (1977) investigated several aspects of hare biology, including the reproductive status of males and females, in March on Axel Heiberg Island.

My study of hare behaviour, begun in 1985 at Sverdrup Pass on Ellesmere Island, includes a detailed analysis of courtship behaviour in groups and in single pairs in April-May (D.R. Gray, unpublished data). Late winter studies begun in 1969 at Polar Bear Pass, where the hare population is scattered and small but predictable in terms of location, are concentrating on the use of snow-dens by hares during late winter. Snow-dens are known from several localities but no significant new information on their use has been published since Fielden's (1877B) description.

Arctic Wolf

The nature of the wolf and its environment account for the great gaps in our knowledge of this species. Studies of arctic wolves in Canada have been limited to incidental observations made while studying other species (Riewe 1975), observations at dump sites near weather stations (Grace 1976), and studies relating wolf behaviour to that of their prey (Gray 1983).

FIGURE 5: Wolf pups investigating an old muskox skeleton, September 28, 1977.

The presence of the High Arctic Research Station on Bathurst Island over many years has meant that substantial data on wolf behaviour in winter have accumulated. Wolves were observed at intervals throughout the winter of 1970-1971, and we watched them kill two muskoxen in March (Gray 1987). In September 1977, the activities of a pack of 10, including five pups, centred on our study area. In a 20-day period, we recorded 13 hunts, five interactions with muskoxen, and two kills. As well as learning much about the behaviour of the pups (Figure 5), we found that muskox kills were used as rendezvous for the pups when the adults left on hunting trips (D.R. Gray, unpublished data).

A recent study of the behaviour of a wolf pack at a den near one of the arctic weather stations on Ellesmere Island (Mech 1987) is expected to continue, and the observation period is to be expanded into the late winter months and the period of courtship (Mech 1988). With Mech's experience in the use of radio-tracking techniques, this study has great potential for expanding our knowledge of wolf behaviour in winter. I hope that the pursuit of photographs will not limit the potential for marking and tracking individuals.

Lemming

That lemmings are active beneath the winter snow is well known. The extent of their surface activities in mid-winter is less clear. While travelling between the Arctic Islands in mid-April 1929, Joy saw great numbers of lemming tracks on the sea ice and even on icebergs, sometimes more than a day's journey from land (Royal Canadian Mounted Police 1929). On Bathurst Island, lemmings or their tracks were seen above ground regularly between September and March. In February 1971, tracks of an individual were followed across the snow for at least of 500 m. Data on population fluctuations in relation to burrow availability and weather conditions, as well as studies of snow depths and temperatures at winter nesting areas, indicate that lemming population fluctuations are far from predictable or cyclical (D.A. Gill, unpublished data).

Muskox

Despite three winter studies and several investigations in early or late winter, our knowledge of muskoxen is still far from complete. These studies have clarified winter feeding behaviour and energy demands (Gray 1987, Hubert 1977), the relationship with wolves as major predators (Gray 1983), and the behaviour of muskoxen during winter storms (Gray 1987) (Figure 6). Unfortunately the results of these studies are still not widely known and the popular literature dealing with muskoxen still uses faulty and out-of-date information.

FIGURE 6:   At the end of a late winter blizzard on Ellesmere Island, a herd of muskoxen remains lying down, some individuals partially covered by drifting snow.

Perhaps the most frustrating example to me is continued use of the story that muskoxen form a defense circle with adult males on the outside and females and young at the centre, not only when faced by wolves but also during winter blizzards. This misconception, apparently based on Pedersen (1958), still appears in general texts, children's books, and more seriously, in new mammal books and even respected journals. Another aspect of late winter about which we need more information is the weaning of calves ("short yearlings") before the birth of the new calves in mid-April or later. Young muskoxen continue to suckle as yearlings if a new calf is not born in the spring. On Bathurst Island we have observed yearlings suckling in October at about 18-months old. However, we know nothing about the timing of weaning when the calf's mother is pregnant. Observations at Sverdrup Pass of yearlings accompanying pregnant cows suggest that weaning occurs during the winter as no suckling attempts were seen in April.

Peary Caribou

This is only arctic land mammal officially declared endangered. It is also the poorest known form of caribou. Canadian Wildlife Service studies (Miller *et al.* 1977; Miller, this volume; Parker *et al.* 1975) have shown the seriousness of the problem at a population level. Observations at Polar Bear Pass have also indicated gaps in our knowledge. In September, small herds of caribou cross the pass to wintering areas thought to be in the southwestern part of the island. Males are in the rut then but little is known of their behaviour. Further, we lack information on the nature of their northward movements and the calving-grounds. Our observations indicate that caribou were a significant prey species for wolves before the population decline of 1973-1974 (Figure 7). The role of wolf predation in the slow recovery since then is unknown.

FIGURE 7: David Gray examining the carcass of a bull Peary caribou killed by wolves in Polar Bear Pass.

Ermine

Winter activities of ermine are directly tied to those of the lemming. Ermine were not seen during winter studies at Bathurst Island, though they were common there in some summers. Riewe (1977) found several ermine tracks on Devon Island in February and March 1971, and also in September and early October. Based on spring observations of lemming winter nests, predation was common, but the under-snow behaviour in relation to that predation is a mystery.

Wolverine

The presence of the wolverine in the High Arctic in winter (or at any time) is doubtful. Although distribution maps in general texts routinely show the wolverine to be present on most of the northern islands (e.g. Banfield 1974), the only records are a sighting on Little Cornwallis Island in 1961 (Tener 1963) and a cranium found on Melville Island in 1819 (Fisher 1821). The species is rare and may not have resident populations in the High Arctic islands (van Zyll de Jong 1975).

Marine Animals

Though marine mammals (including polar bears) and seabirds are beyond the scope of this paper, I would like to acknowledge the work of several investigators who have made significant contributions to our knowledge of seabirds and marine mammals in winter, especially Gaston and Nettleship (1981), Harington (1968), Stirling and his associates (Kiliaan and Stirling 1978; Calvert and Stirling 1985), and Smith and Memogana (1977). Work on the significance of polynyas to winter birds and mammals is of particular importance (Stirling and Cleator 1981).

PROBLEMS AND SOLUTIONS

Environmental and logistical problems of studying birds and mammals in the Canadian Arctic Islands in winter are obvious - intense cold, low light-levels , ice fog, as well as problems of establishing and supplying a camp, transportation, and choosing suitable personnel.

Environment

Although studying animals in the High Arctic in winter will never be easy, some recent developments have changed the situation for the better. In 1970, when we attempted to watch muskoxen during the dark period, special equipment that would have made those studies more successful, such as night vision scopes and radio telemetry were beyond reach of our budget and, at the same time, too cumbersome to be of much practical value. Today such equipment is readily available, less expensive, and much more efficient. The period of winter "darkness" is not as impeding as many think. The long periods of twilight together with the moonlight provide many hours each month that could be suitable for travel and observation.

Coping with the cold is another area where high technology clothing has made a great difference, though I consider traditional Inuit clothing to be superior to the modern.

Logistics

The excellent logistical support offered to researchers by the Polar Continental Shelf Project (Hobson, this volume) means that the necessary field support is available at both ends of the winter, since Polar Shelf usually opens its Resolute base in February or March and closes in September. Unfortunately, in years when there are no major winter projects, the base may open only at winter's end and close before winter settles in. Safe operation of aircraft using off-strip landings restricts the non-wintering biologist to the period before November and after February, depending on location.

The establishment of permanent field research stations at several places in the Arctic Islands means that winter studies can occur without a great expenditure of time and resources. For example, the National Museum of Natural Sciences and the Arctic Institute of North America encourage the use of their research stations, on Bathurst and Devon islands respectively, by other researchers (especially university students) as long as the work conforms to station policy.

In spite of the deplorable reduction in the number of arctic weather stations, these long-established bases still offer unique opportunities as centres for winter biological studies. In the early days of arctic biological investigation these weather stations were of great importance as the only "permanent" bases for field work (MacDonald 1952, 1961).

With regard to the policy of establishing large government research stations in northern communities (e.g. Igloolik and Inuvik), I agree with the assessments of Hattersley-Smith (1974) and Tener (1982) that such a policy is of limited use in terms of biological science. There is usually little or no wildlife within a great distance of these settlements, and the expenditure of similar funds on smaller, remote permanent stations or portable, temporary stations would yield far greater returns for money spent. To make significant progress we do not require elaborate quarters. We could easily get by on the level of accommodation provided to explorers 100 years ago (Figure 8). Our experiences with the versatile and portable Parcoll huts under extreme winter conditions have demonstrated that all one really needs for winter study accommodation is a three- or four-section Parcoll for a two-person team.

FIGURE 8:   Greely's corner at Fort Conger, Ellesmere Island, October 1881 (Public Archives of Canada, C-5499).

Cooperation

If we are to greatly advance our knowledge of arctic animals in winter, we will have to exploit cooperative programs. Cooperation with oil exploration companies, for example, has led to new sources of funds, logistic support and even new data. With the expansion of the Northwest Territories Renewable Resources regional biologist program to more communities, there are increasing opportunities for joint research projects.

An area of potential cooperation that, in my experience, has proved to be mostly negative, is with the Canadian Armed Forces (Editor's note: but see Morrison and Davidson, this volume). On Bathurst Island in past years, and recently on Ellesmere Island, CAF helicopters have repeatedly interfered with research programs and harassed animals under study. Perhaps with a new command structure in the northern region and better communication, this situation can be changed to benefit northern science.

Above all, cooperation between northern biologists and the Inuit is important. Inuit hunters in particular have contributed a great deal to polar bear (Harington 1968) and marine mammal (Smith 1977) studies. The hunters' knowledge of birds and mammals, particularly prey species should be better used and recorded. Observations made during winter hunts have provided much interesting data that would be difficult to obtain by professional biologists, as Gunn, Arlooktoo and Kaomayok (1988) have indicated. By participating in the regular winter muskox hunts on Ellesmere Island, Rowell (1980) was able to collect rare and useful data on muskox reproduction.

THE FUTURE

It seems likely that most future studies involving an overwintering period will, as in the past, be done by university students on thesis projects. The length of time required to obtain sufficient data and the length of a winter make footloose graduate students ideal for this work. Programs initiated by the Northern Heritage Foundation (McCreadie 1987) will help ensure that northerners will be able to take part in future winter studies.

It is encouraging to note that several winter-oriented studies by students are underway presently. Martin Raillard (personal communication) is investigating the effect of winter grazing of muskoxen on plant communities at Sverdrup Pass; Becky Sjare (personal

583

communication) will study winter behaviour of walruses, and Ursula Peterson (personal communication) is collecting information on Snowy Owl migrations and winter habits in the North.

As this volume is intended to provide ideas for future research planning in the Canadian Arctic Islands, and originated through the National Museum of Natural Sciences, it is appropriate to consider future programs of NMNS vertebrate ethologists, and the High Arctic Research Station at Bathurst Island in relation to winter research.

We intend to operate the Bathurst Island station at current levels for the next five years, or at least until the level of protection for the Polar Bear Pass National Wildlife Area has been established. At present, a wooden laboratory building with a small observation tower, and a Parcoll hut are the station's nucleus. Two Parcoll hut frames are standing and can be used when needed.

Necessarily, biological research at the station has focused on the summer season, in order to understand the breeding behaviour and ecology of migratory birds. However, valuable data for both bird and mammal studies have come from the time spent there during, and at both ends of, the winter. It is important to continue and expand our early and late winter observations.

Thus, future NMNS research projects will include the arctic hare behavioural study, particularly breeding behaviour and the use of snow-dens in late winter. Wolf studies at Bathurst Island will continue as opportunities permit, especially on feeding behaviour and predation in relation to the island's population of endangered Peary caribou. Surveys near a possible den site in the National Wildlife Area will continue.

Bird studies will concentrate on the early and late winter behaviour of several migratory bird species. As part of this project, the bird-banding program begun in 1968 will be continued, and in relation to it, information on winter behaviour of birds will be collected from various sources.

It is clear from this review that our knowledge of birds and mammals in the Canadian Arctic Islands in winter is inadequate. It is also evident that more information exists (in unpublished form): (1) at Inuit communities; (2) in the records of Northwest Territories regional biologists; (3) in incidental observations of weather station personnel and the Royal Canadian Mounted Police. These sources, and some of the more obscure records of early explorers, will have to be better used to increase our understanding of Canada's North.

584

As Roots (1969) has suggested, one has to be generous and assume that the lack of winter investigations is due to the increased costs and difficult logistics of winter work rather than the discomforts. In the report, "Canada and Polar Science", Adams *et al.* (1987) stressed the serious effect of current funding restrictions on arctic biology - even the essential work carried out by small parties using simple methods. It is precisely this kind of research that the NMNS is best equipped to carry out. I hope that those responsible for securing adequate support for arctic scientists can work with them to achieve an acceptable level of knowledge of the fauna of the Canadian Arctic Islands.

ACKNOWLEDGEMENTS

I acknowledge the support and encouragement given to me during my own winter studies by S.D. MacDonald and E.F. Roots. Logistic support for winter work by the Vertebrate Ethology Section of the National Museum of Natural Sciences continues to be generously provided by the Polar Continental Shelf Project. I also thank David A. Gill for his contribution to this paper and the NMNS High Arctic research programs. Others who helped me collect winter data were: Donald Cockerton, John Morgan, Richard Popko, Looty Pijamini, Janice Rowell, and Thomas Sadler. Anne Gunn provided unpublished data on winter observations and on the subject of the contribution to research by Inuit hunters.

REFERENCES

Adams, W.P., P.F. Burnet, M.R. Gordon, and E.F. Roots. 1987. Canada and polar science. Indian and Northern Affairs Canada, Ottawa. 129 pp.

Banfield, A.W.F. 1974. The mammals of Canada. University of Toronto Press. Toronto. 438 pp.

Bernier, J.E. 1910. Report on the Dominion of Canada Government Expedition to the Arctic Islands and Hudson Strait on board the D.G.S. *Arctic*. Government Printing Bureau. Ottawa. 529 pp.

Calvert, W. and I. Stirling. 1985. Winter distribution of ringed seals (*Phoca hispida*) in the Barrow Strait area, Northwest Territories, determined by underwater vocalizations. Canadian Journal of Fisheries and Aquatic Sciences 42(7):1238-1243.

Cook, F.A. 1913. My attainment of the Pole. Mitchell Kennerley, New York and London. 610 pp.

Fielden, H.W. 1877A. List of birds observed in Smith Sound and in the Polar Basin during the Arctic Expedition of 1875-76. Zoologist, Series 4, 1:401-412.

_____. 1877B. On the Mammalia of North Greenland and Grinnell Land. Zoologist, Series 3, 1:313-321, 353-361.

Fisher, A. 1821. Journal of a voyage of discovery to the Arctic regions, in His Majesty's Ships *Helca* and *Griper*, in the years 1819 and 1820. Longmans, Hurst, Rees, Orme and Brown, London.

Gaston, A.J. and D.N. Nettleship. 1981. The Thick-billed Murres of Prince Leopold Island, a study of the breeding ecology of a colonial High Arctic seabird. Canadian Wildlife Service, Monograph Series, Number 6:1-350.

Godfrey, W.E. 1966. The birds of Canada. National Museum of Canada, Bulletin 203. Ottawa. 428 pp.

_____. 1986. The birds of Canada. Revised edition. National Museum of Natural Sciences, Ottawa. 595 pp.

Grace, E.S. 1976. Interactions between men and wolves at an arctic outpost on Ellesmere Island. Canadian Field-Naturalist 90(2):149-156.

Gray, D.R. 1971. Winter research on the muskox (*Ovibos moschatus*) on Bathurst Island, 1970-71. Arctic Circular 21(3):158-163.

_____. 1977. The status of the muskox and Peary caribou on Canada's Arctic Islands. In: Canada's Threatened Species and Habitats. Edited by: T. Mosquin and C. Suchal. Canadian Nature Federation, Special Publication 6:57-62.

_____. 1983. Interactions between wolves and muskoxen on Bathurst Island, N.W.T., Canada. Acta Zoologica Fennica 174:255-257.

_____. 1987. The muskoxen of Polar Bear Pass. National Museum of Natural Sciences, and Fitzhenry and Whiteside, Toronto. 192 pp.

Gray, D.R. and H. Hamilton. 1982. Hare revelations: the bizarre behaviour of the arctic hare. Nature Canada 11(1):48-54.

Greely, A.W. 1886. Three years of arctic service. Volume 2. Charles Scribner's Sons, New York. 444 pp.

Gunn, A., G. Arlooktoo, and D. Kaomayok. 1988. The contribution of the ecological knowledge of Inuit to wildlife management in the Northwest Territories. In: Wildlife and Native People. Edited by: L. Carbyn and M.M.R. Freeman. Boreal Institute, Occasional Papers 23.

Harington, C.R. 1961. History, distribution and ecology of the muskoxen. M.Sc. thesis. McGill University, Montreal. 489 pp.

_____. 1968. Denning habits of the polar bear (*Ursus maritimus* Phipps). Canadian Wildlife Service, Report Series 5:1-30.

Hattersley-Smith, G. 1974. North of Latitude Eighty. Defence Research Board, Ottawa. 121 pp.

Hummel, M. 1984. Arctic wildlife. Key Porter, Toronto. 160 pp.

Hubert, B.A. 1974. Estimated productivity of muskox on northeastern Devon Island. M.Sc. thesis, University of Manitoba, Winnipeg. 118 pp.

_____. 1977. Estimated productivity of muskox on Truelove Lowland. In: Truelove Lowland, Devon Island, Canada: A High Arctic Ecosystem. Edited by: L.C. Bliss. University of Alberta Press, Edmonton. pp. 467-491.

Kiliaan, H.P.L. and I. Stirling. 1978. Observations on overwintering walruses in the eastern Canadian High Arctic. Journal of Mammalogy 59:197-200.

MacDonald, S.D. 1952. Report on biological investigations at Mould Bay, Prince Patrick Island, N.W.T., in 1952. Annual Report, National Museum of Canada, 1952-53, Bulletin 132:214-238.

_____. 1961. Biological investigations at Isachsen, Ellef Ringnes Island, N.W.T. National Museum of Canada, Bulletin 172:90-97.

_____. 1980. Scientific progress: terrestrial biology, an overview. In: A Century of Canada's Arctic Islands, 1880-1980. Edited by: M. Zaslow. Royal Society of Canada. pp. 171-186.

Macpherson, A.H. 1969. The dynamics of Canadian arctic fox populations. Canadian Wildlife Service, Report Series 8:1-52.

Manning, T.H., E.O. Hohn, and A.H. Macpherson. 1956. The birds of Banks Island. National Museum of Canada, Bulletin 143:1-144.

McCreadie, M. 1987. Financial aid for northern scientific assistants: the Northern Heritage Society and the Science Institute of the Northwest Territories collaborate. In: The Canadian Arctic Islands: Canada's Missing Dimension. Program and Abstracts. p. 105.

Mech, L.D. 1987. At home with the arctic wolf. National Geographic 171(5):562-593.

Mech, L.D.   1988.   Ellesmere Island; life in the High Arctic.   National Geographic 172(6):750-767.

Miller, F.L., R.H. Russell, and A. Gunn.   1977.   Distributions, movements and numbers of Peary caribou and muskoxen on western Queen Elizabeth Islands, Northwest Territories, 1972-74.   Canadian Wildlife Service, Report Series 40:1-55.

Osborn, S.   1856.   The discovery of a North-West Passage by H.M.S. *Investigator*, Capt. R. M'Clure, during the years 1851, 1852, 1853, 1854.   William Blackwood and Sons, London.   358 pp.

Parker, G.R.   1977.   Morphology, reproduction, diet, and behaviour of the arctic hare (*Lepus arcticus monstrabilis*) on Axel Heiberg Island, Northwest Territories.   Canadian Field-Naturalist 91(1):8-18.

Parker, G.R., D.C. Thomas, E. Broughton, and D.R. Gray.   1975.   Crashes of muskox and Peary caribou populations in 1973-74 on the Parry Islands, Arctic Canada.   Canadian Wildlife Service, Progress Notes 56:1-10.

Parmelee, D.F. and S.D. MacDonald.   1960.   The birds of west-central Ellesmere Island and adjacent areas.   National Museum of Canada, Bulletin 169:1-103.

Parmelee, D.F., H.A. Stephens, and R.H. Schmidt.   1967.   The birds of southeastern Victoria Island and adjacent small islands.   National Museum of Canada, Bulletin 222:1-229.

Pedersen, A.   1958.   Der Moschusochs (*Ovibos moschatus* Zimmermann).   A. Ziemsen Verlag, Wittenberg.   54 pp.

Riewe, R.   1975.   The High Arctic wolf in the Jones Sound region.   Arctic 28:209-212.

_____.   1977.   Mammalian carnivores utilizing Truelove Lowland.   In: Truelove Lowland, Devon Island, Canada: A High Arctic Ecosystem.   Edited by: L.C. Bliss.   University of Alberta Press, Edmonton.   714 pp.

Roots, E.F.   1969.   The role of logistics in northern research.   In: Proceedings of the Second National Northern Research Conference.   Edited by: J.J. Bond.   Boreal Institute, Edmonton.   pp. 65-77.

_____.   1987.   The natural realm and arctic heritage.   In: Arctic Heritage, Proceedings of a Symposium.   Association of Colleges and Universities for Northern Studies.   Ottawa.   pp. 164-176.

Rowell, J.   1980.   A preliminary study of the reproductive anatomy of the female muskox (*Ovibos moschatus*).   M.Sc. thesis, University of Ottawa.   Ottawa.   190 pp.

Royal Canadian Mounted Police.   1929.   Report of the Royal Canadian Mounted Police for the year ended 30 September, 1929.

Smith, T.G. 1973. The birds of the Holman Region, western Victoria Island. Canadian Field-Naturalist 87(1):35-42.

Smith, T.G. and J. Memogana. 1977. Disorientation in ringed and bearded seals. Canadian Field-Naturalist 91(2):181-182.

Stirling, I. and H. Cleator. 1981. Polynyas in the Canadian Arctic. Canadian Wildlife Service, Occasional Papers 45:1-73.

Tener, J.S. 1963. Queen Elizabeth Islands Game Survey, 1961. Canadian Wildlife Service, Occasional Papers 4:1-50.

_____. 1982. Arctic biology. Transactions of the Royal Society of Canada 20:429-434.

van Zyll de Jong, C.G. 1975. The distribution and abundance of the wolverine (*Gulo gulo*) in Canada. Canadian Field-Naturalist 89(4):431-437.

Illustrated by Brenda Carter

THE DECLINE AND RECOVERY OF CARIBOU AND MUSKOXEN ON VICTORIA ISLAND

Anne Gunn[1]

Abstract: Numbers of caribou and muskoxen on Victoria Island reached a low between the 1920s and the 1930s. The Dolphin-Union caribou herd which used to migrate seasonally between southern Victoria Island and the mainland had disappeared. The causes of the decline and the slow recovery are difficult to confirm, but hunting and severe winters were factors. It was not until the 1970s that hunters began to report increases in muskox and caribou numbers, and both species have recolonized southern Victoria Island. The decrease and increase in the numbers of muskoxen and caribou is consistent with trends elsewhere in the Northwest Territories. In Greenland, similar cyclic fluctuations in wildlife are suggested to be responses to climatic changes. The Kitikmeot Hunter's and Trapper's Association harvest study documents the continued importance of caribou hunting to the communities of Holman and Cambridge Bay. The commercial use of muskoxen and caribou is rising as guided non-resident hunting and commercial meat sales increase. The Government of the Northwest Territories' emphasis on development of the renewable resource economy highlights the need to understand the numbers of caribou and muskoxen in relation to climatic changes.

Résumé: La population de caribous et de boeufs musqués de l'île Victoria a atteint un minimum dans les années 1920 et 1930. La harde de caribous de Dolphin et Union qui avait l'habitude de migrer entre le sud de l'île Victoria et le continent avait disparu. Les raisons qui pourraient expliquer cette baisse et cette lente remontée sont difficiles à prouver, mais on croit que la chasse et les hivers rigoureux ont pu être des causes. Ce n'est que vers les années 1970 que des chasseurs ont commencé à signaler des augmentations du nombre de caribous et de boeufs musqués et que ces deux espèces ont repeuplé le sud de l'île Victoria. La diminution et l'augmentation du nombre de caribous et de boeufs musqués correspondent à des variations qu'il y a ailleurs dans les Territoires du Nord-Ouest. Au Groënland, on retrouve ces mêmes variations cycliques de la faune qui résultent probablement de changements climatiques. L'étude sur la récolte des caribous faite par la Kitikmeot Hunter's and Trapper's Association confirme l'importance de la chasse au caribou pour les collectivités de Holman et de Cambridge Bay. La chasse avec guide des non-résidents de l'Arctique et les ventes de viande font augmenter l'usage commercial que l'on fait des caribous et des boeufs musqués. L'accent que met le gouvernement des Territoires du Nord-Ouest sur le développement d'une économie basées sur des ressources renouvelables souligne la nécessité de bien établir le lien qui existe entre, d'une part, la population de caribous et de boeufs musqués et, d'autre part, les changements de climat.

INTRODUCTION

The numbers of caribou (*Rangifer tarandus* spp.) and muskoxen (*Ovibos moschatus*) on Victoria Island decreased from the end of the nineteenth century, and remained low until the 1970s. The evidence for the decline and subsequent recovery mostly comes from Inuit oral history and hunters' recent observations. Scientific studies of wildlife were few until the mid-1980s.

Europeans rarely visited Victoria Island until the establishment of trading posts in the 1920s. Its rather central geographic location among Canada's Arctic Islands virtually isolated it from the early probes for the North-West Passage, searches for the Franklin Expedition, exploration for the North Pole and whaling. Further, the relative lack of commercially

---

[1] Department of Renewable Resources, Government of the Northwest Territories, Coppermine, Northwest Territories X0E 0C0

valuable hydrocarbons and minerals left Victoria Island without the environmental studies spawned by industrial exploration and development elsewhere in the Arctic Islands.

The virtual isolation of Victoria Island from scientific studies hampers any reconstruction of fluctuations in wildlife numbers. An understanding of population changes would be a sound basis for future wildlife management. Victoria Island is the second largest of the Canadian Arctic Islands and the southernmost of the larger western islands. Sustained use of its natural resources could play a significant role in fostering the continued occupation and development of the islands.

This paper describes the evidence for fluctuations in numbers of caribou and muskoxen from anthropological and wildlife sources. I speculate on the causes of the changes in numbers and their implications for future management of caribou and muskoxen.

MATERIALS AND METHODS

I drew heavily on the Inuit Land Use and Occupancy Project (Freeman 1976) for information on the prehistory and history of the human occupation of Victoria Island. I supplemented this information with other references and the personal recollections of local people from Coppermine, Holman and Cambridge Bay. Other wildlife data are from: published papers; unpublished reports in the files of Canadian Wildlife Service and Northwest Territories Wildlife Service (now the Department of Renewable Resources); unpublished reports of consultants for the Polar Gas Project; and studies currently underway, including the Kitikmeot Harvest Study.

RESULTS

Archaeological Information

The archaeological record for Victoria Island is too sparse in time and space to evaluate the status of either caribou or muskoxen. Southern and western coasts were occupied during pre-Dorset, Dorset and Thule times (McGhee 1976). Bones from those sites reveal the presence and the use of both caribou and muskoxen.

Anthropological Information

Pre-trading Era

People living along the south coast of Victoria Island (Freeman 1976) moved to the coast in fall to intercept groups of caribou gathering to cross to the mainland once the sea ice had formed. In April, people moved from sealing camps on the ice to the coast to hunt the returning caribou. Farther north, three Inuit groups that would eventually settle in Holman also relied on caribou. In the fall, Inuit hunted caribou along the northern margin of Minto Inlet and Prince Albert Sound. In spring, caribou and muskoxen were hunted northward toward Richard Collinson Inlet and Glenelg Bay (Figure 1).

FIGURE 1: Place names on Victoria Island mentioned in text.

On eastern Victoria Island, people depended more on sealing and fishing. Hunters had to travel long distances to the vicinity of Hadley Bay for caribou. The area north of Albert

592

Edward Bay toward Gateshead Island was known for muskoxen. People on southeastern Victoria Island hunted caribou that migrated between the island and the mainland in spring and fall.

Manning (1960) compiled historical information on numbers of caribou involved in the migrations between the island and the mainland. There is virtually no information on the caribou populations that were resident on the island during the winter (Manning 1960). Eye-witness accounts, and extrapolation based on the area of Victoria Island, led Manning (1960) to suggest that some 111,000 caribou spent the summer on Victoria Island before the 1920s.

Trading Era

Introduction of rifles extended the hunting seasons for caribou to the winter. The shift from a hunting to a hunting and trapping lifestyle increased the travelling in winter as trap-lines grew in length. Consequently, the trappers needed larger dog-teams and more dog food. The location of winter camps shifted from the sea ice of Dolphin and Union Strait and Coronation Gulf to permanent camps along the southern coast of Victoria Island. Travel inland for caribou and fish during the summer decreased in favour of hunting and caching seals along the coast for dog food.

The pattern of caribou hunting on Victoria Island changed after the opening of trading posts. The first trading posts in the area were established in 1916 at Bernard Harbour, Banks Island and at Rymer Point on Victoria Island in 1919. Trading ships had preceded the trading posts - for example Klengenberg wintered on southwestern Victoria Island in 1905-1906 and Mogg at Walker Bay in 1907-1908. The migration of caribou across Dolphin and Union Strait and Coronation Gulf ceased a few years after the establishment of the trading posts on the southwestern coast of Victoria Island and along the western mainland coast (Manning 1960; Freeman 1976). The migration of caribou from Kent Peninsula across Dease Strait to near Byron Bay stopped about 1930 (Freeman 1976).

The loss of the Dolphin and Union herd that had migrated across Wollaston Peninsula, and possibly as far north as Minto Inlet, left those areas without caribou. People from the Prince Albert Sound and Minto Inlet areas switched to hunting the resident Victoria Island caribou farther north and inland toward Shaler Mountains. Other people from the Read Island area either moved to the mainland or made trips to hunt caribou on the mainland.

The people on eastern Victoria Island continued to travel widely to hunt resident Victoria Island caribou or to the mainland. Many of the recollections of people about changes in hunting after the establishment of trading posts refer to caribou being considered scarce during the 1940s and early 1950s (Freeman 1976). Muskoxen were scarce from at least 1923 to 1939 near Minto Inlet, where they had been hunted previously. Muskox hunting areas contracted during the same period on southeastern Victoria Island, but there are few details on the reduction of muskoxen. Stefansson (1923) recounted that in 1911, Eskimos at Prince Albert Sound believed muskoxen were almost extinct in the area, which suggests muskoxen declined before caribou.

The scarcity of caribou and muskoxen until the 1960s is illustrated by some hunters' comments. D. Komoayok (personal communication) tells of how once hunters crossed a caribou trail, they would track it for days, if necessary, to kill it. Other hunters had to travel to the mainland for caribou meat and hides. Hunters recollect that it was not until the 1960s or even early 1970s when they saw the first muskoxen north of Cambridge Bay.

Wildlife Surveys

Wildlife surveys were not undertaken on Victoria Island until 1979, but A.H. Macpherson (1960 unpublished report, Canadian Wildlife Service) compiled the wildlife observations of geologists during extensive (18,400 km aerial) reconnaissance flights in 1959. The flights crossed large areas of Victoria Island and were flown at altitudes from 30-300 m above ground level. The geologists only recorded 76 muskoxen in six herds, as well as a single animal, and 10 caribou.

In 1976 and 1979, the Northwest Territories Wildlife Service responded to reports of increasing muskox sightings with aerial reconnaissances in the vicinity of Holman and Cambridge Bay (Spencer 1976; Boxer 1979, unpublished reports, Northwest Territories Wildlife Service). Those surveys revealed increasing numbers of muskoxen. The trend in the numbers could not be quantified properly, however, until estimates of numbers were obtained from systematic surveys.

The first systematic aerial survey of wildlife on Victoria Island was part of the environmental evaluation for the Polar Gas Pipeline. The pipeline was proposed to carry gas from the High Arctic across western Victoria Island to the mainland. Jakimchuk and

594

Carruthers (1980) estimated 12,160 ± 2,890 (Standard Error) muskoxen and 7,936 ± 1,839 caribou in August 1980.

The Department of Renewable Resources resurveyed most of the areas in March and August 1983 (Jingfors 1984, 1985) and in March 1988 (A. Gunn, unpublished data). The results are not comparable to Jakimchuk and Carruther's (1980) results which were from a survey of summer distribution. Those authors covered only a small percentage of their survey area (about 6%) compared to the 20% in 1983 and 30% in 1988, which further reduces the comparability of the surveys.

Jingfors (1985) concluded from his estimate of 6,430 ± 498 muskoxen on northwestern Victoria Island, that the muskox population was stable. The proportions of calves, yearlings and two-year olds in the population in 1986, however, supported the hunters' contention that the population is increasing (A. Gunn, unpublished data). The 1983 and 1988 surveys and hunters' reports attest to a rapid recolonization of muskoxen on southwest Victoria Island, where Jingfors (1984) estimated 3,300 ± 345 in March 1983 and I estimated 11,988 ± 2,078 muskoxen in March 1988.

We have more information on muskoxen than caribou partly because of the greater ease of surveying muskoxen, but also because of the quotas. Muskoxen can only be hunted under a quota system, and requested changes to quotas are evaluated by surveys. Inuit subsistence hunting of caribou is not regulated by quotas, and without the need to evaluate quotas there was less impetus for caribou surveys. The difficulties of precisely estimating numbers of the inconspicuous caribou scattered over inconveniently large areas also hindered such surveys. The first step in improving the design of surveys for caribou was to describe seasonal distributions, especially during calving and rutting. Caribou gather for the rut and cows for calving, which facilitates counting and survey design at these times.

Caribou populations are conventionally defined on the basis of their annual return to traditional calving grounds (Thomas 1969; Gunn and Miller 1986). Definition of populations is an essential step in relating harvesting to the trends in population size, and historical information was insufficient to determine the discreteness of separate populations. The seasonal movements of 10 adult cows fitted with satellite-tracked transmitters in March 1987 were monitored (A. Gunn, unpublished data) to locate calving and rutting areas. Four cows moved toward Prince Albert Sound for calving and postcalving and then returned to the south coast of Victoria Island for the winter. Two cows spent the year on Wollaston

Peninsula; an area that was devoid of caribou in the 1930s (Freeman 1976) but used by caribou before the 1920s (Manning 1960). Two caribou cows calved and rutted north of Minto Inlet suggesting that they belong to a different population from the caribou south of Minto Inlet (Figures 2, 3).

Manning (1960) described the Dolphin and Union herd as distinct from, but more related to, mainland caribou than Banks Island Peary caribou. He suggested that the remnants of the Dolphin and Union herd were either absorbed into the mainland caribou or the resident Victoria Island caribou. This raises the question as to the subspecific as well as the population status of the caribou currently on Victoria Island. I am investigating the taxonomy by examination of serum proteins to measure genetic heterogeneity (Roed 1985), and by measuring skulls. Preliminary adult cow skull measurements (A. Gunn, unpublished data) clearly separate the caribou wintering on southern Victoria Island from mainland barren-ground caribou and High Arctic Peary caribou. The greatest resemblance is to the caribou measured from Prince of Wales Island and Boothia Peninsula (Manning 1960; Thomas and Everson 1982).

Harvest Information

Harvest information was not consistently collected until the inception of the Kitikmeot Harvest Study in 1982. Usher (1965) estimated from hunters' reports that some 150-200 caribou were harvested by the about 135 people living in Holman during 1962-1963. The population of Holman has about doubled since then, and the annual caribou harvest has more than tripled (625 ± 00, 1982-1987).

DISCUSSION

Changes in numbers and distributions of caribou and muskoxen on Victoria Island fall into three phases. Coincident with the establishing of coastal trading posts, caribou numbers sharply declined. The Dolphin and Union herd and the caribou crossing Dease Strait (which may, or may not, have been part of the former herd) ceased their seasonal migrations to winter on the mainland. Little is known about the decline of the muskoxen, though it may have preceded that of the caribou. Possibly, the muskox decline on western

596

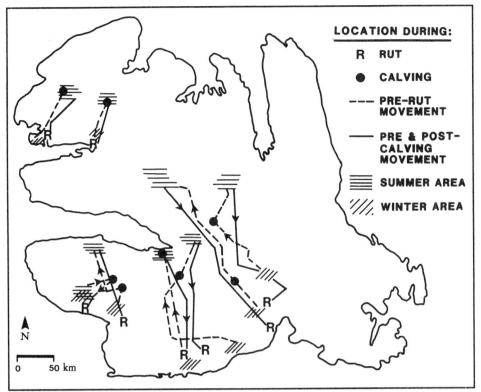

FIGURE 2: Movement of adult cow caribou with satellite-tracked collars, Victoria Island.

FIGURE 3: Applying a satellite radiocollar to a female caribou.

597

Victoria Island coincided with the reduction of Banks Island muskoxen by the mid-1880s for unknown reasons. From 1920 to the early 1960s, caribou numbers farther north on Victoria Island continued to decline or stabilize at a low level, and the numbers of muskoxen also remained low or further declined (Freeman 1976). The third phase was one of increases in numbers of both species and a recolonization of southern Victoria Island.

Numbers of caribou and muskoxen have decreased and increased in the first half of this century on the mainland Northwest Territories. Those changes in population sizes are usually interpreted as the result of lifestyle changes among Inuit hunters that accrued from European influence. On Victoria and Banks islands, this explanation is not completely substantiated by the timing of the declines and the human cultural changes.

Clark (1986) described a "blip" in fur-seal (*Callorhinus ursinus*) bones found in kitchen-middens on Kodiak Island. The interpretation of the blip shows the need for precise dating before correlating changes in use patterns with conspicuous cultural changes. The use of fur seals only preceded European contact by perhaps a few decades. A less than precise analysis of the timing could lead to the conclusion that the introduction of the Asian and European influence triggered the utilization of the fur seals. More likely, an ecological change in the marine environment brought the seals within harvesting reach of the Kodiak natives (Clark 1986).

The timing of the reduction of the Dolphin and Union herd correlates with the establishing of trading-posts, and the effect of the firearms on the caribou is supported by eye-witness accounts (Manning 1960). Ascribing the subsequent declines in the more northern caribou and muskox populations to increased hunting pressure may be an oversimplification. The importance of finding whether ecological factors caused or compounded the decline in the caribou and muskox populations is of immediate management significance today.

Caribou and muskoxen (Figure 4) can double their populations every five to six years when conditions are good and mortality is minimal. Yet despite this potential, the populations have taken decades to recover. Once a population is reduced, however, even relatively low levels or mortality could hold it down.

Two considerations raise doubts about the prolonged decline in caribou and muskox populations being solely attributed to the effects of hunting. Firstly, the declines appeared relatively widespread over Victoria Island and possibly east on the mainland, though the

598

extent that the reduction of each species is synchronized is uncertain.

Secondly, at the time of low ungulate populations from the 1930s to the late 1950s, human population had also decreased after exposure to European diseases (Usher 1965). Large northern and western inland areas of Victoria Island were not used for hunting or trapping (Freeman 1976).

FIGURE 4: Muskox cow with a calf and a yearling, Victoria Island.

The nadir in the human population of Holman and Coppermine was in the early 1930s: not until the mid-1950s did the population return to the pre-contact level. Even in the early 1960s only 70-80 people lived along the northern and southern coasts of Dolphin and Union Strait, and about 135 people occupied the Holman area.

In the early 1950s, when the human populations began to recover, the prices of long furs had crashed. A comparison of the dispersion of traplines before and after 1955 suggests a contraction in areas covered and therefore hunted (Freeman 1976). The number of hunters with firearms to deplete widespread caribou and muskoxen seems low, although hunters travelled widely during the trapping season. After the loss of the large migratory herds, the caribou apparently did not concentrate seasonally in large numbers, which would have increased their vulnerability to overhunting (Freeman 1976). Finally, there were areas not apparently hunted which would have been refuges for caribou and muskoxen.

Hunters from Coppermine, Cambridge and Holman partly attribute the disappearance of caribou and muskoxen to exceptionally severe winters. Those discussions do not specify in which years the caribou died. Weather data shed no light on whether severe winters may have compounded the effect of hunting in depressing the populations in the 1920s and 1930s. Weather records in Holman cover the periods 1941-1969 and 1979 onward. In

Cambridge Bay, weather recording started in 1929, although there are many months without data until 1947.

On western Victoria Island there was, however, a series of severe winters with above average snowfall that persisted into June in the early 1960s and to a lesser extent in the 1940s. In Holman, winters with a total snowfall exceeding 100 cm occurred in 1943-44, 1947-48, 1958-59, 1959-60, 1960-61 (227.6 cm), 1961-62 and 1963-64. In Cambridge Bay, the range in annual snowfall is not so marked as on western Victoria Island, but snowfall exceeded 100 cm in the winters of 1940-41, 1963-64 and 1964-65. Those winters with above average snow depths in the 1940s and 1960s may have contributed to the slow recovery of the caribou and muskox populations.

Ocean-current temperature changes such as the West Greenland current (e.g. Vibe 1967; Dunbar and Thomsen 1979), and alterations in the upper atmospheric pressure systems (e.g. Barry *et al.* 1975) cause shifts in the trend of arctic temperatures and precipitation. Shorter-term changes such as one to two-year decreases in temperature and precipitation, and persistence of sea ice in the summer were caused by the dust-veil after the eruption of major volcanos in 1815, 1835, 1883, 1902, 1907, 1912 and 1963; in some cases compounded by anomalous atmospheric pressure conditions (e.g. Bradley and England 1978; Skinner 1985; Catchpole 1985, 1988). So far, most descriptions of shifts in climate have centred on the eastern Arctic (Greenland, Baffin Island, Hudson Bay and the High Arctic).

Efforts to correlate climate on Victoria Island with changes in the past numbers of caribou and muskoxen are tenuous. The relationships are barely known between the available meteorological measurements such as snow depth or snowfall and ungulate survival. There are relatively few instances where a winter die-off has been documented and the weather conditions known. Relationships are poorly known between snow depth and density; groundfast ice and ice lenses; their timing and duration and the forage availability for caribou (Miller *et al.* 1982) and muskoxen. Peary caribou and muskoxen died on the western Queen Elizabeth Islands during the winter of 1973-1974 (Parker *et al.* 1975); Miller *et al.* 1977). The winter of 1973-1974 started with a fall ice storm, followed by exceptionally deep snowfall that was late in melting. Caribou succumbed before muskoxen in late winter (Miller *et al.* 1977).

Caribou and muskoxen respond differently to severe winters. Conditions severe enough to kill caribou may not cause mortality of muskoxen. The 1972-1973 and 1976-1977 winters had snow deep enough to reduce forage availability for caribou to the point of fatal malnutrition on Banks Island, but not for muskoxen.

This comparative aspect of the ecology of caribou and muskoxen and the relationship of their strategies for winter survival are little understood. Yet, clearly there are such pronounced differences in feeding behaviour and comparative morphology that different winter survival strategies are inevitable. Differences in the peaks and valleys in annual fat cycles (e.g. Adamczewski 1987; Thing *et al.* 1987) and the timing of annual life-cycle phases, such as calving and the rut, further support the idea of dissimilar survival strategies.

Differences in the climate across Victoria Island are sufficient that Maxwell (1981) could divide the island into three climatic regions. The western is under Pacific maritime influence. Eastern Victoria Island has a more continental climate marked by greater annual extremes in temperature and lower precipitation. These climatic differences make attempts to relate the changes in numbers of caribou and muskoxen to climate more difficult.

Predation is a potentially important mortality factor in caribou and muskoxen ecology. Little is known about wolves (*Canis lupus bernardi*) on Victoria Island, but they were a subspecies rather closely related to the High Arctic wolf (*C.l.arctos*) (Nowak 1983). Banfield (1978) speculated that an immigration of the High Arctic wolf had swamped *C. l. bernardi*. Freeman (1976) refers to wolves as scarce but hunted near Minto Inlet from the 1930s onward. Five wolf pelts were sold between 1968 and 1980 from Holman, and seven pelts from 1981 to 1985. Sale records for the pelts underestimates the number of wolves harvested as the species was also killed because of its depredations along fox traplines in the 1960s and 1970s (personal communication, T.G. Smith).

In the 1980s, sightings of wolves are increasing, and Read Island and Holman trappers have complained about damage to trapped foxes by wolves (personal communications, D. Kuptana, J. Atatahak). In December 1986, four wolves were shot along a trapline on the southwestern coast of Victoria Island. Wolves now den at Wellington Bay (personal communication, D. Kaomayok) and packs of up to nine have been sighted at Wellington Bay and Minto Inlet (A. Gunn, field notes).

The sparse information is that wolves were not numerous on Victoria Island. Even low numbers of wolves can, however, exert significant pressure on a low prey population, but there is no evidence for or against this occurring in the 1930s to 1960s on Victoria Island.

Surprisingly, wolves are only slowly increasing despite the large prey base and the high potential rate of increase of wolves (Keith 1983).

The same pattern: decline of caribou and muskoxen in the 1920s and 1930s; low numbers until the 1960s; then recovery in the 1970s and 1980s, occurs elsewhere in the Canadian Arctic. Aerial surveys have documented the increase in caribou numbers near Boothia Peninsula, King William Island and the Back River Lowlands. The compilation of historical accounts and recollections of older hunters document an earlier decrease in numbers (Gunn and Lambert, in press; Gunn and Ashevak, in press). The decline and recovery of caribou numbers is also apparent among the large mainland herds of barren-ground caribou (Gates 1985; Heard et al. 1986) and on Baffin Island (personal communication, M. Ferguson).

The most complete evidence for cycling in caribou numbers comes from the documentation of four cycles of increase and decrease in a 250-year period in Greenland (Meldgaard 1986). However, the cycles are not completely periodic and there were regional differences in the synchronization of peaks and troughs. Meldgaard (1986) rejected hunting and predation in favour of climatic changes as driving the cycles.

Die-offs and reproductive failures as consequences of exceptionally severe winter weather are occasionally documented (e.g. Miller et al. 1977; Parker et al. 1975). The more subtle interactions between less dramatic trends in winter weather, survival and reproduction are little known. Thomas (1982), Adamczewski (1987) and others, however, have started to untangle the interactions between the effects of winter weather on forage availability, body condition and reproduction. Little is known about responses of caribou or muskoxen to the influences of summer weather on forage quality and phenology.

Subsistence use of caribou and muskoxen has been stable for Holman and Cambridge Bay in the 1980s despite the increase in numbers of caribou wintering close to the settlements. The annual replacement cost of the meat harvested is one million dollars - not accounting for the intangible values.

The dollar value of commercial use of caribou and muskoxen to the communities exceeds face value because of the importance of cash in the local economies. Most people are unemployed, which magnifies the importance of any source of cash. Local meat sales to hotels or community feasts, the sales of horns for carvings, and guided non-resident hunting were the only commercial uses of caribou and muskoxen. Commercial use of

602

caribou and muskoxen expanded in 1987 with the opening of a small meat processing facility in Cambridge Bay. Central Arctic Meats Ltd. is affiliated with the Hunter's and Trapper's Association and hires hunters to harvest meat which is sold as jerky or frozen cuts.

People's cash expectations, and the justification of capital investments could provide momentum for commercial projects, even as the "resources" begin a downward swing in their population cycle. The Department of Renewable Resources gives priority to subsistence over commercial use, and would limit commercial use in the event of a population decline. Early warning of the state of the harvested population will be available from studies monitoring the health and physical condition of the caribou population. Population parameters (e.g. calf survival), and skeletal measurements (e.g. mandible or metatarsal length) respond to the availability of resources during different population phases (Meldgaard 1986; Couturier *et al.* 1987).

Our experience with population cycles of caribou and muskoxen is too short to determine whether the cycles are regular and periodic. Additionally, there are the uncertainties stemming from the prediction that anthropological factors may affect the climate. For example, the "greenhouse effect" from rising concentrations of carbon dioxide and other greenhouse gases in the atmosphere may cause increases in mean temperatures.

Monitoring of population-size trends is only one part of managing cyclic populations, as the rapidity of population changes may exceed the feasible frequency of monitoring population size. Phases of population increase and decrease only averaged 10 years in Greenland, though there were variations (Meldgaard 1986). The annual collection of skeletal measurements and other condition indices is an economical approach to monitoring the population phase. Other measures of body and reproductive condition are also easily taken and help track a population's response to prevailing climate.

Awareness of the response of caribou and muskoxen to climatic change (Harington 1986) has to be part of planning their utilization. The memories of the previous declines in caribou and muskoxen and government responses are a strong thread running through the current relationship between government and public (Clancy 1987). The potential of anthropological factors to alter climate hastens has the need to better understand the role of climate regulating, long-term changes in the numbers of caribou and muskoxen in the Northwest Territories.

ACKNOWLEDGEMENTS

This paper grew out of conversations with hunters from Cambridge Bay, Coppermine and Holman, and I especially thank David Kaomayok and Colin Adjun. I thank George Hobson and his staff (Polar Continental Shelf Project (PCSP)) for their support of arctic science. Involvement with PCSP has led to stimulating contacts and friendships which helped in writing this paper. In particular, Bea Alt (Geological Survey of Canada) helped me track down the snow data. C.R. Harington (National Museum of Natural Sciences) directed me to helpful references on climatic change. Janet Troje (J&T Graphics, Yellowknife) produced the illustrations, and Frank L. Miller (Canadian Wildlife Service) reviewed the manuscript.

REFERENCES

Adamczewski, J. 1987. Body composition in relation to seasonal forage quality in caribou (*Rangifer tarandus groenlandicus*) on Coats Island, Northwest Territories. M.Sc. thesis, University of Alberta, Edmonton. 139 pp.

Banfield, A.W.F. 1978. The mammals of Canada. University of Toronto Press, Toronto. 438 pp.

Barry, R.G., R.S. Bradley, and J.D. Jacobs. 1975. Synoptic climatological studies of the Baffin Bay area. In: Climate of the Arctic. Edited by: G. Weller and S.A. Bowling. 24th Alaska Science Conference, University of Alaska, Fairbanks. pp. 82-90.

Bradley, R.S. and J. England. 1978. Recent climatic fluctuations of the Canadian High Arctic and their significance for glaciology. Arctic and Alpine Research 10(4):715-731.

Catchpole, A.J.W. 1985. Evidence from Hudson Bay region of severe cold in the summer of 1816. In: Climatic Change in Canada 5. Edited by: C.R. Harington. Syllogeus 55:121-146.

_____. 1988. Occurrence of severe ice in Hudson Strait and Hudson Bay following major volcanic eruptions, 1751 to 1889 A.D. Climatic Fluctuations and Man 3:67.

Clancy, P. 1987. Native hunters and the state: the 'caribou crisis' in the Northwest Territories. Studies in National and International Development, Queen's University, Kingston. SNID, Occasional Paper 87-101:1-32.

Clark, D.W. 1986. Archaeological and historical evidence for an 18th-century "blip" in the distribution of the northern fur seal at Kodiak Island, Alaska. Arctic 39:39-42.

Couturier, S., J. Brunelle, and G. LaPointe. 1987. Decline of physical condition and decrease of recruitment in the George River caribou herd. Paper presented at the Third North American Caribou Workshop (Chena Hot Springs, Alaska, 4-6 November, 1987).

Dunbar, M.J. and D.H. Thomsen. 1979. West Greenland salmon and climatic change. Meddelelser om Grønland 202(2):5-19.

Freeman, M.M.R. 1976. Inuit Land Use and Occupancy Project. Indian and Northern Affairs Canada, Ottawa. Volume I. 262 pp.

Gates, C.C. 1985. The fall and rise of the Kaminuriak caribou population. Proceedings of the Second North American Caribou Workshop. Edited by: T.G. Meredith and A.M. Martell. McGill Subarctic Research Paper No. 40:215-228.

Gunn, A. and F.L. Miller. 1986. Traditional behaviour and fidelity to caribou calving grounds by barren-ground caribou. Rangifer, Special Issue 1:151-158.

Gunn, A. and J. Ashevak. (in preparation). Abundance and distribution of caribou on Boothia Peninsula and west of Pelly Bay. Northwest Territories File Report.

Gunn, A. and K. Lambert. (in preparation). Abundance and distribution of caribou on King William Island and Adelaide Peninsula. Northwest Territories File Report.

Harington, C.R. 1986. The impact of changing climate on some vertebrates in the Canadian Arctic. In: Impact of Climatic Change on the Canadian Arctic. Edited by: H.M. French. Proceedings of a Canadian Climate Workshop, Atmospheric Environment Service, Downsview. pp. 100-113.

Heard, D.C., T.M. Williams, and K. Jingfors. 1986. Pre-calving distribution and abundance of barren-ground caribou on the northeastern mainland of the Northwest Territories. Arctic 39(1):24-28.

Jakimchuk, R.D. and D.R. Carruthers. 1980. Caribou and muskoxen on Victoria Island. Report prepared for Polar Gas Project by R.D. Jakimchuk Management Associates Ltd., Sidney. 93 pp.

Jingfors, K. 1984. Abundance and distribution of muskoxen on southeastern Victoria Island. Northwest Territories File Report 36:1-24.

_____. 1985. Abundance and distribution of muskoxen on northwestern Victoria Island. Northwest Territories File Report 47:1-22.

Keith, L.B. 1983. Population dynamics of wolves. In: Wolves in Canada and Alaska. Edited by: L.N. Carbyn. Canadian Wildlife Service, Report Series 45:66-77.

Manning, T.H. 1960. The relationship of the Peary and barren-ground caribou. Arctic Institute North America, Technical Paper 4:1-52.

Maxwell, J.B. 1981. Climatic regions of the Canadian Arctic Islands. Arctic 34:225-240.

McGhee, R. 1976. An individual view of Canadian Eskimo prehistory. In: Inuit Land Use and Occupancy Project. Edited by: M.M.R. Freeman, Indian and Northern Affairs Canada. Ottawa. Volume II:109-116.

Meldgaard, M. 1986. The Greenland caribou - zoogeography, taxonomy, and population dynamics. Meddelelser om Grønland, Bioscience 20:1-88.

Miller, F.L., E.J. Edmonds, and A. Gunn. 1982. Foraging behaviour of Peary caribou in response to springtime snow and ice conditions. Canadian Wildlife Service, Occasional Paper 48:1-41.

Miller, F.L., R.H. Russell, and A. Gunn. 1977. Peary caribou and muskoxen on western Queen Elizabeth Islands, N.W.T. 1971-74. Canadian Wildlife Service, Report Series 40:1-55.

Nowak, R.M. 1983. A perspective on the taxonomy of wolves in North America. In: Wolves in Canada and Alaska. Edited by: L.N. Carbyn. Canadian Wildlife Service, Report Series 45:10-19.

Parker, G.R., D.C. Thomas, E. Broughton, and D.R. Gray. 1975. Crashes of muskox and Peary caribou populations in 1973-74 on the Parry Islands, Arctic Canada. Canadian Wildlife Service, Progress Notes 56:1-10.

Roed, K. 1985. Genetic variability in Norwegian semi-domestic reindeer (*Rangifer tarandus* L.). Hereditas 192:177-184.

Skinner, W.R. 1985. The effects of major volcanic eruptions on Canadian climate. In: Climatic Change in Canada 5. Edited by: C.R. Harington. Syllogeus 55:75-106.

Stefansson, V. 1923. My life with the Eskimos. MacMillan, New York. 538 pp.

Thing, H., D.R. Klein, K. Jingfors, and S. Holt. 1987. Ecology of muskoxen in Jameson Land, northeast Greenland. Holarctic Ecology 10:95-103.

Thomas, D.C. 1969. Population estimates and distribution of barren-ground caribou in Mackenzie District, N.W.T., Saskatchewan and Alberta - March to May 1967. Canadian Wildlife Service, Report Series 9:1-44.

_____. 1982. The relationship between fertility and fat reserves of Peary caribou. Canadian Journal of Zoology 60(4):597-602.

Thomas, D.C. and P. Everson. 1982. Geographic variation in caribou on the Canadian Arctic Islands. Canadian Journal of Zoology 60:2442-2454.

606

Usher. P.D. 1965. Economic basis and resource use of the Coppermine-Holman region, N.W.T. Northern Co-ordination and Research Centre, Department of Northern Affairs and National Resources, Ottawa. 290 pp.

Vibe, C. 1967. Arctic animals in relation to climatic fluctuations. Meddelelser om Grønland 170:1-227.

Illustrated by Brenda Carter

INTER-ISLAND MOVEMENTS OF PEARY CARIBOU: A REVIEW AND APPRAISEMENT OF THEIR ECOLOGICAL IMPORTANCE

Frank L. Miller[1]

Abstract: Evidence is reviewed regarding the presence and persistence of seasonal inter-island migrations and sporadic inter-island movements at all times of the year by caribou (Rangifer tarandus sp.) in the Canadian Arctic. Inter-island migrations and movements by Peary caribou (R. t. pearyi) and their intergrades (R. t. pearyi x R. t. groenlandicus or R. t. groenlandicus x R. t. pearyi) in the Canadian Arctic Islands and the coastal mainland of Arctic Canada are emphasized. Early evidence indicates that mass migrations persisted between the mainland and the southern tier of islands; some smaller-scale migrations and sporadic movements between or among islands occurred or continued to occur within both the southern and the northern tiers of islands; but movements over the sea ice of Viscount Melville Sound, Barrow Strait, or Lancaster Sound were infrequent. Subsequent studies detailed inter-island populations of Peary caribou in the Melville-Eglinton-Prince Patrick islands region and Peary caribou, or their intergrades, in the Prince of Wales Island-Somerset Island-Boothia Peninsula region. These studies indicated that movements of caribou between the southern and northern tiers of islands remain infrequent. Evidently inter-island migrations and movements of caribou: (1) maximize seasonal use of the best ranges; (2) provide the greatest opportunities for relief from widespread environmental stresses; and thus (3) maximize the magnitudes and durations of population highs and minimize the lows. Inter-island movements are seen as "ecological manoeuvres" by Peary caribou and their intergrades to cope with and prosper in their harsh surroundings on the Canadian Arctic Islands.

Résumé: On passe en revue les éléments qui attestent de la présence et de la persistance de migrations saisonnières et de mouvements sporadiques du caribou (Rangifer tarandus) entre les îles de l'Arctique canadien en tout temps de l'année. L'accent est mis sur les migrations et les mouvements entre les îles du caribou de Peary (R. t. pearyi) et de ses croisements (R. t. pearyi x R. t. groenlandicus ou R. t. groenlandicus x R. t. pearyi) dans les îles de l'Arctique canadien et sur la côte du continent du Canada arctique. Les toutes premières indications montrent que les migrations de masse ont continué entre le continent et la partie sud des îles. Quelques migrations à plus petite échelle et des mouvements sporadiques à l'intérieur des îles ou entre elles ont eu lieu et se produisent encore dans les parties sud et nord des îles, par contre, les mouvements sur la glace de mer des détroits du Vicomte de Melville, de Barrow et de Lancaster ont été peu fréquents. Des études subséquentes ont porté sur les populations de caribous de Peary qu'il y avait entre les îles dans la région des îles Melville, Eglinton et Prince-Patrick de même que sur les caribous de Peary et leurs croisements dans la région des îles Prince-de-Galles et Somerset et de la péninsule de Boothia. Ces études ont démontré que les mouvements des caribous entre le sud et le nord des îles demeuraient peu fréquents. Bien entendu, les migrations entre les îles et les mouvements des caribous ont pour effet: (1) de faire un usage saisonnier optimal des meilleurs pâturages, (2) de fournir les plus grandes chances possibles de compenser le stress environnemental généralisé et donc (3) de favoriser l'ampleur et la durée des maximums de populations et d'en réduire les minimums. On considère les mouvements entre les îles des caribous de Peary et de leurs croisements comme des "manoeuvres écologiques" visant à affronter le dur environnement sur les îles de l'Arctique canadien et y prospérer.

INTRODUCTION

That caribou and reindeer (*Rangifer tarandus* spp.) are capable of extensive travel over sea ice is evident by their presence on most circumpolar arctic islands. The most impressive, and reasonably well documented account is for reindeer migrants on Spitsbergen having arrived there by travel over the sea ice from Nova Zemlya (Wollebaek 1926; Lønø 1959 in Banfield 1961; Banfield 1954, 1961). An individual reindeer shot on Spitsbergen had a gull's foot tied to one antler, which apparently was a ceremonial decoration put on reindeer by Samoyeds of Nova Zemlya during certain rituals. The most probable route

---

[1] Canadian Wildlife Service, 4999-98 Avenue East, Edmonton, Alberta T6B 2X3

from Nova Zemlya to Spitsbergen necessitates crossing at least 380 km of sea ice from Nova Zemlya to Franz Josef Land, then another 340 km to Spitsbergen. Otherwise the reindeer would have had to travel about 800 km without feeding. Hakala *et al.* (1985, p. 9) give the distance as, "Novaya Zemlya to Kong Karls Land via Franz Joseph Land is 380 + 340 km and a further 90 km to Edgeoya".

I restrict the term "migration" to those movements of caribou that are traditional, seasonal, and annual and which are most likely perpetuated by learned behaviour. The term "movement" applies to all displacements of caribou whether traditional migrations, or periodic or sporadic responses to social intolerance (most likely density-dependent), or widespread forage unavailability (environmentally forced and can be either density-dependent or density-independent (Miller *et al.* 1982)). Also I have adjusted early taxonomic references to *Rangifer* to agree with Banfield's (1961) revision of the genus. That is, all caribou belong to the species *tarandus* and the subspecific forms considered for Canada are *R. t. pearyi*, *R. t. groenlandicus* and their intergrades (both *pearyi* x *groenlandicus* and *groenlandicus* x *pearyi*).

Now, let us review the evidence for consistent inter-island movements of Peary caribou, and subsequently speculate about how such movements make the continued survival and evolutionary divergence of *pearyi* and *pearyi* x *groenlandicus* possible.

CIRCUMSTANTIAL EVIDENCE FOR MIGRATIONS AND MOVEMENTS OF CARIBOU ACROSS SEA ICE

Evolutionary and Historical Background

Banfield (1961, p. 65) indicated that Peary caribou (*R. t. pearyi*) and the now-extinct East Greenland reindeer (*R. t. eogroenlandicus*) were closely related. More recently, Willemsen (1983) and Hakala *et al.* (1985) have remarked on the similarity among *pearyi*, *eogroenlandicus*, and the Svalbard reindeer (*R. t. platyrhynchus*), thus indicating a close taxonomic affinity among all three forms of arctic island caribou. Further support for this relationship has been put forth by Røed *et al.* (1986) with the finding that one of only two alleles that coded for transferrin in the Svalbard reindeer is held in common with *pearyi* (neither are found in continental reindeer or caribou). Thus, progenitors of Peary caribou were capable at some time, of making sea ice crossings, most likely, from the

Canadian Arctic Archipelago to at least northern and eastern Greenland and eventually to the Spitsbergen Archipelago.

By comparison, ancestral Peary caribou had only to make short sea ice crossings from coastal mainland areas to reach the southern tier of islands in the Canadian Arctic Archipelago. Those southern islands of Banks, Victoria, King William, Prince of Wales, and Somerset are only a few hours travel, on the sea ice, away from the north coasts of Boothia, Adelaide, and Kent peninsulas. However, crossing almost anywhere along Dolphin and Union, Rae and Franklin straits; or even Coronation and Queen Maud gulfs would require only several hours to a day's travel on the sea ice without feeding. (I have observed caribou coming off the ice of Peel Sound after travelling about 50 km from Somerset Island to Prince of Wales Island, and they showed no outward signs of hunger, working slowly inland and feeding casually as they moved.)

The second basic step in occupying most of the Arctic Islands (there is no evidence for Peary caribou ever having established themselves on Baffin or Bylot islands) required more extensive travel on sea ice in the west across Viscount Melville Sound from Banks or Victoria islands to Prince Patrick or Melville islands, and in the east across Lancaster Sound from Somerset Island to Devon Island. However, relatively short island-hopping treks across the Barrow Strait ice were possible from Prince of Wales Island to Bathurst or Cornwallis islands. For example, caribou could travel from the north shore of Prince of Wales to Russell, then via Russell-Hamilton-Young-Lowther-Garrett-Moore islands onto the south shore of Bathurst Island. Such a trip would involve a maximum of about 30 km of sea ice travel without landing for feeding in the 190 km (overall minimum) trek from Prince of Wales Island to Bathurst Island.

Most likely during the last (Wisconsin) glaciation, Peary caribou found refuge in the Canadian Arctic Archipelago - probably on Banks and Prince Patrick islands (Harington 1970, 1978), and possibly on northern Ellesmere Island and northern Greenland (e.g., Rand 1954; Banfield 1961, 1963; Macpherson 1965; Harington 1971; Hakala et al. 1985). However, Degerbøl (1957) and more recently Meldgaard (1986) have argued against northern Greenland or the Canadian Arctic Islands having served as refugia for Peary caribou during the Wisconsin glaciation.

Following the last glaciation, precursors of the current Peary caribou radiated out from wherever their refugium or refugia existed to colonize or recolonize the Canadian Arctic

Archipelago (except Baffin and Bylot islands). At least during the last phase of caribou dispersal in the Canadian Arctic Islands, the southern tier of islands was occupied to varying degrees by both *pearyi* and *groenlandicus* forms, and eventually by intergrades of both forms (*pearyi* x *groenlandicus*). Some intergrades favour the characteristics of *pearyi* (e.g., the Banks Island caribou) and some favour the characteristics of *groenlandicus* (e.g., caribou of the Dolphin and Union herd).

The annual seasonal migrations of the Dolphin and Union herd from winter ranges on the mainland to calving areas and summer ranges on Victoria Island (and possibly Banks Island), and return in the autumn (Manning 1960) attests to the relative ease by which such sea ice crossings are made by caribou. Other groups of caribou (apparently both *pearyi* x *groenlandicus* and *groenlandicus* forms) also made, or are still making, regular annual seasonal migrations or only sporadic crossings from Adelaide, Boothia, and Kent peninsulas to island calving areas and summer ranges on eastern Victoria, King William, Somerset, and Prince of Wales islands (Manning 1960; Banfield 1961; Manning and Macpherson 1961; Miller and Gunn 1978, 1980; Miller and Kiliaan 1980A, 1981; Miller *et al.* 1982; Thomas and Everson 1982; personal communication, A. Gunn). There is no evidence to suggest that caribou ever migrated across Viscount Melville Sound, Barrow Strait, and Lancaster Sound between northern and southern islands of the archipelago. However, human habitation ceased in the area several hundred years before the coming of European explorers in the 1800s and was only reestablished in the 1950s (Bissett 1968). Therefore, the likelihood of routine seasonal migrations on an annual basis before the 1950s is unknown. There is indirect evidence from cast caribou antlers and caribou fecal droppings, along with rapidly changing numbers of caribou on several of the small islands of Barrow Strait, that caribou have made at least sporadic treks over sea ice to those islands (Bissett 1968; Freeman 1974; Miller and Gunn 1978, 1980). However, the origins, final destinations, and directions of travel are usually undetermined.

There is no evidence that *groenlandicus* individuals were ever successful at establishing themselves on the Queen Elizabeth Islands (QEI). However, *groenlandicus* caribou established themselves on Baffin and Bylot islands, whereas *pearyi* caribou have not (possibly deeper snow cover on Baffin Island, compared to islands in the western archipelago, favours the survival of the relatively long-legged barren-ground form over the short-legged Peary caribou of the High Arctic).

Probably the answer lies mainly in the relative abundance and higher quality of summer ranges on the large southern islands, especially Banks and Victoria, compared to those on the QEI. The ability of summer ranges on the southern islands to support high densities of caribou is evident by the prolonged history of wintering mainland caribou calving and summering there. Additional benefits afforded those caribou likely were relative freedom from biting and blood-sucking insects, wolves (*Canis lupus*), and brown bears (*Ursus arctos*) compared to possible adjacent mainland summering ranges.

Frequent waves of barren-ground caribou migrated over the sea ice, pushing northward to the southern tier of islands. They usually remained only seasonally, but in the long run intergraded with resident Peary caribou and became the dominant southern island form (*pearyi* x *groenlandicus*). For unknown reasons barren-ground caribou only have been successful in colonizing the extreme eastern portion of the Arctic Islands (Baffin and Bylot) on a year-round basis. Whether Peary caribou have attempted to colonize those areas or have been excluded by the barren-ground form is unknown. Elsewhere on the southern islands the barren-ground form is known only to be successful as a summer migrant. Year-round occupation seemingly favoured the merging of *pearyi* and *groenlandicus* features, thus apparently creating a better adapted intergrade. I am not aware of evidence suggesting that caribou on Victoria Island are possibly "environmentally modified" *R. t. groenlandicus*. The original Peary caribou that occurred on the southern islands had their gene pool contaminated to varying degrees by the barren-ground form. Seemingly, this contamination has been unfavourable in terms of survival on the High Arctic islands, as no intergrades (or barren-ground caribou) are known to have established themselves on the QEI. So Peary caribou on the QEI remain essentially pure, and exhibit typical characteristics of the *pearyi* form (Banfield 1961; Thomas and Everson 1982).

Thus, the stage is set for the further evolution of *pearyi* on the QEI through physiological and behavioural adaptations to their more demanding surroundings. It is obvious from the foregoing that the ability of caribou to periodically or sporadically travel extensively over sea ice has made widespread occupation of the Canadian Arctic Archipelago possible.

Migration and Movements between the Mainland and Southern Islands

Habitation by indigenous peoples shortly before and after contact with Europeans was restricted largely to coastal mainland areas and the southerly portions of the southern islands in the archipelago, until Resolute Bay and Grise Fiord were settled in the High Arctic in the 1950s. Also, sea ice crossings by caribou between the mainland and the southern islands were massive and used by more people; so probably because they were obvious and important, they were more often reported. Most direct observations and circumstantial evidence in the literature support persistent periodic seasonal migrations or sporadic movements of caribou throughout the year on the sea ice between the mainland and the southern islands. The best documented early evidence is for the Dolphin and Union herd (Manning 1960; Gunn, this volume).

First reports of extensive caribou migrations over sea ice between Victoria Island and the mainland were made by Franklin (1823, p. 395), Sabine in Franklin (1823, p. 665), and Simpson (1843, pp. 277-278). However, Rae (1852, p. 79) was apparently the first to actually observe caribou crossing the sea ice of Dolphin and Union Strait in spring 1851. Collinson (1889, pp. 244, 290) offered the first evidence for fall migration of caribou from eastern Victoria Island south across the frozen waters of Dease Strait to Kent Peninsula in 1853. Over 50 years passed before additional information was obtained on such migrations (Manning 1960, p. 7).

In the early 1900s, there were a number of brief accounts on migrations and movements of caribou - primarily between the mainland and Victoria Island, but also King William Island, and to a lesser extent Banks Island. Those records include information on migrations and movements of caribou from and to the mainland across the sea ice of Dolphin and Union Strait, Coronation Gulf, Dease Strait, and to a lesser extent Queen Maud Gulf. More specifically the records included data on: (1) the northward spring migrations and southward fall migrations; (2) numbers of caribou involved, including group-sizes; and (3) the dying out of the major migrations (Anderson 1913A, p. 6, 1913B, pp. 502-503, 1920, p. 544, 1922, pp. 73-74; Stefansson 1913A, pp. 94-95, 99, 106, 1913B, pp. 203-204, 277, 1914, pp. 41, 54, 1920, pp. 135-136, 1921, pp. 401-402; Chipman 1920, p. 101; Jenness 1920, pp. 167-168, 1922, pp. 15, 244, 1928, pp. 12-13, 187-190; Johansen 1920, pp. 136-137; Hoare 1920, pp. 76, 80, 1925, p. 1-3, 7, 10-11, 1927, pp. 33, 36; O'Neill 1920,

p. 37; Storkerson 1920, pp. 277; Rasmussen 1927, p. 246; Godsell 1937, pp. 288-289, 1943, pp. 273-274; and Clarke 1940, p. 98).

Inuit mentioned large numbers of caribou passing by Sachs Harbour in November 1951 and travelling onto the sea ice south of Banks Island. Apparently some returned to Banks Island later in the winter and died there (or others that stayed on the island died). A Holman Island Inuk reported that some Banks Island caribou crossed to Victoria Island and to the mainland near Herschel Island then. McEwen (1955, pp. 45-46) reported a large number of caribou on the sea ice off southwestern Banks Island in October 1952. In addition, he obtained reports from local Inuit of Banks Island caribou in November and December 1952 at Holman Island, Cape Parry, Baillie Islands, Cape Dalhousie, and possibly Herschel Island. Youngman (1975, p. 167) records *R. t. pearyi* (most likely from Banks Island) as an occasional migrant in the Yukon Territory, occurring at least as far south as Old Crow. An adult female was killed during winter 1963-1964 near Old Crow, which most closely resembled a Dolphin and Union herd intergrade.

M'Clintock (1859, pp. 250, 252) mentions migration of caribou from the mainland to King William Island. Macpherson and Manning (1959, pp. 55-56) summarize circumstantial evidence and observations by others on caribou crossing sea ice between the mainland and King William Island. There appeared to be at least two main routes across Simpson Strait: one from Eta Island (Gilder 1881, pp. 196-197; Amundsen 1908, Volume 1, p. 104; Rasmussen 1927, p. 214); and one past Todds Island (Amundsen 1908, Volume 1, pp. 97-105, 247). Herds apparently staged in the Gjoa Haven area from September to October (Gilder 1881, pp. 196-197; Amundsen 1908, Volume 1, pp. 84-99, 104, 106, 247-248). Migrations of barren-ground caribou from winter ranges on the mainland to calving areas and summer ranges on King William Island were drastically reduced by the 1920s (Hoare 1927, p. 37) and apparently ceased about the late 1920s and early 1930s (Burwash 1931, p. 66; Gibson 1932, p. 405).

Migration and Movements among the Southern Islands (Including Boothia Peninsula)

Manning and Macpherson (1958, pp. 65-67) summarize evidence for movements between Banks and Victoria islands. Armstrong (1857, pp. 297, 336) recorded three caribou crossing via the Princess Royal Islands on 6 January 1851 - apparently coming from Banks Island. M'Clure (1856, p. 156) also reported a crew member seeing "a small herd" of caribou trotting toward the Princess Royal Islands. Collinson (1889, p. 200) saw several caribou trails coming from Banks Island on the sea ice near Peel Point, Victoria Island on 31 May 1852.

M'Clintock (1859, p. 186) saw caribou apparently waiting for the freeze-up of Bellot Strait to continue their southward migration from Somerset Island to Boothia Peninsula.

Manning and Macpherson (1961, pp. 219, 221, 222, 226-227) summarize circumstantial evidence and a few direct observations. Inuit of Resolute Bay knew of spring sea ice crossings by caribou from Somerset to Prince of Wales islands in the 1950s. Hearsay evidence was also offered for regular migrations and crossings of mainland caribou from Boothia Peninsula to Somerset Island: northward in spring before break-up and southward again before, during, and after freeze-up. They also reported that caribou (presumed to be Peary caribou) were seen on Boothia Peninsula: one was killed on Matty Island between Boothia Peninsula and King William Island. Fresh caribou tracks were reportedly seen on the ice of Bellot Strait between Somerset Island and Boothia Peninsula in mid-October.

Knowledge of inter-island migrations and movements among Somerset Island, Prince of Wales Island and Boothia Peninsula, as well as observations of caribou tracks on the sea ice in spring and autumn (reported by others) were also mentioned by Macpherson (1959), Bissett (1968), Fischer and Duncan (1976), Miller and Gunn (1978, 1980), Thompson and Fischer (1980), and Gunn and Miller (1983).

Manning and Macpherson (1961, p. 227) presumed little gene flow among caribou between Victoria Island and Prince of Wales Island via ice on M'Clintock Channel. However, Cambridge Bay Inuit who had lived or travelled in the area believe that caribou cross the sea ice of M'Clintock Channel between Victoria and Prince of Wales islands via Gateshead Island (personal communication, A. Gunn).

Queen Elizabeth Islands

The lack of early circumstantial evidence for inter-island movements of Peary caribou for the QEI stems from a near absence of observers. Inuit knowledge only extends from the 1950s until present (e.g. Bissett 1968; Freeman 1975; Miller and Gunn 1978, 1980). Indirect evidence for inter-island movements comes from changing numbers of caribou seen during aerial surveys from the late 1950s to the 1980s (e.g. Macpherson 1961; Tener 1963; Miller *et al.* 1977A).

Parry (1821, pp. 107, 110, 173) mistook autumn intra-island caribou movements to coastal areas for migration from eastern Melville Island to the mainland in autumn and their return in spring.

M'Dougall (1857, p. 398) saw five caribou on 25 May 1854 crossing McDougall Sound from Bathurst Island to Cornwallis Island.

McMillan in Bernier (1910, p. 475) reported that caribou tracks were frequently seen on the sea ice, and herds were seen crossing from "... one island to another" (possibly among Melville, Byam Martin, and Bathurst islands).

Stefansson (1921, p. 554) observed caribou tracks 5 km south of Jenness Island (off the west coast of Borden Island) in September 1915.

A.H. Joy of the Royal Canadian Mounted Police, based on extensive sled journeys in the QEI in the late 1920s, made detailed remarks on the numbers and migration of Peary caribou among some of those islands (Harington 1982, p. 558).

Tener (1963, p. 28) saw caribou tracks leading out onto the sea ice from Mackenzie King to Borden Island in 1961, and suggested that the high density of caribou on Borden Island could have been caused in part by "occasional or seasonal immigration". Macpherson (1961, pp. 12) also suggested that inter-island movements were the cause of varying caribou numbers on Brock, Borden and Mackenzie King islands.

Riewe (1978, pp. 635-636) reported that Inuit knew of caribou movements over the sea ice from the south coast of Ellesmere Island to Smith and Cone islands and then to the area around Starnes or Fram fiords.

Manning (1960, p. 43), when reviewing the relationship between Peary and barren-ground caribou, stated that because of the short distances involved in making sea ice crossings among the QEI, no serious barriers to free movements existed. He concluded that the QEI population should be homogeneous, and that it was homogeneous based on specimens available then. Banfield (1961, p. 63), in his revision of the genus *Rangifer*, stated, without giving sources, that free interchange among the QEI by inter-island crossings on the sea ice had been observed in a "few cases and clearly indicated in many others".

I conclude from this early evidence, that migrations across the sea ice of tens of thousands of caribou (possibly 100,000-200,000 at peaks) occurred in the spring (March-June) from mainland winter ranges to calving areas and summer ranges on Victoria, King William, and possibly Banks islands, returning each fall (end of October to December) to the mainland. Apparently those migrations continued uninterrupted from at least the early 1800s to the early 1900s, a minimum of about 75 years. Also, there were large migrations of caribou between northern Boothia Peninsula, Somerset and Prince of Wales islands - northward in spring and southward in fall. Then, apparently as a result of drastically increased kills made possible by the introduction of firearms, those migrations essentially ceased. However, recently Gunn (this volume) has argued that changing climate could have played a role in the drastic caribou reductions in the region, and thus in the cessation of large-scale migrations. Nevertheless, I think that the migratory caribou could not have sustained the levels of killing that took place in the early 1900s, regardless of environmental pressures then. Perhaps both factors worked together to decimate these caribou.

Early evidence does not indicate large seasonal migrations between Banks and Victoria islands, but it does indicate sporadic movements across Prince of Wales Strait throughout the winter. Although no early direct evidence exists to support seasonal caribou migrations between Somerset and Prince of Wales islands, Inuit knowledge after the 1950s argues for such migrations. The evidence does not suggest regular migrations across Viscount Melville Sound, Barrow Strait, or Lancaster Sound. Caribou sporadically crossed to the small islands of Barrow Strait, if not completely across the strait or sounds. Apparently travel was both north and south. It could be argued that movements between the southern islands and the QEI occurred at low frequencies and numbers based on indirect information. Evidence for inter-island movements among the QEI before the 1970s is based on a few early observations. Large seasonal caribou migrations among the QEI were suggested (1950s to 1970s) by both the taxonomic homogeneity of the specimens from the QEI and the observed changes in seasonal and annual numbers and distributions of caribou seen on various islands during aerial surveys.

INVESTIGATIONS OF INTER-ISLAND MIGRATIONS OR MOVEMENTS

Circumstantial evidence and incidental observations accumulated for over 150 years before the first actual investigation of inter-island movements of caribou in the Canadian Arctic Archipelago was initiated. While carrying out aerial surveys of the western QEI in 1972 and 1973, Miller *et al.* (1977A) noted that differences in numbers and distributions of caribou between March-April and July-August suggested that seasonal migrations were occurring among Melville, Eglinton, and Prince Patrick islands.

By aerial dye-spraying, Miller *et al.* (1977B) marked nearly 230 caribou in April 1974 (about 130 green-marked on Prince Patrick Island, and about 100 red-marked on Eglinton Island). Aerial searches flown in fixed-wing aircraft between 8 June and 23 July resulted in 41 sightings of dye-marked caribou (Miller *et al.* 1977B). Subsequently red-marked caribou were seen on Melville and Prince Patrick islands, as well as being relocated on Eglinton Island, while green-marked caribou were located on Melville and Eglinton islands as well as being relocated on Prince Patrick Island. Unmarked caribou were observed travelling on the sea ice in May and June. Caribou trails led to and from the northern two-thirds of the west coast of Eglinton Island and the opposing section of the east coast of Prince Patrick Island. Other trails led directly from the east coast of Prince Patrick Island, north of Eglinton Island and directly to Marie Heights and Canrobert Hills on western Melville Island. Still other trails led from northeastern Eglinton Island to western Melville Island (Canrobert Hills and the area south of Ibbett Bay). A few trails left the southern coast of Eglinton Island, apparently reaching Comfort Cove and Cape Russell areas of southwestern Melville Island. (It should be noted that because caribou usually walk in single file - often stepping in each others tracks while migrating - estimating the number of caribou that lay a trail is at best very difficult. If only a few caribou (perhaps 5-10) are involved the number can usually be discerned. However, if about 25 or more used the same trail, the number of caribou cannot be judged accurately in the absence of direct observation).

The longest movement detected involved a green-marked caribou that likely travelled at least 600 km between Prince Patrick Island (where it was marked) and eastern Melville Island (where it was last seen).

Miller *et al.* (1977B) estimated that 50% and 87% of the caribou that had wintered on Prince Patrick and Eglinton islands, respectively, had made inter-island movements sometime in spring and/or early summer. Their findings led them to believe that an inter-island migratory population of Peary caribou existed at least within the Melville, Prince Patrick, Eglinton islands region. These and other results (Miller *et al.* 1977A) in 1972-1974 led them to speculate that during periods of high densities those Peary caribou likely expanded the number of islands used as seasonal range to include Emerald, Byam Martin;

probably Mackenzie King, Borden, and Brock; and at extreme highs might occasionally extend farther northeastward and eastward encompassing most of the QEI (except perhaps for Devon, Axel Heiberg and Ellesmere islands).

Three years passed before the opportunity arose again to investigate inter-island caribou movements. This time the studies took place over four springs from 1977-1980 (Miller and Gunn 1978, 1980; Miller and Kiliaan 1980A, 1981).

In 1977 the investigation of inter-island Peary caribou movements was supplementary to another study (Miller and Gunn 1978, 1979; Gunn and Miller 1980). Search areas included the frozen waters of Peel Sound, Viscount Melville Sound, Barrow Strait and Baring Channel. Low-level (10-25 m above the sea ice) searches in a Bell-206B helicopter were flown over the ice and adjacent coastal areas between 12 and 18 June. Hamilton, Young, and Russell islands were surveyed by helicopter between 15 and 25 August. The search revealed 158 caribou trails on the sea ice and 31 additional trails on land adjacent to sea ice crossings. This confirmed large-scale inter-island movements of caribou in June 1977. The 95 trails across Peel Sound and the 63 trails across Baring Channel involved at least several hundred caribou. Apparently movements were entirely east-west from Somerset Island to Prince of Wales Island; then, south-north for those individuals crossing from Prince of Wales to Mecham and/or Russell islands. Many caribou from Somerset Island moved along the eastern satellite islands of Prescott, Vivian, and Lock to Prince of Wales Island. Evidence for sea ice crossings on Viscount Melville Sound and Barrow Strait were meagre. Trails leading onto the ice from Russell Island toward Young, Lowther, and Bathurst islands were soon obliterated due to obscuring snowcover and could not be followed. In August 1977 aerial searches revealed no caribou on Hamilton Island (but winter fecal pellets were seen), 22 caribou on Young Island, and 20 on Lowther Island. Those caribou had not been seen in May 1977 during similar searches.

The first year's (1977) effort indicated that caribou were indeed making large-scale inter-island movements, most likely from winter ranges on Somerset Island to calving areas and summer-ranges on Prince of Wales and Russell islands (and to a much lesser degree on small islands such as Young and Lowther). Based on that information, a more intensive search was planned for spring 1978.

Low-level searches were flown in a Twin Otter aircraft and a Bell-206B helicopter between 16 May and 1 July 1978 by Miller and Gunn (1980). They found 422 trails on the sea ice, distinguished tracks of at least 1,033 individuals, and saw 53 caribou making inter-island crossings on the sea ice. Most (91.7%) of the trails were associated with sea ice crossings among Somerset Island, Boothia Peninsula, and Prince of Wales Island (including Prince of Wales' eastern satellite islands of Lock, Pandora, Prescott and Vivian). Thirty-two (7.6%) of the trails crossed Baring Channel between Prince of Wales and Mecham or Russell islands. Only three (0.7%) trails were found leaving the north shore of Russell for Barrow Strait but, as in 1977, they were obliterated after several kilometres. No trails were found on the frozen waters of Viscount Melville Sound or Intrepid Passage. Approximately 3.1% of the trails were made between 16 and 31 May; 9.5% between 3 and 14 June; and 87.4% between 17 June and 1 July.

Again in 1979, investigation of spring inter-island movements was carried out supplementary to another study (Miller and Kiliaan 1980A,B). The frozen waters of Peel Sound, Franklin Strait, Baring Channel and Bellot Strait were searched by snowmobile and Bell-206B helicopter at irregular intervals from 5 May to 1 July 1979. Miller and Kiliaan found 103 trails on the sea ice, noted the tracks of at least 300 individuals, and saw 25 caribou making sea ice crossings. Most (73.8%) of the trails were seen on Peel Sound, followed by 19.4% on Franklin Strait, and only 3.9% and 2.9% on Bellot Strait and Baring Channel, respectively. Inter-island caribou movements varied somewhat in the spring of 1979 from those observed in the springs of 1977 and 1978. Nearly half (46.7%) of the observed trails were made in May, and for the first time spring caribou crossings from west to east were detected on both Peel Sound and Franklin Strait. However, whether the caribou that travelled eastward from Prince of Wales Island to Somerset Island or Boothia Peninsula summered there or subsequently returned to Prince of Wales to summer is unknown.

Snowcover remained thin on eastern Prince of Wales Island throughout the winter of 1978-1979 until April-May when it increased markedly. Observations in March 1977, 1978 and 1979 on eastern Prince of Wales Island suggested that there were many more caribou there in 1979 than in 1977 or 1978 (personal communication, D.C. Thomas). Perhaps more caribou than usual remained on Prince of Wales during the winter of 1978-1979 because of the lack of significant snowcover until April-May. Then in May, many caribou responded to the increased snowcover by migrating to Somerset Island or Boothia Peninsula. Probably many of them subsequently returned to their traditional spring calving areas and summer ranges on Prince of Wales in late June or early July 1979.

The fourth and final year of investigation was carried out in association with another study in 1980 (Miller and Kiliaan 1981; Miller *et al* 1982). Low-level searches in a Bell-206B helicopter were flown over the ice of Peel Sound and Franklin Strait between 14 and 22 June 1980. Miller and Kiliaan found 588 caribou trails on the sea ice, recorded tracks of at least 1,799 individuals, and saw 15 caribou making sea ice crossings. Most (96%) of the 406 trails seen on Peel Sound were from east to west, as were all 31 trails seen on Franklin Strait.

This four-year investigation demonstrated the existence of an "inter-island population" of caribou within the Somerset Island-Boothia Peninsula-Prince of Wales Island region. The usual pattern appears to be calving and major use of summer ranges on Prince of Wales Island, an assumed early winter return to winter ranges on Somerset Island and/or Boothia Peninsula. Incidental observations have been made of caribou crossing Peel Sound from west to east on new ice in late October (Miller and Gunn 1980). No attempts have been made to document early winter migrations of caribou because of the unfavourable and unpredictable flying weather then. Also, findings from 1979 suggest that many caribou may remain on summer ranges well into the winter before increasing snow depths trigger their return to traditional winter-areas. In such years the return to winter ranges may be in successive waves or staggered movements rather than a discrete migration.

THE IMPORTANCE OF INTER-ISLAND MOVEMENTS TO PEARY CARIBOU

Caribou have two or three types of inter-island movements on the Canadian Arctic Islands. The first is annual seasonal migration, the second is sporadic environmentally-forced movement, and the third may arise occasionally by chance or due to a seemingly innate "restlessness" of the species.

Annual seasonal migrations usually involve many caribou making inter-island movements from traditional winter ranges in the spring to traditional calving areas and summer ranges, returning in fall to winter areas. Perhaps these periodic migrations or the sporadic inter-island movements (especially the environmentally-forced ones) foster continual gene-flow among QEI caribou and also among intergrades on the southern tier of islands. The apparent lack of constant interchange should, however, ensure continued divergence between *pearyi* on the QEI and intergrades (*pearyi* x *groenlandicus*) on the southern islands.

Theoretically, Peary caribou (and its intergrades) could maximize their chances of survival over time by exploiting as many feasible alternatives as possible. Thus, I would expect to find caribou throughout the archipelago exhibiting different survival strategies: some being truly migratory on an annual seasonal basis; others being essentially sedentary but occasionally undertaking inter-island migrations or movements in periods of severe environmental stress; while still others remained sedentary. What is "good" for a species or race in the long-term is not necessarily always "good" for all individuals involved in those activities in all years. For example, in June 1974 snow and ice conditions on Prince Patrick and Eglinton islands were relatively much more favourable for caribou than on eastern Melville Island in June-July 1974. However, parturient female caribou left Prince Patrick and Eglinton islands, crossed to Melville Island, travelled over its rugged western terrain, and fought deep snow and generally hard travelling conditions to reach their traditional calving and summering areas on eastern Melville Island. Apparently, many of the cows either did not calve or they were so delayed that they calved en route and lost their calves before even reaching eastern Melville Island. Others calved there, but most failed to rear their calves, probably because of the severe physical stress caused by their travels. The result was an almost total loss of the 1974 calf crop and the deaths of many mothers. Had the cows remained on Prince Patrick or Eglinton islands and calved there, they most likely would have been more successful in that particular year. Yet, they responded, with fatal results, to "traditions" that until then had favoured their survival and that of their forerunners over the long-term.

Seasonal alterations in range have several advantages. Abandonment of winter ranges reduces the annual use of those ranges and allows plants to recover from grazing during the summer growing period, thus maximizing available forage during the following winter. Also, the use of small islands for summer ranges maximizes the amount of available range during a period when small landmasses will support relatively high numbers of grazers. Those same islands can only support a small fraction of those animals during the winter, and year-round occupation at high densities could not be sustained. Also, probably seasonal shifts in range might, at least temporarily, provide relief from predation and reduce exposure to parasites and various diseases.

The extent and magnitude of annual seasonal migrations among islands is likely density-dependent, with both increasing innate social intolerances and stresses from limited forage serving as catalysts for such movements. Once established, inter-island movements will be perpetuated through "learned behaviour" as "traditional behaviour patterns" until changes in population size or the environment alter or end the traditional response. Evidence from Greenland supports the possibility that traditional migrations may sometimes originate from an environmentally-forced movement due to a chance event. Vibe (1967, pp. 176-177) states "... a sudden icing-up of the country was apparently the original cause of the migration. Ever since that time the Reindeer have wandered constantly towards the north in November/December, returning in April/May".

The second type of inter-island movement by caribou usually occurs sporadically in response to extreme snow and/or ice conditions that lead to widespread unavailability of forage. Serious forage restrictions brought on by unfavourable snow or ice conditions can occur on one or a few islands, while adjacent islands may be relatively free from such severe conditions. Peary caribou (and possibly all caribou) have retained displacement as a natural response to such situations. Thus, caribou often freely move long distances in search of new forage. In the Canadian Arctic Archipelago such movements often necessarily involve inter-island crossings over sea ice to find favourable forage on other islands.

Late winter conditions during spring breakup consistently lead to the formation of ground-fast ice over extensive areas of the islands. Such ice accumulation is greatest, and thus most severe and restrictive, where there is most vegetation per unit area. Snow depths are greater on protected, heavily vegetated sites, and deeper snow causes greater depths and longer durations of ground-fast ice there. Caribou respond at that time of the year by moving from relatively well vegetated sites to poorly vegetated, windblown sites. Although vegetation is sparse on exposed sites, it is available and the caribou can survive best there. In most years (even if most adult caribou survived) many or most breeding females would either produce nonviable neonates or subsequently fail to rear their young, if they could not move to available forage on exposed sites. In many places the simplest relief from such widespread detrimental conditions is through inter-island movement (e.g. from western Somerset Island winter-range to relief-sites on spring transitional range on eastern Prince of Wales Island). However, the spring condition of ground-fast ice accumulation and widespread forage unavailability is so consistent among years that it cannot be thought of as a sporadic event in the lives of Peary caribou. So, this springtime phenomenon should probably be considered as a common cause of the initiation and maintenance of traditional spring migrations from winter ranges to spring transitional relief ranges. If those spring transitional ranges necessitate inter-island movements, it will likely result in caribou having to remain on the island throughout the summer, before returning to traditional winter range in autumn. Perhaps the selection of calving areas by Peary caribou plays a major role in the choice of summering islands.

A third kind of movement, although not documented, may involve a sporadic inter- or intra-island movement by individuals or small social groups that can occur at any time of the year. Such movements probably arise either by chance or simply from a seemingly innate "restlessness" of caribou. Sea ice crossings, other than extended treks that greatly exceed time intervals between normal foraging periods, are essentially the same as land travel over snow covered terrain. Thus, sporadic events such as, severe storms, encounters with predators, exposures to new stimuli, or simply a drive to seek new range could trigger a chance sea ice crossing.

Traditional behaviour is not necessarily fixed in time or space, so changes in traditions should be expected over time, especially when influenced by significantly different climate. Traditions will continue as long as the results are favourable to the survival of the participants in the long run, or possibly at least neutral in their effects. Traditions such as inter-island migrations can be maintained by only a few individuals during periods of low densities, long after any real need for those movements ceases. In this way reestablishment of large-scale inter-island migrations can be readily reinitiated as densities increase to levels where individuals would benefit from such behaviour. An example is the recent resurgence of caribou movement, involving northward shifts of barren-ground caribou from the mainland to Victoria Island and Victoria Island caribou southward to Kent Peninsula and the Coppermine area (personal communication, A. Gunn). Also, widespread forage restriction (caused by spring ground-fast ice accumulations frequently experienced by Peary caribou) can sometimes cause high mortality regardless of existing density levels. Therefore, some caribou could benefit from seeking relief through inter-island movements to exposed spring transition ranges, even at low densities.

In conclusion, it appears that inter-island movements are beneficial to caribou in the Canadian Arctic Islands, and particularly to Peary caribou on the QEI, as follows:

(1) Inter-island migrations serve to, and are necessary to, maximize the seasonal use of the best ranges (in quantity and quality) that are available on two or more adjacent islands (or between or among the mainland and one or more islands) by the greatest number of caribou on a periodic basis.

(2) Inter-island movements at any time throughout the winter allow sporadic or periodic (spring) relief for large numbers of caribou from widespread forage unavailability.

(3) Thus, inter-island migrations and movements likely contribute strongly to maximizing the height and length of population highs and minimizing the depth and duration of population lows

Individuals of Peary caribou and their intergrades apparently lead a precarious existence in the Canadian Arctic Archipelago, particularly in the QEI. Those caribou could be threatened if human activities prevented them from making inter-island movements during winter. Under such conditions, Peary caribou on the QEI might only persist as remnants, if they could not respond by inter-island shifts to their sometimes extremely severe and always stringent winter surroundings. Caribou managers must think of these caribou as belonging to *inter-island populations* rather than island populations. This leads to the dire need for recognizing possible impacts of intensive ice-breaker activities that could be associated with tanker traffic in the Canadian High Arctic.

Undoubtedly, the most significant factor in the origin of Peary caribou and their evolutionary development in the Canadian Arctic Archipelago has been the ability to migrate long distances over sea ice and their continual use of inter-island sea ice crossings, both as periodic seasonal migrations and as sporadic movements. In fact, inter-island migrations and environmentally-forced movements (which we may view as "ecological manoeuvres" by Peary caribou to cope with and prosper in their harsh surroundings) have been, and will continue to be, the deciding factor in controlling gene flow and thus in shaping our taxonomic perception of their destiny - evolution to the level of a true species.

ACKNOWLEDGEMENTS

Investigations of inter-island movements of caribou in the Canadian Arctic Archipelago between 1972 and 1982 were supported by the Canadian Wildlife Service and Polar Continental Shelf Project (PCSP). I am most grateful to G.D. Hobson (PCSP) for his continued support of my studies. I gratefully acknowledge the assistance of the many field observers and my co-authors in these and related studies. I am especially indebted to Dr. A. Gunn (Department of Renewable Resources, Government of the Northwest Territories, Coppermine) for her assistance in many of these studies, especially for the critical debates regarding the value of inter-island movements to caribou.

REFERENCES

Amundsen, R. 1908. The North-West Passage, being the record of a voyage of exploration of the ship *Gjoa*. 2 volumes. A. Constable, London. 732 pp.

Anderson, R.M. 1913A. Arctic game notes. American Museum Journal 13:4-21.

_____. 1913B. Report on the natural history collections of the expedition. In: Stefansson - My life with the Eskimo. Macmillan, New York. pp. 436-527.

_____. 1920. (Evidence given by). Proceedings Royal Commission to Investigate the Possibilities of the Reindeer and Musk-ox Industry in Northern Canada. Volume 3:514-546.

_____. 1922. Memorandum on barren ground caribou and musk-ox. In: Report of the Royal Commission to Investigate the Possibilities of the Reindeer and Musk-ox Industries in the Arctic and Sub-arctic Regions of Canada. Department of the Interior, Ottawa. 99 pp.

Armstrong, A. 1857. A personal narrative of the discovery of the North-West Passage. Hurst and Blackett, London. 616 pp.

Banfield, A.W.F. 1954. The role of ice in the distribution of mammals. Journal of Mammalogy 35:104-107.

_____. 1961. A revision of the reindeer and caribou, genus *Rangifer*. National Museum of Canada Bulletin 177, Biological Series 66:1-137.

_____. 1963. The post glacial dispersal of American caribou. Proceedings of the XVI International Congress of Zoology, Washington, D.C. 1:206.

Bernier, J.E. 1910. Report on the Dominion Government Expedition to the Arctic Islands and Hudson Strait on board the C.G.S. *Arctic* in 1908-1909. King's Printer, Ottawa. 529 pp.

Bissett, D. 1968. Resolute: an area economic survey. In: Lancaster Sound Survey. Volume II. Industrial Division, Department of Indian Affairs and Northern Development, Ottawa. 175 pp.

Burwash, L.T. 1931. Canada's western Arctic. Department of the Interior, Ottawa. 116 pp.

Chipman, K.G. 1920. (Evidence given by). Proceedings Royal Commission to Investigate the Possibilities of the Reindeer and Musk-ox Industry in Northern Canada. Volume 1:95-108.

Clarke, C.H.D. 1940. A biological investigation of the Thelon Game Sanctuary. National Museum Canada, Bulletin 96, Biological Series 25:1-135.

Collinson, R. 1889. Journal of H.M.S. *Enterprise*, on the expedition in search of Sir John Franklin's ships by Behring Strait, 1850-55. Edited by: T.B. Collinson. S. Low, Marston, Searle, and Rivington, London. 531 pp.

Degerbøl, M. 1957. The extinct reindeer of East-Greenland *Rangifer tarandus eogroenlandicus*, subsp. nov. compared with reindeer from other Arctic regions. Acta Arctica 10:1-66.

Fischer, C.A. and E.A. Duncan. 1976. Ecological studies of caribou and muskoxen in the Arctic Archipelago and northern Keewatin, 1975. Renewable Resources Consulting Services Ltd., Edmonton. Report for the Polar Gas Environmental Program 1975. 194 pp.

Franklin, J. 1823. Narrative of a journey to the shores of the Polar Sea in the years 1819, 20, 21 and 22 with an appendix on various subjects relating to science and natural history. John Murray, London. 768 pp.

Freeman, M.M.R. 1974. Environmental report, Bathurst Island, N.W.T. 1974: Part 1. Caribou. Inuit Land Use and Occupancy Project. 12 pp. (typescript).

_____. 1975. Assessing movement in an Arctic caribou population. Journal of Environment Management 3:251-257.

Gibson, W. 1932. Some further traces of the Franklin retreat. Journal of the Royal Geographical Society 79(5):402-408.

Gilder, W.H. 1881. Schwatka's search: sledging in the Arctic in quest of the Franklin records. C. Scribner's, New York. 316 pp.

Godsell, P.H. 1937. The blond Eskimos and the created want. Natural History 39:285-289.

_____. 1943. Arctic trader. G.P. Putnam's, New York. 329 pp.

Gunn, A. and F.L. Miller. 1980. Responses of Peary caribou cow-calf pairs to helicopter harassment in the Canadian High Arctic. In: Proceedings of the 2nd International Reindeer/Caribou Symposium, Røros, Norway, 1979. Edited by: E. Reimers, E. Gaare, and S. Skjenneberg. Direktoratet for vilt og ferskvannsfisk, Trondheim. pp. 497-507.

_____. 1983. Size and status of an inter-island population of Peary caribou. Acta Zoological Fennica 175:153-154.

Hakala, A.V.K., H. Staaland, E. Pulliainen, and K.H. Røed. 1985. Taxonomy and history of arctic island reindeer with special reference to Svalbard reindeer. Aquilo Series Zoologica 23:1-11.

Harington, C.R. 1970. A postglacial muskox (*Ovibos moschatus*) from Grandview, Manitoba, and comments on the zoogeography of *Ovibos*. National Museum of Natural Sciences, Publications in Palaeontology 2:1-13.

_____. 1971. Ice age mammals in Canada. Arctic Circular 22(2):66-89.

_____. 1979. Quaternary vertebrate faunas of Canada and Alaska and their suggested chronological sequence. Syllogeus 15:1-105.

_____. 1982. A.H. Joy (1887-1932). Arctic Profiles, Arctic 35(4):558-559.

Hoare, W.H.B. 1920. (Evidence given by). Proceedings Royal Commission to Investigate the Possibilities of the Reindeer and Musk-ox Industry in Northern Canada. Volume 1:76-86.

_____. 1925. Report of investigations [affecting Eskimo and wild life, District of Mackenzie] 1924-25. Northwest Territories and Yukon Branch, Department of the Interior, Ottawa. 15 pp.

_____. 1927. Report of investigations [affecting Eskimo and wild life, District of Mackenzie] 1925-1926, together with general recommendations. Northwest Territories and Yukon Branch, Department of the Interior, Ottawa. 44 pp.

Jenness, D. 1920. (Evidence given by). Proceedings Royal Commission to Investigate the Possibilities of the Reindeer and Musk-ox Industry in Northern Canada. Volume 1:155-167.

_____. 1922. The life of the Copper Eskimos. Report Canadian Arctic Expedition 1913-18. Volume 12 (Part A):1-227.

_____. 1928. The people of the twilight. Macmillan, New York. 247 pp.

Johansen, F. 1920. (Evidence given by). Proceedings Royal Commission to Investigate the Possibilities of the Reindeer and Musk-ox Industry in Northern Canada. Volume 1:121-144.

Lønø, O. 1959. Reinen pa Svalbard. Meddelelser Norske Polarinstitutt, Oslo 83:1-31.

Macpherson, A.H. 1959. The caribou of Boothia Peninsula. Canadian Wildlife Service, Edmonton. 16 pp. (Unpublished report).

_____. 1961. On the abundance and distribution of certain mammals in the western Canadian Arctic Islands in 1958-59. Arctic Circular 14(1):1-16.

_____. 1965. The origin of diversity in mammals of the Canadian Arctic tundra. Systematic Zoology 14(3):153-173.

Macpherson, A.H. and T.H. Manning. 1959. The birds and mammals of Adelaide Peninsula, Northwest Territories. National Museum of Canada, Bulletin 161:1-63.

Manning, T.H. 1960. The relationship of the Peary and barren-ground caribou. Arctic Institute of North America, Technical Paper 4:1-52.

Manning, T.H. and A.H. Macpherson. 1958. The mammals of Banks Island. Arctic Institute of North America, Technical Paper 2:1-74.

_____. 1961. A biological investigation of Prince of Wales Island, N.W.T. Transactions of the Royal Canadian Institute 33(2):116-239.

McEwen, E.H. 1955. A biological survey of the west coast of Banks Island - 1955. Canadian Wildlife Service, Edmonton. 56 pp. (Unpublished report).

M'Clintock, F.L. 1859. The voyage of the *Fox* in the Arctic seas. A narrative of the discovery of the fate of Sir John Franklin and his companions. John Murray, London. 403 pp.

M'Clure, R. 1856. The discovery of the North-West Passage by H.M.S. *Investigator* 1850, 1851, 1852, 1853, 1854. Edited by: S. Osborn. M.G. Hurtig, Edmonton. 405 pp. Reprint 1969.

M'Dougall, G.F. 1857. The eventful voyage of H.M. Discovery ship *Resolute* to the Arctic regions in search of Sir John Franklin and the missing crews of H.M. Discovery ships *Erebus* and *Terror*, 1852, 1853, 1854. Longman's, London. 529 pp.

Meldgaard, M. 1986. The Greenland caribou - zoogeography, taxonomy, and population dynamics. Meddelelser om Grønland, Bioscience 20:1-88.

Miller, F.L., E.J. Edmunds, and A. Gunn. 1982. Foraging behaviour of Peary caribou in response to springtime snow and ice conditions. Canadian Wildlife Service, Occasional Paper 48:1-39.

Miller, F.L. and A. Gunn. 1978. Inter-island movements of Peary caribou south of Viscount Melville Sound, Northwest Territories. Canadian Field-Naturalist 91:327-333.

_____. 1979. Responses of Peary caribou and muskoxen to helicopter harassment. Canadian Wildlife Service, Occasional Paper 40:1-90.

_____. 1980. Inter-island movements of Peary caribou (*Rangifer tarandus pearyi*) south of Viscount Melville Sound and Barrow Strait, Northwest Territories, Canada. In: Proceedings of the 2nd International Reindeer/Caribou Symposium, Røros, Norway, 1979. Edited by: E. Reimers, E. Gaare, and S.. Skjenneberg. Direktoratet for vilt og ferskvannsfisk, Trondheim. pp. 99-114.

Miller, F.L. and H.P.L. Kiliaan. 1980A. Inter-island movements of Peary caribou in the Prince of Wales Island-Somerset Island-Boothia Peninsula complex, Northwest Territories, May-July 1979. Canadian Wildlife Service, Progress Notes 107:1-7.

_____. 1980B. Some observations on springtime snow/ice conditions on 10 Canadian High Arctic islands - and a preliminary comparison of snow/ice conditions between eastern Prince of Wales Island and western Somerset Island, N.W.T., 5 May - 2 July 1979. Canadian Wildlife Service, Progress Notes 116:1-11.

_____. 1981. Inter-island movements of Peary caribou in the Prince of Wales Island-Somerset Island-Boothia Peninsula complex, Northwest Territories, June 1980. Canadian Wildlife Service, Progress Notes 120:1-7.

Miller, F.L., R.H. Russell, and A. Gunn. 1977A. Distributions, movements and numbers of Peary caribou and muskoxen on western Queen Elizabeth Islands, Northwest Territories, 1972-74. Canadian Wildlife Service, Report Series 40:1-55.

_____. 1977B. Interisland movements of Peary caribou (*Rangifer tarandus pearyi*) on western Queen Elizabeth Islands, Arctic Canada. Canadian Journal of Zoology 55:1029-1037.

O'Neill, J.J. 1920. (Evidence given by). Proceedings Royal Commission to Investigate the Possibilities of the Reindeer and Musk-ox Industry in Northern Canada. Volume 1:36-48.

Parry, W.E. 1821. Journal of a voyage for the discovery of a North-West Passage from the Atlantic to the Pacific; performed in the years 1819-1820, in His Majesty's ships *Hecla* and *Griper*, under the orders of William Edward Parry ... with an appendix containing scientific and other observations. John Murray, London. 309 pp.

Rae, J. 1852. Journey from Great Bear Lake to Wollaston Land. Journal of the Royal Geographical Society 22:73-82.

Rand, A.L. 1954. The ice age and mammal speciation in North America. Arctic 7:31-35.

Rasmussen, K. 1927. Across Arctic America. Narrative of the Fifth Thule Expedition. G.P. Putnam's, New York. 388 pp.

Riewe, R.R. 1978. The utilization of wildlife in the Jones Sound region by the Grise Fiord Inuit. In: Truelove Lowland, Devon Island, Canada: a High Arctic Ecosystem. Edited by: L.C. Bliss. University of Alberta Press, Edmonton. pp. 621-644.

Røed, K.H., H. Staaland, E. Broughton, and D.C. Thomas. 1986. Transferrin variation in caribou (*Rangifer tarandus* L.) on the Canadian Arctic Islands. Canadian Journal of Zoology 64:94-98.

Simpson,T. 1843. Narrative of the discoveries on the north coast of America effected by the officers of the Hudson's Bay Company during the years 1836-39. R. Bentley, London. 419 pp.

Stefansson, V. 1913A. Victoria Island and the surrounding seas. Bulletin of the American Geographical Society 45:93-106.

_____. 1913B. My life with the Eskimo. Macmillan, New York. 538 pp.

_____. 1914. The Stefansson-Anderson arctic expedition of the American Museum; preliminary ethnological report. Anthropology Paper American Museum Natural History 14(1):1-395.

_____. 1920. (Evidence given by). Proceedings Royal Commission to Investigate the Possibilities of the Reindeer and Musk-ox Industry in Northern Canada. Volume 1:76-280.

_____. 1921. The friendly Arctic. Macmillan, New York. 784 pp.

Storkerson, S.T. 1920. (Evidence given by). Proceedings Royal Commission to Investigate the Possibilities of the Reindeer and Musk-ox Industry in Northern Canada. Volume 1:255-280.

Tener, J.S. 1963. Queen Elizabeth Islands game survey, 1961. Canadian Wildlife Service, Occasional Paper 4:1-50.

Thomas, D.C. and P. Everson. 1982. Geographic variation in caribou on the Canadian Arctic Islands. Canadian Journal of Zoology 60:2442-2454.

Thompson, D.C. and C.A. Fischer. 1980. Numbers and distribution of caribou on the Boothia Peninsula, Northwest Territories. Canadian Field-Naturalist 94:171-174.

Vibe, C. 1967. Arctic animals in relation to climatic fluctuations. Meddelelser om Grønland 170(5):1-227.

Willemsen, G.F. 1983. Osteological measurements and some remarks on the evolution of the Svalbard reindeer, *Rangifer tarandus platyrhynchus*. Zeitschrift für Saügetierkunde 48:175-185.

Wollebaek, A. 1926. The Spitzbergen reindeer (*Rangifer tarandus spitsbergensis*). Resultater av de Norske Statunderstottede Spitsbergenekspeditioner 1(4):1-71.

Youngman, P.M. 1975. Mammals of the Yukon Territory. National Museum of Natural Sciences, Publications in Zoology 10:1-192.

Illustrated by Brenda Carter

MUSKOX (Ovibos moschatus Zimmermann) POPULATIONS ON THE NORTHEASTERN COAST OF DEVON ISLAND

Donald L. Pattie[1]

Abstract: Earlier estimates of muskox numbers along the northeastern coast of Devon Island were compared with 1984 to 1987 surveys over five lowlands in that region. A 10-year record of muskox populations on Truelove Lowland is presented for the years 1978-1987. Density on lowland habitat suitable for muskox grazing varied from a high of 0.9 muskox km^{-2} in 1973 to a low of 0.3 km^{-2} in 1987. Muskox population density on Truelove Lowland during the second half of July ranged from a high of 2.5 km^{-2} in 1980 to a low of 0.2 km^{-2} in 1985 and 1986. Herd composition, consisting of numbers of calves, yearlings and (where possible) bulls and cows, is presented for the years 1984-1987. High calf mortality in some years and fluctuating natality were indicated. A population decline of one third followed the winter of 1984-1985.

Résumé: Les premières évaluations du nombre de boeufs musqués de la côte nord-est de l'île Devon ont été comparées avec les études faites de 1984 à 1987 sur cinq terres basses de cette région. On présente des données sur dix ans (1978-1987) des populations de boeufs musqués dans les basses-terres de Truelove. La densité sur les basses-terres adaptées au pâturage de l'espèce a varié d'un maximum de 0,9 boeuf musqué par km^2 en 1973 à un minimum de 0,3/km^2 en 1987. Pendant la dernière moitié de juillet, la densité de population des boeufs musqués dans les basses-terres de Truelove est passée d'un maximum de 2,5 km^2 en 1980 à un minimum de 0,2/km^2 en 1985 et 1986. On donne, pour les années 1984 à 1987, la composition de la harde, c'est-à-dire le nombre de veaux, le nombre de bêtes d'un an et (quand c'est possible) le nombre d'adultes mâles et femelles. On a trouvé un taux de mortalité élevé chez les veaux pour certaines années et une natalité qui varie. Un déclin d'un tiers de population de boeufs musqués a suivi l'hiver 1984-1985.

INTRODUCTION

Truelove Lowland on Devon Island's northeastern coast has been the site of some of the most intensive long-term scientific studies ever undertaken in the Canadian Arctic Islands. Detailed descriptions of both the physical and biotic features of the lowland appeared in Bliss (1977). Muskoxen, the largest terrestrial herbivores on the island, occupy the coastal lowlands. They have been the subject of various studies since the early 1960s. Harington (1964) collected information from Royal Canadian Mounted Police records and other sources about muskox numbers on the northeastern coast of Devon Island from 1908 to 1960. His published estimates ranged from a low of 20 in 1929 to a maximum of 100 in 1937. Tener (1965) estimated 200 muskox for all of Devon Island. Freeman (1971) estimated the muskox population for the lowlands along the entire shore of Bear Bay (Figure 1) at 230-300. Hubert (1977) carried out intensive counts on five adjacent lowlands between Sverdrup Inlet to the west, and Sverdrup Glacier to the east, from 1970 to 1973. The area Hubert surveyed was considerably smaller than the area Freeman covered, yet the highest of

---

[1] Northern Institute of Technology, 11762-106 Street, Edmonton, Alberta T5G 2R1

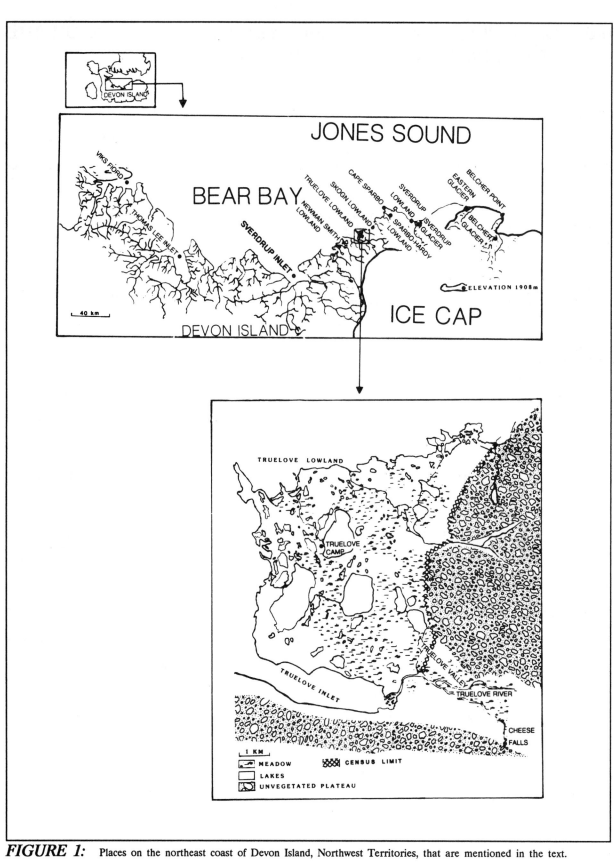

FIGURE 1: Places on the northeast coast of Devon Island, Northwest Territories, that are mentioned in the text.

634

Hubert's counts, 287 in 1973, approached the maximum Freeman had reported. Hubert (1977) also investigated herd composition and movements.

An attempt to count all muskoxen on Truelove Lowland and in Truelove Valley was undertaken from 1978 to 1987, and most or all of the adjacent lowlands where Hubert counted muskoxen were again surveyed during 1984-1987. Together these data provide the longest records of muskox population trends in the Canadian Arctic.

METHODS

The 1978-1987 Truelove muskox counts were conducted during the second half of July. A virtually complete coverage of Truelove Lowland was achieved by having observers walk abreast 100 m apart along predetermined routes marked on a detailed map. Muskoxen in Truelove Valley were typically counted soon after, using a less rigorous technique which involved counting all muskoxen seen during a walk to and from Cheese Falls (Figure 1).

Hubert (1977) used both fixed-wing aircraft and helicopters for his surveys. All of the 1984-1987 data were obtained during helicopter surveys. On these surveys three observers recorded numbers and, where possible, the sex and age of muskoxen seen. The helicopter was flown in a grid pattern for the 1984-1987 counts with 400 m between lines at an altitude of 30-40 m above the surface. Because the 1984-1987 censuses were all conducted during the second half of July, Hubert's July 1970 and 1971 records were selected for comparison. Since he did no July surveys in 1972, we used his 8 May figures, and the 1973 data were from a 16 August survey.

We did not attempt to distinguish the sex of calves or yearlings. Often, because of distance or the orientation of the adults, their sex could not be identified either. They were recorded "adults - sex not determined".

RESULTS

The annual muskox counts for the 58 km^2 Truelove Lowland - Truelove Valley region are reported in Table 1. Presumably the results in some years were affected by significant population movements from or to other nearby lowlands.

TABLE 1: SEX, AGE AND DENSITY OF MUSKOXEN ON THE 58 km² TRUELOVE LOWLAND - TRUELOVE VALLEY REGION BASED UPON WALKED POPULATION SURVEYS (1978-1987).

YEAR	ADULT MALES	ADULT FEMALES	YEARLINGS	CALVES	ADULTS, SEX NOT DETERMINED	TOTAL	ESTIMATED DENSITY (MUSKOXEN PER KM⁻²)
1978	17	11	5	6	18	57	1.0
1979	23	23	5	17	10	78	1.4
1980	3	5	0	26	111	145	2.5
1981	9	-	3	3	48	63	1.1
1982	12	4	-	1	22	39	0.7
1983	-	-	-	2	47	49	0.8
1984	25	17	-	11	-	53	0.9
1985	3	4	-	1	5	13	0.2
1986	5	3	-	0	4	12	0.2
1987	2	9	1	7	-	19	0.3

TABLE 2: MUSKOX POPULATIONS OF FIVE OF DEVON ISLAND'S CONTIGUOUS NORTH COAST LOWLANDS OBSERVED DURING AERIAL POPULATION SURVEYS (1970-1973, 1984-1987)[1].

YEAR	AREA						ESTIMATED DENSITY (MUSKOXEN PER KM²)
	Newman Smith (139 km²)	Truelove (58 km²)	Skogn (15 km²)	Sparbo-Hardy (66 km²)	Sverdrup (22 km²)	Total	
1970	23	17	10	17	65	132	0.4
1971	10	22	13	21	50	116	0.4
1972	29	70	1	99	50	249	0.8
1973	57	27	9	167	18	278	0.9
1984	87	13	10	36	42	188	0.6
1985[2]	-	8	4	40	19	71	0.4
1986	48	12	2	24	57	143	0.5
1987	11	19	12	25	9	76	0.3

[1] 1970-1973 data from Hubert (1977).
[2] No count could be made on Newman Smith Lowland in 1985; density reflects area surveys.

636

Aerial survey data from 1984 to 1987 are listed (Table 2), together with selected results of aerial surveys conducted in 1970-1973 by Hubert (1977). The zones surveyed from east to west include: Sverdrup, Sparbo-Hardy, Skogn, Truelove and Newman Smith lowlands (Figure 1).

Table 3 lists the composition of the various lowland muskox herds to the degree it could be determined from a helicopter. Newman Smith Lowland could not be surveyed in 1985 because of poor weather when the helicopter was available. The density calculation for 1985 is based upon the areas counted.

DISCUSSION

The annual changes in muskox densities might be associated with major movements, differing patterns of habitat use, increases caused by births or immigration, and decreases associated with deaths or emigration. While herd movements from one to another of the lowlands surveyed occurs (Hubert 1977), it is unlikely that there was significant movement to others as there are no large ones nearby. A few small coastal lowlands exist between Sverdrup Glacier and Eastern Glacier (Figure 1), and Hubert (1977) counted a maximum of 13 muskoxen on them in May 1973. Movement to or from that area cannot, however, explain the amplitude of change recorded in Table 2. Population changes seen in Table 1 more likely reflect movements between the contiguous lowlands, as herds occasionally move from one lowland to another. Muskoxen rarely range far up onto the largely-unvegetated plateau in the vicinity of the nearby Devon Island Ice Cap. During a summer helicopter flight, two muskox cows, each with a calf, were seen near the ice cap at least 9 km from the nearest lowland. Since there was less than 1% vegetative cover on that plateau, I suspect they went there to escape mosquitoes or predators, and not to feed. Muskoxen occasionally cross significant expanses of sea ice, for in June 1970 we saw a herd of five on Bear Bay a few kilometres from shore (see Miller, this volume, regarding caribou crossing sea ice). Thus there could be some emigration or immigration. Such movements would help to explain the increase Hubert (1977) reported. Another reasonable explanation is a failure to observe animals that may have been associated with rocky outcrops during some of Hubert's aerial surveys. Rocks and resting muskoxen can be confused easily.

TABLE 3: *RESULTS OF JULY AERIAL MUSKOX CENSUS ON FIVE ADJACENT DEVON ISLAND NORTH COAST LOWLANDS FROM 1984-1987.*

LOWLAND AND (AREA)	1984	1985	1986	1987
Newman Smith (139 km²)				
Males	53	-	25	4
Females	23	-	20	6
Yearlings	2	-	3	1
Calves	9	-	-	-
Sex undetermined; more than 1 year old	-	-	-	-
TOTAL	87	-	48	11
Truelove (58 km²)				
Males	-	3	5	2
Females	-	4	3	9
Yearlings	-	-	-	1
Calves	3	1	-	7
Sex undetermined; more than 1 year old	10	-	4	-
TOTAL	13	8	12	19
Skogn (15 km²)				
Males	-	3	2	3
Females	-	1	-	6
Yearlings	-	-	-	-
Calves	3	-	-	3
Sex undetermined; more than 1 year old	7	-	-	-
TOTAL	10	4	2	12
Sparbo-Hardy (66 km²)				
Males	-	15	10	7
Females	-	18	5	9
Yearlings	-	-	-	1
Calves	7	2	-	8
Sex undetermined; more than 1 year old	29	5	9	-
TOTAL	36	40	24	25
Sverdrup (22 km²)				
Males	-	15	28	3
Females	-	2	23	5
Yearlings	-	1	1	-
Calves	9	1	5	1
Sex undetermined; more than 1 year old	33	-	-	-
TOTAL	42	19	57	9
TOTAL FOR ALL LOWLANDS	188	71[1]	143	76

[1] Does not include Newman-Smith Lowland, which was not surveyed in 1985.

638

The major declines in numbers were related to mortality - apparently accidents, predation and starvation are the most important agents. Muskox predation by wolves and polar bears occurred, and a few accidental deaths were observed (Pattie 1986). However, examples of predation or accident-related deaths were too few to explain the decline in muskox populations from 1984-1987. Based on carcasses or remains examined, starvation appeared to be implicated in most deaths. Detailed analysis of femur fat content or other criteria of body condition at the time of death were not performed, but obviously many of the animals were emaciated. This evidence is corroborated by our observations that scavenging bears, wolves, and foxes often chewed a hole near the back of the ribs and ate only the liver, heart, and lungs, leaving the gastro-intestinal tract, skeletal muscle and bones. Evidently the scavengers did not find that the gain from consuming the rest of the carcass compensated for the effort required to strip the frozen remains.

Hubert (1977) summarized the frequency and severity of mortality, and suggested that starvation during winter was a key factor. Parker *et al.* (1975) also studied Canadian Arctic Islands muskox populations. They suggested starvation was related to: (1) greater than usual snow accumulation in winter feeding areas; (2) icing conditions that made feed unavailable; and (3) reduced production or overharvesting of vegetation. Although only summer weather records are available from 1978-1987, no indication of extreme snow accumulation or icing was noted during that time.

Snow accumulation appeared scant in 1984-1985 and 1985-1986, during which periods the muskox population declined to half the 1984 level.

Empirical data would be required to determine whether overgrazing of vegetation occurred, and such data are not available. Muc (1977) determined that the growth period for sedges and grasses on Truelove Lowland was almost constant, regardless of summer climatic variation, and noted that higher temperatures resulted in increased net production throughout the sedge-moss meadows. Most plant growth took place during July. Svoboda (1977) found that increased plant production on drier Truelove sites was associated with the wettest summers. His data showed that the greatest production of plant biomass was associated with the wettest, but coldest, of the four seasons he studied.

Seemingly the quantity of available winter muskox forage is most affected by summer temperature, and summer forage abundance by the frequency of summer precipitation. Since winter at these latitudes lasts about nine months, summer temperatures may have a disproportionate effect on the muskox population. Summer temperatures show considerable variation. In 1973 the average July temperature was 9.6°C, the highest that has been recorded. In contrast, the average July temperature in 1986, when muskox populations were declining, was 3.1°C. Further study to determine the interaction of climatic factors and muskox populations is needed.

Almost no muskox forage grows above an altitude of 200 m on northeastern Devon Island. The area between the point where Sverdrup Glacier drops to Jones Sound on the east and Sverdrup Inlet joins Bear Bay in the west that is below 200 m has an area of approximately 300 km^2. Of this, only about 50 km^2 is well vegetated meadow. Hubert (1977) reported that muskoxen commonly used these meadows. He recognized that hummocky sedge-meadows with an average available standing crop of 62 g m^{-2} were grazed most, followed by frost-boil sedge-moss meadows that had an average available standing crop of 51 g m^{-2}. The significance of Truelove Lowland to the northeastern Devon Island muskox population is obvious for 17 km^2 (34%) of the 50 km^2 of meadow is there. However, Hubert's (1977) findings revealed that the bulk of grazing on these meadows took place during the period of continuous darkness, maximum snowcover, and the lowest ambient temperatures. Our counts took place during the period of continuous light, minimum snowcover, and maximum ambient temperatures when, I suspect, the bulk of grazing was concentrated in areas where vegetation was less abundant but perhaps more palatable. The significance of this is that it is *easier* to see muskoxen in meadows than in the broken land and rock outcrops they frequent in summer. Practically all muskoxen were seen by the observers walking in the Truelove Lowland, and most were counted in Truelove Valley. No doubt some were missed during surveys from aircraft of the other lowlands. Thus, the counts reported must be regarded as minimal. However, it is doubtful that the numbers not tallied could account for the declines seen during 1984-1987 (Table 2).

One indication of population stability is the annual survival of calves to yearlings. Thirty-one calves were counted in 1984. Of this cohort, only one survived to be counted as a yearling in 1985. In addition, only four calves were seen in 1985 suggesting a crash had occurred like that reported by Parker *et al.* (1975) for Melville, Bathurst, and Byam Martin islands. Parker's group reported high mortality rates, low pregnancy rates, and emaciated animals which, based upon rumen contents, had been feeding on dry habitats with low productivity. The rumen contents were what one would expect from animals grazing the beach ridges of Truelove Lowland rather than the more productive sedge-meadows. Unfavourable conditions for muskox on Devon Island may have persisted through the winter of 1985-1986, for in 1986 we saw only five calves. These data support Hubert's (1977) contention than muskoxen exhibit "occasional increased mortality combined with fluctuating natality".

Observations suggest the muskox population on northeastern Devon Island ranged from a maximum of about 275 in 1973 to a minimum near 75 in 1987. There was no indication that predation or accidents were responsible for major population losses. Carcasses we found were emaciated, suggesting that starvation plays an important part in population regulation.

The population is lightly hunted. The Inuit of Grise Fiord have an annual quota of 27 muskoxen, of which only four males may be taken on northeastern Devon Island. The quota has always been filled.

The Truelove Lowland population exhibits an even greater amplitude of fluctuation than the entire coastal population (Table 1). From a maximum of 145 in 1980, the numbers on Truelove declined to 12 in 1986. Herd movements from or to adjacent lowlands probably played the most important role in these changes. These movements could have been either the seasonal type Hubert (1977) noted, or movements he reported that seemed to be associated with the appearance of polar bears. However, since the surveys were conducted about the same time each year, and there was evidence of bear predation on only four muskoxen between 1979 and 1984, factors other than these two are suggested.

Data presented here support the findings of Parker *et al.* (1975) and those of Hubert (1977), who noted that muskox populations are subject to great fluctuations in both birth and death rates. Apparently the northeastern Devon Island population reached the lowest level since 1970 in 1987. Further study of the role of weather and food availability in muskox population regulation is needed.

ACKNOWLEDGEMENTS

This research was supported by Polar Continental Shelf Project as project 111-80. The Arctic Institute of North America assisted with transportation and provided technical help and accommodation at its field station. Space does not permit me to thank individually all who assisted me in the counts over the years, but their work is appreciated. Special thanks to Colleen Harlton and Jim Trask who, together, directed the work in 1987.

REFERENCES

Bliss, L.C. (Editor). 1977. Truelove Lowland, Devon Island, Canada: a High Arctic ecosystem. University of Alberta Press, Edmonton. 716 pp.

Freeman, M.M.R. 1971. Population characteristics of muskoxen in the Jones Sound region of the Northwest Territories. Journal of Wildlife Management 35(10):103-108.

Harington, C.R. 1964. Remarks on Devon Island muskoxen. Canadian Journal of Zoology 42:79-86.

Hubert, B.A. 1977. Estimated productivity of muskox on Truelove Lowland. In: Truelove Lowland, Devon Island, Canada: A High Arctic Ecosystem. Edited by: L.C. Bliss. University of Alberta Press. Edmonton. pp. 467-491.

Muc, M. 1977. Ecology and primary production of sedge-moss communities. In: Truelove Lowland, Devon Island, Canada: A High Arctic Ecosystem. Edited by: L.C. Bliss. University of Alberta Press, Edmonton. pp. 157-184.

Parker, G.R., D.C. Thomas, E. Broughton, and D.R. Gray. 1975. Crashes of muskox and Peary caribou populations in 1973-74 on the Parry Islands, Arctic Canada. Canadian Wildlife Service, Progress Notes 56:1-10.

Pattie, D.L. 1986. Muskox density and calf numbers on Devon Island's north coast. Journal of Mammalogy 67(1):190-191.

Svoboda, J. 1977. Ecology and primary production of raised beach communities. In Truelove Lowland, Devon Island, Canada: A High Arctic Ecosystem. Edited by: L.C. Bliss, University of Alberta Press, Edmonton. pp. 185-216.

Tener, J.S. 1965. Muskoxen in Canada. Canadian Wildlife Service, Monograph Series 2:1-166.

NURSING BEHAVIOUR OF ARCTIC HARES (Lepus arcticus)

Aniśkowicz, B.T.,[1] H. Hamilton[2], D.R. Gray[3], and C. Downes[4]

Abstract: Nursing behaviour in three arctic hare (Lepus arcticus) families was studied at Polar Bear Pass, Bathurst Island, and Sverdrup Pass, Ellesmere Island during the summers of 1986 and 1987. Additional information was collected at Bathurst Island between 1968 and 1985 and at Borup Fiord, Ellesmere Island in 1988.

Three female hares nursed their three to five young at mean intervals of 19 hours 48 minutes, 18 hours 47 minutes and 18 hours 36 minutes. The young arrived near the nursing site singly or in groups, and congregated 21-90 minutes before their mother arrived. Nursing commenced immediately after the female's arrival. The duration of each nursing bout was short (range: 1-4 minutes). Occasionally, one or several of the young arrived late and missed the nursing. In several instances, when the young were up to four weeks old, the female, while still in the nursing area, allowed a leveret who arrived late to begin nursing as much as 9 minutes after the group suckle had ended. In one case only were some leverets allowed to resuckle. The female ended the nursing bout by hopping away. During the first several weeks after birth the female pulled away from the young immediately after nursing, but remained at the nursing site or close to it. As the young became older, the female quickly left the immediate vicinity of the nursing site when nursing stopped. In early summer the young hares dispersed rapidly after nursing but stayed near the nursing site, gradually increasing their range to an observed maximum of about 1 km in mid-August. Leverets gradually increased the amount of time they spent accompanying the female until, during August, they remained with her for up to 1.9 hours after nursing. Young hares occasionally remained together between nursing bouts. The young were weaned in the second or third week of August at 8-9 weeks old.

Résumé: On a étudié le comportement d'allaitement de trois familles de lièvres arctiques au col de Polar Bear, île Bathurst, et au col de Sverdrup, île Ellesmere, pendant les étés 1986 et 1987. On a également recueilli des renseignements supplémentaires provenant de l'île Bathurst entre 1968 et 1985 et du fjord Borup, îles Ellesmere, en 1988.

Trois femelles lièvres (hases) allaitaient trois à cinq petits à intervalles moyens de 19 heures 48 minutes, 18 heures 47 minutes et 18 heures 36 minutes. Les petits arrivaient près du lieu d'allaitement seuls ou en groupes et se rassemblaient de 21 à 90 minutes avant que leur mère n'arrive. L'allaitement commençait dès l'arrivée de la mère. La durée de chacune des périodes d'allaitement était courte (1 à 4 minutes). Parfois, un ou plusieurs petits arrivaient en retard et manquaient l'allaitement. Dans plusieurs cas, lorsque les petits avaient moins de 4 semaines, la femelle, qui se trouvait encore près du lieu d'allaitement, permettait à un levraut en retard de téter, même 9 minutes après que les autres avaient terminé. Dans un cas, la femelle a permis à la portée au complet de se faire allaiter une seconde fois. La hase terminait la période d'allaitement en s'éloignant par bonds. Pendant les premières semaines après la naissance, elle se retirait immédiatement après l'allaitement, mais restait sur les lieux ou à proximité. Lorsque les levrauts vieillissaient, la femelle quittait rapidement les abords du lieu d'allaitement dès la fin de la tétée. En début d'été, les jeunes lièvres se dispersaient vite après l'allaitement, mais restaient à proximité, s'éloignant graduellement, jusqu'à un maximum observé d'environ 1 km à la mi-août. Les petits accompagnaient leur mère de plus en plus longtemps jusqu'à ce qu'au mois d'août ils restent avec elle après l'allaitement pendant 1,9 heures. Quelques fois les levrauts demeuraient ensemble entre les périodes d'allaitement. Les petits étaient sevrés dans la deuxième ou la troisième semaine du mois d'août, ils étaient alors âgés de 8 à 9 semaines.

INTRODUCTION

Although arctic hares (*Lepus arcticus*) are widely distributed throughout northern Canada, including the Arctic Islands, they have not been studied extensively. Several studies have been conducted on their distribution in Newfoundland (Bergerud 1967; Hearn *et al.* 1987; Mercer *et al.* 1981), demography (Hearn *et al.* 1987), morphology (Parker 1977; Walkinshaw 1947) and population dynamics (Bergerud 1967; Lloyd 1981; Mercer *et al.* 1981). Although

---

[1] R.R. #4, Shawville, Quebec J0X 2Y0
[2] Box 412, Osgoode, Ontario K0A 2W0
[3] Zoology Division, National Museum of Natural Sciences, Ottawa, Ontario K1P 6P4
[4] 197 Glebe Avenue, #4, Ottawa, Ontario K1A 2C4

a few studies describe basic behaviour in this species (Bonnyman 1975; Parker 1977; Walkinshaw 1947), there is very little information on reproduction (Parker 1977; Walkinshaw 1947; Hampson 1968).

Research on other species of *Lepus* indicate that parental care, other than nursing, is virtually non-existent. Female brown hares (*L. europaeus*) (Broekhuizen and Maaskamp 1980) associate with their young only during nursing, which occurs once every 24 hours, soon after sunset. Shortly before nursing, young hares come to the nursing site from different directions and wait in a group. Within-litter variation in time of arrival is small. Very young leverets normally wait for their mother at the place of birth, which serves as the gathering-place, but as they get older they may go to meet the female who usually arrives from the same direction on successive evenings. Consequently, the nursing place gradually shifts. The female sits in an upright posture during nursing, which lasts only a few minutes. Duration of nursing bouts decreases as leverets age. Bouts are ended by the female jumping away from her young. Having nursed once, the female refuses all resuckling attempts. After nursing, the female leaves and the young disperse. The distance over which they range increases with age. Young hares nibble on vegetation from an age of four days onwards, and are weaned at 3-10 weeks, depending on whether they are a first or last litter.

Rongstad and Tester (1971) reported similar behaviour in the snowshoe hare (*L. americanus*). The young assembled 5-10 minutes before the arrival of the female and nursed for up to 10 minutes.

Both studies suggest that the nursing regime is based on cues from the 24-hour light-cycle.

Very little information is available on parental care in *L. arcticus*. Pedersen (1962) mentions that female hares paid close attention to their leverets during the first two or three days after birth and were reluctant to leave them. Hampson (1968) states that a nursing arctic hare on Bathurst Island returned to her leverets at long intervals and nursed them briefly - three minutes in one case. He reports a nursing bout observed at close range. After nursing, the young scattered in all directions. In one instance a leveret followed the mother for about 3 m before leaving her. The female departed abruptly after nursing ended and ran long distances before stopping to feed. Hampson did not observe a single case of the female feeding in the vicinity of her leverets, and noted that only once she dozed about 600 m from the young. He reported that 9-10 day-old leverets ate some fresh vegetation.

The present study gives details on the frequency of nursing and related behaviour in several families of *L. arcticus* in the Queen Elizabeth Islands. In the High Arctic 24-hour daylight occurs throughout the summer, and changes in the intensity of illumination throughout the daily cycle are greatly reduced compared to the pronounced day-and-night cycle experienced by more southerly species.

METHODS

Observations were conducted at the National Museum of Natural Sciences High Arctic Research Station at Polar Bear Pass, Bathurst Island (75°43'N, 98°25'W), in June and July 1986, with incidental observations in 1968, and at Sverdrup Pass, Ellesmere Island (79°08'N, 79°45'W) in July and August 1986 and 1987. Additional data were collected by R. Burton at Borup Fiord, Ellesmere Island (80°52'N, 81°53'W) in June-August 1988.

Observations at Polar Bear Pass in 1986 were made from an enclosed observation tower, 3-4 m above the ground. At Sverdrup Pass and Borup Fiord, the observer sat quietly in the open or partially hidden behind boulders at least 10 m from the nursing site. In all cases, 7x35 binoculars and/or a Bushnel spotting scope were used. Nursing behaviour was documented using super 8 mm, 16 mm and 35 mm photography.

The mother of four arctic hare leverets found at Polar Bear Pass on 28 June 1986 marked herself by brushing against some wet paint, making her identifiable. The young were approximately two days old when first observed and were followed until 11 July 1986. A total of 16 nursing sessions were observed. The young were not marked.

A lactating hare was live-trapped at Sverdrup Pass on 17 July 1986. She was ear-tagged with a small green "Allflex" ear-tag, marked with picric acid stain for recognition at a distance and released. On 26 July she was followed until she nursed five young, which were estimated to be approximately five weeks old. This family was observed until 6 September, and data on 24 nursing bouts were recorded. Young hares were not ear-tagged until early September.

In 1987, hares 2-3 weeks old were followed at Sverdrup Pass until they nursed on 14 July. Subsequently, the three leverets were marked with picric acid stain. The female was not marked. Forty nursing bouts were observed until the young were weaned on 16 August.

At Borup Fiord in 1988, a litter of eight leverets was observed intermittently from 26 June to 23 July. Sixteen nursing sessions were observed.

OBSERVATIONS

Birth Sites

On 24 June 1986 one of two hares which frequented the Research Station area of Polar Bear Pass appeared to be pregnant. Attempts to determine visually whether her mammae were enlarged proved unsuccessful because the belly fur was long and thick. She spent much time resting and seemed reluctant to get up when approached.

Four young arctic hares, estimated to be two days old, were discovered in the early afternoon of 28 June. All were within several metres of each other, but no two were together. Two other very young hares were found dead on 29 June, 1986. They were in an unlined, shallow depression, about 0.3 m in diameter, in trampled moss. This nest resembled that described by Walkinshaw (1947).

Nursing-Sites

The young hares observed in 1986 initially gathered for nursing at the presumed birth site or nest. It was situated on a low ridge on the north side of the pass and approximately 55 m above its floor (80 m asl). In the vicinity of the nursing area the flattish ridge top was about 175 m wide. The surface of this raised-beach (Blake 1974) consisted of fine, silt and limestone gravel. Some rocks, protruding no more than 20 cm above the surface, were scattered about the area (none was present in the immediate vicinity of the nest) and provided little cover - particularly for adult hares. The research station was only 20 m from the nursing site. Both adult and young hares sometimes used the buildings, fuel barrels, boxes and glow cones along the landing strip for shelter.

The nursing area on the ridge top was moderately vegetated (approximately 50% ground cover) with plants characteristic of the upland community (Sheard and Geale 1983).

646

Salix arctica, Saxifraga oppositifolia and *Papaver radicatum* were the predominant vascular plant species. Other common species included: *Dryas integrifolia, Ranunculus* sp., *Oxyria digyna, Cerastium alpinum, Melandrium affine, Draba* sp., *Saxifraga caespitosa, S. cernua, S. flagellaris,* other saxifrage species, grasses including *Alopecurus alpinus, Poa abbreviata, Puccinellia* sp. and *Festuca* sp., as well as various mosses and lichens, providing abundant forage for hares. On the valley floor, about 200 m to the south, virtually 100% of the ground was covered by vegetation. Wet meadows on poorly drained soil surrounding many tundra ponds were lush with sedges and grasses. Hares rarely visited this marsh.

At Sverdrup Pass the nursing site used by a hare family in 1986 was about 1 km north of the main pass, approximately 300 m asl and about 150 m above the floor of the pass. The site was on an exposed, gentle south-facing slope. The substrate consisted was composed of coarse, sharp sandstone, dolomite and limestone gravel. Boulder-strewn areas with granitic erratics and deep ravines were nearby. The site was very sparsely vegetated (<1% ground cover). Species present included: *Saxifraga oppositifolia, S. tricuspidata, S. caespitosa, Dryas integrifolia, Draba corumbosa, Woodsia* sp., *Cerastium* sp., *Salix arctica* and various lichens. Well vegetated, wet meadows (in which adult hares frequently fed) occurred 300 m downslope. The nursing site was seldom visited by hares other than the nursing family.

The 1987 nursing site was approximately 3.5 km southeast of the 1986 site, on a small plateau some 365 m asl and about 215 m above the valley floor. The substrate consisted of predominantly granitic and gneissic rock, and the area was boulder-strewn and sparsely vegetated. This spot was more heavily vegetated than the 1986 site, with approximately 10% cover. Plants were similar but also included: *Cassiope tetragona, Papaver radicatum, Carex nardina* and other unidentified grasses. It was located less than 1 km from the main valley of Sverdrup Pass. Visibility from the nursing site was largely unobstructed for approximately 50 m in most directions. Potential predator-escape terrain was available in steep ravines and moraines bordering the site. Several well vegetated areas and a small glacial meltwater stream and pond were within 70 m. Throughout the summer, the nursing female was the only adult hare seen near nursing site.

The nursing site at Borup Fiord lay among boulders in a gully opening onto a scree fan that spread down the valleyside. It was 213 m asl and 181 m above the large river in the valley.

Congregation of Young Hares

During the first few days, the newborn hares at Polar Bear Pass (1986) stayed within 4 m of the nest, spending most their time sitting still. After two weeks, they spent the non-nursing period at least several hundred metres from the nursing location.

TABLE 1: TIME AT WHICH YOUNG HARES BEGAN CONGREGATING[1] PRIOR TO NURSING.

AGE (weeks)	CONGREGATION OF LEVERETS (weekly mean in minutes)		
	PBP-1986	SP-1986	SP-1987
1	-----	-----	-----
2	52	-----	-----
3	-----	-----	33 (N=8)
4	-----	-----	40 (N=9)
5	-----	59 (N=5)	54 (N=9)
6	-----	57 (N=7)	59 (N=6)
7	-----	52 (N=4)	48 (N=2)

[1] Arrival of first young.
PBP = Polar Bear Pass.
SP = Sverdrup Pass.
N = Number in sample.

Because the young did not stray far from the nest during the first few days of life, it was difficult to determine when they began moving towards the nest in preparation for suckling. During their second week they dispersed ever farther and began making their way towards the nest between 20 and 85 minutes (mean: 52 minutes, N=6) before nursing (Table 1). At Sverdrup Pass during 1986, when young hares were five weeks of age or older, they appeared in the nursing area shortly before nursing. We do not know how far they ranged between nursing bouts. Usually they began congregating about an hour prior to nursing (mean: 56 minutes, range: 32-89 minutes, N=16). In 1987, young hares 3-4 weeks old usually arrived 30-40 minutes (range: 10-71 minutes, N=17) before the female.

This increased to 50-60 minutes (range: 28-90 minutes, N=17) during the fifth and sixth weeks, and remained so until weaning.

Very young leverets usually arrived at or near the nursing spot individually from different directions and at slightly different times. As they matured, two occasionally arrived together, having met before they reached the nursing spot. Once at Sverdrup Pass in 1986, all hares 5-6 weeks old arrived in the nursing area together. In 1987, when the young were perhaps less than 5 weeks old, they arrived and departed from the nursing site separately. The young hares from all three families arrived generally using their own regular routes. As they grew older these routes varied more.

From the beginning of observations at Polar Bear Pass in 1986, the leverets sat in a tight cluster after they had congregated, grooming themselves or nuzzling each other - sometimes apparently attempting to suckle. From five days onward they groomed each other too. As they grew older they spent more time moving about and feeding on vegetation while waiting to be nursed.

Whether the young at Sverdrup Pass (1986, 1987) met at the waiting spot or near it, they frequently ran to each other on first noticing a sibling and "greeted" each other by nuzzling. If several young were involved, the greeting was often followed by the whole group leisurely hopping, single file, in a partial circle. This would last only a few seconds but could be repeated with the arrival of each sibling.

The young hares usually congregated in the open, but on very windy days they tended to wait in the lee of boulders. While waiting for the female to arrive, they sat, backs to the wind, grooming themselves or their siblings, or they hopped about, fed or rested. In several cases they reingested feces. As the nursing time drew near, they would spend increasingly more time sitting close together or in a tight cluster, sometimes touching. Usually they watched for the arrival of the female.

Arrival of Female

Each female hare consistently approached her nursing location from the same direction, and frequently used the same path for the last 100 m or so of the approach. This was not always the shortest distance to the nursing site.

On 28 June 1968 at Polar Bear Pass, a female was observed suckling five very young hares (Hampson 1968). From concealment less than 5 m away, an observer heard her give a short series of low growls as she approached, before the previously motionless young ran to her and began nursing. No vocalization was heard in other circumstances.

At Polar Bear Pass in 1986, the female often spent some time feeding and/or resting several hundred metres from the nest. She made her final approach with a few short pauses, and then dashed directly to the nest where her young waited. When the leverets were older and more active, they ran toward her as she approached. Nursing usually took place immediately at the meeting point. At first the young moved less than 1 m to their mother, but this distance increased gradually. In addition, the female began stopping before the young reached her. So both the spot where the young congregated and the nursing spot gradually shifted away from the nest in the direction of the expected approach of the female. When the young were two weeks old, they congregated about 70 m to the west of the nest and nursed approximately 5 m beyond that.

At Sverdrup Pass, nests were not identified. There in 1986, the female approached the nursing area using one of two routes. She often made a brief stop about 100 m from where the young congregated. The female spent from 1-17 minutes sitting still, grooming and/or feeding a little. She ran the last 90 m or so, either directly or pausing for only a few seconds, and stopped 10-12 m from the young. In this area, too, congregating and nursing spots shifted gradually toward the female's approach route.

In 1987, the doe's behaviour was like that observed in 1986. She consistently approached the nursing site along two routes, with a third route used infrequently. In 1987 the nursing spot shifted approximately 100 m during the five weeks of observations (from the time the young were approximately three weeks old to weaning).

Nursing

When a female arrived at the nursing area, the young hares suckled immediately. The nursing female typically sat upright, with ears erect, eyes open, hind feet in a wide "V" under her haunches, front legs fully extended and front feet rather far apart on the ground.

When the female approached, older leverets (Sverdrup Pass 1986, 1987) she often stopped 10-12 m from them and waited a few seconds in the nursing position until the young reached her. During this time she often laid her ears back against her head and kept her eyes partly closed. The young immediately ran to her, sometimes almost bowling her over. As the young nursed, the female raised her ears and opened her eyes.

650

After an initial period of intense suckling, one or more leverets would stop (probably when the teat from which it was suckling became dry) and move around rapidly, burrowing between its siblings or climbing on their backs in an attempt to reach another nipple. During each nursing bout, such activity increased with time, probably as milk became scarce. Activity also increased with the age of the leverets. Hares five weeks old and older (Sverdrup Pass 1986, 1987) pushed and shoved a great deal, making it difficult for the

FIGURE 1: Ear-tagged female arctic hare nursing two eight-week-old leverets at Sverdrup Pass, Ellesmere Island, 19 August 1986. Photograph by David R. Gray, NMNS.

mother to stay still. She sometimes could not keep both front feet on the ground and would temporarily rest one front paw on the back of the young (Figure 1).

When the leverets were very young, (Polar Bear Pass 1986), the female frequently licked and/or nosed them on the back or head while they were nursing. Urine licking, as described in *L. europaeus* (Broekhuizen and Maaskamp 1980) was not seen. As the leverets grew older, grooming of the young by the mother became less frequent. By the time the young were five weeks old (Sverdrup Pass 1986), the female still briefly lowered her head but without making contact. This remnant of the grooming movement was performed less frequently until, during the sixth week and later, the female consistently lowered her head only once a few seconds before terminating each nursing bout.

Duration of Nursing Bouts

The duration of nursing bouts at Polar Bear Pass in 1986 varied from approximately 10 seconds to 6.5 minutes (N=15). These extremes occurred in cases which could not be considered normal. In the 10-second bout, which occurred on 5 July, only one leveret was involved; the others failed to appear. This youngster was very sluggish. So were its siblings when they were found later that day. One was found dead the following day, but the remaining three leverets behaved almost normally when they congregated for the next nursing.

On 10 and 11 July, all of the young hares nursed, but not together (see Frequency of Nursing, below). This resulted in a combined nursing period for each bout of approximately 6.5 and 6.0 minutes, respectively, while all other bouts at that age lasted for 2.5-3.0 min.

If the above-mentioned cases are excluded from calculations, the young hares at Polar Bear Pass nursed for an average of 3 minutes (range: 2.5-4.0 minutes, N=11). Table 2 shows that the duration of nursing-bouts decreased from 3.5 minutes (N=4) in the first week of life to 2.8 minutes (N=7) in the second week. In 1987 the duration of nursing for leverets 2-3 weeks old averaged about 2.5 minutes, then levelled off in the fifth and sixth week to about 1.5 minutes and remained constant until weaning. In 1986 the duration of nursing bouts of hares 5-7 weeks old remained almost constant at 1.4 minutes until a few days before weaning, when it declined to 1 minute. Young hares 1-5 weeks old at Borup Fiord nursed for an average of 1.8 minutes (range: 1.2-2.1 minutes, N=16).

Frequency of Nursing

At Polar Bear Pass in 1968, very young leverets were observed nursing on 28 June and again on 29 June. The 18 hours 35 minutes between these two nursing bouts probably constituted a nursing interval. In 1986 the female at Polar Bear Pass nursed her young at a mean interval of 19 hours 48 minutes (range: 19 hours 4 minutes to 20 hours 58 minutes, N=15) (Table 3). In 1986, nursing by the young hares during the first two weeks of life was disrupted on several occasions by the appearance of a wolf or the presence of people. One such case occurred on 30 June. The female arrived at the nest at 0205 hours but found no young. She hopped around and fed within 100 m of the nest and returned to it at 0321 hours when only one young hare nursed. The interval between this suckle and

TABLE 2: CHANGE IN DURATION OF NURSING BOUTS WITH AGE.

AGE (weeks)	DURATION OF NURSING BOUTS (weekly mean in minutes)		
	PBP-1986	SP-1986	SP-1987
1	3.5 (N=4)	-----	-----
2	2.8 (N=7)	-----	-----
3	-----	-----	2.5 (N=12)
4	-----	-----	2.5 (N=10)
5	-----	1.4 (N=7)	1.6 (N=9)
6	-----	1.4 (N=8)	1.5 (N=9)
7	-----	1.3 (N=4)	1.6 (N=4)
8	-----	1.0 (N=4)	

PBP = Polar Bear Pass.
SP = Sverdrup Pass.

TABLE 3: NURSING SCHEDULE - POLAR BEAR PASS, 1986.[1]

DATE	TIME OF NURSING	NURSING INTERVAL	NO. OF YOUNG NURSED
June 29	0645		4
30	0205	19 hrs 20 min.[2]	1
	2115	19 hrs 10 min.[2]	4
July 1	1734	20 hrs 19 min.	4
2	1318	19 hrs 44 min.	3
3	0910	19 hrs 52 min.	3
4	0455	19 hrs 45 min.	4
5	0045	19 hrs 50 min.	4
	2047	20 hrs 02 min.	1
6	1551	19 hrs 04 min.	3
7	1147	19 hrs 56 min.	2
8	0732	19 hrs 45 min.	3
9	0318	19 hrs 46 min.	3
	2244	19 hrs 26 min.	3
10	1942	20 hrs 57 min.	2+1
11	1552	20 hrs 10 min.	2+1+(2)

[1] Observations by B.T. Aniśkowicz.
[2] Arrival of female, not time of nursing, was used to calculate interval (see text for details).

( ) Resuckle.

the previous one was 20 hours 36 minutes, but the interval between her first arrival and the previous suckle was 19 hours 20 minutes, very close to the mean. Thus, the female arrived at the predicted time. Moreover, she subsequently returned to the nest 17 hours 54 minutes after the preceding suckle but 19 hours 10 minutes after her first arrival for the preceding nursing-bout - again close to the mean. It was this interval between arrivals of the female (which, in the absence of disturbance, coincides with the nursing interval) that was used for calculating the mean for this family.

At Sverdrup Pass, the mean nursing interval in 1986 was 18 hours 47 minutes (range: 18 hours 30 minutes to 19 hours 12 minutes, N=21) (Table 4). In 1987 it was 18 hours 36 minutes (range: 18 hours 8 minutes to 19 hours 8 minutes, N=37) (Table 5). At Borup Fiord the interval was 18 hours 23 minutes (range: 18 hours 6 minutes to 18 hours 42 minutes, N=13). Variations in these intervals were small, and some were the result of disturbances such as a predator near or in the nursing area. In one case in 1986, the female was delayed by the presence of other adult hares that tried to accompany her despite her apparent efforts to leave them behind. She spent approximately 20 minutes running about on a high, boulder-strewn plateau until she left the two pursuing hares behind. Then she headed directly to the nursing site.

Missed Suckles

The young usually nursed together. If a leveret arrived late, it almost invariably missed the suckle. This occurred occasionally in all three families observed. Three of the four young at Polar Bear Pass (1968) missed a nursing session when 4 days old. One or several young missed a suckle in four other instances during the first two weeks of life. In 1986 at Sverdrup Pass, a single leveret missed a nursing bout in two instances, one during the fifth week of life and the other during the sixth week. Three other instances of late arrival which resulted in missed nursing occurred in 1987, when the young were 2-4 weeks old.

Even leverets 4 days old did not appear to suffer from missing a nursing session. At that age, and perhaps even earlier, they were eating some fresh vegetation. By the time they were 2 weeks old they ate dry grasses too. As they grew older they spent more time foraging and were observed feeding on dried flower and seed heads, as well as on fresh flowers of: *Dryas integrifolia, Papaver radicatum, Arenaria* sp., *Oxyria digyna, Saxifraga*

TABLE 4: NURSING SCHEDULE - SVERDRUP PASS, 1986.[1]

DATE	TIME OF NURSING	NURSING INTERVAL	NO. OF YOUNG NURSED
July 26	1529		5
27	1000[2]	18 hrs 31 min.[2]	-
28	-	- - - - - -	-
	2339	- - - - - -	4
29	1828	18 hrs 49 min.	3
30	1323	18 hrs 55 min.	4
31	0819	18 hrs 56 min.	4
Aug. 1	0331	19 hrs 12 min.	4
	2228	18 hrs 57 min.	4
2	1743	19 hrs 15 min.	4
3	1213	18 hrs 30 min.	3
4	- - - -	18 hrs 33 min.[3]	-
5	0149	18 hrs 33 min.[3]	4
	2041	18 hrs 52 min.	4
6	1540	18 hrs 59 min.	3
7	1015	18 hrs 35 min.	3
8	0440	18 hrs 25 min.	3
	2340	19 hrs 00 min.	3
9	1816	18 hrs 36 min.	3
10	1256	18 hrs 40 min.	3
11	0759	19 hrs 03 min.	3
12	0252	18 hrs 53 min.	3
17	1434	- - - - - -	2
18	0933	18 hrs 59 min.	2
19	-	- - - - - -	-
	2321	- - - - - -	2
20	1820	18 hrs 59 min.	2
21	1333	19 hrs 13 min.	2

[1] Observations from 26 July to 12 August by B.T. Aniśkowicz. Subsequent observations by D.R. Gray.
[2] Approximate.
[3] Calculated mean.

TABLE 5: NURSING SCHEDULE - SVERDRUP PASS, 1987.[1]

DATE	TIME OF NURSING	NURSING INTERVAL	NO. OF YOUNG NURSED
July 14	0928	- - - - - -	3
15	0416	18 hrs 48 min.	3
	2230	18 hrs 14 min.	3
16	1735	19 hrs 05 min.	3
17	1202	18 hrs 27 min.	3
18	0652	18 hrs 50 min.	3
19	0128	18 hrs 36 min.	3
	2011	18 hrs 43 min.	3
20	1446	18 hrs 35 min.	3
21	0926	18 hrs 40 min.	3
22	0400	18 hrs 34 min.	3
	2225	18 hrs 25 min.	3
23	1701	18 hrs 36 min.	3
24	1122	18 hrs 21 min.	3
25	0612	18 hrs 50 min.	3
26	0038	18 hrs 26 min.	3
	1928	18 hrs 50 min.	3
27	1403	18 hrs 35 min.	3
28	0838	18 hrs 35 min.	3
	0243	18 hrs 05 min.	3
29	2129	18 hrs 46 min.	3
30	1607	18 hrs 38 min.	3
31	1048	18 hrs 41 min.	3
Aug. 1	0530	18 hrs 42 min.	3
2	0009	18 hrs 39 min.	3
	1840	18 hrs 31 min.	3
3	1316	18 hrs 36 min.	3
4	0810	18 hrs 54 min.	3
5	0234	18 hrs 24 min.	3
	2112	18 hrs 38 min.	3
6	1555	18 hrs 43 min.	3
7	1026	18 hrs 31 min.	3
8	0458	18 hrs 32 min.	3
	2315	18 hrs 17 min.	3
9	1753	18 hrs 38 min.	3
10	1250	18 hrs 57 min.	3
11	- - - -	- - - - - -	-
12	0153	- - - - - -	3
	2030	18 hrs 37 min.	2
13	1531	19 hrs 01 min.	2
14	- - - -	- - - - - -	-
15	0435	- - - - - -	2

[1] Observations by H. Hamilton and C. Downes.

oppositifolia, Salix arctica and *Carex nardina*. Leaves and roots of *Salix, Dryas, Saxifraga* and *Oxyria* were also consumed.

Young that arrived after the group suckle had ended usually had to wait till the next nursing session. However, two females made exceptions. At Polar Bear Pass (1968), the female allowed a leveret 2 weeks old (who arrived 4 minutes after the group suckle had ended) to nurse. The following day, a leveret again missed the group suckle and was allowed to nurse 5 minutes after the regular bout had ended. Then the female allowed two of the young to resuckle - the only recorded instance of such behaviour. In addition, in five instances in 1987 (when the leverets were approximately 3 weeks old), the female allowed a single young to nurse after it missed the group suckle. In three cases in 1987, the second suckle occurred within 4-5 minutes of the initial suckle. In two instances, there was a gap of 9 minutes and the female had started to leave the nursing site when she returned and nursed the late young. In all cases, the late suckle was of comparable duration to the group suckle, demonstrating flexibility, at least during the first four weeks of nursing.

Termination of Nursing Bouts and Dispersal

The female terminated the nursing bout in all cases, except for two in 1987, when a young hare stopped suckling and left before the others had finished. When the female was about to end a nursing bout she got up on all fours while turning. Then she hopped away, leaving the young behind.

When the leverets were very young, the Polar Bear Pass female frequently stopped about 1 m from the nursing spot, groomed her belly in the region of the mammae and then fed - interspersed with hopping, resting and/or grooming as she gradually moved away from the young. She spent most of the time between nursing bouts alternately feeding and resting several hundred metres from the nest. She disappeared only when a wolf came on 29 June and on several subsequent days, and stayed away for up to 13 hours. By the time the young were 10 days old, the female remained in the nursing area for about 2 hours after each nursing bout. She continued to do this fairly regularly until observations ended when the young were approximately 2 weeks old. When observations began at Sverdrup Pass in 1986, the female nursing young 5 weeks old left the nursing site (and usually the nursing area) immediately after nursing ended.

All three females usually departed along one of several routes they used for approaching their respective nursing sites. However, for a given nursing session a female often would arrive by one route and leave by another.

At first, the leverets at Polar Bear Pass remained in the nest for up to a few minutes before scattering several metres in different directions, or they dispersed immediately after nursing had ended. When about a week old, some of the leverets began following the female for a short time. As one of the leverets came close to its mother, the adult usually hopped away a short distance. This sequence could be repeated a number of times before the young ceased following the mother. By the time they were 2 weeks old some leverets spent up to 2 minutes following the mother after nursing.

Five-week-old young (Sverdrup Pass 1986, 1987) did not always attempt to follow their mother. Sometimes they stayed together for varying lengths of time, feeding close to each other and/or resting. Eventually, they would disperse individually, or two would leave together.

More often, they ran quickly after the mother, who could readily out-distance them. The female either ran until she was out of sight, or she stopped at some distance to groom, rest or feed. At least one young would often attempt to follow her. If any leverets came close, the mother would get up and hop farther away. She would continue until all the young had dropped out. Even when the young caught up with their mother, they rarely attempted to resuckle. If they did, the female invariably moved away. The doe usually did not aggressively rebuff the young, but twice in 1987 this was observed. In both cases, the leveret attempted to suckle again after following the female some distance from the nursing area. The female lunged aggressively at it with her forepaws, although not coming into direct contact. The leveret responded by racing wildly in many directions within a few metres and jumping up. This occurred for several seconds before it abruptly stopped and the young fed quietly near the female. The doe watched this behaviour and when it was over also began to feed quietly nearby.

Both the time the young spent with the mother and the distance they followed her increased with age. By the sixth week (Sverdrup Pass 1986), the young usually followed the female away from the nursing site (Figure 2). At least one young spent 1 hour 25 minutes feeding in the company of its mother and two other adults. In 1987 the young were observed to spend up to 1 hour 15 minutes with the female after nursing.

658

FIGURE 2: Two young hares following their mother as she leaves the nursing site at Sverdrup Pass, 18 August 1986. Photograph by David R. Gray, NMNS.

Whenever leverets from all three families left the nursing area without following the mother, they tended to disperse in different directions along regularly used individual routes. Patterns of route use began to emerge when leverets were in their second week at Polar Bear Pass, but became most evident in older leverets - especially the individually marked ones observed at Sverdrup Pass in 1987. Variations in routes increased with age. In 1987 two of the leverets tended to spend more time together between nursing, and on at least one occasion the whole interval between suckling was spent together.

The dispersal distance also increased as the young hares matured. In 1987, young about 6 weeks old were seen foraging up to 1 km from the nursing site.

Duration of Nursing Period

Weaning of young hares took place in mid- to late-August. Both litters at Sverdrup Pass nursed for about 8 to 9 weeks. On 22 August 1986 and on 16 August 1987, the female did not appear at the nursing site, though in both cases the female was observed in the usual feeding areas. In 1986 both young hares stayed at the site in the absence of the female for 10 hours before leaving. One appeared at the site at the appropriate time the following day and then stopped coming.

On 15 August 1987, two young were at the nursing site when an arctic fox came into the area just before the projected arrival of the female. The fox chased the two leverets out of the area along the path on which the female usually arrived. The female did not appear and the suckle did not occur. Approximately 30 minutes later the female was observed feeding several hundred metres from the site. The next day the same two young were present, but the female did not appear. The young did not appear on the following day.

At Borup Fiord in 1988, determination of weaning was complicated by an arctic fox attacking the young. On 22 July a fox killed a leveret after chasing several at the nursing area. The doe suckled three leverets after the attack, as well as on the following day. Three leverets spent 2 hours at the site on 24 July and two appeared at the appropriate time on 25 July, after which none of the hares was seen again, despite extensive searching.

Contact with Adults Apart from the Mother

Contact of leverets in the nursing area with other adult hares was rare. In 1987, other adults were never observed at or near the nursing site. Although several adult hares occasionally approached both nursing sites in 1986, few contacts occurred. One case of leverets apparently attempting to suckle a strange hare was observed at Polar Bear Pass in 1986. At Sverdrup Pass (1986), adult hares apart from the mother were observed at or near the nursing site on several occasions when the young were in their fifth and sixth weeks. Only on 8 August did the young interact with an adult. Approximately 20 minutes before nursing, two young hares were at the nursing site when an adult came out of the canyon entrance frequently used by their mother. Both young ran toward it. The adult hopped a few steps with the young following, then stopped and both young rushed to it. One young hare wedged its head under the adult, which was standing in a horizontal position, and attempted to nurse. The adult lowered its head toward the young hare and appeared to sniff it, then hopped away with the two young following closely. When a third leveret came out of the canyon entrance, its siblings ran to it, crouched as if to suckle, then nuzzled and sniffed it. Subsequently, the same adult approached again and sniffed one of the leverets, which hopped a short distance away. This was repeated several times and several young were involved. After 7 minutes, the adult fed near the young but no longer attempted to sniff them. Three minutes later the adult left. As far as could be determined, the hare was not lactating and may not even have been a female. After it departed, the young continued to wait for their mother.

As the young grew, they followed their mother for increasing distances until they accompanied her to feeding areas used by other hares. Here, the young contacted other adults. In 1986 this was first observed on 5 August, when the young were in their sixth week. In 1987 the first observed contact occurred on 1 August. On 11 August, two young were observed feeding with two adults (one a marked male and one possibly their mother) about 0.5 km from the nursing site. The hares stayed together for 6.5 hours, during which the male several times chased the young for a short distance.

DISCUSSION AND CONCLUSION

Parental behaviour in the arctic hare (*Lepus arcticus*) is similar to that described for the brown hare (*L. europaeus*) (Broekhuizen and Maaskamp 1980) and the showshoe hare (*L. americanus*) (Rongstad and Tester 1971) with one notable exception: *L. arcticus* does not nurse on a 24-hour cycle. Other hare species live at latitudes with distinct day-and-night periods. Studies have shown that in these species nursing is linked with sunset (Broekhuizen and Maaskamp 1980; Rongstad and Tester 1971). At high latitudes in the Queen Elizabeth Islands, 24-hour daylight exists from well before the time hares are born until weaning. Nursing cycles of *L. arcticus* varied between 18 hours 5 minutes and 19 hours 48 minutes, but were remarkably constant for each family. Such cycles are, necessarily, independent of the daily light regime. The few data on delayed nursing suggest that the female follows an internal clock and is not greatly influenced by the time at which she actually nurses her young.

The 18 or 19-hour nursing cycle may be an important survival factor in the short arctic summer because it increases the number of suckles per unit time. For example, over 8 weeks, arctic hare leverets on an 18-hour cycle would be nursed 75 times, whereas the young of species on a 24-hour cycle would be nursed only 56 times. This extra nursing may accelerate growth and maturation.

The shorter nursing cycle also ensures that the time of nursing is more difficult to predict than when young are nursed at a constant time of day. In addition, the brief amount of time the conspicuous adult spends with the young hares, that are initially cryptically coloured, further reduces the chance of predation.

The location of nesting/nursing sites on exposed ridges and slopes away from areas regularly used by other hares helps to ensure that leverets are not approached undetected at the nursing location. It may serve to minimize leveret mortality, since predators tend to visit areas where prospective prey is abundant. It also results in minimal contact of young hares with adults apart from their mother. Limited observations indicate, however, that young hares at the nursing site will attempt to suckle strange adults, and adults are not aggressive towards strange young.

Young hares that miss a nursing bout are not usually suckled until the next nursing session. Although resuckling is highly unusual, it can occur.

Female brown (*Lepus europaeus*), snowshoe (*L. americanus*), and mountain (*L. timidus scoticus*) hares nurse their final litters of a season (when not pregnant) for 6-8 weeks, although they usually wean earlier litters at 3-4 weeks (Broekhuizen and Maaskamp 1980; Flux 1970; Rongstad and Tester 1971; Severaid 1942 (in Rongstad and Tester 1971)). The 8-to-9-week nursing-period of the arctic hare (*L. arcticus*) is not unusually long as hares in the study area have only one litter per year.

ACKNOWLEDGEMENTS

This project was carried out under the auspices of the National Museum of Natural Sciences (NMNS). The authors gratefully acknowledge the invaluable logistical support provided by the Polar Continental Shelf Project. Additional logistical support was generously provided by First Air of Ottawa. The authors are grateful to S.D. MacDonald and D.A. Gill (NMNS) for collecting some data from Bathurst Island and to R. Burton (British Joint Services Expedition to Borup Fiord) for collecting additional material from that part of Ellesmere Island. The first author is indebted to S.D. MacDonald for the opportunity to work at Polar Bear Pass, and thanks S.A. Edlund for helpful comments on this paper.

REFERENCES

Begerud, A.T. 1967. The distribution and abundance of arctic hares in Newfoundland. Canadian Field-Naturalist 81(4):242-248.

Blake, W., Jr. 1974. Periglacial features and landscape evolution, central Bathurst Island, District of Franklin. Geological Survey of Canada, Paper 74-1B:235-244.

Bonnyman, S.G. 1975. Behavioural ecology of *Lepus arcticus*. M.Sc. thesis, Carleton University, Ottawa. 35 pp.

Broekhuizen, S., E. Bouman, and W. Went. 1986. Variation in timing of nursing in the brown hare (*Lepus europaeus*) and the European rabbit (*Oryctolagus cuniculus*). Mammal Review 16(3/4):139-144.

Broekhuizen, S. and F. Maaskamp. 1980. Behaviour of does and leverets of the European hare (*Lepus europaeus*) whilst nursing. Journal of Zoology 191:487-501.

Flux, J.E.C. 1970. Life history of the mountain hare (*Lepus timidus scoticus*) in northeast Scotland. Journal of Zoology 161:75-123.

Hampson, C.G. 1968. Notes on the behaviour of arctic hares on Bathurst Island, Summer 1968. National Museum of Natural Sciences. Unpublished report. 43 pp.

Hearn, B.J., B.K. Lloyd and O.J. Rongstad. 1987. Demography and ecology of the arctic hare (*Lepus arcticus*) in southwestern Newfoundland. Canadian Journal of Zoology 65(4):852-861.

Lloyd, B.K. 1981. Population dynamics of hares. In: Proceedings of the World Lagomorph Conference (Guelph, Ontario, 1979). Edited by: K. Myers and C.D. MacInnes. pp. 395-440.

Mercer, W.E., B.J. Hearn and C. Finlay. 1981. Arctic hare populations in insular Newfoundland. In: Proceedings of the World Lagomorph Conference (Guelph Ontario, 1979). Edited by: K. Myers and C.D. MacInnes. pp. 450-468.

Parker, G.R. 1977. Morphology, reproduction, diet, and behavior of the arctic hare (*Lepus arcticus monstrabilis*) on Axel Heiberg Island, Northwest Territories. Canadian Field-Naturalist 91(1):8-18.

Pedersen, A. 1962. Polar animals. Harrap, London. 180 pp.

Rongstad, O.J. and J.R. Tester. 1971. Behavior and maternal relations of young snowshoe hares. Journal of Wildlife Management 35(2):338-346.

Severaid, J.H. 1942. The snowshoe hare; its life history and artificial propagation. Maine Department of Inland Fisheries and Game, Augusta. 95 pp.

Sheard, J.W. and D.W. Geale. 1983. Vegetation studies at Polar Bear Pass, Bathurst Island, N.W.T. I. Classification of plant communities. Canadian Journal of Botany 61:1618-1636.

Walkinshaw, L.H. 1947. Notes on the arctic hare. Journal of Mammology 28(4):353-357.

Illustrated by Brenda Carter

HUMAN PREHISTORY

THE PEOPLING OF THE ARCTIC ISLANDS

Robert McGhee[1]

Abstract: Arctic Canada was the last major region of the habitable world to be occupied by mankind. Early Indian occupants of Canada inhabited the Arctic mainland on a seasonal basis by at least 8,000 years ago, but did not penetrate the Arctic Archipelago. The first people to have developed a year-round Arctic adaptation were Paleo-Eskimos who probably came from Asia about 4,000 years ago, basing their Arctic adaptation on two Asiatic inventions: the bow-and-arrow, and finely tailored skin clothing. For the following 3,000 years, Paleo-Eskimos were the primary occupants of most arctic regions, including all but the northwestern islands of the Arctic Archipelago. The Paleo-Eskimos disappeared from the Arctic Islands about 1,000 years ago an event which is related to the expansion of Neo-Eskimo peoples from Alaska, the ancestors of the present Canadian Inuit. These people had developed an extremely efficient maritime adaptation in the marine mammal-rich waters of the Bering Sea, and this adaptation was transferred to much of the Arctic Islands. The development of the Inuit way of life in Arctic Canada occurred over the past millennium during a period of deteriorating climate, which resulted in an impoverishment of the earlier Inuit economy and culture. This process culminated in the Little Ice Age (1600-1850), which saw the Inuit abandon the High Arctic islands.

Résumé: Le Canada arctique est la dernière grande région habitable du monde à être peuplée par l'homme. Il y a au moins 8 000 ans, les Indiens du Canada en occupaient la partie continentale de façon saisonnière, mais ils ne pénétrèrent pas dans l'archipel arctique. Les premiers hommes à vivre en permanence dans l'Arctique furent les Paléo-Esquimaux. Sans doute venus d'Asie voilà environ 4 000 ans, il s'adaptèrent au milieu arctique grâce à deux inventions asiatiques: l'arc et des vêtements de peau finement façonnés. Trois mille ans durant, les Paléo-Esquimaux furent les principaux occupants de la plupart des régions arctiques, y compris tout l'archipel arctique à l'exception des îles du nord-ouest. Ils disparurent des îles il y a environ 1 000 ans, à l'époque de l'expansion des peuples Néo-Esquimaux d'Alaska, ancêtres des présents Inuit du Canada. Les Néo-Esquimaux s'étaient extrêmement bien adaptés à un milieu maritime, celui de la mer de Béring aux eaux riches en mammifères marins, et transportèrent leurs usages dans une grande partie des îles arctiques. Les Inuit du Canada arctique ont développé leur mode de vie au cours du dernier millénaire, période durant laquelle le climat s'est détérioré, entraînant un appauvrissement de l'économie et de la culture antérieures des Inuit. La situation devait continuer de se dégrader jusqu'au Petit âge glaciaire (1600-1850) qui vit les Inuits abandonner les îles de l'Extrême-Arctique.

The Arctic Islands are the homeland of the Inuit. According to Inuit tradition, they have lived in the area since the beginning of the world. The view of the Inuit in popular Canadian culture is somewhat similar. Schoolchildren are taught of the Inuit as the supreme example of the human ability to adapt to their environment; the impression is given that these people have lived in Arctic Canada for countless generations, gradually developing a technology and a way of life which has made them as much at home in the Arctic as are the seals and the caribou. The story of the peopling of the Arctic Islands that comes from archaeological research is quite different; it is a story which is much more complex, and much more human, than that told by either Inuit tradition or popular culture.

Humans are tropical animals. Our ancient ape-like ancestors first stood upright, developed large brains, and learned how to use sticks and stones as tools in the savannahs of the equatorial belt. It is not surprising that the Arctic tundras, polar deserts and icefields

---

[1] Archaeological Survey of Canada, Canadian Museum of Civilization, Ottawa, Ontario, K1A 0M8

were not occupied until mankind had developed fully modern skills, and a technology which allowed survival in northern climates. It was at some time during the last Ice Age, between about 80,000 and 15,000 years ago, that humans developed these capabilities.

Arctic Canada was the last major region of the habitable world to be occupied by people. Although the westernmost part of the area, unglaciated throughout the last Ice Age, saw the first Paleo-Indian immigrants to North America at some time between 12,000 and 20,000 years ago, little trace of their passing has been clearly identified. In the warming climates of the early postglacial period, the descendants of these people began to push northward into the mainland Arctic, leaving traces of Paleo-Indian occupation on the Barren Grounds west of Hudson Bay, and on coastal Labrador, as early as 8,000 years ago.

By this time, most of the Arctic was as habitable as it is today. For the following 4,000 years, however, the Arctic coast and islands remained unoccupied. The Indian groups which inhabited the mainland Barren Grounds appear to have done so on a seasonal basis, much as did the Chipewyan of the Historic period. In the summer they followed the caribou north into the tundra, and in the autumn they retreated to treeline, where the forests provided fuel and shelter from the winter. No group had yet learned how to survive the entire year north of treeline. When such people did appear, it seems likely that they came from Asia, and they based their Arctic adaptation on two Asiatic inventions which were not known previously in the New World: the bow-and-arrow, and finely-tailored skin clothing of an Old World pattern.

The first immigrants were a people who are known to archaeologists as Paleo-Eskimos ("Old Eskimos"), as distinct from the Neo-Eskimo ("New Eskimo") ancestors of the Canadian Inuit. The Paleo-Eskimos are a strangely intriguing people, if only because we know so little about them. They may not have even been Eskimos, in the sense that they may not have spoken a language of the Eskimo family, although they probably spoke a related language; and in physical type were of the same northern Asiatic stock. The Paleo-Eskimos were the first to occupy the islands of the Canadian Arctic Archipelago. They appear suddenly in the archaeological record across Arctic North America, from Alaska to Greenland, approximately 4,000 years ago. Their technology hints at Siberian origins. The tools which they chipped from flint are very distinctive, and resemble those which have been excavated by Soviet archaeologists from 5,000 year old Neolithic sites in eastern Siberia. Their Asiatic origin is also reflected in the remains of their tents, as found archaeologically

FIGURE 1: Remains of an early Paleo-Eskimo tent with central hearth and midpassage structure. Porden Point, Devon Island.

on Arctic beaches. These so-called midpassage structures are marked by a central box-hearth built of stone slabs, with two sides extended to form a central work-area separating two living or sleeping areas on either side (Figure 1). This is a characteristic northern Asiatic form, similar to the traditional Sammi (Lapp) house of northern Europe, and of the Samoyedic peoples of Siberia. The Paleo-Eskimos brought with them from Siberia an adaptation which allowed people to live on all but the most remote northwestern Arctic Islands. For the following 3,000 years, their descendants were the primary occupants of most arctic regions, occasionally expanding southward as far as Lake Athabaska in the west, and the island of Newfoundland in the east.

The early Paleo-Eskimos seem to have led lives of terrifying simplicity and endurance, lacking many of the technological items that allowed later Inuit occupants of the Arctic to live in relative comfort. Although the Arctic climate of 4,000 years ago was slightly warmer than at present, it was still a treeless country where winter temperatures regularly fell below -30°C for weeks on end, through the darkness of the winter night. Yet the Paleo-Eskimos seem to have lived throughout the year in skin-covered tents, heated only by occasional small fires of animal fat, bones, chips of driftwood and willow twigs. There is no evidence that they possessed boats or dog-hauled sleds, which must have limited not only their hunting capabilities but their ability to move in order to escape starvation if local game resources failed. Their main weapons were the bow, and the harpoon with hand-held retrieving line, lacking the harpoon-float equipment which allowed the later Inuit to kill sea mammals larger than seals with relative ease. Settlements seem to have been very small and temporary. Their total population may have consisted of only a few hundred people scattered over several million square kilometres of Arctic landscape. Yet the Paleo-Eskimos managed to survive, although marginal regions such as the High Arctic islands seem to have been largely abandoned after the climatic deterioration which began some 3,500 years ago.

Although the archaeologist may be appalled by the remains of such an apparently meagre way of life, the meagreness does not show in the artifacts that we find around the camps of these Arctic pioneers. Their craftsmen seem to have been interested in more than the functional aspects of these tools: they selected multicoloured stones, chipped them very evenly and symmetrically, often with decorative edge serration, and their extremely small size suggests that great

FIGURE 2: Small chipped-stone points for lances, arrows and harpoons. Early Paleo-Eskimo, Port Refuge, Devon Island.

value was placed on the skill necessary to create such miniature pieces (Figure 2). Flintworking is one of our oldest and most difficult crafts, yet few cultures have surpassed the early Paleo-Eskimos in their skill in handling this intractable material. If we can call this an art form, then its usefulness and portability would seem to have been perfectly suited to the lifestyle of these first occupants of Arctic North America. These beautifully-crafted tools are welcome evidence that we are looking at the remains of people who not only survived, but who enjoyed their lives.

Beginning nearly 2,500 years ago, Paleo-Eskimos across Arctic Canada began to develop techniques that must have made their lives more comfortable and secure. Winter houses with stone and turf walls were used in some areas, and dwellings were now heated and lighted by oil lamps carved from soapstone. There is slight evidence that they may have possessed dogs, and perhaps kayaks, which must have greatly increased the efficiency of their hunting. The remains of their settlements are larger and represent more permanent habitations than did those of their ancestors. These later Paleo-Eskimos are known as the Dorset people - named after the Baffin Island community of Cape Dorset where their archaeological remains were first recognized. The Dorset culture dominated Arctic Canada until it suddenly disappeared from most regions about 1000 years ago.

The Dorset culture developed in the eastern Arctic during a period when the climate was rapidly cooling. For an ice-hunting people such as the Paleo-Eskimos, such a change may have provided greater hunting opportunities, a challenge to the usual assumption that colder climates make living conditions more difficult for northern peoples. The Dorset people spread southward as far as Newfoundland, where they were the primary occupants for 1,000 years, and northward to Ellesmere Island and northern Greenland. Wherever they went, they left in the ruins of their camps unique pieces of art: tiny, exquisite sculptures in ivory, antler and wood, representing humans, other animals, and spirits.

These carvings appear to have been made during the 1,500 years that Dorset people occupied Arctic Canada: but during most of this time, only a few scattered examples of such carvings are known. However, during the final two or three centuries of the Dorset period, approximately 1,000 years ago, there was a great explosion of artistic production. This coincides with a major expansion of Dorset occupation to many parts of the Arctic Archipelago which appear to have been abandoned, or very sparsely populated, during the preceding centuries. For a few generations, Dorset people lived from Labrador to northwestern Greenland, and across the Arctic Islands to the shores of Amundsen Gulf. It is these people who produced most of the carvings that make up our collections of Dorset art. It was an artistic tradition rooted in the Paleo-Eskimo past, but which flourished for only a few generations, and was remarkably standardized across the Arctic, apparently through widespread communication networks, and perhaps even through trade in carvings themselves.

The carvings, which appear to have been intimately associated with shamanistic religion, afford us a rare insight into the beliefs of the Dorset people: wooden masks probably used by a shaman in rituals of curing or hunting magic; sets of carved animal teeth designed to be held in the human mouth in order to give the impression of transformation into an animal; small wooden carvings of people or animals which have been magically "killed" with a slit in the throat or chest (the slit sometimes contains a spike of wood); and the skeletal motif added to many carvings, particularly those of bears, perhaps relating to the importance of the skeleton in shamanic thought.

The meaning and use of other objects is less clear. Portions of caribou antler carved with up to 60 human or human-like faces may be cartoon-like portraits of the members of a local community, representations of a pantheon of spirits, or a shaman's record of his varied spirit-helpers. Pendants in the form of animals may have been used as personal amulets. Other carvings of animals may simply have been playthings, or objects made for the delight of the artist or his audience. Using vague estimates of community size and duration of occupation from a Dorset site that I excavated a few years ago on Bathurst Island in the High Arctic, I have calculated that between approximately 0.1 and 1 carvings were lost or abandoned per person per year at the site. This figure suggests that carvings were produced or acquired with about the same frequency that present-day Canadians acquire wrist-watches or pocket-calculators: somewhere between once a year and once every ten years. It is tempting to guess that these carvings may have had a similar level of significance, or usefulness, to the Dorset people as that which we apply to such personal items. From these carvings we obtain a rare glimpse of the aesthetic and spiritual life of an extinct people, a people whose world was populated with humans and animals whose spirits could be magically controlled by shamans in order to combat illness, bad weather, or poor luck at hunting.

The great florescence of Dorset carvings about 1,000 years ago also marked the approaching end of the Dorset people, and may perhaps be in some way related to the stresses produced by a changing environment and the arrival of newcomers in their lands. So the Dorset Paleo-Eskimos disappeared from most Arctic regions about 1,000 years ago, surviving only in the Ungava Peninsula of northern Quebec and Labrador until perhaps 500 years ago. The disappearance of the Dorset people coincided with, and is almost certainly related to, the expansion into their territory of Neo-Eskimos from Alaska, the ancestors of the present Canadian Inuit. These people were descended either from Alaskan Paleo-Eskimos, or from an earlier group of people who had crossed the Bering Isthmus and established a maritime hunting way of life in southern Alaska. By the final millennium B.C. (about 3,000-2,000 years ago), these people found themselves between, and in at least occasional contact with, two rapidly developing culture areas: to the west, the Bronze and Iron Age peoples of Siberia, and to the south the Indian peoples of the Northwest Coast. Between roughly 2,500 and 1,000 years ago, they developed an extremely efficient maritime adaptation in the marine mammal-rich waters of the Bering Sea, and had evolved most of the technology characteristic of later Eskimo cultures: half-buried (semi-subterranean) winter houses covered with turf and heated by oil-lamps; skin-covered kayaks and larger umiaks capable of pursuing whales or carrying an entire camp; efficient float-harpoon gear, sinew-backed bows; and other hunting and fishing weapons. These people could no longer be classified as belonging to the stone age, since their technology was dependent on small pieces of metal obtained by trade from the civilizations of China or Central Asia.

About 1,000 years ago the Arctic climate became somewhat warmer, in step with that of Europe where the time is characterized as the Mediaeval Warm Period. This warming may have resulted in a decrease in sea ice in Arctic Canada and a consequent extension of the range of the bowhead whale, the 10 to 20 m long animal that was a prime prey of the Eskimos of northern Alaska. These conditions may have encouraged the movement of Alaskan Eskimos eastwards into Arctic Canada. There is a possibility, however, that the warming climate and decreased sea ice merely allowed such a movement, and that the impetus behind the invasion of Arctic Canada was the presence of metal in the eastern Arctic: meteoritic iron from the Cape York meteorite fall in northwestern Greenland. It is interesting that what appear to be the earliest Thule sites known in the eastern Arctic occur in northwestern Greenland and on adjacent Ellesmere Island, and contain quantities of not only meteoritic iron but of smelted metal obtained from the Greenlandic Norse.

Whatever the reason behind the Eskimo expansion eastward, the evidence suggests swift occupation of most Arctic regions, and the archaeological disappearance of the Dorset people. Inuit legends tell of their ancestors killing or driving away a race of people called *tunnit* who were the previous occupants of Arctic Canada. If we can identify the legendary *tunnit* with the archaeologically-known Dorset people, then legend and archaeology appear to support one another: the Paleo-Eskimos were killed or driven to extinction about 1,000 years ago, at the hands of the early Inuit invaders.

These whale-hunting immigrants, the ancestors of the Inuit, are known as the people of the Thule culture, named for the community in northern Greenland where their remains were first discovered. The Thule expansion eastward resulted in the wholesale transfer of an Alaskan culture and way of life across the Canadian and Greenlandic Arctic. Permanent winter villages similar to those of their Alaskan ancestors were established, but the houses were built from boulders and whale bones rather than driftwood logs (Figure 3). Adapting their hunting technology to local conditions, they were capable in most regions of maintaining a way of life comparable to that of their Alaskan relatives. By about 800 years ago, this way of life had been established across all but the most remote northwestern Arctic Islands.

The Dorset *tunnit* were not the only people whom the Inuit met in the Arctic Islands. Very soon after they arrived in Arctic Canada, they encountered the Norse who had recently established colonies in southwestern Greenland, and who appear to have made at least occasional visits to northeastern Canada over a period of a several centuries. A few items of European origin are found in most Thule villages: small pieces of smelted iron or copper, fragments of chain mail, boat-nails, and objects such as a portion of a bronze trader's balance found on Ellesmere Island. Visits by the Norse to the Arctic Islands are suggested by an Inuit carving of a person in European clothing, found in a thirteenth century Thule village on Baffin Island. In Greenland, there is growing evidence that the Inuit and the Norse shared the country in apparent peace for at least two centuries.

But despite their apparent success, the Thule Inuit occupation of Arctic Canada was essentially the transposition of a way of life that was adapted to the coasts of the Bering and Beaufort seas, to a region which could only temporarily support such an existence. After the twelfth century, the climate began to deteriorate, sea ice increased in both extent and seasonal duration, and the ranges of large whales must have been considerably restricted. Whale stocks may have been further reduced by European hunting in the North Atlantic, which began on a large scale during the sixteenth century. By the seventeenth century, when Europe entered a period of cold climate called the Little Ice Age, Thule people throughout the Arctic Islands had begun to revert to a way of life similar to that of their

FIGURE 3: Reconstructed Thule winter house with whale mandible roof supports. Brooman Point, Bathurst Island.

Dorset predecessors. Summers were no longer spent hunting whales (Figure 4) and other large sea mammals from boats in open water, but hunting inland caribou, muskoxen or fishes. The lack of summer-stored food made the occupation of large permanent winter villages of whale bone and turf houses impossible, and people began using temporary snow-houses on the sea-ice, from which they could hunt small ringed-seals, the only abundant prey during the arctic winter. Only in the relatively warm and ice-free regions of Greenland, Labrador, and portions of Baffin Island, were people capable of maintaining an essentially Thule way of life until the time of European contact.

When European explorers began to penetrate the Arctic Islands during the eighteenth and nineteenth centuries, they described a series of Inuit cultures which were so meagre, and so ingenious in their adaptations to the harshest habitable region of the world, that it was generally considered that such ways of life were the result of millennia of adaptation to such a severe environment. What we have learned from archaeology is that this is

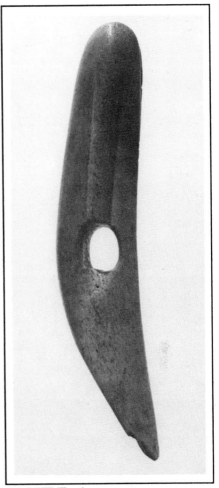

FIGURE 4: Whaling harpoon head carved from whale bone. Early Thule culture, Porden Point, Devon Island.

not true: traditional Canadian Inuit ways of life are the remnants of what, a few centuries ago, was a much richer and more sophisticated culture, and one that adjusted rapidly through a series of make shift adaptations to a deteriorating climate and environment, during the centuries immediately preceding European contact.

As I mentioned at the beginning of this paper, the development of Inuit culture in Arctic Canada was neither simple nor direct. It is not a story of simple and gradual, animal-like adaptation to a harsh environment. Rather it is a complex story involving population expansions into unused areas, survival or retreat when things went badly, invasions, and learning to live with and profit from strange peoples. It is a story which, although unique, involved processes which were not all that simpler than, or different from, those affecting the histories of most human populations.

REFERENCES

Dumond, D.E. 1977. The Eskimos and Aleuts. Thames and Hudson, London.

Maxwell, M.S. 1986. Eastern Arctic prehistory. Academic Press, Orlando.

McGhee, R. 1978. Canadian Arctic prehistory. Van Nostrand Reinhold. Toronto.

July 20 1977
Whalebone from Thule site

Illustrated by Brenda Carter

THULE PIONEERS IN THE CANADIAN ARCTIC

Charles D. Arnold[1] and Karen McCullough[2]

Abstract: Archaeological investigations on Banks Island in the western Canadian Arctic and on Ellesmere Island in the east have revealed evidence for pioneering groups of Thule Inuit in each of those areas. The Banks Island occupation represents the initial expansion of Thule into the Canadian Arctic, and the sites on Ellesmere Island contain archaeological remains of a later group that migrated eastward from Alaska. These data show the complex nature of processes involved in the prehistoric development of Inuit culture.

Résumé: Des recherches archéologiques sur l'île Banks, dans l'ouest de l'Arctique canadien, et sur l'île Ellesmere dans l'est, ont montré avec certitude la présence de groupes de pionniers inuit de Thulé à ces endroits. L'occupation de l'île Banks représente l'expansion, dans les débuts, de Thulé dans l'Arctique canadien, alors que les sites de l'île Ellesmere renferment des vestiges archéologiques d'un groupe postérieur, migrant de l'Alaska vers l'est. Ces informations illustrent la complexité des processus qu font partie du développement préhistorique de la culture des Inuits.

INTRODUCTION

Geographical shifts were a common fact of life for Inuit in pre-contact times. Nomadic groups of Inuit migrated to follow or to intercept game, to seek out new hunting grounds, to obtain raw materials from distant sources, and for many other reasons. Inuit often moved on foot, but they also possessed a well-developed transportation technology that included dog-drawn sledges and skin-covered boats which allowed them to move whole camps. They also had an open, flexible social system which facilitated the movement of people by accommodating newcomers.

Most of these movements probably took place within a known geographic area, but periodically in the history of the Canadian Arctic there were long-distance migrations of people, which took them into unoccupied or only sparsely occupied territories. In addition to expanding the geographic range of a culture, the process of colonizing new territory also served as an agent for cultural change. This paper summarizes investigations of two pioneering episodes involving the immediate ancestors of the present-day Inuit, whose culture is known archaeologically by the term "Thule". These investigations took place at opposite ends of the Canadian Arctic (Figure 1), and so provide us with a unique perspective on the early movements of the Thule people into their new homeland.

[1] Prince of Wales Northern Heritage Centre, Yellowknife, Northwest Territories X1A 2L9
[2] The Arctic Institute of North America, University of Calgary, Calgary, Alberta T2N 1N4

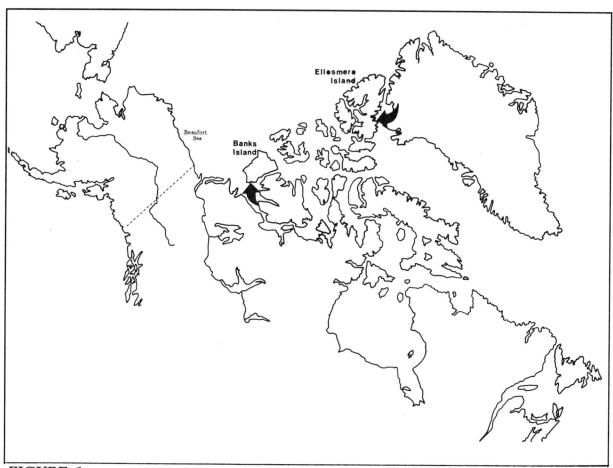

FIGURE 1: The study areas. The Nelson River site is indicated by the arrow pointing to southeastern Banks Island, and the Skraeling Island sites are situated at the tip of the arrow pointing to eastern Ellesmere Island.

EARLY THULE MIGRATIONS

Origin and Expansion of Thule

The Thule people were not the first to live in the far northern parts of Canada. An earlier migration that began about 4,000 years ago saw even more ancient people whom archaeologists call "Paleo-Eskimos", move out of western Alaska into the Canadian Arctic and Greenland, eventually extending along the northeastern coast of North America and into Newfoundland (Figure 2; McGhee, this volume). Within this vast geographic expanse, local Paleo-Eskimo cultures developed and changed as time progressed. Some of the most far-reaching cultural developments took place in the Bering Sea and Bering Strait regions of western Alaska. There, about 2,000 years ago, Paleo-Eskimos devised, or perhaps borrowed, the techniques and technology to hunt large sea mammals from boats. Accompanying this development were shifts in population, settlement and other factors which gave rise to what

678

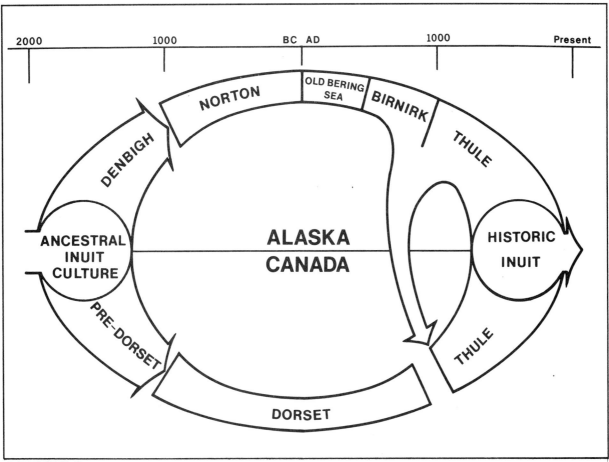

FIGURE 2: The way of life of the Thule people had its roots in earlier Neo-Eskimo cultures (Old Bering Sea and Birnirk) in Alaska, and in even more ancient Paleo-Eskimo cultures (Denbigh, Norton, Pre-Dorset, and Dorset).

have been termed the "Neo-Eskimo" cultures.

Nearly 1,100 years ago (about 900 AD), the regional expression of Neo-Eskimo culture known as Thule was poised at the western edge of the Canadian Arctic, then only sparsely occupied as the Paleo-Eskimos there had undergone a marked decline in geographic extent and numbers. The immediate ancestor of Thule culture was a phase, or variant, of Neo-Eskimo called Birnirk which had appeared several centuries before in northern Alaska, where people had adapted efficiently to the resources and environment of that area.

Archaeologists who have studied Thule culture have advanced several theories to account for the transition from Birnirk to Thule in northern Alaska, and for the subsequent movement of Thule people into the Canadian Arctic. One of these, which has gained a high degree of popularity, attaches considerable importance to evidence suggesting that those events occurred during a climatic trend underway by 900 AD which saw average temperatures in the Arctic become substantially warmer than those of today.

679

A climatic shift of this nature would have altered the distribution and availability of marine mammals in several important ways. According to a model developed by Robert McGhee (1969-1970), changes in the availability of bowhead whales were of paramount importance to the appearance of Thule culture. During the Birnirk period in northern Alaska, techniques were devised to hunt whales in spring when they began to move eastward through narrow leads that develop along the southern edge of the pack ice. Before 900 AD, when the climate was like today's, these leads probably were inshore and bowhead whales were easy to spot and chase using umiaks launched in the open water leads. But the actual kill must have been a dangerous affair. The model supposes that the post-900 AD warming would have shifted the position of pack ice northward, so the spring open water leads might have been too far offshore for such hunting to be feasible. In order to continue the whale kill, a shift to a summer hunt in the open water would have been required. The normal summering grounds of bowheads are in the eastern Beaufort Sea. If a shift to open water hunting was made, then those waters would have presented better opportunities for hunting than would the northern coast of Alaska, where whales are found only briefly during spring and fall migrations.

These and other interdependent events may have triggered the development and initial expansion of Thule. Until recently it was difficult to assess this model, since the archaeological trail left by early Thule migrants was sparse, and the meagre evidence controversial. Now, we have clear evidence of pioneering Thule groups from at least two parts of the Canadian Arctic, southern Banks Island and northeastern Ellesmere Island, which can be used to evaluate and perhaps to refine this model.

Nelson River Thule

In 1980 and 1981, Arnold (1986) conducted fieldwork on southern Banks Island, searching for archaeological remains from the early Thule period. There were several good reasons to suppose that such evidence could be found there.

Banks Island is the westernmost of the islands in the Canadian Arctic Archipelago, and as such is the closest to the Alaskan Thule homeland. It is richly vegetated by most arctic standards, and the plant life in turn supports an abundance of wildlife of economic interest to people, including the world's largest concentration of muskoxen. Peary caribou are also common, and multitudes of various species of waterfowl nest in the wet, low-lying parts of the island. Nutrient-rich waters flowing into the Beaufort Sea from the west bring migratory bowhead whales close to the southern shores, and more sedentary ringed and bearded seals are common. Given these biological and geographical factors, it seemed reasonable to expect that Banks Island would have been occupied by the pioneering Thule groups from Alaska.

Fieldwork designed to test this possibility focused near Nelson River on the southeastern coast of the island, in part because it juts out into the Beaufort Sea, and also because excavations at an archaeological site there in the 1950s had hinted at an early Thule presence. Altogether five Thule sites were investigated there during two field seasons. One in particular, the Nelson River site, seems to be from the culture's initial stage. Only one house at the Nelson River site was well preserved, but it yielded an abundance of information about the culture of the early pioneers.

The surface deposits on Banks Island are mainly sedimentary in origin, and geological forces have contributed to redeposition of sands and silts across the landscape. The remains of the Nelson River house, found in a low sand dune, were covered by as much as 1 m of overburden (Figure 3). They were firmly encased in permafrost, resulting in excellent preservation of architectural details, animal bones and artifacts. Excavations revealed the floor and parts of the walls of a substantial dwelling of two rooms, joined by their entrance tunnels (Figure 4).

According to our excavations, evidently the dwelling had been erected over a depression that had been dug into the ground. The main structural elements were posts and beams of driftwood which can be found in places along the shore of this part of the island. Adzed planks were used for the floor and walls, and perhaps for the roof. Next to one of the rooms we found a concentration of scorched rocks and charcoal cemented by seal oil, which we interpreted to have been a kitchen floor. Evidently walls did not enclose the kitchen, so perhaps cooking was done in a tent attached to the dwelling. This would have prevented smoke from driftwood cooking fires from polluting the main structure, and cooking in a tent also would have reduced the hazard of sparks igniting the dry driftwood structure of the house. The main part of the dwelling was covered with an insulating layer of sod blocks, weighted down with stones (Figure 5). Such structures are known to have been used throughout the Arctic as cold-season dwellings.

FIGURE 3: Archaeologist uncovering the remains of the Nelson River Thule house buried beneath approximately 1 m of overburden.

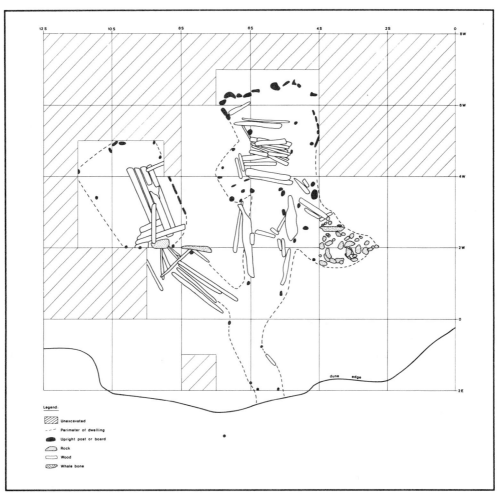

FIGURE 4: Plan view of the remains of the Nelson River house. Driftwood was used almost exclusively in the construction of the dwelling.

683

FIGURE 5: Artist's reconstruction of the driftwood Nelson River house, covered over with an insulating layer of turf.

More than 20,000 bones were excavated from the interior of the house and from an outside midden. A 10% sample was analyzed, on the assumption that this would clarify the overall economic pattern of the Nelson River Thule people (Figure 6). In terms of

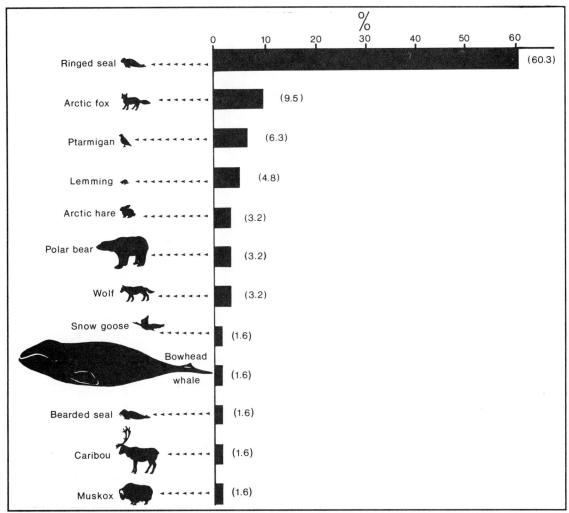

FIGURE 6: Percentages of animal species represented by bones excavated from the Nelson River house.

overall contribution to their diet, hunting sea mammals was of paramount importance. Ringed seals were by far the most frequently killed species, although bowhead whales probably contributed a larger amount of meat and oil (Savelle and McCartney, this volume). Even with this emphasis on sea mammals, the faunal assemblage showed that probably most of the vertebrates in the area had been hunted. Notably absent were fish bones, although we found (to our dismay) that fishing is unproductive near Nelson River. The low frequency of caribou in the assemblage seems anomalous, since caribou skins are almost essential for warm, lightweight winter clothing. Remembering, however, that this was a winter house, and since fall caribou pelts are the most desirable for making clothing, perhaps caribou were hunted earlier in the season, before the Nelson River Thule people moved to their winter quarters.

Abundant artifacts were recovered, representing a variety of hunting and domestic activities (Figure 7). Many artifacts had been made using techniques and materials that were closely related to Alaskan tool industries. Tools made of wood, and for working wood, were common. This reflects a ready access to driftwood, which is characteristic of Alaskan Thule. Many of the stone tools were shaped by flaking, a common western technique, although ground stone tools of the kind that later dominated the stone tool industry of the eastern Arctic Thule culture were also found. Lamps and cooking pots were made from clay - a common western Arctic trait - rather than from soapstone which was usually used for these purposes farther east.

The kinds of artifacts found

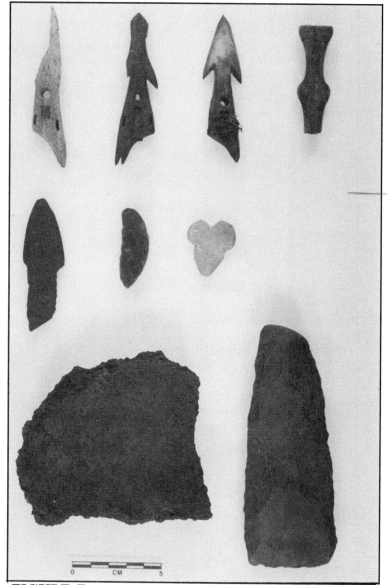

FIGURE 7: Artifacts from the Nelson River House. Top (left to right): harpoon heads, some of which retain Birnirk traits, Alaskan-style needle-case. Middle (left to right): ground stone knife blade, chipped stone scraper, whale effigy? Bottom (left to right): pottery sherd, adze blade.

are much like those made by the late Birnirk and early Thule peoples in Alaska. Harpoon heads in particular show this affiliation, suggesting a fairly early date for the Nelson River site. Radiocarbon age determinations support this suggestion. The average uncorrected date on four samples is 920 AD, with a correction factor advancing that date to 940. The transition from Birnirk to Thule is thought to have happened about 900, so apparently the Nelson River site was occupied shortly after that event.

To summarize, the Nelson River site is not far removed culturally or geographically from Birnirk in northern Alaska. For instance, the people who lived there retained the use of driftwood for housing and woodworking, made stone tools by flaking and by grinding, and used pottery. Specific artifact resemblances are apparent as well.

There are differences, too. Erosion at the Nelson River site has destroyed some of the houses, but we can guess by the generally small size of other house clusters in the area that it was smaller than most Birnirk settlements. Smaller camp sizes are predicted by McGhee's model for the transition from ice-lead to open-water whale hunting. Whales are less concentrated in the open water, and if the hunt should be unsuccessful the group's chances of survival are maximized if it is small enough to be sustained by other resources. Further differences include new and changed artifact types, but they are expected as adjustments are made to new environmental situations, and as lines of communication with people on the north Alaskan coast became attenuated.

The Nelson River site, then, conforms well to McGhee's model for Thule development and expansion. In its first phase this involved a shift into an area not too different from the north Alaskan homeland of the Thule culture, although new hunting strategies and resultant patterns of settlement were required. Other archaeological sites in the western Canadian Arctic, including several elsewhere on Banks Island, southern Victoria Island and on the mainland coast near Cape Parry, show that the Nelson River cultural configuration was not unique, and that this early pioneering movement was successful in colonizing the eastern margins of the Beaufort Sea.

Ruin Island Thule

The expansion of early Thule culture into the Canadian Beaufort Sea region was only the first step in its spread through most of the Canadian Arctic. Recent archaeological investigations of Thule culture sites in the vicinity of Alexandra Fiord on Ellesmere Island (at the eastern end of the Canadian Arctic; Figure 1) have revealed evidence of another, later pioneering episode.

The relatively low, dissected plateau area around Alexandra Fiord (79° North) represents one of the few, major unglaciated areas along the mountainous east coast of Ellesmere Island. Skraeling Island, near the entrance to Alexandra Fiord, contains two large Thule culture winter settlements with over 40 house ruins relating to various stages of occupation.

The earliest Thule culture houses on Skraeling Island belong to a distinctive period known as the Ruin Island phase, after an island by that name located off the coast of northwestern Greenland where its remains were first discovered in the early 1930s by the Danish archaeologist, Erik Holtved. The Ruin Island phase is characterized by a distinctive winter dwelling and by the retention of many western-related traits such as: Alaskan-style needle cases; harpoon heads with ornamental spurs and western design motifs; and the use of pottery for vessels and lamps.

The typical Ruin Island winter dwelling was half-buried (semi-subterranean) with broad exterior walls constructed of a double row of boulders (Figure 8). Since driftwood logs were scarce on eastern Ellesmere Island, large boulders and bowhead whale bones were used as structural supports for the roof which was covered with a thick, insulating layer of sod. The floor of the main room was generally unpaved except for a single piece of stone flagging which marked the edge of the sunken entrance passage (Figure 9). The presumed sleeping area at the back of the main room was marked by a slight rise in the sandy gravel floor, with a thin layer of heather used as part of the bedding. In a few cases, slab-stone sleeping platforms supported by stone uprights were built, although this was a more common occurrence in later Thule winter houses. The most distinctive feature of the Ruin Island winter houses was the construction of a separate kitchen extension paralleling the entrance passage (Figure 10). Each kitchen

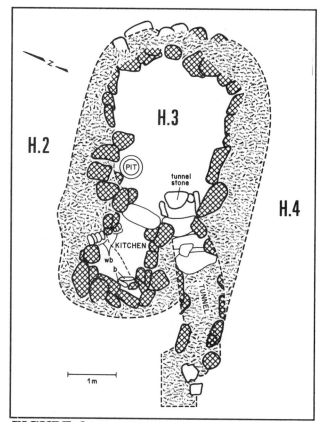

FIGURE 8: Skraeling Island Site, House 3.

688

FIGURE 9: Aerial view of House 6, Skraeling Island Site.

FIGURE 10: Skraeling Island Site, House 11, kitchen.

had its own short entrance, often capped with one or two boulders. This suggests that the kitchen was roofed separately from the main room, perhaps with a skin flap allowing smoke to escape. The small kitchens contained raised platforms where food was cooked over open fires fuelled by bone, wood and marine mammal oil (Figure 11).

The analysis of over 15,000 identifiable mammal and bird bones from the winter house ruins shows that, like the people who lived at Nelson River, the Thule inhabitants of Skraeling Island depended mainly on sea mammals, particularly ringed seal, for their livelihood. Microscopic examination of seal canine tooth thin-sections showed that most seals were killed during spring, summer and fall, suggesting that meat stored in caches may have provided the bulk of winter sustenance. Migratory waterfowl and land mammals such as arctic fox, arctic hare, and muskox lent variety to the predominantly sea mammal diet.

Winter houses with well-defined kitchen extensions, are, to date, unknown in other areas of the eastern Canadian Arctic but are found in contemporaneous Thule sites in western Alaska. The similarities in house form, harpoon-head styles, and several other artifact traits, suggest that the Ruin Island phase represents a migration of people from western Alaska, rather than from the northern coast of Alaska.

Although the western cast of their buildings and artifacts suggest that the Ruin Island phase Thule people were recent immigrants, several radiocarbon age determinations on a variety of material from the Skraeling Island houses indicate an average age of late twelfth or early thirteenth centuries - approximately 200 to 300 years after Thule people had first entered the Beaufort Sea region. Nor were the Ruin Island phase people the first Thule in the eastern Arctic, as archaeological sites in the Barrow Strait/Lancaster Sound region contain evidence of other cultural variants that apparently predate the Ruin Island phase by at least a century. So, while the Ruin Island phase Thule people may have been the first Thule to enter the Alexandra Fiord area, and did so following a rapid migration from Alaska, other Thule groups were already present throughout most of the Canadian Arctic. Thus, archaeological evidence from southern Banks Island, eastern Ellesmere Island and other areas of the central and eastern Arctic suggests that the Ruin Island phase is only one of several pioneering movements from various regions of Alaska into the Canadian Arctic.

FIGURE 11: Skraeling Island Site, House 5, kitchen cooking platforms.

DISCUSSION

Comparing the Nelson River data with evidence from Skraeling Island shows that no single theory yet advanced satisfactorily accounts for the spread of the Thule culture throughout the Canadian Arctic. The Nelson River data suggest that the earliest pioneering Thule groups simply expanded their range eastward a short distance from Alaska, possibly due to ecological pressures. Seemingly originating from a different area and in a different period, however, the Ruin Island phase migrants do not fit neatly into the ecologically-based model for the expansion of Thule. Other causes which could account for their appearance in the east include a search for raw materials such as iron, depletion of resources in their former territory, or troubles in their homeland, such as feuding.

One can search for other explanations to account for this later wave (or waves) of migrants, but more productive lines of inquiry can be pursued as well. Archaeologists are interested in studying these migrations not only because of our curiosity about how cultures came to be in a particular place, but also because migrations are themselves strong causal factors promoting cultural change. For as long as Inuit have been known to a wider world, anthropologists and ethnologists have marvelled at their adaptability, which is shown in part by accommodation to particular conditions found in different parts of the Arctic. The time depth added by archaeology lets us see that migrations which brought people into contact with fresh environmental situations stimulated new cultural responses. This, in turn, contributed to the diversity which eventually came to characterize regional Inuit groups. Further, if we are correct in reading the evidence from Nelson River, Alexandra Fiord and elsewhere as indications that the Thule ancestors of the historic period Inuit stemmed from several different parts of the Alaskan homeland at different times, we can see this, too, as a factor in the emergence of cultural diversity in the Arctic.

ACKNOWLEDGEMENTS

The archaeological work on Banks Island was undertaken by Charles Arnold and funded by the Social Sciences and Humanities Research Council of Canada and the University of Toronto Connaught Fund. Karen McCullough and Peter Schledermann directed the

Ellesmere Island archaeological investigations with financial assistance from the Social Sciences and Humanities Research Council of Canada, the National Geographic Society and the Arctic Institute of North America. The Polar Continental Shelf Project provided logistic support for both projects.

REFERENCES

Arnold, C. 1986. In search of the Thule pioneers. In: Thule Pioneers. Edited by: E. Bielawski, Carolynn Kobelka and Robert Janes. Prince of Wales Northern Heritage Centre, Occasional Papers No. 2:1-93.

McGhee, R. 1969-1970. Speculations on climatic change and Thule culture development. Folk 11-12:173-184.

McCullough, K.M. 1986. The Ruin Island phase of Thule culture in the eastern High Arctic. Unpublished Ph.D. dissertation, University of Toronto, Toronto, Ontario.

Illustrated by Brenda Carter

PREHISTORIC THULE ESKIMO WHALING IN THE CANADIAN ARCTIC ISLANDS: CURRENT KNOWLEDGE AND FUTURE RESEARCH DIRECTIONS

James M. Savelle[1] and Allen P. McCartney[2]

Abstract: Prehistoric Thule Eskimo subsistence in the Canadian Arctic Islands is often considered synonymous with bowhead whaling, due to the highly visible and impressive remains of winter dwellings constructed from bowhead whale bones. Despite the considerable body of data relating to Thule culture that has been compiled since its initial definition and description in 1927, the role of the bowhead whale in the Thule subsistence economy is poorly understood. Indeed, many researchers consider an assessment of its importance beyond our present interpretative capabilities.

Here, we outline the nature of archaeological whale bone and review past interpretations of Thule subsistence and bowhead whaling. Bowhead whales are then examined as part of the Thule economy, within the context of recent human ecological models. Specifically, by analyzing Thule whaling from the perspective of predator-prey relationships and economic zonation strategies, bowheads are shown to be central to the economy of Thule Eskimos living beside many major straits and bays of the central and eastern Canadian Arctic. In doing so, we emphasize the importance of expanding future Thule subsistence studies to include a regional, as opposed to a site-specific approach.

Archaeological whale bones are useful evidence of the range and relative frequency of bowheads in different parts of the Canadian Arctic prior to commercial whaling. Archaeology provides material remains of bowheads that lived some 700-800 years before those described in whalers' journals and explorers' accounts of the nineteenth century. While bowheads of the historic period are loosely documented, they are not represented in material form for further examination today. Thus, archaeological whale bones furnish whale biologists with valuable diachronic data about these largest of arctic mammals that were almost extinguished by nineteenth and early twentieth century commercial whaling.

Résumé: La survie des Eskimos préhistoriques de Thulé dans les îles de l'Arctique canadien est souvent associée à la chasse à la baleine boréale, à cause des restes hautement visibles et imposants d'habitations d'hiver construites d'os de baleines boréales. Malgré le grand nombre d'informations compilées sur la culture de Thulé depuis sa première définition et description en 1927, le rôle de la baleine boréale dans l'économie de subsistance de Thulé n'est pas bien compris. En effet, bien des chercheurs croient que l'évaluation de son importance dépasse nos capacités d'interprétation actuelles.

Tout d'abord, nous donnons un aperçu de la nature de l'os de baleine, sur le plan archéologique, puis nous passons en revue les précédentes interprétations de l'économie de subsistance et de la chasse à la baleine à Thulé. Par la suite, nous examinons les baleines boréales et leur rôle dans l'économie de Thulé, dans le contexte de récents modèles écologiques de l'espèce humaine. Plus spécifiquement, lorsque l'on fait l'analyse de la chasse aux baleines de Thulé du point de vue des relations prédateurs-proies et des stratégies de zone économique, les baleines boréales apparaissent comme le pivot de l'économie des Eskimos de Thulé vivant à proximité des principaux détroits et baies du centre et de l'est de l'Arctique canadien. Cette manière de procéder met l'accent sur l'importance d'élargir les futurs champs de recherche sur la subsistance de Thulé, de manière à adopter une approche axée sur la région plutôt que sur le site même.

Les vestiges d'os de baleines apportent des preuves utiles sur le territoire et la fréquence relative des baleines boréales dans les différentes parties de l'Arctique canadien avant l'apparition de la chasse commerciale. L'archéologie offre des restes physiques de ces baleines qui existaient quelque 700 à 800 ans avant celles décrites dans les journaux des pêcheurs de baleine et dans les comptes rendus des explorateurs du 19e siècle. Cependant, bien qu'il existe une vaste documentation sur les baleines boréales de la période historique, on ne retrouve plus, de nos jours, de restes matériels pour les étudier plus à fond. Par conséquent, les vestiges des os de baleines apportent aux biologistes des données diachroniques de prix sur ces mammifères les plus gros de l'Arctique, dont l'espèce a été presque détruite par la chasse commerciale à la baleine au 19e siècle et au début du 20e siècle.

INTRODUCTION

Prehistoric Thule Eskimos of the Canadian Arctic (about 1000-1600 AD) are often considered to be preeminent whalers. The initial development of Thule culture in Alaska prior to about 1000 AD, the migration of Thule Eskimos across northern Canada and into

---

[1] Department of Anthropology, McGill University, Montreal, Quebec H3A 2T7
[2] Department of Anthropology, University of Arkansas, Fayetteville, AR 72701, U.S.A.

prior to about 1000 AD, the migration of Thule Eskimos across northern Canada and into Greenland (Arnold and McCullough, this volume), and the subsequent 'decline' of the human population and abandonment of the High Arctic between approximately 1400-1600 AD, for example, have all been directly related to bowhead whale availability. This paper: (1) reviews the evidence for Thule whaling as traditionally presented; (2) reviews past interpretations of this evidence; (3) introduces a study that we feel can contribute to a more comprehensive understanding of Thule whaling; and (4) suggests ways that whale bone data are of use to cetacean biologists.

THE BOWHEAD WHALE AS A PREY SPECIES

The bowhead whale (*Balaena mysticetus*) is, in several respects, unique in the Arctic Islands as a prey species. These animals are by far the largest of arctic mammals, with mature adults attaining lengths of up to 20 m (Nerini *et al.* 1984) and weighing up to 40,000-50,000 kg. Furthermore, the very large size of the individual bones of the skeleton (Figure 1) make them ideal for construction materials for dwellings in an area lacking trees

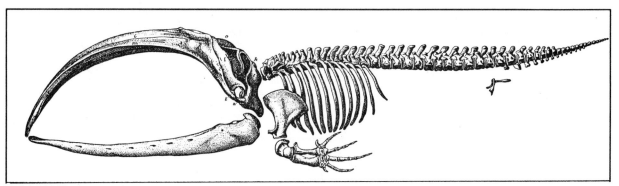

FIGURE 1: Bowhead whale (Balaena mysticetus) skeleton, showing the relative size of the various elements. (From Scammon 1874; based on an original drawing published in 1866 by D.F. Eschricht and J.Reinhardt).

or significant quantities of driftwood. Finally, bowhead whales are slow swimmers (averaging 2-4 knots), feed near the surface, are relatively easy to approach,and float remarkably well when killed (McVay 1973; Marquette 1978; Reeves *et al.* 1983). Three separate bowhead stocks are known in the Canadian Arctic during historic and recent times: Beaufort Sea, Davis Strait, and Hudson Bay stocks (Mitchell 1977; Mitchell and Reeves 1982). Each of these had a separate commercial whale fishery (Ross 1979).

Given that the most important attributes to hunter-gatherers in determining prey species are weight, density, aggregation, mobility, fat content, and non-food yields (Jochim 1976, p. 7, 23 and following pages), the bowhead whale is an obvious prey choice, given an appropriate technology.

TRADITIONAL EVIDENCE FOR THULE WHALING

Thule culture was originally defined and described by Therkel Mathiassen (1927), and the presence of architectural and other whales bones and baleen in winter house sites (Figures 2, 3) influenced Mathiassen's interpretation of the culture:

> "Whaling has apparently been one of the principal occupations; this is proved both by the construction of the houses, in which whalebones play such a great part, and by the material used for implements, whalebone and baleen apparently being the most important; in particular, however, the composition of the refuse heap, the large masses of baleen and whalebones which appear especially in the lower strata, indicate that whaling has been one of the most important means of livelihood of the population. The hunting of other marine mammals, especially walruses and seals, has also been of great importance to them, and the same may be said of caribou hunting." (Mathiassen 1927A, p. 85)".

While Mathiassen did not ignore non-whaling variants of Thule culture, noting for example that Thule Eskimos at Malerualik on King William Island "... based their lives upon caribou hunting, whereas marine mammal hunting retired into the background" (Mathiassen 1927A, p. 321), there is no question that, for the most part, he interpreted large baleen whale hunting as the primary subsistence activity. This is undoubtedly due to the fact that the major prehistoric sites he studied (Naujan at Repulse Bay, and Qilalukan and Mitimatalik at Pond Inlet) were on waters frequented by bowheads, thus making them available to prehistoric hunters.

The evidence for Thule whale hunting (in contrast to using stranded carcasses) includes direct and indirect evidence (see McCartney 1980A for detailed discussion).

FIGURE 2: A winter house ruin at the PcJq-5 (Cape Garry) site, southeastern Somerset Island. Jumbled stones and whale bones lie scattered from the original house construction.

FIGURE 3: The excavated house ruin shown in Figure 2, from approximately the same view. The entranceway (upper) is flanked by four whale skull bases and enters the house proper through the linteled doorway. Two platforms face the flagstone floor, one at the rear (lower) and one at the right side of this view. The string grid sections measure 2 x 2 m.

Direct Evidence

Direct evidence for whaling includes the presence of specialized whaling gear and depictions of whaling scenes.

Specialized Whaling Gear

Thule has been described as one of the most gadget-oriented of prehistoric cultures (Maxwell 1985, p. 262), and several Thule implements have been identified as having been used specifically for whaling. Whaling gear originally identified by Mathiassen (1927A) includes whaling harpoon heads, whaling harpoon foreshafts, whaling lance heads, and whaling harpoon and lance endblades. While rare in archaeological contexts, these items have been recovered from Thule sites in Alaska, the Canadian Arctic, and Greenland.

Depictions of Whaling Scenes

Although pictorial representations of Thule Eskimo activities on artifacts are rare, at least five have been recovered that depict scenes of active whaling (Collins 1951, p. 63; McCartney 1980A, p. 523; McGhee 1984, p. 76; Maxwell 1983, 1985, p. 268). Four of these show umiak crews in the process of chasing or harpooning bowhead whales (Figure 4), while the fifth (Maxwell 1985, p. 268) depicts a bowhead whale being towed tail-first by an umiak.

Indirect Evidence

In addition to direct evidence, there are also various forms of indirect evidence for whaling. These are outlined as follows.

Site Location

Besides the occurrence of whale bone and baleen in considerable quantities at many Thule winter sites, the location of these sites corresponds closely with the historic (and probably prehistoric; see Harington, this volume) distribution of bowhead whales. Thule sites which contain few little or no bowhead whale products, on the other hand, correspond closely with those areas where bowheads were historically absent or only occasionally reported. This correspondence may be seen on a larger scale for the Canadian Arctic

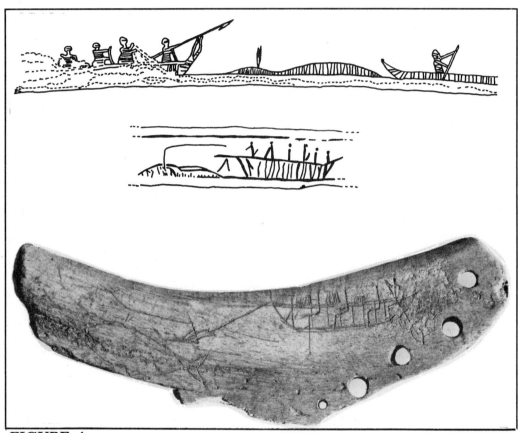

FIGURE 4: Depictions of Thule whaling scenes from the Canadian Arctic. Upper: Scene from an ivory bow drill handle found by Father Guy Mary-Rousseliere and Lawrence Oschinsky at a site on Admiralty Inlet, Baffin Island. Middle: Scene from an ivory bow drill handle found by Peter Schledermann at a site near the head of Cumberland Sound, Baffin Island. Lower: Scene from a snow knife handle piece found by Henry Collins at a site near Resolute Bay, Cornwallis Island. (Drawings by Phyllis Clancy; photo courtesy of Henry Collins and the Department of Anthropology, Smithsonian Institution).

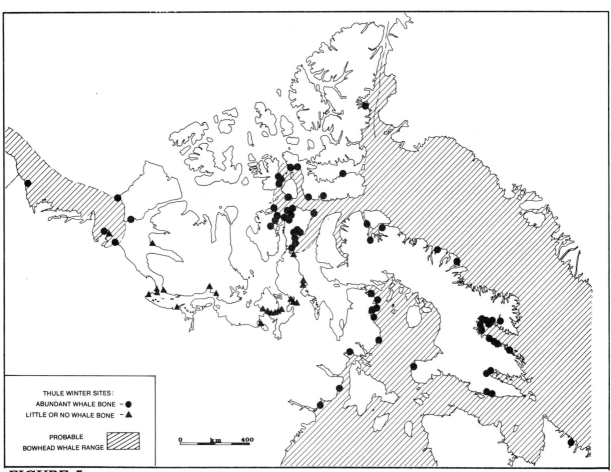

FIGURE 5: Distribution of whale bone at permanent winter sites in relation to the probable contemporary bowhead whale range. Sites with little or no whale bone are shown for the areas bordering or outside the bowhead whale range only.

(Figure 5), or on a small scale such as the Boothia Peninsula-Somerset Island area (McCartney and Savelle 1985, p. 52).

Resource Utilization

The massive size of even immature bowheads, such as those we have measured at Somerset Island sites (see below) that averaging about 8.5 m long and probably weighing 10,000-12,000 kg, totally overshadowed all other available fauna. Conservatively assuming that half of an immature whale's weight was usable as meat and blubber, then the resulting 5,500 kg of edible food or fuel equalled the usable weight of about 120 caribou or 180 ringed seals. Since bowheads provide so much human and dog food, fuel, and bone and baleen for tools, sled parts, and containers, we would expect Thule Eskimos to pursue bowheads whenever they had the opportunity.

Ethnographic Continuity

Ethnographic analogy has been referred to previously in relation to whaling gear. Another example of analogy between recent and prehistoric features is the *karigi* (men's ceremonial house) that northern Alaskan whaling crews used (Spencer 1959). Several structures that appear to have been *karigi* have been reported from Thule sites (Savelle 1987). These structures are also reported for nineteenth century Canadian Inuit (Parry 1824, p. 284).

Further, because Thule Eskimos were the direct cultural and biological ancestors of recent Canadian Inuit, many of whom whaled in the central and eastern Canadian Arctic, we would expect that native whaling is an old tradition and a subsistence activity practised by the ancestral people. Although early ethnographic accounts of native whaling and associated gear are relatively rare, there are examples such as the writings of Henry Ellis (in the 1740s) for the Hudson Strait Eskimos (Oswalt 1979), and William Parry (1824) for the Central Eskimos that clearly indicate early historic period native whaling before stocks were decimated by Euroamerican whaling.

Permanent Settlements and Associated Meat Caches

Thule winter house settlements were established close to shore, and thus near open summer waters and winter sea ice. From the midden deposits that surround these settlements, the latter appear to have been occupied for many winters. In order to maintain a permanent settlement, in contrast to temporary igloo winter settlements at places where seals were available (as occupied by historic Inuit), there must be a regular and large amount of storable meat for winter consumption. The settlements with whale bones, stone, and peat block houses mark points on straits and bays where bowheads migrated and summered with some regularity (and thus, from the Eskimos' perspective, predictability). The large number of meat caches associated with winter settlements would be used for storing whale meat and blubber acquired during the summer and early fall, as well as smaller game products. Caches are usually of three types: stone cairns above ground; half-buried pits or 'ice cellars'; and simple, shallow depressions excavated in loose gravel. The shallow depressions (Figure 6) are especially common at Thule sites. As many as 200-300 such

FIGURE 6: Aerial view of surface caches (stone clusters) and subsurface caches at the PaJs-2 (Mount Oliver) site, southeastern Somerset Island. (Photo courtesy of Dr. William Kerr, Geological Survey of Canada 1976).

caches are known from sites on southeastern Somerset Island, and they could have stored the meat and blubber of 15-25 whales (Savelle 1987). Clearly, such storage capacities are consistent only with active whaling rather than the occasional use of stranded whales.

Community Size and Prerequisite Whaling Crews

Thule winter settlements in the central and eastern Canadian Arctic vary greatly in numbers of house ruins (3-50), but 10-20 are common. Even if all the houses were not contemporaneously occupied, probably several umiak crews per settlement could have been organized for whale hunting and towing (Bockstoce 1976).

Prerequisite Sea-Mammal Hunting Gear

No whale hunting using harpoons and drag gear could occur prior to the development of this technology. This gear complex includes inflation nozzles for seal-skin drag floats, wooden bars for lashing floats to drag lines, as well as umiaks and their respective gear (Maxwell 1985, pp. 266-267). Although the various float items and umiaks could also serve in the procurement of smaller sea mammals, they and more specialized whale harpoons and lances were available for use on bowheads (Bockstoce 1973).

Whale Bone Modification

Diet-related butchering marks on whale bones have rarely been recorded, primarily because it is extremely difficult to distinguish such modifications from marks related to shaping and working whale bones for house construction and/or tool manufacture. However, one type of whale bone alteration has been reported that does suggest butchering related to soft organ extraction. During excavations and surveys of Thule sites on southeastern Somerset Island, McCartney (1980A) found that 125 of 129 crania examined exhibited a large, irregular hole in the braincase just superior or anterior to the foramen magnum. Savelle (1987) found similar modifications on 94 of 98 crania examined in the same area. Many of these holes shows definite chop-marks, and the most likely interpretation of such modification is for brain extraction, or possibly the symbolic release of the whale's soul. Both interpretations would be consistent with active hunting. Some of the holes, on the other hand, lack definite chop marks and may have resulted from drying and cracking of the thin supraoccipital bones (McCartney and Savelle 1985, p. 46).

PAST INTERPRETATIONS OF THULE WHALING

Mathiassen's (1972) original interpretation of Thule subsistence stressed bowhead whaling to the extent that it could be considered the "preeminent facet of Thule economy" (Maxwell 1985, p. 248). Furthermore, he suggested a western Arctic (Alaska-Siberia) origin for Thule culture, partly on the basis that in that area only was there sufficient wood to construct umiaks (used in whale hunting). Jenness (1940), following Mathiassen, equated the eastward expansion of Thule culture with whaling. Further, Jenness suggested that Thule culture replaced the preceding Dorset culture (which Mathiassen at that time did not recognize) in the central and eastern Arctic, primarily due to the greater ecological advantage enjoyed by the latter as a result of whaling and dog-sled traction (Taylor 1963).

The whaling emphasis of Thule subsistence was further reinforced by Larsen and Rainey (1948), who, on the basis of excavations in Alaska, introduced the term "Arctic Whale Hunting culture", which in turn included Thule as a "phase".

Since Mathiassen's pioneering study, dozens of preliminary reports and site monographs on the Thule culture have appeared, especially over the past three decades (see for example Dekin 1978, Savelle 1980, Morrison 1983, and particularly Maxwell 1985 for summaries of the history of research). Excavation of Thule sites in the Canadian Arctic, such as those by Collins at Frobisher Bay (Collins 1950) and Resolute Bay (Collins 1951, 1952, 1955), Lowther (1962) at Cape Sparbo, and Manning (1956) on Banks Island all appeared to confirm the "preeminent facet" of Thule whaling. Although not disputing the hunting of bowhead whales per se, Taylor (1966) was the first to stress that not *all* Thule Eskimos were whale hunters. Instead, he suggested that Thule society could best be classified as "omnivorous", such that "... the degree to which different species are exploited reflects primarily the environment, the faunal resources, and only secondarily an economic heritage" (Taylor 1966, p. 118).

Studies since then have confirmed 'whaling' and 'non-whaling' variants of Thule economy. This discrepancy in the apparent emphasis placed on bowheads may well prove, with additional research, to be more a gradation than a dichotomy. Currently, we know that bowheads were rarely used at western Canadian Arctic Thule sites of the Mackenzie Delta-Coronation Gulf region (Taylor 1966; McGhee 1975; Morrison 1983) and at sites along the continental margin (Savelle 1987). At the latter sites, seals and caribou were important in the diet, whereas bowheads were more frequently represented at central and eastern Canadian Arctic Archipelago sites. This difference in the relative importance of bowheads makes it nearly impossible to generalize about *all* Canadian Thule winter sites. The discussion presented here applies to the central and eastern sites where bowheads are typically found associated with winter house sites.

Despite the recognition of non-whaling variants of Thule subsistence, the bowhead whale is considered instrumental in Thule development. McGhee (1969/1970, 1972, 1975) and McCartney (1971, 1977), in particular, stressed the primacy of bowheads in the initial expansion of Thule Eskimo society out of Alaska about 1000 AD, and the subsequent 'decline' or 'transition' of Thule culture to historic Inuit cultures. Briefly, they related the development of a bowhead whaling industry in Alaska about 1000 AD and subsequent expansion across Canada and into Greenland with a warming trend (Neo-Atlantic period). This warming apparently resulted in a decrease in the extent and duration of summer sea ice cover, which in turn led to an increase in the abundance and distribution of bowhead whales. Conversely, the decline in whaling and abandonment of the High Arctic beginning about 1400 AD was equated with a cooling trend (Neo-Boreal period). That is, the cooling resulted in an increase in sea ice cover, which in turn resulted in a decrease in the abundance and distribution of bowheads and a shift in the Thule economy to alternate sea and land resources.

Subsequent studies by other researchers have tended to be based on and/or reinforce this general scenario (e.g. Dekin 1972; Schledermann 1975, 1979; Stanford 1976; Sabo 1981; Savelle 1987). However, McGhee (1983, p. 23; this volume) suggested that the early migration, at least, may well have been triggered by other causes, in particular the availability of meteoritic iron in northern Greenland, a suggestion also put forward by Blaylock (1980, p. 85) and McCartney (1982). Nevertheless, the standard practice until recently was to equate bowhead whale bone at a dwelling site with active bowhead whaling. This facile interpretation changed, however, with the publication of a critique by Freeman (1979) of Thule Eskimo whaling.

LIMITATIONS OF WHALING INTERPRETATIONS

The view of Thule as an active whaling culture, with the exception of Taylor's (1966) caveat, was not seriously questioned until Freeman (1977, 1979) suggested that arctic archaeologists had placed undue emphasis upon the presence of whale bone in Thule sites when interpreting Thule subsistence. That is, the "... distinction between a whale bone utilizing people and a whale hunting people does not appear to be explicitly recognized in the reconstructions advanced to date" (Freeman 1979, p. 279). Freeman presented several other related objections, but the whale bone use vs active whale hunting distinction was the most critical. While McCartney (1980A) has responded to these criticisms, Freeman's article focused the attention of archaeologists on the problems of the logical development from data to archaeological/ethnographic generalizations.

Consequently, arctic archaeologists have become much more cautious in their interpretations of whaling. For example, in discussing the faunal remains from the Learmonth site on Somerset Island, Taylor and McGhee (1979, p. 114) noted: "... we do not know how much of that food [represented in the houses and middens], if any, came from whales whose bones were found in a house." Staab (1979, p. 362), in discussing the faunal remains from the Silumiut site, concluded that "... food and raw material procurement primarily involved the hunting and processing of seal and caribou." Nevertheless, she added that "... were it possible to definitely establish the role of the great baleen whales in the [subsistence] economy, seals and caribou might be relegated to secondary importance."

Faunal material recovered by McCartney (1979A) from several sites on Somerset Island was analyzed by Rick (1980, p. 114), who suggested "... it is hard to assess the importance of whales to a particular house's economy ... since the whale bones in individual dwellings ... could have been collected by the Thule builders from abandoned houses and beached carcasses as well as from freshly killed whales." Accordingly, she excluded bowhead whales from her assessment of the contribution to the diet represented by the archaeofauna.

Morrison (1983, p. 224), while noting baleen in the recovered material from his excavations on Coronation Gulf, concluded that the "... importance of this species in Thule subsistence economies cannot be validly quantified ..." Thus, he excluded bowheads from a discussion of Thule subsistence in that region.

Finally, McGhee (1984, p. 81), despite recording a minimum of 20 bowhead whales represented at the Brooman Point site on Bathurst Island, asserted that the site "... provides little evidence of the importance of large whales in local subsistence."

A recent review of faunal (dietary) remains identified at Thule sites across the Arctic (Savelle and McCartney, in press) shows that by excluding whale bones from faunal analyses, 90% of the bones are of small seals, caribou, and foxes. Are we to assume that 90% of the Thule diet was based on these three kinds of animals? We have little alternative unless bowhead bones are evaluated and included as dietary evidence.

Clearly, if archaeologists are unable to determine past subsistence at the individual site level, then generalizations regarding subsistence for broad regions, whether explicit or implicit, must necessarily be very tenuous. We must have at least *some* knowledge of the nature and extent of subsistence and the role of whaling in it if we are to interpret other, non-subsistence aspects of Thule society, such as social, demographic, and ideological behaviour.

FUTURE RESEARCH DIRECTIONS

The major problem in Thule whaling studies is not lack of careful research or insufficient data. The studies noted above, for example, individually represent significant contributions in many areas of Thule archaeology. The main problem is that these studies have not been designed *specifically* to examine the question of Thule whaling; they have as a rule been site-specific studies, designed with other, primarily cultural-historical, questions in mind. Therefore, factors such as architectural vs diet-related whale bone, scavenged whale skeletons/carcasses vs hunted animals, and the 'schlepp' effect (wherein non-useful parts of large animals such as bones, unless utilized for building purposes, were left at the processing sites; see Daly 1969) cannot be adequately addressed through such studies.

In order for the problems of bowhead interpretation to be addressed adequately, two factors must be recognized. The first is that Thule subsistence strategies must not be regarded in isolation, but rather as articulating with other aspects of Thule culture. Traditional Thule studies have focused on one type site only, the winter residential site, with emphasis on settlement dates, house descriptions, artifact types, traded materials, and evidence of migrations. Historically, however, Inuit whaling was a complex activity that involved logistically organized groups operating over large areas and performing specialized tasks. As discussed by Binford (1980, 1982), such activities produce characteristic site types and characteristic site distributions. Thus, in order to fully investigate Thule whaling, the entire range of associated activities and sites must be examined. This, in turn, requires a *regional* as opposed to a site-specific approach.

A second factor that should be recognized is that quantification of fauna in *absolute* (nominal) terms suffers from a number of serious problems (e.g. Lyman 1982; Grayson 1984). Consequently, relative (ordinal) data are best employed in inspecting such aspects as faunal frequencies, abundances, and meat weights. When dealing with large fauna such as whales, where various parts have multiple uses (e.g. subsistence and architecture), even relative comparisons between these and other fauna are invalid. Accordingly, archaeological whale bone at one site/area can be compared with archaeological whale bone at other sites/areas, but cannot be directly compared with other faunal remains.

The following section summarizes the results of recent studies of Thule Eskimo whaling initiated by us and developed with the above two factors as guiding principles. We believe this approach can contribute to a better understanding of this aspect of arctic prehistory.

THULE ESKIMO WHALING ON SOMERSET ISLAND: AN EXAMPLE OF A REGIONAL APPROACH

The regional study described here examines Thule whaling from the perspective of predator-prey relationships. If examined through a series of archaeological expectations, this in turn allows us to determine predation (active hunting) from scavenging, and to determine the *relative* extent of whaling spatially and/or temporally. If Thule Eskimos in a region indeed actively hunted whales, then we should find evidence of:

(a) site types and site patterning indicative of active whaling, according to the presumed extent of active whaling;

(b) deliberate prey selection, and;

(c) bone distribution patterns indicative of active whaling.

There are additional archaeological correlates of active whaling, but these three will serve to demonstrate the value of a regional approach.

Site Types and Site Patterning

As an example of the relationships between hunter-gatherer site types, site patterning, and prey species, Binford (1980, 1982) defined two kinds of systems: collecting and foraging. Collecting systems are based on 'specialized' subsistence strategies which involve logically organized task groups intercepting specific, generally large and/or abundant prey animals. These animals result in large, storable surpluses. Such systems generate five site types:

(1) residential bases, which are the principal residential localities or settlements for social groups;

(2) locations, which are the principal places where resources are procured and, often, initially processed;

(3) stations, which are the principal places from which information on resources is gathered (e.g., observation points);

(4) field camps, which are temporary encampments for specialized task groups, such as whaling crews, and;

(5) caches, which are localities where various products are stockpiled, such as meat and blubber.

Binford also discussed the spatial arrangement of such sites, and suggested that the residential bases or settlements will tend to be at the centre of foraging zones of approximately 10 km radius and logistical zones of approximately 20 km radius. Foraging zones contain those sites relating to activities conducted on a regular basis and/or within a day's 'foraging' or walking, while logistical zones contain sites that are used by groups organized for temporary tasks, intercepting resources, and initially processing resources. Furthermore, Binford suggested that the movement of residential base sites will result, over time, in a sequential pattern of zone sets or groups of settlements, their stations, camps and caches (Figure 7). As Savelle (1987) has suggested, however, contemporaneous zone sets also reflect territoriality. That is, each local band's territory will be separated from adjacent bands' territories by the zone sets.

710

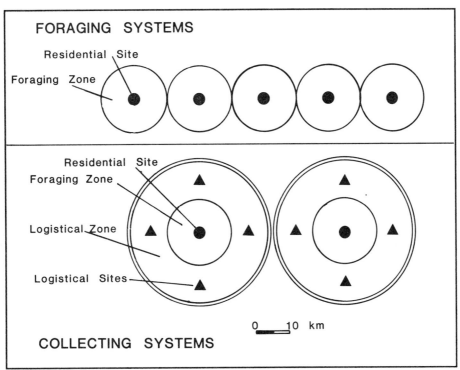

FIGURE 7: Idealized patterns of economic zones associated with: (a) foraging systems and (b) collecting systems. After Binford 1982.

The second type of system, the foraging system, is fundamentally different in that it is related to a generalized subsistence strategy. In this system, prey species tend to be harvested when encountered rather than when intentionally intercepted. Prey species tend to be smaller and/or less abundant and offer comparatively little surplus for storage. Such systems typically lack logistical zonation (Figure 7), and sites tend to be primarily residential bases and procurement locations.

The above systems are 'ideals' in that rarely will any hunter-gatherer society be either of the two extremes (e.g. Kelley 1983). However, active whaling societies, such as those of Thule Eskimos who whaled and created enormous surpluses, should exhibit collecting tendencies, while societies engaged in less, or no, active whaling should exhibit foraging tendencies (the !Kung San and Australian Aborigines are examples of foraging peoples).

In order to examine Thule society from the collecting vs foraging perspective, two areas on Somerset Island have been compared: Creswell Bay and Aston Bay (Figure 8). We have conducted detailed investigations here since 1975. Thule occupations at Creswell Bay have previously been demonstrated to be classic Thule, that is, relating to the period of maximum bowhead whale distribution and abundance (McCartney 1979A; Taylor and

McGhee 1979). The Thule occupation at Aston Bay, on the other hand, appears to be of a later period, when bowhead whales were becoming less abundant and more restricted in distribution (Savelle 1987). Neither Creswell Bay nor Aston Bay sites have been sufficiently radiocarbon dated, but we estimate that most of the Creswell Bay sites date to about 1200--1300 AD, while the Aston Bay sites date to about 1400-1500 AD. Furthermore, Aston Bay is near the western extreme for the eastern Arctic bowhead whale stocks, such that even if the occupations relate to the classic Thule period, they are nevertheless within an area where bowheads were probably less predictable and abundant.

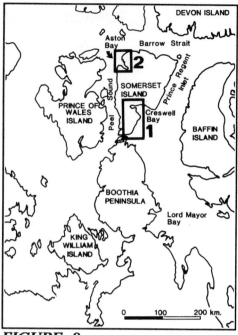

FIGURE 8: Survey regions in the study area: 1 - Creswell Bay; 2 - Aston Bay.

The distribution of various site types in these two areas are represented in Figures 9 and 10, and the relative frequencies are shown in Figure 11. For purposes of comparison, permanent residential bases are defined as half-buried winter house sites and temporary residential bases are those containing three or more summer tent rings or winter snow-houses. Locations are those sites or site components containing bowhead bones in non-dwelling contexts (for instance, whale beaching-butchering spots), and caches are sites of stone cairns or gravel depression features (Figure 6). Finally, field camps are those sites or site components containing one or two tent rings. The distinction between field camps and temporary residential sites is based on nineteenth century ethnographic literature suggesting that small task groups (male hunting crews, for example) overnighted in two or less tents (or igloos). Larger groups, such as three or more families camping at a river for fishing, represent temporary settlements in as many tents (Savelle 1987). Obviously, this is a fine archaeological distinction between two and three tent rings, and greater differences (for example, between two and six or more rings) would be more clearcut. No stations were identified, which is to be expected, given their low archaeological visibility (Binford 1978).

Dealing first with the relative frequencies of the different sites or component types, there is a clear contrast between the few logistically-related sites such as field camps and

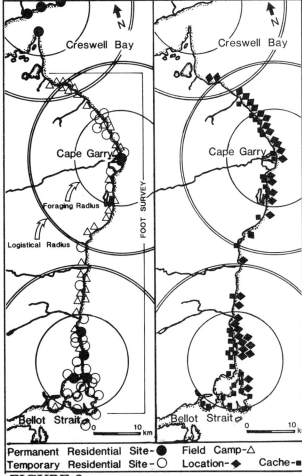

FIGURE 9: Thule site characteristics in the Creswell Bay area, with foraging and logistical radii from major permanent residential site clusters indicated. From Savelle and McCartney (in press).

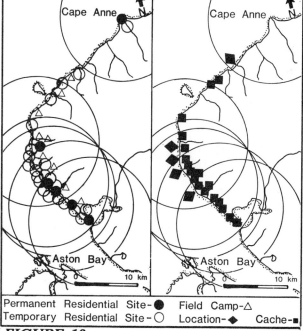

FIGURE 10: Thule site characteristics in the Aston Bay area, with foraging radii from major permanent residential site clusters indicated. From Savelle and McCartney (in press).

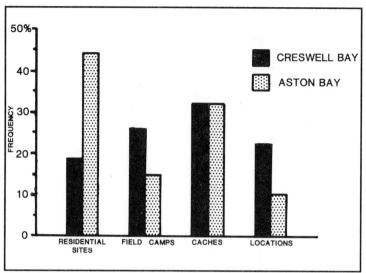

FIGURE 11: Site type frequencies at Creswell Bay and Aston Bay.

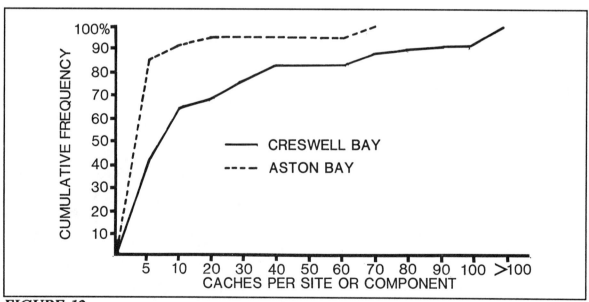

FIGURE 12: Cache site frequencies according to site size for Creswell Bay and Aston Bay. From Savelle and McCartney (in press).

locations (whale processing sites) at Aston Bay and the greater number of residential sites at Creswell Bay. Furthermore, although the relative proportions of cache sites or components are similar, there is a much greater frequency of large cache sites at Creswell Bay (Figure 12).

Looking now at zonation, in the Creswell Bay area major winter house settlements are concentrated in three regions: (1) to the south near Bellot Strait; (2) midway along the coast at Cape Garry; and (3) along the north coast of Creswell Bay (Figure 9). The three centres are separated by almost exactly two logistical radii (40 km). In addition, of the various sites or component types occurring within these zones, almost all temporary residential sites (large tent ring sites) occur within foraging zones, while almost all field camps (small tent ring sites) occur within logistical zones.

The pattern at Aston Bay, on the other hand, while displaying a separation of residential centres along the Aston Bay coast proper and Cape Anne, does not incorporate well-defined logistical zones. Instead, the permanent residential sites are more closely spaced than at Creswell Bay, primarily within overlapping zones (Figure 10). Essentially all other site types occur within these foraging zones.

According to the collecting vs foraging model, the prehistoric Thule society in the Creswell Bay area was logistically organized as a collecting system, which is appropriate to active whaling. Thule society at Aston Bay, on the other hand, was logistically organized as a foraging system, which is appropriate to less active whaling and more reliance on smaller animals.

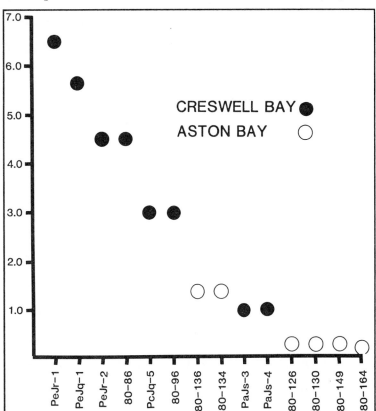

FIGURE 13: Average minimum number of bowhead whales per dwelling at sites at Creswell Bay and Aston Bay. (Note that PeJr-2 is probably contemporaneous with the Aston Bay occupations). After Savelle and McCartney (in press).

Finally, in support of the differences in the extent of whaling, we can compare the minimum numbers of bowheads represented at individual residential sites in the two areas. Assuming approximately similar occupation spans for the two areas (but not chronological periods; see Savelle 1987), the decrease in the importance of bowhead whales between Creswell Bay and Aston Bay is pronounced. This is indicated through the comparison of the average number of whales represented per dwelling (Figure 13).

Prey Selection

A second area of interest in determining active whaling vs whale scavenging is in prey selection. Specifically, if whale bone at Thule sites resulted from scavenging beached carcasses, then the demographic profile represented by whales at Thule sites should reflect the demographic profile of stranded whales.

Unfortunately, cetacean biologists know relatively little about bowhead whale stranding-patterns (Mitchell and Reeves 1982), but random strandings would be unlikely to affect only certain age-classes. On the other hand, ethnographic studies suggest that active whale hunters select certain age-classes, especially immature or small animals. During surveys of the Creswell bay area, McCartney (1978) measured 197 crania, 327 mandibles, 47 cervical vertebrae, and 110 scapulae of bowhead whales. Regression models based on Alaskan bowhead skeletons of approximate known whole animal size were applied to these bones and their original body lengths were estimated. Almost 97% of the bowheads represented are estimated to have been 7-10 m in length, which suggests they were immature whales (mostly yearlings but some two-year-old whales), since adult bowheads average greater than approximately 12 m (McCartney 1980B; Nerini *et al.* 1984).

Bone Distribution Patterns

Bone distribution patterns relate primarily to the question of active hunting vs scavenging. Specifically, if whale bone at archaeological sites was scavenged from beached carcasses or skeletons, then whale bone elements present at Thule dwelling sites should be correspondingly underrepresented at beach sites, while elements at the latter sites should be underrepresented at dwelling sites. Figure 14 compares the bowhead whale bone elements at the various beach sites where whale bones occur at Creswell Bay and Aston Bay and at two completely excavated half-buried dwellings at Creswell Bay. The element distribution is characteristic of a whale hunting as opposed to a whale bone scavenging pattern. That is, there is nothing approaching a 1:1 articulation of over-represented elements with underrepresented elements between beached bone

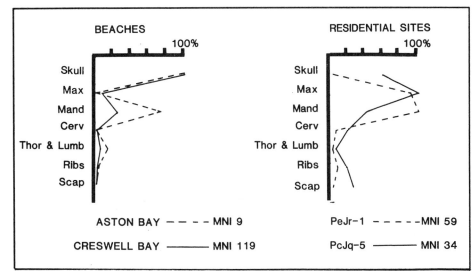

FIGURE 14: Bowhead whale element frequencies (as percent MNI) from semisubterranean dwelling sites and beach processing sites. From Savelle and McCartney (in press).

sites and the half-buried dwellings. There is, however, considerably difference in relative abundance between mandibles and crania at the two residential sites. Much of this variation may be due to removal of whale bones by recent Inuit carvers (McCartney 1979A) or, at least for crania from PeJr-1, subsequent removal for garmang (temporary, shallow bone and skin dwellings) construction at nearby PeJr-2 (McCartney 1978).

ARCHAEOLOGICAL WHALE BONES: THEIR RELEVANCE TO CETACEAN BIOLOGY

Whereas early historic accounts of Eskimo whaling are valuable, if often sketchy, testimony to the occurrence of native whaling, is rare. Ships' logs, whalers' journals, and Hudson's Bay Company records tell much about the frequency and range of bowheads (Ross 1974, 1979; Reeves et al. 1983). Archaeological whale bones add time depth and a material dimension to the diachronic study of bowhead stocks in the Canadian Arctic. Dated archaeological bone sites have been used by cetacean biologists to reconstruct past ranges, frequencies, and native predation of bowheads (Reeves and Mitchell 1985). Based on the assumption that heavy whale bones were used near the butchery locations where animals were beached, their distribution, frequency, and size can contribute to a better knowledge of the stocks before commercial whaling severely affected them. Because the modern Canadian bowhead stocks are relatively small compared to pre-commercial whaling numbers and have grown slowly since whaling ceased about 1915, archaeological whale bones spanning the earlier part of this millennium are valuable indicators of bowhead dynamics, including the relationship between ranges and fluctuating climatic episodes. Edward Mitchell (Arctic Biological Station, Quebec) and the second author began a study of archaeological whale bone measurements during the mid-1970s (McCartney 1980B), which is being expanded with the first author's participation.

FUTURE THULE WHALING RESEARCH

We have only begun to sample archaeological whale bones that may tell us much about bowhead procurement by prehistoric Eskimos, settlement patterns, as well as whale range and abundance. From studies of the King William Island-Boothia Peninsula-Somerset Island area, we believe that other Canadian Arctic areas could be profitably studied for similar and comparative data. Savelle (1987) has demonstrated the feasibility of foot surveys of shore-lines to locate whale bones and associated features. By extending such surveys to other areas, we can better understand the variation that may exist in prehistoric use patterns and sizes of bowheads taken across the Canadian Arctic. A program of radiocarbon dating to provide better temporal control for Thule period whaling is crucial to future research.

Finally, more Inuit should be involved in studies of bowhead predation. Northern natives are familiar with bowheads (as they occur today) and maintain much oral tradition about past whaling. Whether anthropological and historical or biological and managerial, Inuit participation in all phases of bowhead studies can contribute significantly to a clearer knowledge of past use, as well as promoting future conservation.

ACKNOWLEDGEMENTS

The first author's research was supported by the Polar Continental Shelf Project, the Boreal Institute for Northern Studies, the Social Sciences and Humanities Research Council of Canada, the Science Advisory Board of the Northwest Territories, and the Arctic Institute of North America.

The second author's research was supported by the Archaeological Survey of Canada (Canadian Museum of Civilization), the Department of Indian and Northern Affairs, and the Polar Continental Shelf Project.

We are grateful to these institutions for their generous support.

Edward D. Mitchell (Arctic Biological Station, Quebec) has been of great assistance over the years in providing expertise on whales for our archaeological projects.

Figures 9, 10, 12, 13, and 14 are reproduced with the kind permission of Barry L. Isaac, editor, *Research in Economic Anthropology*.

REFERENCES

Binford, L.R.   1978. Dimensional analysis of behavior and site structure: learning from an Eskimo hunting stand. American Antiquity 43:330-361.

_____.   1980. Willow smoke and dogs tails: hunter-gatherer settlement systems and archaeological site formation. American Antiquity 45:4-20.

_____.   1982.   The archaeology of place. Journal of Anthropological Archaeology 1:5-31.

Blaylock, S.K.   1980. A Thule bone and antler industry from Somerset Island, central Canadian Arctic. Unpublished M.A. thesis, Department of Anthropology, University of Arkansas.

Bockstoce, J.   1973. A prehistoric population change in the Bering Strait region. Polar Record 16(105):793-803.

_____.   1976. On the development of whaling in the Western Thule Culture. Folk 18:41-46.

Collins, H.B.   1950. Excavations at Frobisher Bay, Baffin Island, Northwest Territories. National Museum of Canada, Bulletin 118:18-43.

_____.   1951. Excavations at Thule Culture sites near Resolute, N.W.T. National Museum of Man Mercury Series, Archaeological Survey of Canada, Paper 123:49-63.

_____.   1952. Archaeological excavations at Resolute, Cornwallis Island, N.W.T.   National Museum of Canada, Bulletin 126:48-63.

Collins, H.B. 1955. Excavations of Thule and Dorset Culture sites at Resolute, Cornwallis Island, N.W.T. National Museum of Canada, Bulletin 136:22-35.

Daly, P. 1969. Approaches to faunal analysis in archaeology. American Antiquity 34:146-153.

Dekin, A.A. 1972. Climatic change and cultural change: a correlative study from Eastern Arctic prehistory. Polar Notes 12:11-31.

_____. 1978. Arctic archaeology: a bibliography and history. Garland Press, New York.

Freeman, M.M.R. 1977. A critical view of Thule Culture and ecological adaptation. Paper presented at the 10th Annual Meeting of the Canadian Archaeological Association (Ottawa, May 1977).

_____. 1979. A critical view of Thule Culture and ecological adaptation. In: Thule Eskimo Culture: An Anthropological Retrospective. Edited by: A.P. McCartney. National Museum of Man Mercury Series, Archaeological Survey of Canada, Paper 88:278-285.

Grayson, D.K. 1984. Quantitative zooarchaeology. Academic Press, New York.

Jenness, D. 1940. Prehistoric culture waves from Asia to America. Journal of the Washington Academy of Sciences 30:1-15.

Jochim, M.A. 1976. Hunter-gatherer subsistence and settlement. Academic Press, New York.

Kelley, R.L. 1983. Hunter-gatherer mobility strategies. Journal of Anthropological Research 39:277-306.

Larsen, H. and F.G. Rainey. 1948. Ipiutak and the Arctic Whale Hunting Culture. Anthropological Papers of the American Museum of Natural History 42.

Lowther, G.R. 1962. An account of an archaeological site on Cape Sparbo, Devon Island. National Museum of Canada, Bulletin 180:1-19.

Lyman, R.L. 1982. Archaeofaunas and subsistence studies. Advances in Archaeological Method and Theory 5:331-393.

Manning, T.H. 1956. Narrative of a second Defence Research Board expedition to Banks Island, with notes on the country and its history. Arctic 9:3-77.

Marquette, W.M. 1978. Bowhead whale. In: Marine Mammals of Eastern North Pacific and Arctic Waters. Edited by: D. Haley. Pacific Search Press. pp. 70-81.

Mathiassen, T. 1927A. Archaeology of the Central Eskimos: Part I. Descriptive. Report of the Fifth Thule Expedition, Volume 4, Copenhagan.

Mathiassen, T. 1927B. Archaeology of the Central Eskimos: Part II. The Thule Culture and its position within the Eskimo culture. Report of the Fifth Thule Expedition, Volume 4, Copenhagen.

Maxwell, M.S. 1983. A contemporary ethnography from the Thule period. Arctic Anthropology 20:79-87.

_____. 1985. Prehistory of the Eastern Arctic. Academic Press, New York.

McCartney, A.P. 1971. Thule Eskimo prehistory along northwestern Hudson Bay. Ph.D. dissertation, Department of Anthropology, University of Wisconsin-Madison.

_____. 1977. Thule Eskimo prehistory along northwestern Hudson Bay. National Museum of Man Mercury Series, Archaeological Survey of Canada, Paper 70.

_____. 1978. Study of whale bones for the reconstruction of Canadian arctic bowhead whale stocks and whale use by prehistoric Inuit. Report submitted to Northern Environmental Protection Branch, Indian and Northern Affairs Canada, Ottawa.

_____. 1979A. Archaeological whale bone: a northern resource. University of Arkansas, Anthropological Papers 1.

_____. 1979B. A processual consideration of Thule whale bone houses. In: Thule Eskimo Culture: An Anthropological Retrospective. Edited by: A.P. McCartney. National Museum of Man Mercury Series, Archaeological Survey of Canada, Paper 88:301-323.

_____. 1980A. The nature of Thule Eskimo whale use. Arctic 33:517-541.

_____. 1980B. Study of archaeological whale bones for the reconstruction of Canadian Arctic bowhead whale stocks and whale use by prehistoric Inuit. Final report submitted to Northern Environmental Protection Branch, Indian and Northern Affairs Canada, Ottawa.

_____. 1982. Re-evaluation of metal use by Thule Eskimos of the Canadian Arctic. Paper presented at the Annual Meeting of the Society for American Archaeology, Minneapolis.

McCartney, A.P. and J.M. Savelle. 1985. Thule Eskimo whaling in the central Canadian Arctic. Arctic Anthropology 22:37-58.

McGhee, R. 1969/1970. Speculations on climatic change and Thule Culture development. Folk 11/12:173-184.

_____. 1972. Copper Eskimo prehistory. National Museum of Man, Publications in Archaeology 2. Ottawa.

_____. 1975. An individual view of Canadian Eskimo prehistory. Canadian Archaeological Association, Bulletin 7:55-75.

McGhee, R. 1983. Eastern Arctic prehistory: the reality of a myth? Musk-Ox 33:21-25.

_____. 1984. The Thule village at Brooman Point. National Museum of Man Mercury Series, Archaeological Survey of Canada, Paper 125.

McVay, S. 1973. Stalking the arctic whale. American Scientist 61:24-37.

Mitchell, E.D. 1977. Initial population size of bowhead whale (*Balaena mysticetus*) stocks: cumulative catch estimates. Report of the International Whaling Commission 33:1-113.

Mitchell, E. and R.R. Reeves. 1982. Factors affecting abundance of bowhead whales *Balaena mysticetus* in the eastern Arctic of North America, 1915-1980. Biological Conservation 22:59-78.

Morrison, D.A. 1983. Thule culture in western Coronation Gulf, N.W.T. National Museum of Man Mercury Series, Archaeological Survey of Canada, Paper 116.

Murdoch, J. 1892. Ethnological results of the Point Barrow Expedition. In: Ninth Annual Report of the Bureau of Ethnology (1887-88).

Nerini, M.K., H.W. Braham, W.M. Marquette, and D.J. Rugh. 1984. Life history of the bowhead whale, *Balaena mysticetus* (Mammalia: Cetacea). Journal of Zoology 204:443-468.

Oswalt, W.H. 1979. Eskimos and explorers. Chandler and Sharp Publishers, Novato, California.

Parry, W.E. 1824. Journal of a second voyage for the discovery of a Northwest Passage from the Atlantic to the Pacific; performed in the years 1821-22-23, in His Majesty's Ships *Fury* and *Hecla* under the orders of Captain William Edward Parry. John Murray, London.

Reeves, R.R. and E.D. Mitchell. 1985. Shore-based bowhead whaling in the eastern Beaufort Sea and Amundsen Gulf. Report of the International Whaling Commission 35:387-404.

Reeves, R.R., E.D. Mitchell, A. Mansfield, and M. McLaughlin. 1983. Distribution and migration of the bowhead whale, *Balaena mysticetus*, in the eastern North American Arctic. Arctic 36:5-64.

Rick, A.M. 1980. Non-cetacean vertebrate remains from two Thule winter houses on Somerset Island, N.W.T. Canadian Journal of Archaeology 4:99-117.

Ross, W.G. 1974. Distribution, migration, and depletion of bowhead whales in Hudson Bay, 1860 to 1915. Arctic and Alpine Research 6:85-98.

_____. 1979. The annual catch of Greenland (bowhead) whales in waters north of Canada 1719-1915; a preliminary compilation. Arctic 32:91-121.

Sabo, G. 1981. Thule Culture adaptations on the south coast of Baffin Island, N.W.T. Ph.D. dissertation, Department of Anthropology, Michigan State University.

Savelle, J.M. 1980. An appraisal of Thule archaeology. M.A. thesis, Department of Anthropology, University of Arkansas.

_____. 1987. Collectors and foragers: subsistence-settlement system change in the central Canadian Arctic, A.D. 1000-1960. British Archaeological Reports, International Series No. 358.

Savelle, J.M. and A.P. McCartney. (in press). Geographical and temporal variation in Thule Eskimo subsistence economies: a model. Research in Economic Anthropology 10.

Scammon, C.M. 1874. The marine mammals of the northwestern coast of North America. John H. Carmany and Company and G.P. Putnam's Sons, New York. (Reprinted by Dover Publications, New York, 1968).

Schledermann, P. 1975. Thule Eskimo prehistory of Cumberland Sound, Baffin Island, Canada. National Museum of Man Mercury Series, Archaeological Survey of Canada, Paper 38.

_____. 1979. the Baleen Period of the Arctic Whale Hunting Tradition. National Museum of Man Mercury Series, Archaeological Survey of Canada, Paper 88:134-148.

Spencer, R.F. 1959. The North Alaskan Eskimo: a study in ecology and society. Bureau of American Ethnology, Bulletin 171.

Staab, M.L. 1979. Analysis of faunal material recovered from a Thule Eskimo site on the island of Silumiut, N.W.T. National Museum of Man Mercury Series, Archaeological Survey of Canada, Paper 88:349-379.

Stanford, D.J. 1976. The Walakpa Site, Alaska. Smithsonian Contributions to Anthropology 20. Smithsonian Institution Press, Washington, D.C.

Taylor, W.E. 1963. Hypothesis on the origin of the Canadian Thule Culture. American Antiquity 28:456-464.

_____. 1966. An archaeological perspective on Eskimo economy. Antiquity 40:114-120.

Taylor, W.E. and R. McGhee. 1979. Archaeological material from Creswell Bay, N.W.T., Canada. National Museum of Man Mercury Series, Archaeological Survey of Canada, Paper 85.

_____. 1981. Deblicquy: a Thule Culture site on Bathurst Island, N.W.T., Canada. National Museum of Man Mercury Series, Archaeological Survey of Canada,, Paper 102.

ENVIRONMENTAL AND CULTURAL CHANGE IN THE LARGE LAKES REGION OF BAFFIN ISLAND: A PROGRESS REPORT

J.D. Jacobs[1], D.R. Stenton[2], and W.N. Mode[3]

Abstract: The interior of south-central Baffin Island in the vicinity of the large lakes, Nettilling and Amadjuak, is an unusually productive ecosystem in a landscape of abundant glacial and marine deposits and relatively warm summer climate. Located at the northern extremity of the Low Arctic bioclimatic zone, the region is an important range for caribou, and figures prominently in the nearly 4,000-year record of human occupation of Baffin Island. Preliminary results of paleoenvironmental and archaeological investigations suggest a mid-Holocene maximum of vegetation development and tundra productivity, with a significant presence of Pre-Dorset Culture people. A transition to a cooler, drier climate around 3,000 years ago made the area less habitable, but in the subsequent millennium the more arctic adapted Dorset Culture people used the area at least occasionally. During the last 700 or more years, the region became an important element in the annual settlement subsistence cycle of the Thule Culture, with year-round occupation occurring in some periods. This pattern of land-use persisted with the Inuit of southern Baffin Island into the present century, until transformed by the disruptive influence of sustained Euro-American contact.

Résumé: L'intérieur du centre-sud de l'île de Baffin à proximité des grands lacs de Nettilling et Amadjuak, est un écosystème remarquablement productif dans un paysage d'abondants dépôts glaciaires et maritimes et dans un climat relativement clément. Situé à l'extrémité nord de la zone bioclimatique du Bas-Arctique, cette région est très fréquentée par les caribous et constitue un élément dominant dans l'histoire de l'occupation de l'île de Baffin par les humains, depuis presque 4,000 ans. Les résultats préliminaires d'études archéologiques et paléoenvironnementales semblent indiquer un maximum de développement de la végétation et de la productivité de la toundra vers le milieu de l'Holocène, avec une présence marquée de peuples de culture pré-Dorset. Le climat étant devenu plus frais et plus sec, il y a environ 3,000 ans, la région s'est montrée moins habitable, mais, dans le millénaire suivant, les peuples de culture Dorset mieux adaptés à l'Arctique l'ont fréquentée au moins à l'occasion. Dans les 700 dernières années ou plus, cette région est devenue un élément important du cycle annuel d'établissement et de subsistance de la culture de Thulé et, à certaines périodes, a été occupée toute l'année. Ce modèle d'utilisation du territoire s'est poursuivi avec les Inuit du sud de l'île de Baffin jusqu'au siècle actuel, en fait jusqu'à sa transformation sous l'influence perturbatrice du contact régulier avec les Euro-Américains.

INTRODUCTION

Baffin Island, with an area of about 500,000 km^2, is the largest of the Canadian Arctic Islands. Spanning 12° of latitude and bioclimatic zones from Low Arctic to High, the island contains examples of nearly every arctic landscape and habitat type. A predominately Inuit population is distributed around the island in coastal settlements and outpost camps, and there is a distinctly maritime orientation to the traditional economy. The vast interior of the island is nonetheless important, particularly as range for barren-ground caribou (*Rangifer tarandus groenlandicus*).

Ethnographic accounts of late summer and autumn caribou hunting trips far inland are readily confirmed by Inuit elders. This testimony indicates more than just seasonal use of

[1] Department of Geography, University of Windsor, Windsor, Ontario N9B 3P4. Present address: Department of Geography, Memorial University of Newfoundland, St. Johns, Newfoundland A1B 3X9.
[2] Department of Anthropology, University of Alberta, Edmonton, Alberta T6G 2H4
[3] Department of Geology, University of Wisconsin, Oshkosh, Wisconsin 54901, U.S.A.

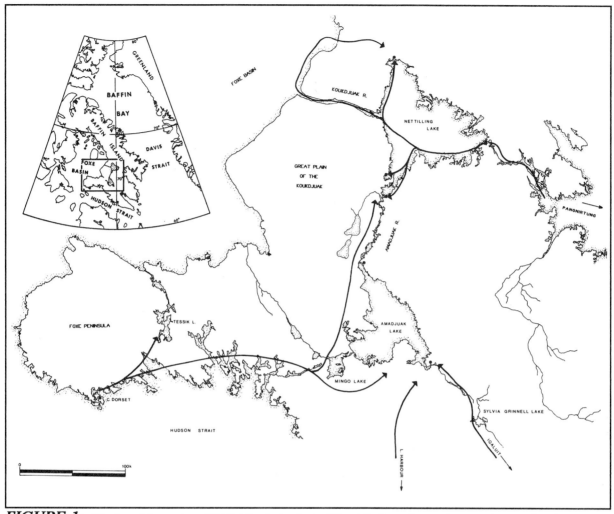

FIGURE 1: The large lakes region of Baffin Island, showing traditional Inuit travel routes between the coastal settlement areas and the interior.

the interior, however, in that there are also accounts of year-round occupation, an unusual practice by eastern Canadian Inuit standards. The particular region involved here is the south-central part of the island which contains the two large lakes, Amadjuak and Nettilling (Figure 1). Franz Boas (1888, p. 430) published Inuit accounts of both summer use near, and winter settlements on, Nettilling Lake in the nineteenth century, and a Royal Canadian Mounted Police report of the 1940s refers to possibly as many as 15 families occupying several camps around the lake for at least a year (McLauchlan 1944).

Such accounts imply that this interior region was a locally productive one and that southern Baffin Island Inuit were uniquely adapted to these circumstances. Given what is generally known of the impacts that fluctuations in climate may have on traditional kinds of Inuit economies, we hypothesized that this interior location would be a marginal one and thus a good locale in which to develop and test climate-impact models and theories of human adjustments to changing resources.

In 1984, we began a study of the physical environment and archaeology of what we call the large lakes region of Baffin Island (Figure 1). This initiative was a logical step following our work in coastal areas, particularly around Frobisher Bay, where a complicated picture of late- and postglacial climate and vegetational succession has emerged (Jacobs *et al.* 1985A), and where archaeological work (Stenton 1983) revealed the importance of interior caribou to the prehistoric people of the coastal region (Stenton 1983, 1987; Jacobs and Stenton 1985). Thus, a program was planned to detail the archaeological and paleo-environmental records and to understand their relationship.

Four field seasons have provided us with a wealth of data, much of which remains to be analyzed, and there is much more field work to do. Here we present our preliminary findings and the conceptual framework that guides the work.

LANDSCAPE

The interior of south-central Baffin Island consists of low, glaciated granitic hills of the Precambrian Shield, flanked on the west by mainly flat, drift-covered Paleozoic limestone of the Foxe Lowland. Deglaciation of the lakes occurred sometime between 7,000 and 5,000 years ago, with the last remnants of the south Baffin Ice Dome east of Amadjuak Lake vanishing soon thereafter (Blake 1966). Inundation by the sea to an elevation of about 100 m above present sea level occurred during deglaciation, with subsequent emergence due to isostatic recovery. These events produced several kinds of surface features of particular significance in this study: (1) extensive sediments in the lowlands, including marine silt, which is a good substrate for vegetation development; (2) a complex drainage system of rivers, lakes and ponds; and (3) extensive linear features (moraines, eskers, and beach ridges) that stand above the wet lowlands (Figure 2). Thus, the legacy of the glacial and sea-level history includes relatively rich and varied habitats, as well as natural highways between them.

FIGURE 2: Major washed moraine at the mouth of the Amadjuak River, looking eastward. This feature, an important caribou highway and river-crossing, has the largest concentration of archaeological features so far reported in the region.

BIOGEOGRAPHY

The interior lowlands lie mostly within the Low Arctic bioclimatic zone as described by Porsild (1958), among others (see Bliss, and Edlund, this volume). Northeast and southeast of the lakes are areas of granite-gneiss bedrock with tundra-heath vegetation. Limestone areas to the west support a sparse cover dominated by mountain avens (*Dryas integrifolia*) and purple saxifrage (*Saxifraga oppositifolia*). Vast wetlands forming the Great Plain of the Koukdjuak extend westward from Nettilling Lake to Foxe Basin. This is a nesting area for many bird species, notably the Snow Goose (*Chen caerulescens caerulescens*). Arctic char (*Salvelinus alpinus*) are abundant in lakes and rivers, and a freshwater population of ringed seals (*Phoca hispida*) inhabits Nettilling Lake. The entire region is a summer range for caribou.

The warm summer climate suggested in regional climate maps (Maxwell 1980) has been confirmed by our field observations. Not surprisingly, we have found populations of several Low Arctic indicator species, such as dwarf birch (*Betula glandulosa*) and alpine azalea (*Loiseleuria procumbens*), well beyond their previously reported limits. Shrub-tundra characteristic of the Low Arctic bioclimate, is limited to areas underlain by acidic crystalline rock that are favourable because of moisture supply, protection from wind, and southerly exposure. Quantitative vegetation surveys have been carried out in an attempt to describe these patterns.

Surface pollen samples (moss and lichen polsters) have been collected around the western and southern ends of Nettilling Lake and on the south side of Amadjuak Lake. These are being analyzed and related to the presence or absence at the collection site of such indicator species as *Betula glandulosa*. Near Frobisher Bay, a statistically-significant difference in *Betula* pollen percentage was found between samples taken at sites where shrub-birch was present and those from sites with no birch (Jacobs *et al.* 1985B). Preliminary results show a similar relationship in Nettilling Lake samples, but with somewhat lower percentages. These results enable paleoecological interpretation of the fossil pollen record because they define a threshold *Betula* percentage which distinguishes Low Arctic from High Arctic bioclimates.

CLIMATOLOGY

The inland location, some 100 km from the icy waters of Foxe Basin, and low elevation contribute to a warm summer climate. The lakes, with their large thermal capacity, also play an important role in moderating the local climate, particularly in late summer and autumn. Our data from the Burwash Bay area, at the extreme southern end of Nettilling Lake, suggest a long-term average July temperature of about 9°C (Jacobs and Grondin 1988). Summer precipitation is light, with July totals at Burwash Bay of 23 mm in 1985 and 9 mm in 1986. Winds in summer are variable, but frequently from the south, and average about 5 m s^{-1}. Clear to partly cloudy days are not uncommon and solar radiation is consequently high, an average daily flux of 19.6 MJ m^{-2} d^{-1} having been recorded in July of 1986 (Jacobs and Grondin 1988). Observations in the region over four summers point to a large year-to-year variability in weather, as is generally the rule in the eastern Arctic.

A more complete climatic picture will result from installation of automatic stations at two places during the summer of 1987 (Figure 3). These instruments operate year-round on 3-hourly and daily programs to record standard climatic readings, as well as solar radiation and ground temperatures. The results will be used in developing a mesocale climate model that will have application in calibrating the fossil pollen record and in determining the local responses to regional changes in climate.

PALEOENVIRONMENTS

The principal method of determining past regional environmental conditions is through the stratigraphic analysis of fossil pollen in sediments. Past climate can then be inferred from relative abundances of various plant taxa in the pollen record, on the assumption (not always valid) that present climate-vegetation-pollen relationships apply to the past. With few exceptions, paleoclimatic reconstructions in the eastern Canadian Arctic have been based on fossil pollen sequences in terrestrial peats, and have shown considerable disagreement across the region (Short *et al.* 1985). By contrast, we have found good stratigraphic

FIGURE 3: An automatic climatological station at the south end of Amadjuak Lake. It and a similar station on Nettilling Lake sample and store data on a 3-hourly and daily basis for recovery during the following summer.

agreement between a lake sediment core taken from Hikwa Lake[1] on Frobisher Bay (Mode and Jacobs 1985) and one described by Davis (1980) from Iglutalik Lake, near Pangnirtung.

Lake sediment cores were taken in Burwash Bay (Nettilling Lake) in 1986 and from South Bay (Amadjuak Lake) in 1987. Analysis has begun on the first, a 1 m-long core spanning the past 5,000 years. We expect the Nettilling and Amadjuak lake cores to confirm our interpretation of the general regional pattern, while showing special interior influences. This will be an important addition to the Holocene record for the eastern Arctic.

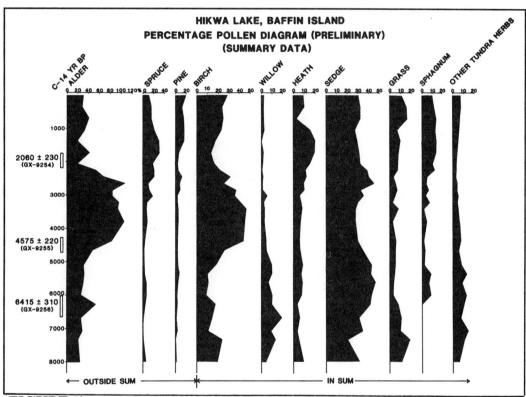

FIGURE 4: Percentage pollen diagram from Hikwa Lake on Frobisher Bay. Cores taken from Nettilling and Amadjuak lakes are expected to yield similar pollen records with some differences intrinsic to the interior region.

Pending those results, we can summarize what the Hikwa Lake record (Figure 4) tells us about developments in southern Baffin Island, and suggest how these apply to the large lakes region. Apparently Low Arctic vegetational elements (e.g. *Betula*) were present in a predominantly herbaceous tundra around the glacier margins of southern Baffin Island before

---

1 Hikwa Lake is the unofficial name for a small (425 m x 150 m) lake located in Ward Inlet, on the north side of Frobisher Bay (63.5°N, 67.6°W).

7,000 yr B.P. Expansion of vegetation and a transition to shrub-tundra, at least in lower elevations, coincided with deglaciation. This trend reached its climax around 3,500 yr B.P., and subsequently shrub-tundra became more restricted, although a recovery may have begun in this century.

The Burwash Bay core consists of an algal gyttja containing scattered moss macrofossils that become more abundant with depth. Radiocarbon dates from two levels are: 2,825 ± 230 yr B.P. (S-2879) at 35 cm and 4,290 ± 315 yr B.P. (S-2878) at 85 cm. Extrapolation from the latter date shows that deglaciation occurred before 6,000 yr B.P. and was followed by a period of relatively rapid sedimentation and plant production that peaked between 4,000 yr B.P. and 3,500 yr B.P. Thereafter, the sedimentation rate decreased to less than half the earlier rate, and organic production declined. So perhaps a rather warm, wet climate prevailed soon after deglaciation and lasted until after 3,000 yr B.P., when climate rapidly became colder and drier. In outline, this is consistent with the record of the Hikwa Lake core. It remains now to determine through pollen analysis whether the shrub-tundra maximum and associated maximum of tundra primary productivity occurred simultaneously in both areas. Even more exciting is the prospect of being able to ascertain, with a resolution of a century or better, the sequence of changes that occurred in what during the mid-Holocene must have been a decidedly different environment from the present.

ARCHAEOLOGY

Two main cultural traditions are recognized in the prehistory of Arctic Canada: Paleo-Eskimo and Neo-Eskimo. The origins of both traditions, which collectively span some 4,000 years, have been traced to Alaska, from which a series of eastward migrations have occurred (see McGhee, this volume). These peoples were widely dispersed throughout the Arctic Islands and mainland where they adapted to various tundra and boreal forest environments (Maxwell 1985).

The Paleo-Eskimo tradition dates between about 4,000 and 900 yr B.P., and includes several temporal and/or regional variants (e.g. Independence I, Pre-Dorset, Dorset). Archaeological evidence from Independence I and Pre-Dorset sites indicates a greater reliance on terrestrial resources such as caribou and muskox than appears in the later Dorset period (about 2,800 - 900 yr B.P.). In the latter case, a stronger commitment to the maritime environment is seen as an adaptive response to climatic cooling and is reflected in the appearance of such items as snow-knives, sled-shoes, stone cooking vessels and ice creepers, used in procurement of marine mammals at the floe-edge or in open leads.

The second major tradition (Neo-Eskimo) developed in northern Alaska and appeared in the Canadian Arctic about 1,000 AD. Through processes that are not completely clear, these latest arrivals (the Thule Culture) supplanted the existing Dorset Culture. A primary distinction between the Thule and their Dorset predecessors was the ability of the former to harvest large baleen whales with a complex technological and social arsenal (cf. Minc 1986; Savelle and McCartney, this volume). An emphasis on hunting large whales may have developed as a response to their increased availability through an expansion of habitat during the warm Neo-Atlantic climatic episode (McGhee 1969/1970). Thule people were equally adept, however, at harvesting smaller marine mammals as well as other aquatic and terrestrial resources. The pronounced flexibility of their socio-economic system played a central role in their cultural development when the economic importance of large whale hunting diminished.

The archaeological part of our research focuses primarily on Thule land-use patterns. Traditionally, analyses of Thule socio-economic systems have been restricted to the coastal-winter dimension, and to correlating group behaviour with changes in climate and the ecology of certain marine resources. This approach has clearly established the central role of the maritime economy in Thule cultural development. However, it was not of exclusive importance, and its continued domination of Thule research is based primarily on a priori assumptions regarding the scarce inland archaeological record. As a result, we lack detailed information on the forms of inland adaptations, especially those surrounding caribou use. Despite recognition of this species as a critical subsistence resource during the pre-contact era, and its potential for dramatic fluctuations through time, little information is available beyond descriptions of caribou procurement methods and archaeological data on frequencies of caribou and bird remains.

Archaeological investigation of the large lakes region was prompted by Inuit oral traditions and ethnographic accounts that cite its importance to the seasonal round of three regional populations in southern Baffin Island (Figure 1) and by the demonstrated importance of caribou in coastal Thule winter settlement sites in upper Frobisher Bay (Stenton 1983,

1987; Jacobs and Stenton 1985). These sites are far from the resource-rich floe-edge in winter, and good local availability of caribou has been advanced as an argument for continued occupation of the upper bay region until the early contact period. The primary catalyst for travel to the interior was a need for caribou skins for winter clothing. But it is also clear that maintenance of social relationships through various forms of interaction (e.g. marriage, trade partnerships) also guided such behaviour (Boas 1888, pp. 15, 54-62).

Prior to this study, there had been no archaeological surveys in the interior lowlands, although travellers such as Hantzsch in 1910 (Millward 1930; Neatby 1977) and Soper in 1925 (Soper 1981, p. 60) reported finding cultural features on the lake shores. We conducted surveys along the northwest shore of Nettilling Lake and at its south end, as well as at the south end of Amadjuak Lake. Nearly 100 habitation sites have thus far been described (Stenton 1987), most of them in Burwash and Tikera bays of Nettilling Lake. With few exceptions, these sites are associated with prominent esker/moraine systems which provide good views of the surrounding area, some relief from swarms of mosquitoes and, because caribou travel along these features in the course of their movements around the lakes, the opportunity to intercept them at predetermined strategic locations such as river crossings (Figure 2).

The oldest site discovered so far is "Sandy Point" (L1Dv-10) on Burwash Bay (Figure 5), which is more than 3,000 years old, based on a radiocarbon date of 2,815 ± 65 yr B.P. (S-2780) from a buried soil overlying the cultural layers. Typing of lithic artifacts indicates that it represents an early to middle Pre-Dorset occupation (Figure 6) (Stenton 1986). Another productive site is L1Dv-4 near the mouth of Amadjuak River, which typologically is in the late Dorset cultural phase of about 1,000 to 1,100 yr B.P. Pre-Dorset and Dorset artifacts have been found at other sites too, so there is little doubt that this region was frequently inhabitated in the Paleo-Eskimo period.

The Thule Culture is represented at many sites on Nettilling and Amadjuak lakes. One of the largest is on the washed moraine complex at the mouth of Amadjuak River (Figure 2), where more than 150 features of various types (Figure 7) and artifact assemblages (Figure 8) attest to an economy based mainly on caribou, but using abundant fishes, waterfowl, and other resources. At other sites tangible evidence in the form of Thule-style winter half-buried (semi-subterranean) dwellings confirms early reports of occasional year-round settlements on the lakes (Figure 9).

FIGURE 5: Aerial view of "Sandy Point" on Burwash Bay, Nettilling Lake. This is the location of a Pre-Dorset occupation that is at least 3,000 years old. Most of the site has eroded into the lake, but artifacts have been recovered <u>in situ</u> in the banks of the small island to the right, on the beach, and from the water.

FIGURE 6: Selected Pre-Dorset artifacts from the "Sandy Point" site, including burins, end-blades, knives, and scrapers.

FIGURE 7: Concentration of caches, tent-rings and cairns on the crest of a moraine at the Amadjuak River mouth. They indicate intensive and repeated occupation of this site which overlooks a major caribou-crossing point.

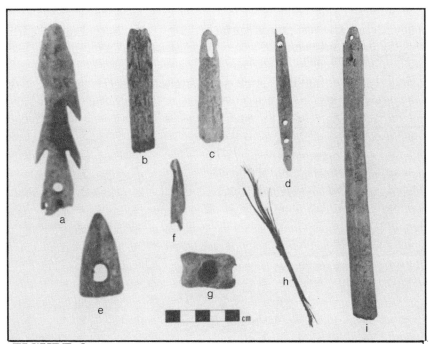

FIGURE 8: Thule Culture artifacts from the Burwash Bay area include: a sealing harpoon head (a), leister barbs (b,f), a dog trace buckle (e), a bow-drill mouthpiece (g), and a lance head (i) that are indicative of the range of subsistence activities. The harpoon head is common to Thule assemblages dating between about 1300 and 1600 AD.

FIGURE 9: A Thule-style half-buried autumn/winter dwelling on Burwash Bay, one of a number of such structures that have been found on Nettilling and Amadjuak lakes.

Evidence of occupation during the early part of this century has been found at several sites. This typically includes considerable surface debris, rifle and shotgun cartridges (but also bow and arrow parts!), saws and files, as well as the use of metal and wood instead of stone and bone in otherwise familiar Thule-style implements (Figure 10). Although use of

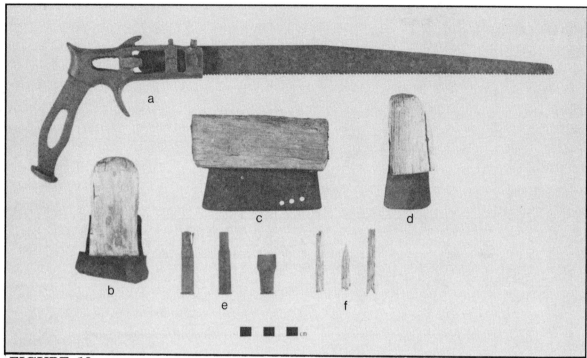

FIGURE 10: Evidence of occupation early in this century has been found at several sites. In addition to obviously modern implements such as the saw (a) and cartridge cases (e), there are two wood and steel scrapers (b,d) that were traditionally fashioned from caribou scapulae and a cutting and scraping tool (c) with a steel blade replacing what would have been slate in the past, as well as arrow parts (f).

the interior region has declined recently, Inuit elders from Iqaluit, Pangnirtung and Cape Dorset vividly recall their experiences in travelling overland in summer to the interior.

Although many of the archaeological field data are still under analysis, clearly settlement in the large lakes region was a periodic option through the last four millennia. Our ethnographic evidence suggests that movement to the interior is triggered by changes in the number and distribution of caribou. Studies in Alaska and Greenland (Burch 1972; Meldgaard 1986) have demonstrated the cyclic nature of caribou population dynamics, and have related these fluctuations to increased predation and overgrazing. However, effects of climatic fluctuations on primary production and especially on winter range conditions are seen as the primary influence. There is evidence of similar fluctuations in caribou numbers and distribution in Baffin Island; therefore, our archaeological study is organized within an ecological-interpretive framework, modelling human behaviourial adjustments as responses to changing herd conditions.

CORRELATION

It would be premature to propose a detailed chronology of the large lakes region at this early stage in our investigations. Archaeological surveys are far from complete, and many promising sites have yet to be tested or excavated. Likewise, the paleoenvironmental record is still under study, as we analyze and calibrate the pollen record against a regional climatology that is itself being studied. However, we can offer a tentative interpretation of the available archaeological evidence against a paleoenvironmental sequence inferred mainly from the Frobisher Bay pollen record (Figure 11).

Deglaciation and emergence came late to the interior lowlands, but plant colonization and succession were rapid. The first people to arrive, the

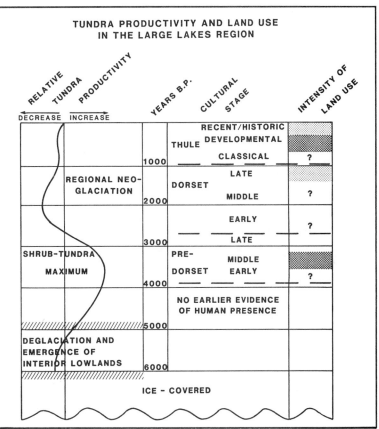

FIGURE 11: A tentative chronology of environmental and cultural developments in the large lakes region. Some gaps in the cultural record (?) may be filled as a result of further surveys and excavations.

Pre-Dorset, found a highly-productive land in a milder-than-present climate, under which conditions they flourished for perhaps a millennium or more. With regional cooling around 3,000 yr B.P., winter occupation of the interior became untenable. Perhaps there was a long hiatus until Dorset people, better-adapted to colder climate, found their way into the interior on a seasonal basis. Their successors, people of the Thule Culture, showed little hesitation in exploiting the interior seasonally and, when short-term conditions were favourable, year-round.

So much for the outline. There is an intriguing inland arctic ecosystem that humans evidently occupied over much of the last four millennia. The nature of that system and how it has changed over time remain to be more fully determined.

ACKNOWLEDGEMENTS

This work has benefited greatly from information provided by the people of Iqaluit, Kingnait, and Pangnirtung, and from discussions with Michael Ferguson, Baffin Regional Wildlife Biologist. Assistance in the field has been given by students from our and other institutions and from the northern communities. Financial and material support has been provided by the Natural Sciences and Engineering Research Council, the Social Sciences and Humanities Research Council, Indian and Northern Affairs Canada (through both the Northern Scientific Training Grants and the use of the Iqaluit Laboratory), the Atmospheric Environment Service, the Government of the Northwest Territories, the Boreal Institute for Northern Studies, the Faculty Development Program of the University of Wisconsin at Oshkosh, and the University of Windsor Research Board.

REFERENCES

Blake, W., Jr. 1966. End moraines and deglaciation chronology in northern Canada with special reference to southern Baffin Island. Geological Survey of Canada, Paper 66-26:1-31.

Boas, F. 1888. The Central Eskimo. Sixth Annual Report of the Bureau of American Ethnology. Smithsonian Institution. pp. 400-675.

Burch, E.S., Jr. 1972. The caribou/wild reindeer as a human resource. American Antiquity 37:339-368.

Davis, P.T. 1980. Late Holocene glacial, vegetational, and climatic history of Pangnirtung and Kingnait Fiord area, Baffin Island, N.W.T., Canada. Ph.D dissertation, University of Colorado, Boulder.

Jacobs, J.D. and L. Grondin. 1988. The influence of an arctic large lakes system on mesoclimate in south-central Baffin Island, N.W.T., Canada. Arctic and Alpine Research 20:212-219.

Jacobs, J.D., W.N. Mode, C.A. Squires, and G.H. Miller. 1985A. Holocene environmental change in the Frobisher Bay area, Baffin Island, N.W.T. Géographie physique et Quaternaire 39:151-162.

Jacobs, J.D., W.N. Mode, and E. Dowdeswell. 1985B. Contemporary pollen deposition and the distribution of *Betaula glandulosa* at the limit of Low Arctic tundra in southern Baffin Island, N.W.T., Canada. Arctic and Alpine Research 17:279-287.

Jacobs, J.D. and D.R. Stenton. 1985. Environment, resources, and prehistoric settlement in upper Frobisher Bay, Baffin Island. Arctic Anthropology 22:59-76.

Maxwell, J.B. 1980. Climate of the Canadian Arctic Islands and adjacent waters, Volume 1. Atmospheric Environment Service, Downsview, Ontario.

Maxwell, M.S. 1985. Prehistory of the eastern Arctic. Academic Press, Orlando, Florida.

McGhee, R.J. 1969/1970. Speculation on climatic change and Thule culture development. Folk 11/12:173-184.

McLauchlan, D.P. 1944. Report of patrol from Lake Harbour to Cape Dorset, Nettilling Lake, Pangnirtung, and Frobisher Bay by dog team, March 27th - May 25th, 1944. National Archives of Canada files, "G" Division, Royal Canadian Mounted Police.

Meldgaard, M. 1986. The Greenland caribou - zoogeography, taxonomy, and population dynamics. Meddelelser om Grønland, Bioscience 20:1-88.

Millward, A.E. (Editor). 1930. Southern Baffin Island: an account of exploration, investigation and settlement during the past fifty years. Department of The Interior, Ottawa.

Minc, L. 1986. Scarcity and survival: the role of oral tradition in mediating subsistence crises. Journal of Anthropological Archaeology 5:39-113.

Mode, W.N. and J.D. Jacobs. 1985. Holocene vegetation and climate, southern Baffin Island, N.W.T., Canada. Geological Society of America, Abstracts with Programs 17:319.

Neatby, L. H. 1977. My life among the Eskimos: the Baffinland journals of Bernard Adolph Hantzsch 1909-1911. Mawdsley Memoir Series 3. Institute for Northern Studies, University of Saskatchewan, Saskatoon.

Porsild, A.E. 1958. Geographical distribution of some elements in the flora of Canada. Geographical Bulletin 11:57-77.

Short, S.K., W.N. Mode, and P.T. Davis. 1985. The Holocene record from Baffin Island: modern and fossil pollen studies. In: Quaternary Environments: Eastern Canadian Arctic, Baffin Bay and Western Greenland. Edited by: J.T. Andrews. Allen and Unwin, Ltd. Boston.

Soper, J.D. 1928. A faunal investigation of southern Baffin Island. National Museum of Canada, Bulletin 53.

_____. 1981. Canadian Arctic recollections: Baffin Island 1923-1931. Mawdsley Memoir 4. Institute for Northern Studies, University of Saskatchewan, Saskatoon.

Stenton, D.R. 1983. An analysis of faunal remains from the Peale Point Site (KkDo-1), Baffin Island, N.W.T. M.A. thesis, Department of Anthropology, Trent University, Peterborough, Ontario.

_____. 1986. Mitigation of the Sandy Point Site (L1Dv-10), Baffin Island, N.W.T. Report on file, Prince of Wales Northern Heritage Centre, Yellowknife, N.W.T.

_____. 1987. The Nettilling Lake Archaeological Project, Baffin Island, N.W.T. Report to the Archaeological Survey of Canada. Department of Anthropology, University of Alberta, Edmonton, Alberta.

Illustrated by Brenda Carter

HISTORY AND RECENT EXPEDITIONS

DISCOVERIES AND EXPLORATIONS OF THE CIRCUMPOLAR LANDS AND SEAS FROM ANTIQUITY TO THE TWENTIETH CENTURY

J.R. Weber[1] and E.F. Roots[2]

Abstract: This paper sumarizes information on expeditions that led to the discovery and exploration of the Arctic Ocean and its margin since the voyage of Pytheas about 320 BC. The exploration of the Canadian Arctic Islands is viewed in this perspective. It took more than three centuries to map all of those islands beginning with Frobisher's exploration of southwestern Baffin Island in the sixteenth century and virtually ending with Stefansson's discovery of several islands in the northwestern extremity of the archipelago during the Canadian Arctic Expedition of 1913-1918. However, Prince Charles, Air Force and Foley islands remained undiscovered until 1948, when a Royal Canadian Air Force Lancaster spotted them.

Résumé: Cet article résume l'information sur les expéditions qui ont permis la découverte et l'exploration de l'océan Arctique et de ses marges, depuis le voyage de Pythéas vers l'an 320 A.C. C'est dans cette perspective qu'est examinée l'exploration des îles de l'Arctique canadien. Il a fallu plus de trois siècles pour cartographier l'ensemble de ces îles, depuis l'exploration par Frobisher du sud-ouest de l'île Baffin, au 16e siècle, jusqu'à la découverte par Stefansson de plusieurs îles dans l'extrémité nord-ouest de l'archipel pendant l'expédition de 1913 à 1918 dans l'Arctique canadien. Cependant, les îles Prince-Charles, de l'Aviation et Foley ne furent découvertes qu'en 1948, lorsqu'un avion "Lancaster" de l'Aviation royale du Canada les a repérées.

INTRODUCTION

The history of geographical exploration of the arctic regions has been told many times, and there is an enormous literature dealing with expeditions and geographical discoveries. This is a summary of those expeditions, starting with the earliest recorded voyages, that led to the discovery of the Arctic Ocean and its scientific exploration during the last two centuries. Among the circumpolar lands, the Canadian Arctic Islands and northern Greenland, because of their intricate geography and ice conditions that are so much more severe than elsewhere, were the most difficult to explore. It took more than three centuries to map all of the Arctic Islands starting with Martin Frobisher's exploration of Hudson Strait and southwestern Baffin Island in the sixteenth century, and ending with Vilhjalmur Stefansson's discovery and mapping of the last of the Queen Elizabeth Islands during the First World War. For a more complete history of the geographical discovery and scientific exploration of the Arctic Ocean region, see Weber and Roots (1989).

The reader is referred to the maps on the inside covers of this book for geographical place-names used in this section.

[1] Geophysics Division, Geological Survey of Canada, 1 Observatory Crescent, Ottawa K1A 0Y3
[2] Science Advisor, Environment Canada, Ottawa, Ontario K1A 0H3
Geological Survey of Canada Contribution No. 50588

FROM ANTIQUITY TO MERCATOR AND BARENTS

The first polar explorer on record was Pytheas from the Greek colony of Massilia, the modern Marseilles. About 320 BC, he sailed in search of the tin which had mysteriously appeared from time to time in the markets of Massilia, coming, so rumour said, south through Gaul from some remote and unknown northern land. Navigating by sun and stars he steered his square-sailed Greek galley to Brittany and to Cornwall, the source of the tin. After sailing northward from the British Isles for six days, he reached another land, which he identified as Thule, where the nearby sea was frozen. Whether this was Iceland or northern Norway has been much debated; but the consistency with which the wealth of information brought back by Pytheas was reported and used by many contemporaneous sources leaves no doubt that he reached arctic latitudes and spent some time there. Observations on the relative positions of the stars, the midnight sun, the differing lengths of days and nights as the seasons progressed, the connection between the tides and the phases of the moon, large sea mammals, the unexpected phenomenon of the freezing of the sea was mystifying and terrible to warm-ocean sailors. These observations were completely new to Mediterranean geographers and scholars, so that the words to describe some of them had to be borrowed from Pytheas' Celtic and Norse contacts. So convincing was his information that this one extended voyage significantly enlarged the known world and brought arctic phenomena into what was then the mainstream of European scientific knowledge and literature (Chevallier 1984).

Pytheas' observations paved the way for Eratosthenes (220 BC) to portray the Earth as a sphere of finite size and to devise ways to calculate its circumference and axial tilt (Figure 1). Later geographers and cartographers such as

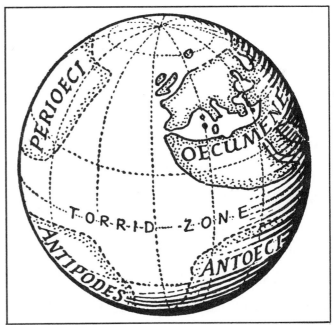

FIGURE 1: Greek conception of the Earth after Pytheas' discoveries and Eratosthenes' calculations: the globe as described by Crates (about 150 BC). It satisfied symmetry by inventing, in addition to the known inhabited world (the Oecumene), three other populated continents: Perioeci (peoples around the globe from the Oecumene), Antoeci (peoples below the Oecumene), and the Antipodes (peoples on the opposite of the globe) (Raisz 1948).

Strabo and Ptolemy incorporated this information, embellished with fanciful details and reports from various other sources, to develop a European concept of the arctic regions that remained essentially unchallenged for the next thousand years.

Apparently Iceland was already settled by Irish monks, when the Norsemen arrived about 870 AD. The settlement of Greenland by Eric the Red around 985 AD was soon followed by the discovery of Baffin Island, Labrador, Newfoundland and possibly Nova Scotia by Norsemen. Norse travellers from West Greenland reached St. Helena Island at the west end of Jones Sound in the central Canadian Archipelago and Bache Peninsula on Ellesmere Island.

The earliest account of a penetration into the Arctic Ocean Basin is in the writings of King Alfred the Great of England, who about 890 AD was informed by a Norwegian chieftan named Othere (Ottar), from Halagoland in southern Norway, that some decades earlier he had followed the Scandinavian coast to the north and east - "he was anxious to know how far the land extended, and whether any people lived beyond the wasteland" (Bosworth 1855; Sweet 1883, p. 30). Othere sailed around the North Cape and the Kola Peninsula into the White Sea, where he encountered the Finns from whom he thereafter annually collected produce and tribute. This voyage was followed by considerable coastal trade, and the extension of Norwegian sovereignty from the White Sea to Iceland. Norway's rule became absolute. A royal proclamation in 1294 forbade foreigners to sail north of Bergen and forced English and Dutch merchants to buy produce from all northern waters and lands in the harbour of that town. Even Norwegian ships were subjected to royal restrictions in venturing northward. This principle of mare clausum appears to have effectively prevented further exploration of the Arctic Ocean until well into the sixteenth century (Blom 1984).

Speculation on the geography of northern regions continued, however, and there were several attempts to compile known and imagined records. Early in the fifteenth century, a Dane, Claudius Clavus, made two maps of the North extending Ptolemy's atlas which showed only Terra Incognita and Mare Congelatum north of 63° latitude (which perhaps was Pytheas' northern limit). Presumably using information gathered from traditional Norse mariner's sailing stories, Clavus placed Iceland midway between Norway and Greenland. Norse knowledge of impenetrable sea ice across the northern North Atlantic may also have been the basis for the interpretation that a continuous land bridge between Greenland and

746

Europe closed off <u>Mare Congela-</u><u>tum</u>. A map showing both sides of the Atlantic in reasonable scale and proportions based on Norse and English voyages to North America was drawn in Iceland by Sigurdur Stephansson in 1570 (Figure 2), but it retained the land bridge. Other maps of the time, for example that of Ortelius published the same year, do not show land connecting Europe and Greenland. Greenland is depicted as a modest island of realistic shape, and a long marine passage leads around the north of North America to the "Strait of Anian" and the Pacific Ocean.

FIGURE 2: Map of the North Atlantic region drawn in Iceland by Sigurdur Stephansson in 1570. Note the rectangular coordinate system used for latitude and longitude. Stephansson appended explanatory notes to this map in which he remarks that the Atlantic Ocean was closed by Jotunheiman (the home of giants). Royal Library, Copenhagen.

In 1588, Nicolo Zeno published a story, now considered fiction, of the voyages of two of his ancestors to the Arctic in 1380. He illustrated the story with an imaginative "chart" based partly on the maps of Clavus and later cartographers. The popularity of this drawing was such that "Zenian geography" was accepted as an improvement on previous maps. Genuine contemporary discoveries, such as those of Frobisher, were force-fitted into Zeno's map and, thereby, falsified (Wallis 1984).

From the time of the early Greek and Roman globes that showed an all-encompassing ocean beyond the known and unknown lands (Figure 1), little attention had been given to what lay beyond the travelled world, including the polar region (Rey *et al.* 1984). Scandinavian legends, however, in which a polar maelstrom swirled about a central rock, surrounded by four islands, peopled by pygmies, and between which strong currents of water rushed to the Pole, had become known in southern Europe through a widely quoted book,

"De Inventione Fortunata qui liber incipit a gradua 54 usque ad polum" ("... which book begins in the description at latitude 54 degrees and goes as far as the pole") attributed to Nicholas of Lynne and published in Italy in 1360. The book is of interest today because it shows that, in the fourteenth century, degrees of latitude were already in widespread use for geographical description and that the North Pole was a widely understood concept. The mythical geography of the north polar regions, however, described in this book became the chief source of ideas for cartographers wishing to fill in blanks on the arctic map.

One of the earliest attempts to draw a map of the polar basin was by Johannes Ruysch of the Netherlands, whose 1507 map is included as Plate 1 in the 1508 edition of "Ptolemy's Geography" published in Rome. Ruysch quotes his authority for the central part of his map by a legend on the map:

> "In the book 'De Inventione Fortunata' it may be read that there is a high mountain of magnetic stone, 33 German miles in circumference. This is surrounded by flowing 'mare sugenum' which pours out water like a vessel through openings below. Around it are four islands of which two are inhabited. Extensive desolate mountains surround these islands for 24 days' journey, where there is no human habitation" (translation in Nansen 1911, Volume 2, p. 289).

The most influential of the map-makers to take their ideas from "De Inventione Fortunata" and similar stories was the Flemish cosmographer and cartographer Gerhard Kremer (Mercator), who in 1569 produced a world chart with a polar projection insert of the Arctic Ocean. This map differs in important ways from his earlier 1538 map. Although his 1569 map shows known land and seas as accurately as knowledge then permitted, the central Arctic Ocean is a fanciful cartoon based on "Inventione Fortunata" and the Scandinavian legends. The result was to mislead generations of later explorers. Over the next 30 years, Mercator improved his map and added details from successive discoveries of the known coasts and lands, but never abandoned the imaginary central ocean land masses (Figure 3). Other well-known world maps of the period, notably that of Ortelius, 1570, also fill the Arctic Ocean with four mythical islands. More cautious map-makers, notably the Dutch navigator Willem Barents, produced circumpolar maps depicting only the known and verified lands, at least within the sector of the then discovered lands, between Davis Strait and Novaya Zemlya (Figure 4). However, these more accurate renditions had less influence on geographers' concepts of the Arctic Ocean Basin.

FIGURE 3: Gerhard Mercator's revised circumpolar map of the Arctic Ocean, <u>Septentrionalium terrarum descriptio</u> (1595). National Archives of Canada, NMC-29431.

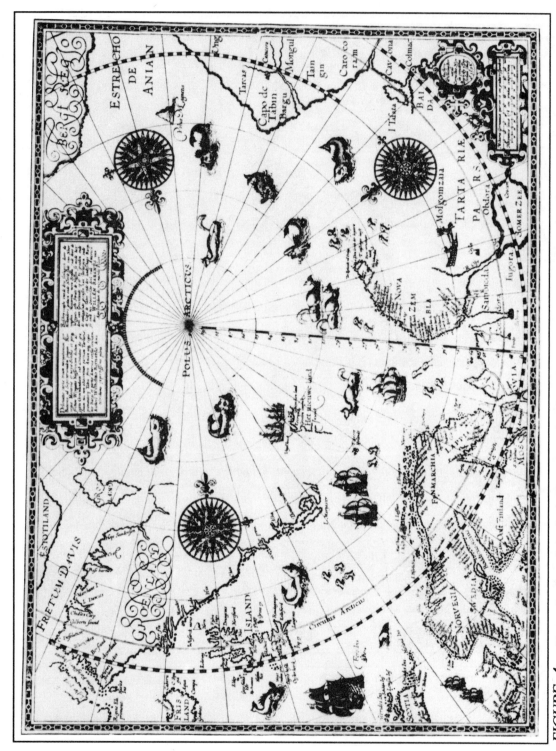

FIGURE 4: Circumpolar map of the Arctic Ocean drawn by Willem Barents (1598). National Archives of Canada, NMC-10299.

750

An interesting detail of Mercator's arctic maps, and of many other European maps of the period, is the inclusion of the "Strait of Anian" that connects the Arctic Ocean with the Kingdom of Japan. The concept of a strait separating Asia from North America was first embodied on maps about 1540, prior to any recorded discoveries in the region (Falk 1984). Many maps produced during the next 60 years show this strait, and on several of these the geographical position and outlines bear quite close resemblance to Bering Strait. Many modern scholars feel that the representations are pure speculation and the resemblance to actual geography is coincidental (Fisher 1984).

The fanciful ideas from the Scandinavian legends and "De Inventione Fortunata" have been very durable. The concept of a magnetic mountain as an attractor for the compass persisted long after William Gilbert showed that the Earth as a whole generated the magnetic forces. The notion of an open north polar sea was a driving force for centuries of later exploration. The concept of an aperture at the pole that led to the interior of the Earth developed later into "Symmes Hole", and still further into the idea of a hollow earth, popular with science fiction writers from Jules Verne ("Adventures of Captain Hatteras", 1864; see Barr, this volume) to Richard Lupoff ("Circumpolar!", 1984). A number of apparently serious quasi-philosophical tracts that ignore scientific evidence still find a ready popular sale among those wishing to believe in, or be titillated by, a "hole at the Pole" (Bernard 1976).

SEARCH FOR THE NORTHERN SEA ROUTE TO THE KINGDOMS OF CATHAY

In the sixteenth century, a fresh impetus was given to arctic exploration by the search for a northern route to the Indies, China and Japan, or the kingdoms of Cathay as they were called. This search was, in part, the result of the Treaty of Tordesillas in 1494, which divided the right of exploration and acquisition of the then known world into two domains, the western being granted to Spain, the eastern to Portugal. Although the treaty extended from Pole to Pole, the Papal bull giving international sanction to the treaty excluded lands already in possession of a Christian power and did not prevent northern nations from exploring the coasts of lands that they claimed (Theutenberg 1984). Discovery of a northern route to the Orient would, thus, circumvent the Spanish and Portugese blockades. Until the eighteenth century, the main motive of arctic voyages remained the search for a northern passage to the Pacific and the oriental kingdoms of Cathay. The concept of a navigable northern trade route to the Orient was first strongly promoted in 1527 by the English merchant adventurer Robert Thorne. In addition to political motives, it was bolstered by two misconceptions that, despite growing evidence, were to persist for centuries: (1) that sea ice formed only near coasts and that continuous arctic summer sun would maintain an open ice-free polar sea; and (2) a mistaken notion of the distance to China based, apparently, on Marco Polo's erroneous description of the width of Asia (Saladin d'Anglure 1980). This led to an assumption that a route through the North-West Passage would be much shorter than one to the east.

During the reign of Elizabeth I, in the second half of the sixteenth century, the British ventured both to the northeast and to the northwest. Richard Chancellor sailed as far as the southern tip of Novaya Zemlya, where he was forced back by an ice barrier at the entrance to the Kara Sea. In three voyages, 1576-1578, Martin Frobisher, probing Hudson Strait and the bays of southeastern Baffin Island, made the first contribution to arctic economic geology by bringing back pyritiferous mica schist that was mistaken for gold ore. This discovery precipitated two further expeditions in a frantic attempt to find gold - the first arctic gold rush.

In three carefully documented voyages, 1585 to 1587, John Davis explored the coasts of Greenland along Davis Strait. In 1594, four Dutch ships under the command of Willem Barents managed to penetrate the Kara Sea. Two years later, another Dutch expedition, commanded by Jon Rijp and Jacob Heemskerck with Barents as pilot, sailed beyond 80°N. On their way south, they discovered Spitsbergen with its waters abounding with seals, walruses and whales. Exploring further to the east, Heemskerck and Barents sailed around the northern tip of Novaya Zemlya, thus completing the outline of the major land areas north of Eurasia.

In 1609, the Netherlands forced Portugal to grant her full rights to the trade in eastern waters. Thus, the Dutch had no further need for the arctic sea route, and abandoned its search for a northern route to the Indies. The British, however, were still opposed by Spain and continued the quest, and in 1616 Robert Bylot, with William Baffin as navigator, nearly solved the problem of the North-West Passage. Bylot was by this time on his fifth arctic exploratory voyage, Baffin on his sixth. They navigated the 50-ton ship *Discovery* along

Greenland's west coast to Melville Bay, rounded the head of what is now Baffin Bay, crossed Smith Sound at the south end of Nares Strait and explored the eastern ends of Jones and Lancaster sounds. Naming all the major land and water features, they recorded most of the outline of western Greenland and the eastern Canadian Arctic Islands. Baffin's detailed maps and journals from this voyage, however, were not preserved. The only record of his survey that can be identified today is in the circumpolar chart "Polar Map or Card" produced in 1635 by Luke Foxe, an acquaintance of Baffin, to illustrate his own 1631-1632 explorations in Hudson Bay. The map shows in excellent detail the then-known arctic coastlines of North America, Spitsbergen and Scandinavia (Taylor 1955; Wallis 1984). Otherwise, and in part possibly due to commercial rivalry, Baffin's findings were forgotten or doubted. They were not rediscovered until the nineteenth century.

The seventeenth century arctic maritime discoveries, launched by merchant guilds and city companies seeking a trade route to the Orient, were supplemented by the unrecorded voyages of whalers and sealers who followed into subarctic and arctic waters. The Dutch discovery of rich marine resources in the Barents Sea and around Spitsbergen soon led to a fierce rivalry between English and Dutch whalers and sealers. The extension of whaling grounds into Melville Bay, western Baffin Bay and Hudson Strait was mainly an English operation, although Dutch, Danish, French and Portugese ships are known to have been active. On land the men of the Hudson's Bay Company (founded in 1670), and other trappers, hunters and voyageurs, had already started to push the North American frontier towards the Arctic Ocean. Similarly, the Russian economic empire was expanding eastwards across Siberia and along the Asian arctic coast.

EIGHTEENTH CENTURY STRATEGIC EXPLORATIONS

With the onset of the eighteenth century, motives and methods of polar exploration changed. Exploration became largely an instrument of government policy, and the national navies of Britain, France and Russia replaced the private groups and merchant adventurers of former years. In Britain, the dominant role of the Royal Navy in the organization and conduct of polar exploration became a tradition that has continued almost to the present day. Most important, however, the eighteenth century saw the beginning of scientific exploration. The new national academies of science that sprang up in England, France and Russia played a very important part as advisors of governments in all scientific matters, and as initiators of exploration.

The eighteenth century was one of Russian achievement in the Arctic. All activities, however, were land-based or coastal. The question of whether Asia and America are joined had been solved by a Siberian Cossack, Simon Dezhnev. In 1648, he sailed from the Kolyma River on the eastern Siberian arctic coast around East Cape (Mys Dezhneva) through Bering Strait to the mouth of Anadyr River. Dezhneva's discovery was reported to the authorities in Yakutsk but remained officially unknown in Europe until well into the first half of the eighteenth century, although rumours of the voyage may have reached the Imperial Court in St. Petersburg earlier. Such rumours may have stimulated Tsar Peter the Great to launch a series of grandiose projects of exploration. The first of these under the leadership of Vitus Bering, was a huge expedition that included 200 horses, which left St. Petersburg in 1725 and crossed Siberia overland. After immense hardships, it reached the coastal town of Okhotsk. In 1729, Bering was able to circumnavigate Kamchatka Peninsula and sail up Bering Strait as far as Mys Dezhneva, but due to the lateness of the season and dense fog, he had to return without having sighted the Alaskan coast. In 1732, on a separate expedition, Ivan Fedorov and Mikhail Gvozdev charted Cape Prince of Wales, and King Island and the Diomede Islands in Bering Strait, thus completing the exploration of Bering Strait. It was not until 1740, on a subsequent expedition, that Bering made landfall in Alaska. These expeditions were supplemented by many surveys by the Imperial Admiralty College, and by 1746 the whole of the Siberian arctic coast from the River Ob to Mys Dezhneva, Bering Strait and the Anadyr and Kamchatka peninsulas had been explored and charted.

In eastern Siberia and Bering Strait, exploration was followed by trade, and by the formation of trading companies. Catherine the Great encouraged a new brand of Russian imperialism across Bering Strait and southward along the North American coast during the second half of the eighteenth century. By the first quarter of the nineteenth century, Russia - in the form of the government sponsored Russian-American Company - was firmly established in Alaska. A rigorous ukase, or ban, proclaimed by Tsar Alexander I in 1818, effectively closed the North Pacific to non-Russians (Roots 1986), and the problem of finding a North-West Passage around the northern extremity of Canada became a strategic priority for Great Britain. The search for this passage was to preoccupy the British Navy for more than half a century following the Napoleonic Wars.

Among the remarkable advances in science of the eighteenth century, the study of magnetism was one of the most important. The formulation of general laws, or principles, of planetary magnetism and the construction of magnetic charts led to a need for widespread, simultaneous observations of magnetic variation and dip. Consequently, the recording of magnetic observations became a prime duty of naval expeditions. The re-emergence of scientific astronomy, and the study of the relation of the Earth to the motions of other planets and "heavenly bodies" became another powerful scientific incentive for global exploration and voyages to distant locations to observe eclipses and make celestial observations.

Advances in technology, such as the invention of John Hadley's reflecting quadrant in 1731, the introduction of John Harrison's chronometer in 1762, the publication by Nevil Maskeleyne in 1767 of the first nautical almanac, the availability of better ships, including rot-resistant rope for rigging, and the techniques of preventing scurvy during long voyages, boosted exploration.

Between 1770 and 1772, Samuel Hearne of the Hudson's Bay Company, accompanied by Indian guides, made an overland trip from Churchill to the Coppermine River in search of the source of native copper, and also to determine whether a low-latitude North-West Passage could be found north of Churchill. In July 1771, Hearne reached the mouth of the Coppermine River, the first white man to stand on the north coast of the American continent. His explorations showed conclusively that there was no easily navigable passage between eastern North America and the Pacific Ocean (Keating 1970). Hearne brought back a sample of copper but the company made no attempt to exploit the copper deposits.

In 1773, Captain Constantin John Phipps led a scientific expedition into the Arctic Ocean. The plan was for a "voyage made towards the North-Pole to be of service to the promotion of natural knowledge" (Royal Society 1782, p. 158). The voyage was sponsored by the Royal Society of London and approved by the Admiralty and King George III. Prevented by heavy ice from reaching more than a short distance north of Spitsbergen, his two ships, the sloops *Racehorse* and *Carcass*, explored the ice edge from near Greenland to White Island. Among the better known results of Phipps' expedition were: the first scientific description of the polar bear (*Ursus maritimus* Phipps); measurement of the gravity difference between northernmost Spitsbergen and Greenwich; the first measurements of the West Spitsbergen and East Greenland currents; and the first temperature and salinity profiles and depth-soundings of Arctic Ocean waters. Although there were no new geographical discoveries, the expedition is mentioned because it was an important event in the story of Arctic science. It represented the first multidisciplinary field research expedition into the Arctic Ocean region and set the pattern for nineteenth century polar expeditions.

Except for Phipps' expedition, no British ships ventured into the High Arctic during the eighteenth century. A number of voyages were undertaken into Hudson Bay in search of the North-West Passage, motivated primarily by a desire to outflank the French fur trade in the south. During that time, British exploratory interests were mainly preoccupied with the great Pacific and Antarctic voyages of James Cook and with operations to oust the French and secure dominion over Canada.

BRITISH ROYAL NAVY EXPLORATIONS OF THE NINETEENTH CENTURY

Following the battle of Waterloo, military or territorial goals became closely connected to trade, and except for the North Pacific the seas were for the first time free to all ships. Exploration expanded dramatically. Interest in scientific knowledge among the emerging middle classes (a development influenced by the industrial revolution) found an expression in private societies in which scientific discoveries were followed by a popular, as well as professional, membership. Geographical societies, in particular, became centres of influential and informed public opinion and took a leading role in promoting polar exploration. The first was the Société de Géographie in Paris, founded in 1821, followed by the Gesellschaft für Erdkunde in Berlin (1828) and the Geographical Society of London (1830). Polar exploration during the first half of the nineteenth century was predominantly a naval affair, and naval officers with experience of polar voyages were among the most active members of the new geographical societies. The membership also included many owners of whaling and sealing ships. Through these members a wealth of practical knowledge accumulated and the geographical societies became centres of advice on the organization and techniques of polar exploration.

The British Navy was foremost in the revival of polar exploration. The motive was no longer simply a search for a passage to Cathay but included the delineation of the Arctic coast of British North America and the discovery of new lands of exploitable resources. Britain was keenly aware of its potential rivals, the youthful and ebullient United States to the south, and the Russian Empire to the west. The latter was in control of Alaska and the coasts of the North Pacific from Vancouver Island to Vladivostok and had extended trading posts as far south as San Francisco. By taking the initiative in northern exploration, the British Admiralty hoped to forestall rival operations in the Arctic.

It is indicative of the politics and mood of the times that British naval interest in Arctic Ocean exploration was sparked by commercial whaling interests and made possible by a surplus of new, well-built, capable vessels and trained officers left from the close of the Napoleonic wars in 1815. The Second Secretary of the Admiralty, Sir John Barrow, was dedicated to the discovery and traverse of the North-West Passage, and was a principal exponent of the widely held view that polynyas in the pack-ice of the North Atlantic were evidence of "a freedom of movement to the north, including open water in the neighbourhood of the Pole" (Kane 1856, Volume 1, p. 307). Barrow stated with conviction that "... if, therefore, the great polar basin should be free of land, the probability is that it will also be free of ice" (Barrow 1818, p. 374). The whaling captain and scientist William Scoresby, Jr., who had more than 20 years experience in the ice and who had made a careful survey of the coasts of Greenland and compiled the first technical description of polar ice, on the other hand considered the idea of an open polar sea to be "altogether chimerical". He proposed to "... reach the Pole by travelling across the ice from Spitzbergen" (Scoresby 1818, p. 328). Scoresby noted strong variations in the severity of ice between different decades, and urged taking advantage of the then comparatively ice-free situation to search for a North-West Passage. Together with his friend Sir Joseph Banks (president of the Royal Society and a colleague of Phipps), who had been a Lord of the Admiralty, Scoresby was able to revive scientific interest in polar exploration. However, his difference of opinion with Barrow appears to have prevented his taking further direct part (Taylor 1955, p. 22; Martin 1988; Levere 1988). As a result, in 1818, the British parliament passed an act to promote polar exploration. The government dispatched two major polar expeditions, one under Captain John Buchan, with Lieutenant John Franklin as second-in-command, to continue Phipps' work of 45 years earlier "to try to reach the Pacific by a northern route across the

Pole" (Smith 1877, p. 41), and the other, led by Commander John Ross, with Edward Parry as second-in-command, to check on Baffin's findings of 200 years before.

Buchan and Franklin, in *Dorothea* and *Trent*, barely got north of Spitsbergen before they were, like Phipps, stopped by impenetrable ice. Ross and Parry, however, in *Isabella* and *Alexander*, sailed up Davis Strait and rounded the head of Baffin Bay. Although they did not get as far north as their Elizabethan predecessors Bylot and Baffin, they confirmed Baffin's discoveries and applied his names to the main geographical features of the eastern Canadian Arctic Islands. Ross, however, failed to penetrate far into Lancaster Sound and inexplicably turned back, allegedly stopped by a chain of mountains he named Crokers Mountains.

The following year the Admiralty sent two ships, *Hecla* and *Griper*, under the command of Edward Parry to check on Ross' findings. Parry sailed through Lancaster Sound into Barrow Strait to discover Prince Regent Inlet, Wellington Channel and Cornwallis Island. He continued into Viscount Melville Sound, until stopped by ice at 110° longitude. The two ships wintered at Winter Harbour on Melville Island and the following summer, after penetrating a little farther west but finding ice still barring the way, they returned to England. Parry had with him, as he had also the year before, Captain Edward Sabine of the Royal Artillery, "... a gentleman well skilled in Astronomy, Natural History and various branches of knowledge" (Ross 1819, p. 10). Besides charting and sounding, Sabine measured water and air temperatures, studied the movement of tides and currents, made magnetic observations, and observed the effect of the Aurora Borealis on the electrometer and magnetic needle. While wintering on Melville Island, Sabine took pendulum measurements from which he subsequently determined the elipticity of the earth (Sabine 1821). Geological observations were made in Lancaster Sound and on a traverse to the interior of Melville Island.

Parry made two more attempts to navigate the North-West Passage. He sailed into Prince Regent Inlet and later entered Foxe Basin, on the southwest side of Baffin Island, where he discovered Fury and Hecla Strait, but ice conditions in each case prevented his sailing farther west.

The experiences of Phipps and Buchan did not dispel the idea of an open polar ocean. In 1827, encouraged by handsome rewards offered by the British Parliament for an attempt to reach the Pole, Parry and his crew sailed for Spitsbergen in the *Hecla*. From there, using two ships' boats fitted with iron runners and provisioned for 71 days, they sailed north until they reached solid pack ice. Hauling the boats on foot over the ice and launching them in intervening open water, they toiled for five weeks. They made very slow progress against the strong Transpolar Current, whose drift rate and direction they carefully recorded, and on July 26, 1827, having reached 82° 45' North latitude, they turned back.

John Ross made another, privately-funded attempt to find a passage to the west in 1828. He sailed in *Victory*, a paddle steamer that had been used in commercial service around the British coast. His second-in-command was his nephew, James Clark Ross, a specialist in the study of magnetism. Sailing south into Prince Regent Inlet, Ross mistook Bellot Strait, the key to the transit to Amundsen Gulf and the North-West Passage, for a bay (Savelle and Holland 1987), and continued to Boothia Peninsula where the *Victoria* was beset by ice. The ship remained icebound for three winters and was finally abandoned. During those years, James Clark Ross made long sled journeys with the Inuit. On one of these trips, to King William Island on 31 May 1831, he determined the location of the North Magnetic Pole.

While shipborne expeditions explored the northern waterways, overland parties, led mostly by naval officers, assisted by men of the Hudson's Bay Company, carried out many great journeys on the Arctic mainland. Chief Factor Peter Warren Dease, Dr. John Richardson and George Back travelled with Lieutenant John Franklin, and later led their own parties; and John Rae made extensive natural history observations as he filled in all but short stretches of the unknown coasts. Dease, Richardson, Back, Rae and Thomas Simpson were among these land explorers, who contributed most to the discovery and mapping of mainland Arctic Canada. By 1847, the arctic coasts of Alaska and Canada from Prudhoe Bay to Boothia Peninsula, including the southern shores of Victoria and King William islands, had been explored. During these explorations, the main areas of crystalline (Precambrian Shield) and sedimentary rocks along the North American Arctic coast became known.

The search for the North-West Passage along the southern route, via Coronation Gulf, had narrowed to the gap between Barrow Strait and Queen Maud Gulf. It was Sir John Barrow, promoter and organizer of the Ross and Parry expeditions, who persuaded the Admiralty to launch yet another expedition in search of the North-West Passage. Approval was motivated partly by the concern that ships of the growing American and Russian fleets might win the honour of the Passage; partly by the opportunity for testing, under adverse conditions, ships outfitted with the new screw propellers; and partly as a naval training exercise. In 1845, HMS *Erebus* and *Terror*, under the command of Sir John Franklin, left England for Lancaster Sound, where they were last sighted. From Barrow Strait, *Erebus* and *Terror*, after having circumnavigated Cornwallis Island, headed south along Peel Sound and eventually became beset in Victoria Strait. Weakened by scurvy and threatened by starvation, the men abandoned the ships in April 1848 and headed for the mainland in hope of reaching a Hudson's Bay post. None of the 134 men of the original ship's companies was ever seen again, although there is evidence that they may have encountered a small band of Inuit before they perished. As it turned out, Franklin had linked the eastern and western approaches to the North-West Passage.

By 1857, some 40 expeditions had been launched in search of Franklin and his men. The searchers converged by land and by sea from Bering Strait, Lancaster Sound and Hudson Bay, so that by 1860 almost all of the intricate geography of the Canadian Arctic Archipelago had been mapped. The commanders and ships best remembered from this period were Britishers: James Clark Ross (*Enterprise* and *Investigator*, 1847); Henry Kellett (*Herald* and *Plover*, 1847-1850; *Resolute* and *Intrepid*, 1852-1855; see Barr, this volume); Richard Collinson (*Enterprise*, 1850-1855); John Ross (*Felix*, 1850-1851); Horatio Austin (four ships, led by *Resolute*, 1850-1851); William Penny (*Lady Franklin* and *Sophia*, 1850-1851); Edward Belcher (five vessels, led by *Resolute* and *Assistance*, 1852-1854); Edward Inglefield (*Isabel*, 1852; *Phoenix*, 1854); Francis McClintock (*Fox*, 1857-1859); and Americans: Edwin deHaven (*Advance* and *Rescue*, 1850-1851); Elisha Kane (*Advance*, 1853-1855). Travelling overland from the south, John Richardson and John Rae (1847, 1848-1849, 1851, 1853-1854) discovered firm evidence indicating where Franklin had disappeared and added many details to geographic and scientific knowledge. In 1852, aboard *Isabel*, Commander Inglefield, on a private expedition sponsored by Lady Franklin, advanced into Nares Strait and showed that this channel led northwards into the Arctic Ocean, confirming earlier Norse maps and the sixteenth-century charts of Mercator and Ortelius.

LAST DISCOVERIES OF LANDS AND COASTS

By 1870, all the circumpolar mainland coasts, Novaya Zemlya, and most of the Canadian Arctic Islands had been explored. There still remained large unexplored and unmapped areas: the northern and northeastern coasts of Greenland and its vast interior, Ellesmere Island, the northwestern Queen Elizabeth Islands, much of Spitsbergen, Severnaya Zemlya and Franz Josef Land. Although the south coast of Ostrov Kotel'nyy had been visited in 1773 (Gorshkov 1980), the remaining New Siberian Islands had not been explored.

In 1871, the American explorer Hall sledged with Inuit to the northwesternmost limits of the Greenland Ice Cap, discovered Hall Land and saw Lincoln Sea. He also approached the Pole in his ship *Polaris* reaching latitude 82°11'N. In 1875, Captain George S. Nares sailed his ships, *Alert* and *Discovery*, north through Nares Strait to the edge of the Arctic Ocean. One object of the British expedition was to plant the Union Jack beyond America's farthest north. Equally important, however, were scientific objectives. Like their predecessor Parry 50 years earlier, parties of the expedition, led by Lieutenant Albert Markham, man-hauled boats over the pack ice and reached a point (83°20'N) a few miles beyond Hall's and Parry's highest latitudes. More significant to science, however, was their exploration and mapping of the northern coasts of Ellesmere Island and Greenland, where they carried out astronomical, geological, magnetic, tidal, meteorological, zoological, botanical and ethnological studies (Nares 1876, 1878). The site of their expedition base, Discovery Harbour (later named Fort Conger), was to become an important centre for scientific observation in the North American Arctic.

Baron A.E. Nordenskjöld was a Swedish chemist and mineralogist who became interested in Arctic science. He conducted a number of scientific expeditions to Spitsbergen and Greenland, later turning his attention to the problem of navigation of the North-East Passage. For Russia, Nordenskjöld argued, the navigation of the North-East Passage could be of vital importance; it might open up a commercial highway along the Siberian coast over which the mineral resources of the immense territories of eastern Russia could be brought cheaply to industrial Europe. In addition, there were strong scientific arguments for an expedition: namely, research in geography, oceanography, geology and natural history. Nordenskjöld gained the support of the king of Norway and Sweden, his patron Baron Oscar Dickson and a rich Russian merchant. In 1878, Nordenskjöld sailed from Tromsö in the

357-ton steam and sailing ship *Vega* with scientists from five nations. Sailing close to the coast, and encountering little ice, the *Vega* made good progress. Off the mouth of the Yenesey River he found a secure island anchorage, which he named Dickson Island after his Swedish patron. He correctly prophesied that the anchorage would "... one day be of great importance for commerce of Siberia" (Nordenskjöld 1882, p. 145). The site is the modern port of Dickson. By late fall, *Vega* came within 200 km of Mys Dezhneva before becoming beset by winter ice. In July, the following year, she sailed through Bering Strait. Nordenskjöld did not discover any new land, but we mention his multidisciplinary, multinational voyage because it marked a resurgence of Arctic Ocean research. Since Phipps' expedition 100 years earlier, polar research had been nearly eclipsed by the attention given to geographical exploration and national prestige.

In 1872, two young Austrian scientists, Navy Lieutenant Karl Weyprecht and Army Lieutenant Julius Payer, sailed into the Barents Sea on board the steamer *Tegethoff*. They were going to investigate the famous German geographer A.H. Petermann's claim of a relatively ice-free approach to the North Pole in this part of the Arctic Ocean - the revival of a 300-year old idea. Petermann's theories were not substantiated but the Austrians discovered and mapped part of the Franz Josef Land archipelago. Weyprecht and Payer put forward the hypothesis that this archipelago might be an outlier of a much greater landmass that included the North Pole. Weyprecht became convinced that scientific study should take precedence over geographical discovery in polar exploration. He began a personal campaign that led to the International Polar Year, 1882-1883, with 20 simultaneous expeditions in the polar regions, supported by 11 countries. None of these, however, was in the Arctic Ocean Basin.

In 1898, two expeditions attempted to sail into Nares Strait, Robert E. Peary aboard U.S.S. *Windward* and Otto Sverdrup aboard the Norwegian ship *Fram*. Peary's aim was the conquest of the Pole, whereas the Norwegians planned to explore and map the northern and northeastern coasts of Greenland. Ice prevented both ships from penetrating Kane Basin. Peary was obsessed by his desire to become the first to reach the Pole and achieve personal fame. Although Sverdrup had no intention of making a dash to the Pole, it was inconceivable, in Peary's view, that the Norwegians would not try, and he regarded Sverdrup's plans of exploration as an intrusion into "his" territory. The following summer, to prevent embarrassing complications, Sverdrup focused on exploration of western Ellesmere Island and the islands to the west, and sailed into Jones Sound. During the next three years, travelling by ship and by dog-team, the Norwegians accurately mapped that part of the Queen Elizabeth Islands now known as Sverdrup Islands (Norsk Videnskap-Akademi 1907-1919; Sverdrup 19893A,B, 1904). Per Schei, the geologist of the expedition, conducted reconnaissance geological surveys and established the first stratigraphic succession in the North American Arctic (Schei 1903). Peary, in turn, explored northern and northeastern Greenland, thereby settling any doubt about the insularity of Greenland (Hayes 1929).

Russian polar expeditions under the leadership of E. Toll, explored the New Siberian Islands between 1900 and 1903, and in 1913 the crews of two Russian vessels *Tamir* and *Vaigach* discovered and explored Severnaya Zemlya (Gorshkov 1980).

A new territorial awareness and interest in her northern frontiers felt by Canada led the Canadian government to sponsor a number of expeditions. In 1903 and 1904, A.P. Low of the Geological Survey of Canada sailed in the steam-powered *Neptune* into Hudson Bay, Smith Sound and Lancaster Sound, following which between 1906 and 1911, Captain J.E. Bernier in the D.G.S. *Arctic* visited many of the islands of the archipelago. The main objective of these expeditions was the establishment of sovereignty, but they also enabled Low in the *Neptune* and J.G. McMillan, geologist aboard *Arctic*, to study the geology of the regions traversed by the ships and produce the first regional geological maps of the Canadian Arctic Archipelago.

The Canadian Government, through its Geological Survey, also financed Vilhjalmur Stefansson's Canadian Arctic Expedition of 1913-1918. An ambitious program was devised in which a northern party, led by Stefansson, would search for new lands in the Beaufort Sea north of the already discovered islands of the archipelago, while a southern party, under the leadership of Dr. R.M. Anderson, would explore and carry out geological and biological field work along the mainland Arctic coast. The *Karluk*, the northern party's ship became trapped in the ice near Point Barrow and drifted westward, while Stefansson was hunting on the mainland. Stefansson and his men were unable to return, and *Karluk* drifted across the Chukchi Sea, eventually sinking near Herald and Wrangel islands in February 1914. Fewer than half the company of 28 survived. During this drift, the expedition's oceanographer, James Murray, obtained water depths, dredged bottom sediments and collected biological and water samples. The soundings were recorded in the ship's log and preserved but the samples sank with *Karluk*, and Murray's notes were lost with him when he attempted to reach the Siberian mainland on foot (personal communication, W.L. McKinley, 1980). Over the next four years, Stefansson discovered and mapped the remaining Queen Elizabeth Islands: including Brock, Borden, Mackenzie King, Meighen and Lougheed. Anderson, meanwhile, surveyed the southwestern islands of the archipelago, initiating a program of geological mapping that has continued, with some interruptions, to the present day. With Stefansson, the last major areas of unknown Arctic lands had been found, except for the surprising discovery from aircraft, after the Second World War, of previously unrecognized islands in Foxe Basin and Hudson Bay.

ACKNOWLEDGEMENTS

Useful in providing the historical setting for the growth of scientific knowledge of the Arctic Ocean areas are compilations by Kirwan (1959), who furnishes insights into the economic, strategic, political and personal motives behind many of the explorations; and the scholarly analyses, edited by Rey *et al.* (1984) tracing the development of geographic and scientific knowledge of the Arctic as a result of myths, conjectures, genuine discoveries and observations from antiquity to the eighteenth century. Figure 2 is reproduced by courtesy of the Royal Library, Copenhagen. We gratefully acknowledge permission from the National Archives of Canada to reproduce the map (Figures 3, 4).

REFERENCES

Barrow, J. 1818. A chronological history of voyages into the Arctic regions. London, John Murray. 379 pp.

Bernard R. 1976. The hollow earth. 2nd Edition. Citadel Press, New York. 225 pp.

Blom, G.A. 1984. The participation of the kings in the early Norwegian sailing to Bjarmeland (Kola Peninsula and Russian Waters), and the development of a royal policy concerning the northern waters in the Middle Ages. Arctic 37:385-388.

Bosworth, J. 1855. Description of Europa and the voyage of Othere and Wulfstan by King Alfred the Great. London, Murray. 80 pp.

Chevallier, R. 1984. Greco-Roman conception of the North from Pytheas to Tacitus. Arctic 37(4):341-346.

Falk, M.W. 1984. Images of pre-discovery Alaska in the work of European cartographers. Arctic 37(4):562-573.

Fisher, R.H. 1984. The early cartography of the Bering Strait region. Arctic 37(4):574-589.

Gorshkov, S.G. (Editor-in-chief). 1980. World ocean atlas, Volume 3: Arctic Ocean. Department of Navigation and Oceanography, Ministry of Defence, U.S.S.R., Pergamon Press, Oxford. 203 pp.

Hayes, J.G. 1929. Robert Edwin Peary, a record of his explorations, 1886-1909. Richards Tomlin, London. 448 pp.

Kane, E.K. 1856. Arctic explorations - the Second Grinnell Expedition in search of Sir John Franklin, 1853, 1854, 1855. Childs and Peterson, Philadelphia, Volume I, 464 pp.; Volume 2, 457 pp.

Keating, B. 1970. The hard death of Anian. In: The Northwest Passage; from the Mathew to the Manhattan. Edited by: B. Keating. Rand McNally and Company, Chicago. pp. 51-67.

Kirwan, L.P. 1959. The white road. A survey of polar exploration. Hollis and Carter, London. 374 pp.

Levere, T.H. 1988. Science and the Canadian Arctic, 1818-1876, from Sir John Ross to Sir George Strong Nares. Arctic 41:127-137.

Martin C. 1988. William Scoresby, Jr., (1789-1857) and the open polar sea - myth and reality. Arctic 41:39-47.

Nansen, F. 1911. In northern mists; Arctic exploration in early times. Heinemann, London. Volume I, 383 pp.; Volume II, 415 pp.

Nares, G. 1876. Captain Nares' report, communicated by the Lords Commissioners of the Admiralty, October 27th. Nature 15:24-28.

_____. 1878. Narrative of a voyage to the Polar Sea during 1875-76 in H.M. Ships Alert and Discovery; with notes on the natural history edited by H.W. Feilden. Low, Marston, Searle & Rivington, London. Volume 1, 395 pp.; Volume 2, 378 pp.

Nordenskjöld, A.E. 1882. The voyage of the Vega around Asia and Europe with a historical review of previous journeys along the north coast of the Old World. Macmillan & Co., New York. 756 pp. (Translated from Swedish by Alexander Leslie).

Norsk Videnskaps-Akademi. 1907-1919. Report of the Second Norwegian Arctic Expedition in the *Fram* 1898-1902, issued in 36 numbers.

Raisz, E. 1948. General cartography. 2nd Edition. McGraw-Hill Book Co., New York. 354 pp.

Rey, L., C.R. Upton, and M. Falk. (Editors). 1984. Unveiling the Arctic. University of Alaska Press, Fairbanks. 292 pp. (Reprinted in Arctic 37:321-613).

Roots, E.F. 1986. Exclusive economic zones; a brief sketch of historical development and current issues. In: Exclusive Economic Zones; Advances in Underwater Technology. Ocean Science and Offshore Engineering 8:5-13.

Ross, J. 1819. A voyage of discovery, made under the order of the Admiralty, in his Majesty's ships *Isabella* and *Alexander* for the purpose of exploring Baffin Bay, and inquiring into the possibility of a Northwest Passage. Murray, London. 425 pp.

Royal Society. 1782. Minutes, Royal Society of London, Volume 6 (1769-1782).

Sabine, E. 1821. An account of experiments to determine the acceleration of the pendulum in different latitudes. Philosophical Transactions of the Royal Society, London. pp. 163-190.

Saladin d'Anglure B. 1980. Le syndrome chinois de l'Europe nordique ou la démesure de l"Amérasie entre le temps de l'Astrolalbe (1480) et l'espace du chronomètre (1780). l'Ethnographie 76:81-82.

Savelle, J.M. and C. Holland. 1987. John Ross and Bellot Strait: personality versus discovery. Polar Record 23:411-417.

Schei, P.E. 1903. Summary of geological results (of The Norwegian Polar Expedition in the *Fram* 1898-1902). Geographical Journal 22:55-65.

Scoresby, W., Jr. 1818. On the Greenland or polar ice. Memoirs, Wernerian Natural History Society, Edinburgh. Volume 2, pp. 261-338.

Smith, D.M. 1877. Arctic expeditions from British and foreign shores; from the earliest times to the expedition of 1875-76. Liddell, Glasgow and Melbourne. 824 pp.

Sverdrup, O.N. 1903A. The Second Norwegian Polar Expedition in the *Fram*. Scottish Geographical Magazine 19:337-353.

_____. 1903B. The Norwegian Polar Expedition in the *Fram* 1898-1902. Geographical Journal 22:38-55.

Sweet H. (Editor). 1883. King Alfred's Orosius. Early English Text Society, (London) Paper 79:1-42.

Taylor, A. 1955. Geographical discovery and exploration in the Queen Elizabeth Islands. Canada, Geographical Branch, Memoir 3:1-172.

Theutenberg, B.J. 1984. Mare clausum et mare liberum. Arctic 37(4):481-492.

Wallis, H. 1984. England's search for the northern passages in the sixteenth and early seventeenth centuries. Arctic 37(4):453-472.

Weber, J.R. and E.F. Roots. 1989. Historical background: exploration, concepts and observations. In: Decade of North American Geology, Volume L, Chapter 2. Edited by: G.L. Johnson, A. Grantz, and J.F. Sweeney. Geological Society of America, Boulder, Colorado.

Illustrated by Brenda Carter

EMILE FRÉDÉRIC DE BRAY AND HIS ROLE IN THE ROYAL NAVY'S SEARCH FOR FRANKLIN, 1852-1854

William Barr[1]

Abstract: In April 1852, Sir Edward Belcher's squadron, consisting of <u>Assistance</u>, <u>Pioneer</u>, <u>Resolute</u>, <u>Intrepid</u> and <u>North Star</u>, sailed from England in the continuing search for Sir John Franklin's expedition aboard <u>Erebus</u> and <u>Terror</u>, missing in the Arctic since the summer of 1845. One of the officers aboard <u>Resolute</u>, commanded by Captain Henry Kellett was a Frenchman, Enseigne de vaisseau Emile Frédéric de Bray, seconded at his own request from the French Navy to take part in the search. <u>Resolute</u> and <u>Intrepid</u> wintered off Dealy Island near the mouth of Bridport Inlet, Melville Island. Prior to the onset of winter, De Bray led a sledge party west to Cape Providence to lay a depot for the following spring's sledge journeys. In the spring of 1853 he was leader of a sledge party which made a much longer journey north across Melville Island and west along its north coast in support of Captain Leopold McClintock. De Bray turned back at Cape De Bray on the northwest coast of Melville Island; he and his men sledged 594 km in 45 days.

The two ships sailed eastward in August 1853 but were soon beset again off Cape Cockburn, the southwest tip of Bathurst Island. After a second wintering, on orders from Sir Edward Belcher <u>Resolute</u> and <u>Intrepid</u> were abandoned in the spring of 1854, all the officers and men retreating to <u>North Star</u> at Beechey Island. During this latter operation De Bray led a sledge party of invalids which covered the 280 km distance in 17 days. He returned to England safely aboard the supply ship <u>Phoenix</u> in October 1854. For his part in the Franklin search De Bray was made an officer of the Legion d'Honneur by Napoleon III. He was also awarded the Arctic Medal by Queen Victoria. He was thus the only living Frenchman to receive that honour, although his better-known compatriot Joseph-René Bellot was awarded it posthumously.

Résumé: En avril 1852, l'escadre de Sir Edward Belcher, formée des navires <u>Assistance</u>, <u>Pioneer</u>, <u>Resolute</u>, <u>Intrepid</u> et <u>North Star</u>, partait d'Angleterre à la recherche de l'expédition de Sir John Franklin à bord de l'<u>Erebus</u> et du <u>Terror</u>, disparue dans l'Arctique depuis l'été de 1845. À bord du <u>Resolute</u> commandé par le capitaine Henry Kellett, il y avait parmi les officiers un Français, l'enseigne de vaisseau Èmile Frédéric de Bray, détaché à sa demande de la marine français pour prendre part à la recherche.

Les navires <u>Resolute</u> et <u>Intrepid</u> passèrent l'hiver au large de l'île Dealy, près de l'embouchure de l'inlet Bridport sur l'île Melville. Avant l'arrivée de l'hiver, de Bray mena une expédition en traîneau vers l'ouest jusqu'au cap Providence, dans le but d'établir de dépôt pour les expéditions en traîneau du printemps suivant. Au printemps de 1853, il conduisit une expédition en traîneau, dont l'itinéraire, beaucoup plus long, traversait l'Île Melville vers le nord et suivait sa côte nord vers l'ouest, afin d'assister le capitaine Léopold McClintock. De Bray fit demi-tour au Cap De Bray sur la côte nord-ouest de l'île Melville; ses hommes et lui avaient, en traîneau, parcouru 594 km en 45 jours.

Les deux navires prirent la mer vers l'est en août 1853, mais furent bientôt, à nouveau, aux prises avec des difficultés au large du Cap Cockburn, à la pointe sud-ouest de l'île Bathurst. Après un deuxième hiver, le <u>Resolute</u> et l'<u>Intrepid</u> furent abandonnés, sur les ordres de Sir Edward Belcher, au printemps de 1854, et tous les officiers et hommes d'équipage regagnèrent le <u>North Star</u> à l'île Beechey. Pendant cette dernière opération, de Bray mena une expédition en traîneau des invalides, qui couvrit 280 km en 17 jours. En octobre 1854, il regagna l'Angleterre, sain et sauf, à bord du ravitailleur <u>Phoenix</u>. Pour sa participation aux recherches pour retrouver Franklin, de Bray fut fait officier de la Légion d'honneur par Napoléon III. La Reine Victoria lui décerna également une récompense: l'"Arctic Medal". Il fut donc le seul Français vivant à recevoir cet honneur, bien que son compatriote mieux connu, Joseph-René Bellot, l'ait reçu à titre posthume.

On 15 April 1852, as Sir Edward Belcher's Arctic Squadron, consisting of the sailing vessels *Assistance*, *Resolute*, and *North Star* and the steamships *Pioneer* and *Intrepid* were heading down the river from Woolwich Basin to Greenhithe, Lieutenant George Strong Nares, a young officer aboard Captain Henry Kellett's ship *Resolute* was hurriedly writing a final note to his father. In the middle of a paragraph containing initial impressions of his fellow officers Nares included the following intriguing and typically ethnocentric remark: "The Frenchman does not seem an <u>Englishman,</u> but I suppose he will improve on

---

[1] Department of Geography, University of Saskatchewan, Saskatoon, Saskatchewan S7N 0W0

acquaintance" (Nares 1852). Since the Frenchman is not named in the letter the casual reader is left wondering who he was and whether he did indeed "improve on acquaintance".

The Frenchman was Enseigne de vaisseau Emile Frédéric de Bray (Figure 1). Born in Paris on 9 March 1829, Emile de Bray was enrolled as a cadet at the École Navale on 1 October 1844. He graduated as Élève de la Marine on 1 August 1846, when he was posted to Brest (De Bray, G., n.d.). On 1 October he joined the corvette *Galathée* and served in the Pacific for the next three years. Returning to Lorient aboard *Galathée* on 17 September 1849, over the next 18 months De Bray served as "aspirant" aboard six vessels, visiting places such as Toulon, Civita Vecchio and Naples. Having passed the requisite examination on 2 April 1851, De Bray was promoted to the rank of Enseigne de vaisseau.

FIGURE 1: Emile Frédéric de Bray, soon after his return from the Arctic. Photo courtesy of Archives de France.

In 1850 the mounting concern in Britain and elsewhere as to the fate of Sir John Franklin's ships *Erebus* and *Terror*, which had disappeared while engaged in a search for the North-West Passage in 1845, resulted in a series of parallel and overlapping expeditions heading into Barrow Strait. Totalling 11 ships, they included one American expedition and both Royal Navy and private British endeavours. Probably the most significant result of this multi-faceted search, all of whose components focused their attention on Wellington Channel and Cornwallis Island, was the discovery that Franklin's ships had spent the winter of 1845-

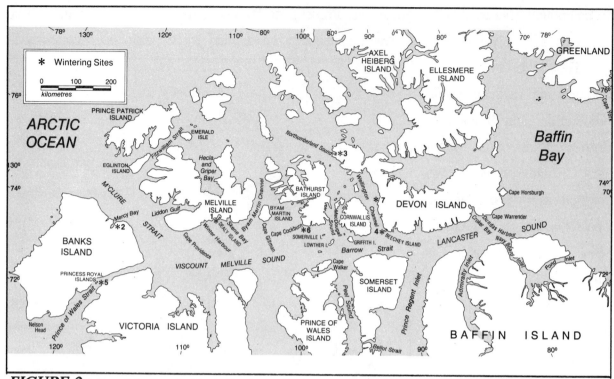

FIGURE 2: Part of the Canadian Arctic Islands, showing the areas of operations and wintering sites of the search expeditions of 1850-1854. 1. <u>Resolute</u> and <u>Intrepid</u>, 1852-1853; 2. <u>Investigator</u>, 1851-1853; 3. <u>Assistance</u> and <u>Pioneer</u>, 1852-1853; 4. <u>North Star</u>, 1852-1854; 5. <u>Investigator</u>, 1850-1851; 6. <u>Resolute</u> and <u>Intrepid</u>, 1853-1854; 7. <u>Assistance</u> and <u>Pioneer</u>, 1853-1854.

1846 at Beechey Island near the southwestern corner of Devon Island (Figure 2) (Sutherland 1852, pp. 303-308; Kane 1854, pp. 162-165; Osborn 1852, p. 109). Among the evidence left by Franklin's party were the graves of three of his men. But the most baffling and frustrating aspect was that not the slightest trace of any record or note was found. The movements of the missing ships after they left Beechey Island, presumably in the summer of 1846, were still a complete mystery.

News of the discovery at Beechey Island reached Britain in October 1850 (Snow 1851). In the light of this information, a further expedition sponsored by Lady Franklin and led by William Kennedy sailed from Aberdeen aboard *Prince Albert* in May 1851 (Kennedy 1853; Bellot 1854, 1855). Significantly the second-in-command was Lieutenant de vaisseau Joseph-René Bellot, who had obtained special leave from the French Navy to participate in the expedition. It was also in the light of the discoveries at Beechey Island that a further Royal Navy expedition was dispatched, under command of Sir Edward Belcher. As we have seen, it consisted of five ships.

770

Probably De Bray's imagination was fired by Bellot's participation in the expedition aboard *Prince Albert*. On learning of the plans to dispatch Sir Edward Belcher's squadron in the summer of 1852, De Bray decided to try to participate, his opening gambit being a letter requesting permission to offer his services to the British Admiralty, addressed to the Minister of the Navy and the Colonies and dated 20 December 1851. His request was forwarded to the British Admiralty who in turn approved it. On 20 January 1852 the British Foreign Minister, Earl Granville, wrote to Count Walewski, the French Ambassador, that De Bray would be allowed to participate in the expedition.

Over the next few months the details were worked out, and on 13 April 1852 De Bray left Paris for London. Thus De Bray came to be aboard *Resolute* as the squadron moved down the Thames on 15 April. After a number of official visits the five-ship squadron finally sailed from the Nore on the afternoon of 22 April, accompanied by the steamers *Basilisk* and *Desperate*, which were to escort the squadron for the first part of the Atlantic crossing.

On 25 April the squadron was lying at anchor off Stromness in the Orkneys. De Bray had started to get to know his fellow officers whom he found "very obliging, since I had only an imperfect command of English, and understanding me required a great deal of good will (De Bray n.d., p. 9). On the 27th, accompanied by Lieutenants Hamilton, Pim and Nares he made an excursion by carriage to Kirkwall where they visited the cathedral.

The squadron set out again on 28 April, *Desperate* and *Basilisk* towing the sailing vessels, so that *Pioneer* and *Intrepid* could conserve fuel. Over the next few days the towlines parted frequently in rough seas and it was not until the 8 May that the squadron reached 20°W where, by prearrangement, *Desperate* and *Basilisk* turned back.

The first ice was sighted on the 20th, some 13 km off Cape Desolation, and on the 24th the coast of Greenland near Godthåb was in view. On the 28th the squadron dropped anchor off Kron Prins Ø, and De Bray met Inuit for the first time. He was greatly impressed by their skill in kayak-rolling and their marksmanship with harpoons, but was nauseated by the stench inside their half-buried houses. The next stop was at Lievely on Disko Ø, where De Bray took the opportunity to climb a snow-capped mountain overlooking the harbour. After a further stop at Upernavik the squadron pushed north along the Greenland coast, encountering increasingly heavy ice. On the evening of 26 June *Resolute* was severely nipped between two floes; since the shuddering of the ship was sufficient to start all her bells ringing, the incident clearly made quite an impression on De Bray. The only damage sustained was a smashed rudder. Once the pressure slackened, the crews cut ice-docks and De Bray has left a detailed description of the technique involved.

On 30 June the Royal Navy squadron came up with a fleet of 14 whaling ships, and De Bray witnessed the crushing and sinking of the American whaler *McLellan*. Throughout June, in company with the whalers, the Navy vessels made fitful progress northward across Melville Bugt, exploiting leads and polynyas whenever possible, mooring to ice anchors or lying in ice-docks when the ice was treacherous.

On the morning of 1 August *Resolute*, *Intrepid*, *North Star* and the whaler *Alexander* moored to fast-ice off Kap York, and De Bray was a member of the party that walked ashore to meet the local Inuit. Before returning to the ship, De Bray climbed to the summit of Kap York in the hope of sighting *Assistance* and *Pioneer*, but without success. That evening *Alexander* parted from the Navy ships, taking their last mail, while *Resolute*, *Intrepid* and *North Star* headed west across the North Water. They sighted Cape Horsburgh on 3 August, then swung west into the mouth of Lancaster Sound. Coasting west past Croker Bay, De Bray made perceptive comments on the landforms of this striking coastline:

> "... the summits of the mountains are all in the same horizontal plane, cut here and there by deep gullies. The slopes of the mountains drop almost sheer into the sea and from a certain distance have quite a strong resemblance to the bastions of a fortress." (De Bray n.d., p. 48)

In the early hours of the 11th, *Resolute* and *Intrepid* dropped anchor alongside *North Star* off Beechey Island. Later in the morning De Bray took a stroll ashore, examining Sir John Ross's yacht *Mary*, the graves of the three members of Franklin's expedition, assorted debris scattered around the wintering site and the sledge-tracks in the gravel first spotted by Captain Erasmus Ommanney's party in 1850. On his way back from Union Bay (Figure 3) De Bray climbed to the summit of Beechey Island, and in one of three cairns there found notes left by Captains Austin and Ommanney in 1850.

Next day while *Resolute* loaded provisions from *North Star*, De Bray undertook an even more ambitious hike. He climbed to the summit of Cape Riley where he built a cairn surmounted by a pole to which he nailed a board with the carved inscription "H.M.S.

Résolue 11 Août 1852" on one side and his initials "E.D.B." on the other. At the foot of the cape he found a cairn containing notes signed by Captains Austin, De Haven and Griffith, and a short distance away a red-painted cross with the inscription "Prince Albert 25 August 1851".

When *Assistance* and *Pioneer* had arrived at Beechey Island and the other four ships had coaled and provisioned from *North Star* (which was to remain at Beechey Island as a depot ship), the squadron dispersed. On 14 August *Assistance* and *Pioneer* started north up Wellington Channel. At noon next day *Resolute* and

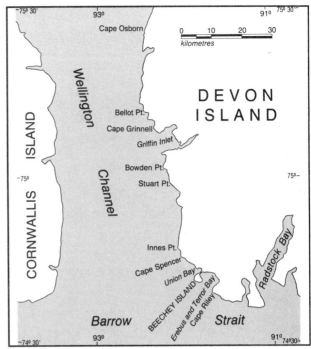

FIGURE 3: Map of the Beechey Island area.

Intrepid (Captain Leopold McClintock) set off westward for Winter Harbour (Figure 2) with orders to establish a major depot for *Investigator* (Captain Robert M'Clure) and/or *Enterprise* (Captain Richard Collinson) which had entered the Arctic Ocean via Bering Strait, also in search of the Franklin expedition, and had not been heard from for two years.

Having left a depot and a whaleboat at Cape Hotham on Cornwallis Island, the ships pushed on west to Assistance Harbour on Griffiths Island. Here *Resolute* ran heavily aground near the top of the tide; to make the situation even worse she was caught by a large drifting floe some 10 km² in area and heeled violently to starboard. She was finally refloated at the cost of about half of her false keel. Next day (17 August) De Bray was a member of a party which built a cairn and left documents on the southern tip of Griffiths Island. After waiting off Lowther Island for about 10 days for ice conditions to improve, the two ships finally continued west on the 28th. Having left depots on southern Bathurst Island and southeastern Melville Island (where several muskoxen were shot), the expedition reached Winter Harbour (Figure 4) on 7 September. A depot was landed near Parry's Rock.

Unfortunately, since solid ice in Winter Harbour precluded its use as winter quarters, Kellett decided to backtrack to Dealy Island, off Bridport Inlet. A suitable wintering site

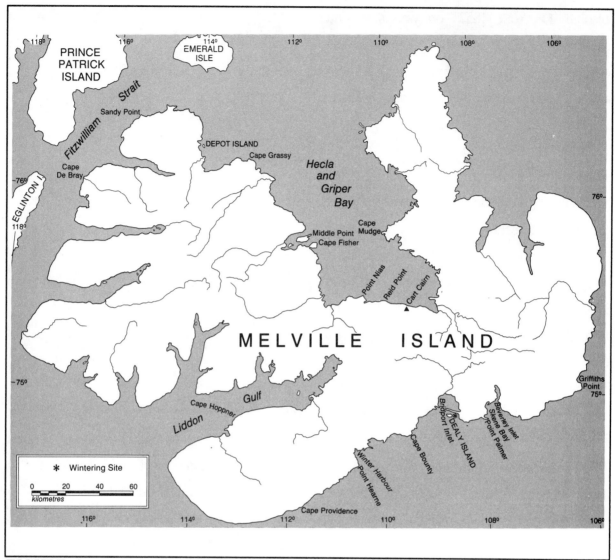

FIGURE 4: Map of Melville Island showing area covered by De Bray's sledge trips.

was found off the east side of the island and on the 9th work began on cutting docks for the ships in the edge of the fast-ice. Normal preparations for an arctic wintering began: sails were unbent and stowed in their lockers; the decks were enclosed by tents, and the ships' boats were moved ashore to Dealy Island.

On 22 September five sledge parties set off in different directions to lay depots for the main sledging operations the following spring. De Bray, in command of the sledge "Marie" with a crew of six, was to accompany Lieutenant Pim in taking supplies westward along the south coast of Melville Island for parties that would cross to Banks Island the following spring. They reached their destination, Cape Providence, safely on 2 October and cached the supplies. On the way back, on 3 October Pim and De Bray shot a muskox, so muskox steaks were on the menu that night. He pronounced it "... the most delicious meat I have ever eaten, although a little tough" (De Bray n.d., p. 77). The two sledge parties reached the ships on 8 October having covered 244 km in 17 days (including a day tentbound by bad weather).

On the morning of 14 October De Bray was taking a stroll on Dealy Island when he sighted a sledge approaching from the west. It was Lieutenant Mecham's party with exciting news; having established his depot at Cape Hoppner on Liddon Gulf as arranged, on his return Mecham had decided to visit Parry Rock. There, in a cylinder on top of the rock he found a message left by Captain Robert M'Clure of *Investigator* the previous April. The message gave a brief précis of *Investigator's* activities since passing through Bering Strait in July 1850. When the message had been left at Parry Rock, *Investigator* had just spent a winter at Mercy Bay on northern Banks Island. The message ended with the information that, if the ice permitted, M'Clure intended to sail eastward to Baffin Bay in the summer of 1852. Since Kellett's expedition had seen no sign of *Investigator*, it was assumed that she was still at Mercy Bay, so Kellett decided to send a rescue party there in early spring.

On 17/18 October De Bray was a member of a hunting party to the head of Bridport Inlet. However, the weather was foul and they returned empty-handed. This in fact was the last hunting trip of the season. Game killed on Melville Island in the fall included 27 muskoxen, 5 caribou, 23 hares, 39 ptarmigan, 1 bear, 1 wolf, 1 fox and 2 lemmings (De Bray n.d., p. 91).

On returning to the ships, the hunting party heard the sad news of the expedition's first death: Walter Moberly, *Resolute's* steward, had died of a heart attack on the 18th. On the 26th the body was sledged ashore at the head of a funeral procession and was buried in a shallow grave piled high with rocks and earth. An oak headboard 90 cm high was erected.

Preparations for the wintering continued. The decks were insulated with a mixture of fine gravel and snow, packed down in a layer 22 cm deep. Snowblocks were built up around the ships' sides to reduce heat loss (Figure 5). On 4 November the upper rim of the sun appeared briefly above the southern horizon at noon for the last time. Winter had now begun and with it the traditional winter activities. Classes in subjects such as navigation, as well as the basics of reading and writing, were offered by various officers, and

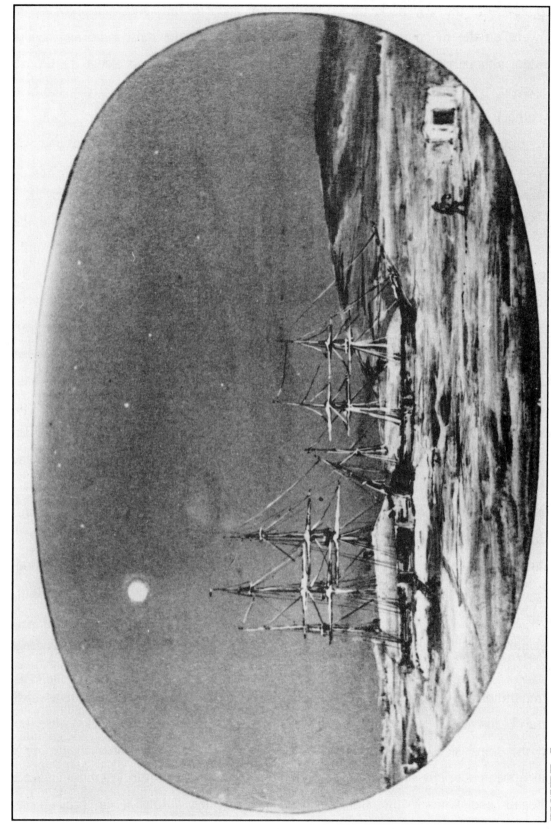

FIGURE 5: De Bray's painting of <u>Resolute</u> and <u>Intrepid</u> in winter quarters at Dealy Island, by moonlight. Courtesy Scott Polar Research Institute.

FIGURE 6: De Bray's painting of the theatre on <u>Resolute</u>'s main-deck. Courtesy Scott Polar Research Institute.

preparations began for the first theatrical performance. This was held on the night of 23 November on *Resolute's* housed-in main-deck (Figure 6). Two stoves managed to raise the temperature to -5°C from the outside temperature of -9°. The officers presented an historical drama, "Charles II" for which De Bray sewed one of the ladies' costumes; he was also responsible for make-up. The men then presented a farce entitled "Who speaks first" but it had to be discontinued when one of the principals got too drunk to play his part.

The beneficial effect of this activity must have been dampened when a second death occurred on 12 December. George Drover, one of *Intrepid's* men became ill after one of the fall sledge trips. He too was buried on Dealy Island, the funeral service being held on the 19th. Although it took place at noon, Captain Kellett needed a lantern to read the service.

Christmas and New Year's were celebrated with appropriate festivities. Muskox, hare, ptarmigan and caribou were served for Christmas dinner; De Bray decided that the caribou was "... the most delicious venison I have ever tasted" (De Bray n.d., p. 101). He also visited the crew's Christmas dinner in the orlop deck and seems to have been startled by the scene: "For a moment one could hear only the noise of knives and forks; at the end of ten minutes the astonished eye had nothing left to contemplate but a vast field of carnage" (De Bray n.d., p. 100).

In the New Year work began on the Dealy Island depot. On 9 January three two-tonne tanks were swayed out of the hold and sledged ashore to the south point of the island. Filled with provisions, they were to become an integral part of the depot. Thereafter sledging provisions ashore became one of the daily chores, the sledges hauling gravel for ballast on the return trip.

The second theatrical performance was held toward the end of January. This time De Bray was promoted to playing one of the female roles, that of 'Lady Lollipop' in a comedy called "King Glumpus", written in verse by Sir John Barrow (Figure 7). De Bray found the performance an ordeal: he was wearing satin slippers and his feet were half frozen; after the show he had to soak them in warm water to restore feeling.

The sun reappeared on 5 February and the tempo of outdoors work was intensified. Hauling and stowing of ballast was a major chore, while dog sledges began hauling sand from Dealy Island to spread on the ice along a strip from the ships towards the open sea, to encourage faster melting of the ice.

778

On 3 March two sledges commanded by Lieutenant Pim and Dr. Domville set off for Banks Island in order to make contact with *Investigator*. On the 21st other spring sledge parties were detailed and their routes outlined. De Bray was placed in charge of the sledge "Hero", which was to travel in support of McClintock across Melville Island, then west along the coast of Hecla and Griper Bay. Under his command were eight men from *Intrepid's* crew.

Seven sledges set off in various directions on the morning of 4 April. In company with McClintock's sledge, De Bray headed north across the "waist" of Melville Island. Progress was slow due to the numerous gullies, and only light snowcover on the rock-strewn plateau. The sledge crews reached Hecla and Griper Bay on the 12th, then headed northwest along the coast. Swinging around the northwest tip of Melville Island, on 2 May the two sledges reached a cape which McClintock named Cape

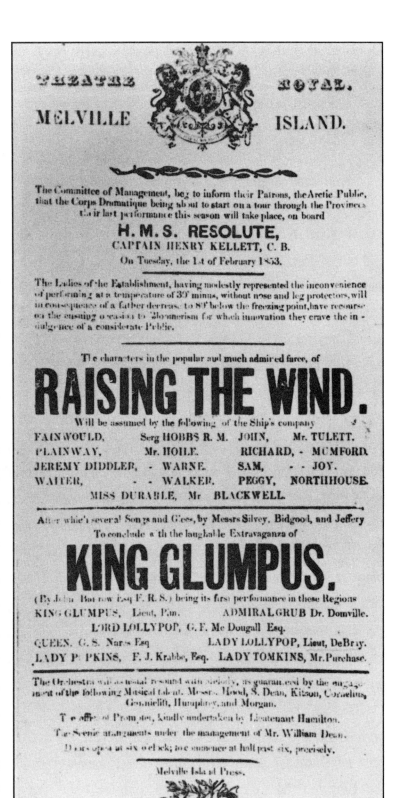

FIGURE 7: Playbill produced on board <u>Resolute</u> for the second theatrical performance of the winter. Photo courtesy Scott Polar Research Institute.

779

De Bray (Figure 4). McClintock ordered De Bray to cache his load there and start for home, while he and his men headed west across the sea ice. On the way back De Bray was ordered to relay a depot forward for several days' march from Point Nias to Cape Fisher.

On the return trip De Bray made excellent progress since the sledge was light. He was even able to hoist a sail to take advantage of frequent favourable winds. But on 12 May, near Point Nias, a crisis occurred. One of the men, Coombes, who had stopped to relieve himself, suddenly dropped unconscious. De Bray did his best to revive him but without success. The man was dead. De Bray was now faced with a difficult decision, especially for a foreign officer not fully acquainted with the norms and expectations of the Royal Navy. His men wanted him to sledge the body straight back to the ship for proper burial, whereas his instructions specified that he should relay a depot forward from Point Nias to Cape Fisher for McClintock's use on his return trip. After deliberation he decided to accede to his men's wishes. On 18 May, sledge-flag flying at half mast, De Bray and his men returned to their ship.

Their sledge trip represented an impressive achievement. In 45 days they had covered 594 km. Taking into account days when they were weatherbound, this represented a mean daily distance of 15.74 km (12.14 on the outward trip and 19.36 on the homeward trip). From the evidence of the track-chart appended to De Bray's report to McClintock (Figure 8), he appears to have been a workmanlike surveyor. Deviations from the modern map are readily explicable in terms of the problems of low, snow-covered coastlines, indistinguishable from sea ice and often obscured by fog and/or blowing snow.

The varying reactions to De Bray's decision to sledge Coombes' body back to the ship rather than completing his tasks are interesting: McDougall, sailingmaster aboard *Resolute* felt that a British officer would have completed his orders then brought the body back (McDougall 1857, pp. 242-243). Most importantly for De Bray's peace of mind, however, both Captain McClintock and Captain Kellett approved of his decision. Coombes funeral was held on 22 May, the grave being located beside the other two on Dealy Island. De Bray led the funeral procession and the body was hauled on a sledge flying De Bray's sledging flag.

A great deal had happened at Dealy Island in De Bray's absence. As a result of Lieutenant Pim's journey, some 22 sick members of *Investigator's* crew had arrived at Dealy

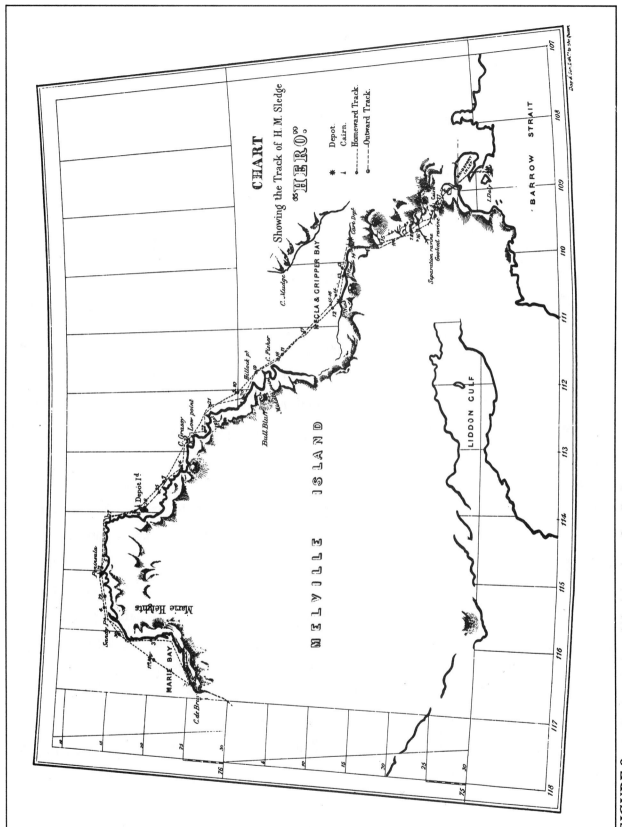

FIGURE 8: De Bray's track-chart of his sledge trip to Cape De Bray.

Island, and to house them, *Intrepid* had been turned into a hospital ship. On 7 May the 10 least fit of these men, led by Lieutenant Creswell of *Investigator* had set off eastward for *North Star* at Beechey Island.

The day after De Bray's return, work began on the foundation of the store-house on Dealy Island. The structure grew steadily, but on 13 June it experienced a setback. Due to the wet nature of the ground and badly designed foundations the entire building collapsed and had to be rebuilt. On 17 June, while De Bray was hunting, the last of *Investigator's* men arrived from the west. As described by Miertsching (Neatby 1967, p. 200) it was a sorry-looking party: eight men were riding lashed on the sledges while others were leaning on the sledges or were supported by their companions. By now preparations for getting the ships ready for sea were in full swing, while a steady sledge traffic moved supplies ashore to the depot (Figure 9). During this period, the last of the sledge expeditions returned. Lieutenant Mecham arrived after an absence of 94 days, during which he had explored Liddon Gulf and the south coasts of Eglinton and Prince Patrick islands. On 18 July McClintock arrived after covering an amazing 1,660 km in 106 days. After parting from De Bray, McClintock had discovered and explored Prince Patrick Island, Eglinton Island and Emerald Isle (Figure 4).

The ice was starting to break up, and by 28 July *Resolute* was afloat again. The men now concentrated on setting up the running rigging and generally making the ships ready for sea. The storehouse on Dealy Island had been stocked with sufficient supplies for 60 men for a winter, in case the crew of *Enterprise* needed them. De Bray drafted a detailed plan of the depot and its contents and compiled an inventory of the contents of every cask and tank (Figure 10). Some of these supplies were still in the building when it was partially excavated and restored in 1978 (Janes 1982). In addition, a cairn 9 m-high, surmounted by a mast had been built on the summit of Dealy Island.

During a gale on the night of 17/18 August the ice began to break up in spectacular fashion; the floe to which the ships were moored began to drive rapidly southwards. Break-up was so sudden and the weather so wild that a pump used for watering the ships, and a small boat were left on shore. After a little work the ships got free of the ice and pitched and rolled with the waves for the first time in months.

They managed to reach Point Griffiths on southeastern Melville Island without much difficulty, but there they encountered ice. Until 10 September the ships were able to make

FIGURE 9: De Bray's painting of the ships in spring, showing supplies being sledged ashore to the depot. Courtesy Scott Polar Research Institute.

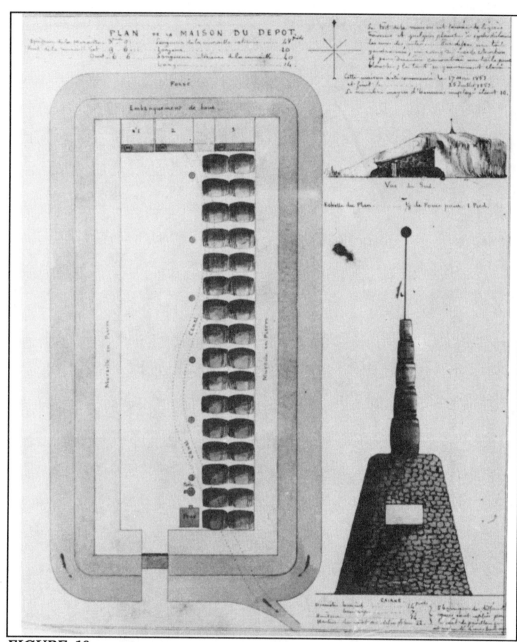

FIGURE 10: De Bray's plan of the depot left on Dealy Island. Courtesy Archives de France.

some progress eastward toward Byam Martin Island. Every opportunity was grasped to hunt muskoxen on Melville Island, and several tonnes of meat were sledged out to the ships.

By the evening of 10 September the ships were solidly beset and drifting east and southeast. Resigning himself to the inevitable, Kellett gave orders to prepare for a second wintering on 20 September. The ships continued to drift southeast, finally becoming immobile at 74° 42'N, 101° 22'W, some 45 km to the southwest of Cape Cockburn on Bathurst Island (Figure 2). The routine was much the same as that of the previous winter with lectures and theatrical performances to help maintain morale. Three deaths occurred during the winter, the bodies in each case being buried through holes cut in the ice.

An interesting innovation, set up by Lieutenant Hamilton and De Bray, was an electric telegraph system rigged between the two ships, which lay about 400 m apart, messages being passed by means of a Morse key. It proved its worth during dinner on New Year's Eve when Thomas Hartnell, one of a trio of musicians on his way from *Intrepid* to *Resolute*, was lost in a blizzard. By using the telegraph it was easy to establish that he had turned back and was safely aboard his own ship.

In the spring there was considerable sledge traffic between *Resolute* and *Intrepid*, *North Star* at Beechey Island, and *Pioneer* and *Assistance*, also wintering for a second time, at Disaster Bay, about 100 km north of Beechey Island. Alarmed at the possibility of yet a third wintering if the ships failed to get free during the summer of 1854, Sir Edward Belcher sent orders to Captain Kellett to make preparations for abandoning both ships. *Resolute's* carpenter began building two new sledges, and an ice-boat was made ready to be cached at Cape Cockburn on Bathurst Island. De Bray was given the task of sledging this boat ashore: he left the ship with a party of nine men and 10 days' provisions on the afternoon of 20 April. Rough pressure-ice made this a slow tedious trip. De Bray and his men often had to unload the sledge and manhandle the boat over hummocks and ridges. It was not until 28 April that they completed their mission and returned to the ship.

On the same day Captain McClintock returned from a visit to *Assistance*, relaying to his officers and men Sir Edward's categorical orders that both ships were to be abandoned as soon as possible. De Bray's views on these orders almost certainly reflect the general feeling aboard the two ships:

"We still had enough provisions and supplies for another year; we were all in perfect health and filled with great anticipation in thinking of our planned spring journey, which would have led to us finding traces of, or even meeting, Captain Collinson. It might even have led to something akin to Captain McClintock's voyage of 1858 when he found the relics of Sir John Franklin on Prince [sic] William Land." (De Bray n.d., p. 224)

Preparations were made for abandoning the ships. On 4 May De Bray was ordered to prepare to leave for Beechey Island with two sledges, nine dogs and nine sick men; he would be accompanied by Dr. Domville. One man, Thomas Morgan, was extremely ill with scurvy, covered with sores and unable to walk. A hanging cot was rigged for him on one of the sledges. The party set off on 8 May. On the first lap to Cape Cockburn they made poor progress due to the rough ice. On the 14th Dr. Domville decided that in view of the deterioration in Morgan's health he should push on ahead with the invalid in forced marches. Following at a more leisurely pace, De Bray and his party reached *North Star* at Beechey Island on the morning of 25 May; the party of invalids had covered 280 km in 18 days. De Bray was saddened to hear that Morgan had died soon after reaching Beechey Island and had been buried beside the graves of the three members of Franklin's expedition.

By now traffic between *North Star* at Beechey Island and *Assistance* and *Pioneer* at Disaster Bay was so frequent that a series of four staging camps was set up between the two points. On 12 June De Bray was sent north with an urgent message for Sir Edward; travelling with a team of 10 dogs, the 100-km trip look only 20 hours. By the 15th De Bray was back at Beechey Island.

The first leads in the ice of Erebus and Terror Bay appeared on 7 August, and by the 21st *North Star* was floating freely in open water. Since there was little prospect of *Assistance* and *Pioneer* fighting free of the ice, Sir Edward decided to abandon them. Their crews travelled south to Beechey Island partly by boat, partly by hiking overland. It was intended that the entire crews of *Resolute*, *Intrepid*, *Assistance* and *Pioneer*, plus part of the crew of *Investigator* would be transported home aboard *North Star*. This would have meant a total complement of 263 men and would have meant unbearable overcrowding.

Fortunately this did not become necessary. On 27 August the resupply ships *Phoenix* and *Talbot* arrived, and some of the officers and men aboard *North Star* were assigned to these vessels. De Bray found himself aboard *Phoenix*.

A memorial tablet to commemorate Lieutenant de vaisseau Joseph-René Bellot, De Bray's compatriot, who had been drowned when blown off a floe in Wellington Channel in August 1853, had arrived aboard *Phoenix*. It was now erected on the monument which had earlier been raised to the memory of Franklin and his men. The ceremony was attended by most of the officers of Sir Edward's squadron along with those of *Phoenix* and *Talbot*. Very fittingly De Bray was invited to unveil the tablet.

The three ships were homeward bound on 28 August. After calling at Lievely on Disko Ø, *Phoenix* dropped anchor at Cork on 28 September. From there Sir Edward, Captain Kellett and Captain M'Clure left immediately for London to face courts martial, standard procedure when Navy ships had been abandoned. De Bray stayed aboard *Phoenix*, reaching London on 2 October 1854 and Paris soon afterwards.

His contribution had been warmly appreciated by the officers and men with whom he had served. On 30 September Sir Edward wrote to the Secretary of the Admiralty "... to speak in the highest terms of praise of the conduct of M. Emile de Bray". Belcher's letter was forwarded to the French Minister of Foreign Affairs, who in turn passed it to Ducos, the Minister of Marine. Ducos wrote De Bray a letter of sincere congratulations on 13 October. He also sent a copy of Belcher's letter to the newspaper *Moniteur Universel*, where it appeared in translation on 12 October.

Thereafter, honours came in rapid succession. Almost immediately De Bray was named Chevalier de la Légion d'Honneur, and on 29 October was received in private audience by the Emperor Napoléon III (Rouch 1944, p. 7). On 5 October 1855 De Bray was promoted Lieutenant de vaisseau, at the age of 26. By then he was serving as first officer aboard the gunboat *La Poudre* on active service in the Baltic. In July 1857 he was awarded the Arctic Medal by Queen Victoria; in the covering letter the Lords of the Admiralty asked that Admiral Hamelin "... convey to M. de Bray the expression of their utter appreciation of this valuable exertion" (Stewart 1857). The Arctic Medal was simultaneously awarded posthumously to Bellot, but De Bray was the only living Frenchman ever to receive this award. On a more personal level, Lady Franklin sent him a framed portrait of her husband with the dedication "En reconnaissant et affectueux souvenir de ses très habiles et zélés services dans la recherche de mon bien aimé mari" (De Bray, G. 1926, p. 4).

De Bray's subsequent naval career was varied. It included three years in command of a fisheries-protection vessel based at Saint Pierre and Miquelon (1858-1861). During the Franco-Prussian War, while in charge of a brigade of the Third Army of Paris, he found himself commanding a battery at St. Quentin during the defence of Paris in December 1870 (Rouch 1938, 1944, 1945). In recognition of these services he was made "Officier de l'Ordre National de la Légion d'Honneur".

De Bray's health had been badly undermined, in part by his arctic experiences, in part by his three years of service based at Saint Pierre and Miquelon. Illness forced him to take early retirement on 7 October 1878 and he died prematurely in 1879 at the age of 50.

The nick-name given to De Bray throughout his later career was "De Bray Pôle Nord" (Rouch 1938). But there were also two more substantive sequels to his arctic experiences. He was friendly with the novelist Jules Verne, who relied heavily on De Bray for technical details while writing his two-part novel on the adventures of Capitaine Hatteras in the Arctic (Verne 1866A,B). On a different level, in the mid-1860s De Bray was approached by Gustave Lambert (1866, 1868), who offered him command of the vessel *Boréal* on his anticipated attempt at the Pole via Bering Strait. De Bray declined but did offer advice and assistance regarding organization. These plans at a polar attempt evaporated with Lambert's death during the Franco-Prussian War.

De Bray's contribution to the search for Franklin, and hence to the exploration of the Canadian Arctic, was significant. His two long sledge trips from Dealy Island, the one to Cape Providence in the fall of 1852 and the one to Cape de Bray in support of McClintock in the spring of 1853, compare favourably with any of those of his British fellow-officers. The chart that he produced during the second of these trips is an excellent piece of work. Furthermore his supplementary sledge journeys, such as the one with the party of invalids from Cape Cockburn to Beechey Island in May 1854, or his dash north by dogteam with urgent dispatches for Sir Edward Belcher later that month, are not only impressive, but demonstrate the trust placed in him by Captain Kellett.

It is noteworthy that in his journal De Bray frequently includes detail which is rarely, if ever, to be found in those of English officers. For example he provides a detailed description of the pitching and arrangement of the tents used during the sledge journeys, even to such charming details as "When all the men are in their bags one spreads a canvas or very light blanket over them, a little larger than the tent ..." (De Bray n.d., p. 114). Elsewhere he explains how to rig a sail on a sledge.

Not the least of De Bray's contributions is in the artistic realm. The two paintings, of which photographs have survived, show that he combined an eye for detail with true artistic talent. These two works of the wintering ships by moonlight in the depths of winter, then by daylight in the spring, are important additions to the rather specialized genre of mid-Victorian arctic expedition paintings.

Of all the letters of commendation on the character of Enseigne de vaisseau Emile Frédéric de Bray that have survived in the Archives de France in Paris, perhaps the most telling was written by Captain Kellett prior to leaving *Phoenix* at Cork on 28 September 1854:

> "My dear De Bray:
>
> I have already expressed to Sir Edward Belcher commanding the Arctic Expedition my opinion of your conduct whilst serving in Her Britannic Majesty's Ship "Resolute" under my command. But I cannot allow you to leave me without expressing to you personally my admiration of your promptness and zeal in undertaking any piece of service and your ability in its execution.
>
> You have Mr. De Bray done credit to the distinguished service to which you belong.
>
> Thrown amongst us a perfect stranger not even speaking our language with ease, you have so perfectly identified yourself with everything common to us, our duties, amusements and teaching as to have won the esteem and regard of all on board and of none more than of yours
>
> Very sincerely,
>
> Henry Kellett, Captain"
>
> (Kellett 1854)

One would hope that, by this time, Lieutenant George S. Nares would have readily admitted that the "Frenchman" had indeed improved on acquaintance. Cape De Bray on the northwest coast of Melville Island is a fitting memorial to a fine man.

ACKNOWLEDGEMENTS

I thank the staff of the Scott Polar Research Institute for the warm welcome and kind assistance extended to me as a visiting researcher. I am especially indebted to M. Phillipe Henrat of the Archives de France in Paris for supplying me with the photograph of De Bray and of his plan of the Dealy Island store-house. My thanks are also due to Mr. Keith Bigelow of the Department of Geography, University of Saskatchewan, for drafting the maps.

REFERENCES

Bellot, J.-R. 1854. Journal d'un voyage aux mers polaires executé à la recherche de Sir John Franklin en 1851 et 1852. Perrotin, Paris. 415 pp.

_____. 1855. Memoirs of Lieutenant Joseph Rene Bellot ... with his journal of a voyage in the polar seas, in search of Sir John Franklin. Hurst and Blackett, London. 392 pp.

De Bray, E.F. n.d. Journal de bord de l'Enseigne de vaisseau Emile Frédéric de Bray à bord de la frégate anglaise "La Résolue". Expédition polaire de 1852-1853 [sic] envoyée à la recherche de Sir John Franklin. Scott Polar Research Institute, MS 864/1. 288 pp. (Typescript).

De Bray, G. n.d. Emile de Bray. Scott Polar Institute, MS 864/3. 4 pp. (Typescript).

Janes, R.R. 1982. The preservation and ethnohistory of a frozen historic site in the Canadian Arctic. Arctic 35(3):358-385.

Kane, E.K. 1854. The U.S. Grinnell Expedition in search of Sir John Franklin: a personal narrative. Sampson Low, Son and Co., London. 552 pp.

Kellett, H. 1854. Letter to Emile de Bray, 28 September 1854. Scott Polar Research Institute, MS 887.

Kennedy, W. 1853. A short narrative of the second voyage of the *Prince Albert* in search of Sir John Franklin. W.H.Dalton, London. 202 pp.

Lambert, G. 1866. Projet de voyage au Pôle Nord. Société de Géographie, Paris. 15 pp.

_____. 1868. L'expédition au Pôle Nord. Société de Géographie, Paris. 25 pp.

McDougall, G.F. 1857. The eventful voyage of H.M. discovery ship *Resolute* to the Arctic regions in search of Sir John Franklin and the missing crews of H.M. discovery ships *Erebus* and *Terror*, 1852, 1853, 1854. Longman, Brown, Green, Longmans and Roberts, London. 530 pp.

Nares, G.S. 1852. Letter to W.H. Nares, 15 April 1852. Scott Polar Research Institute, MS 876 1/6.

Neatby, L.H. (Editor). 1967. Frozen ships. The Arctic diary of Johann Miertsching, 1850-1854. Macmillan Co. of Canada, Toronto. 254 pp.

Osborn, S. 1852. Stray leaves from an Arctic journal; or, eighteen months in the polar regions, in search of Sir John Franklin's expedition, in the years 1850-51. Longman, Brown, Green and Longmans, London. 320 pp.

Rouch, J. 1938. Émile de Bray. La Géographie 59(5-6):257-263.

_____. 1944. Le journal inédit d'Émile de Bray, explorateur polaire français. Bulletin de la Section de Géographie du Comité des Travaux Historiques et Scientifiques (Paris) 59:1-9.

_____. 1945. Deux officiers de marine français, Joseph Bellot et Émile de Bray à bord de navires de S.M. Britannique dans les mers polaires (1852-1854). France - Grande Bretagne 194:1-12.

Snow, W.P. 1851. Voyage of the *Prince Albert* in search of Sir John Franklin: a narrative of every-day life in the Arctic seas. Longman, Brown, Green and Longmans, London. 416 pp.

Stewart D. 1857. Letter to Count Walewski, 25 July 1857. Scott Polar Research Institute, MS 887.

Sutherland, P.C. 1852. Journal of a voyage in Baffin's Bay and Barrow Straits in the years 1850-1851, performed by H.M. Ships *Lady Franklin* and *Sophia* under the command of Mr. William Penny, in search of the missing crews of H.M. Ships *Erebus* and *Terror*. Longman, Brown, Green and Longmans, London. 410 pp.

Verne, J. 1866A. Les Anglais au pôle Nord; aventures du capitaine Hatteras. J. Hetzel, Paris. 338 pp.

_____. 1866B. Le désert de glace; aventures du capitaine Hatteras. J. Hetzel, Paris. 320 pp.

Illustrated by Brenda Carter

THE 1983 ELLESMERE ISLAND ARCTIC EXPEDITION

Tim O. Rockwell[1]

Abstract: On 30 June 1983, the United States,Canadian, National Geographic Society and Explorers Club flags were flown on the north shore of Pim Island, Northwest Territories,during a memorial service to commemorate the 100th anniversary of the First International Polar Year. The ceremony was conducted at a point nearly equidistant from Greely's "Camp Clay" (1883-1884), Sverdrup's Fram Haven (1898), and Peary's Payer Harbour Base (1902). The flags were borne by a nine-person expedition composed of students and faculty of the Mercersburg Academy and a representative of the Explorers Club on a 30 km, five-day hike along the rugged coastline of the Johan Peninsula and a 6 km-trek across the deteriorating ice of Rutherford Bay.

The expedition was conceived and directed by the author (Dean of Students at the Mercersburg Academy, a coeducational independent secondary school in south-central Pennsylvania) as a living tribute to Ross. G. Marvin, former faculty member, who died during Peary's 1908 bid for the Pole.

Résumé: Le 30 juin 1983, les drapeaux des États-Unis, du Canada, de la "National Geographic Society" et du "Explorers Club" ont été hissés sur la rive nord de l'île Pim, dans les territoires du Nord-Ouest, lors de la cérémonie commémorative du 100e anniversaire de la première Année polaire internationale. La cérémonie a eu lieu à un point quasi équidistant du "Camp Clay" de Greely (1883-1884), du "Fram Haven" de Sverdrup (1898) et du "Payer Harbour Base" de Peary (1902). Les drapeaux ont été portés par une expédition de neuf personnes composée d'étudiants et de membres du corps enseignant de la "Mercersburg Academy", ainsi que d'un représentant du "Explorers Club", sur une distance de 30 km lors d'une expédition à pied de cinq jours, le long du littoral accidenté de la péninsule du Johan, suivie d'une étape de 6 km sur les glaces en décomposition de la baie Rutherford.

L'expédition a été conçue et dirigé par l'auteur (Doyen des étudiants à la "Mercersburg Academy", école secondaire mixte indépendante du centre-sud de la Pennsylvanie) en hommage vivant à Ross G. Marvin, ancien membre du corps enseignant, qui mourut lors de la tentative de Peary pour atteindre le Pôle Nord en 1908.

INTRODUCTION

A small expedition composed of students and faculty of the Mercersburg Academy, a secondary independent coeducational boarding school in south-central Pennsylvania, visited the Pim Island-Cape Sabine area of Ellesmere Island during a three-week period in late June and early July, 1983. The purpose was to commemorate the 100th anniversary of the Greely Expedition (Greely 1888); the First International Polar Year, 1882-1883 (Barr 1985); and Ross G. Marvin, Mercersburg Academy faculty member (1907) who died on the Peary North Pole Expedition (Peary 1910). The expedition's primary goals were: (1) to pay tribute to those who opened the arctic frontier; and (2) to kindle at the secondary high-school level an interest in, and knowledge of, the polar regions. Secondary goals were: (1) to replicate Sergeant Long's 1882 trek on the Johan Peninsula (Greely 1886); (2) to conduct field observations and study on flora and fauna - study sessions on these subjects during the preceding school year provided a valuable background for this field work; and (3) to record personal impressions of the arctic environment through diaries and photographs.

---

[1] Mercersburg Academy, Mercersburg, Pennsylvania 17236, U.S.A.

In keeping with the memorial and academic nature of the expedition, contributions to fund the project were solicited from private sources and appropriate scientific or cultural agencies.

The Mercersburg Academy Robert R. Black Alumni Fund for Faculty Summer Study provided faculty stipends. Expedition members were responsible for contributing $1,500 (U.S.) each to meet airfare and personal equipment costs. The National Geographic Society provided a small contingency grant and its official flag. The Explorers Club supplied youth grants for student members and the personal flag of Lowell Thomas, since A.W. Greely had been the Club's first president. The Polar Continental Shelf Project quartered members at Resolute, offered technical advice, reviewed the expedition's plans, and included the expedition in its radio net. The Canadian Embassy in Washington, D.C. supplied maps, general information and a Canadian flag for the ceremony.

Total costs for the nine-person expedition were $23,000 (U.S.) of which $17,000 (U.S.) went to airfare. Transportation involved scheduled commercial flights from Pittsburgh to Resolute via Montreal and Frobisher Bay, as well as a regular schedule flight to Grise Fiord on southern Ellesmere Island. A charter flight to Alexandra Fiord completed this part of the trip. The first attempt to reach Grise Fiord was prevented by heavy ground-fog that delayed the expedition by two days.

In essence, the project demonstrated that a group of highly motivated and properly trained high school students and faculty could plan and accomplish carefully set goals, as well as completing a 10-day 100-km trek in the High Arctic with a minimum of direct support.

As an educational institution at the secondary school level, Mercersburg Academy has had an unusual interest and association with polar affairs. Ross G. Marvin who taught mathematics at the Academy in 1907 (Figure 1) served on Peary's 1905-1906 expedition, and in 1909 perished on Peary's successful 1908-1909 polar expedition (Figure 2). Marvin's death had a lasting impact on the school, since its first Headmaster, Dr. William M. Irvine, held Marvin forth as an example of the school's motto "Integritas, Virilitas, Fidelitas" (Rockwell 1984A).

As early as 1911, Sir Wilfred Grenfell lectured at the school urging and finding support for his humanitarian work in Labrador. His strong relationship with the Academy was further emphasized when a stained glass window depicting Sir Wilfred and the Arctic frontier was included when the Mercersburg Chapel was constructed in 1927, that being a singular

FIGURE 1: Ross Marvin (seated) in southern surroundings. Courtesy of Chemung County Historical Society.

FIGURE 2: Ross G. Marvin in arctic clothing. Courtesy of Chemung County Historical Society.

honor for a living person. Sir Wilfred and Lady Grenfell visited the school for the last time in 1932, shortly before their retirement.

Admiral Peary recounted Marvin's exploits for the student body in 1912, and during the 1930s various lecturers and visitors associated with Byrd's efforts in Antarctica came to the school to share their experiences. Donald MacMillan, who was with Marvin in 1909, rekindled the Arctic interest during the 1950s with various lectures on his past sled trips and then-current sailing ventures in the High Arctic. Commander Calvert, captain of the USS *Skate*, first submarine to surface at the North Pole, lectured Mercersburg students in 1962 (Rockwell 1984B). Thus, the conception, organization, and execution of the 1983 expedition on the 100th anniversary of the First International Polar Year seemed a natural culmination of the school's polar interests, and an apt way to demonstrate its willingness to provide practical arctic field experience for youthful students in history and the natural sciences.

THE DESTINATION OF THE EXPEDITION

Logistics and history dictated the selection of Pim Island and Cape Sabine as the expedition's final destination and the site for its planned commemorative ceremony. Approximately midway between the Arctic Circle and the North Pole, Cape Sabine is the easternmost tip of tiny (6 km x 15 km) Pim Island which lies off the Johan Peninsula on the east coast of Ellesmere Island. With the peninsula, Pim Island forms the narrowest point of the 48 km-wide Smith Sound separating Ellesmere Island from Greenland. Until the time of the Greely Expedition, (Figures 3,4) Cape Sabine was thought to be the eastern point of the Johan Peninsula; however, Sergeant Rice (photographer on the Greely Expedition), during a reconnaissance from Wade Point in 1883, discovered that the area was really a small island separated from the mainland by a narrow strait which now bears his name (Greely 1886).

Lying at the edge of the North Water polynya, the cape's accessibility by water is not always certain. June to July land temperatures near the cape vary from -8° to 5°C.

Because the scientific base at Alexandra Fiord is accessible by Twin-Otter aircraft, it made a perfect staging area from which the novice team of students and faculty could reach Pim Island and Cape Sabine by hiking along the Johan Peninsula.

FIGURE 3: Members of the Greely Expedition. Lieutenant A.W. Greely is fourth from the left in the front row.

FIGURE 4: Greely Expedition field party man-hauling sledges.

Most significant for the commemorative aspects of the expedition was the varied history and prehistory of Pim Island and its approaches. Recent archaeological investigations on the nearby Knud Peninsula and Skraeling Island indicated prehistoric Eskimo activity and possible Norse contact by 1300 AD (Schledermann 1980). As is well known, Greely retreated to Cape Sabine in 1882 from his more northern station at Lady Franklin Bay after two years of important scientific observations, collection, experimentation and discovery. Unfortunately, 19 of the 25 man party perished at "Camp Clay" on the north shore of Pim Island awaiting rescue, which finally arrived too late in 1883 (Greely 1888; Figure 5). Otto Sverdrup in 1898-1899 wintered near the northern entrance to Rice Strait at Fram Haven and discovered the ruins of Eskimopolis on the Johan Peninsula midway between Alexandra Fiord and Pim Island (Sverdrup 1904). Peary in 1898-1902 used Payer Harbour on the south shore of the island as a support camp for his more northern base at Greely's abandoned Fort Conger on Lady Franklin Bay. Donald MacMillan, former assistant of Peary, made one of the first maps of the area in 1961, and during the winter of 1924 crossed from Greenland to erect a National Geographic Society bronze tablet to the memory of the Greely Expedition at "Camp Clay" (MacMillan, M. 1951). Lieutenant Commander Byrd, flying over that spot with MacMillan in 1925 during one of the pioneering trials of aircraft by the United States in the Arctic, commented that he had "never seen a bleaker spot" (MacMillan, D.B. 1925). In the late 1940s MacMillan again made several attempts to reach the island and "Camp

FIGURE 5: Survivors (all seated) of the Greely Expedition following their rescue from "Camp Clay" in 1883. Greely is in the centre of the group.

800

Clay" by sea, succeeding finally in 1950 (MacMillan, M. 1951). Since that time the area has been visited frequently by field teams now having easier access by helicopter. However, the fact remains that the Pim Island and Cape Sabine area with its rich prehistory and association with several early arctic expeditions makes it a physical and symbolic confluence of man's conquest of the Far North.

STRUCTURE AND GOALS OF THE EXPEDITION

As with any expedition operating in isolated, unfamiliar terrain, individual and group safety was a primary consideration. Since few true emergencies can be completely foreseen, adequate training and field discipline were stressed to decrease the likelihood of serious problems. Thus, a number of conditions were set: (1) the expedition would not be more than 30 km from the usable airstrip at Alexandra Fiord; (2) radio contact with Polar Continental Shelf Project in Resolute was maintained twice daily; and (3) other Canadian research posts and agencies had been advised of our itinerary. Further, the summer season of 24-hour daylight provided less stress in an unfamiliar environment as well as conditions favourable to more rapid assistance, if needed. All first aid equipment and safety gear, except the radio, was distributed among members of the group so that complete loss of essential emergency equipment was unlikely. Although recorded summer weather conditions for the area were no more severe than those of a mild winter in the continental United States, all camping and personal gear was of high quality alpine-type and serviceable well below the recorded minimums.

Because the expedition was composed of high school students and faculty inexperienced in the Arctic, much consideration was given to selecting a team whose combined physical and psychological strengths and past experience were likely to make the expedition a success. The four faculty members, besides expertise in archaeology, history, mathematics, chemistry and biology, had field experience in hunting, trapping, mountaineering, and extended trekking in the more southerly parts of Canada. The three 17-year old male students and one 20-year old female alumnus were chosen for their keen interest, high motivation, psychological stability under stress, and demonstrated ability to work as a team. As the Explorers Club wished to honour its first president A.W. Greely, the Club secretary, an experienced arctic mountaineer, rounded out the nine-member expedition (Bruno 1984). All participants had to present a reasonable health record and undergo a physical and dental screening prior to departure. Also all members were trained in CPR and basic first-aid, one faculty member being a certified Emergency Medical Technician.

In brief, the expedition met its several educational and commemorative goals. All along Johan Peninsula the group encountered signs of prehistoric Dorset and Thule cultures from tent-rings to half-buried communal buildings. When time permitted, sketches, photos and notes were taken, such as at Eskimopolis. Extreme care was exercised neither to remove nor to disturb any of the remains. Slides and notes on unusual features, such as two large polar bear traps (Schledermann 1978), were later forwarded to the Arctic Institute of North America. Altogether, these on-site visits had a profound impact on the group's appreciation for the cultures and people of the High Arctic.

Signs of historic activity ranged from inland tower cairns on Cape Rutherford to indications on Pim Island of a "butcher station" mentioned in Sverdrup's account of his stay in Fram Haven (Sverdrup 1904). Unfortunately, refuse, such as soda cans and plywood, was found icebound in several spots well down the peninsula from Alexandra Fiord. These, too, provided important, albeit negative, lessons for the group.

After five days of hiking from Alexandra Fiord, the expedition had to cross to Pim Island on a 2 km-wide ice bridge across Rutherford Bay near Cocked Hat Island. Originally, planning had called for a crossing at the narrower Rice Strait, but early break-up necessitated a detour and shortened the time the group had on Pim Island, since a safe return to the peninsula relied on the stability of the ice bridge. These crossing conditions, large tidal cracks, and deteriorating weather hindered the search for "Camp Clay". Reluctantly, but to insure a safe return, we decided to abandon the search and hold the commemorative service where the 1983 expedition first set foot on Pim Island - a point nearly equidistant from Payer Harbour, Fram Haven, and "Camp Clay".

COMMEMORATIVE CEREMONY AND RESULTS OF THE EXPEDITION

With the Canadian, United States, National Geographic Society, Explorers Club flags and a Mercersburg Academy banner flying, the service was conducted abut noon on 30 June

FIGURE 6: Members of the 1983 Ellesmere Island Arctic Expedition on the north shore of Pim Island. Left to right: Tim Rockwell, Frank Rutherford, Jeff Dailey, Shawn Rockwell, Robin Sarner, Brent Gift, Dan Kunkle and Kurt Nielsen. Photo by Shawn Rockwell.

1983 (Figure 6). A prayer was offered for the dead of the Greely Expedition and for "all who, through their lives, extended mankind's knowledge of the polar regions". A small cairn now encloses a brass plaque stating the purpose of the expedition and recording the memorial service.

Upon our return to the United States, summary accounts of the expedition were published in various national and international scientific, professional and educational journals. Student and faculty members gave various slide presentations and lectures to groups of all ages, reaching nearly 5,000 people. Fossils, faunal remains and Inuit art were deposited in the science department's teaching museum. Plant specimens collected by Sergeant Ralston of the 1883 Greely Expedition, and now in the plant collection of the Pennsylvania Department of Agriculture, were brought to Mercersburg for comparison with those collected 100 years later. Other than personal gear, all expedition equipment was donated to the school's outdoor program, and finds continued use. Thus, the 1983 Ellesmere Island Arctic Expedition demonstrated that High Arctic field experiences by qualified, motivated high-school students and faculty are possible and provide unusual long-term learning experiences well worth the effort and planning needed for their safe success.

ACKNOWLEDGEMENTS

I thank the United States Military Historical Institute, Carlisle War College, for permission to use the Greely photographs, and the Chemung County Historical Society for the pictures of Ross Marvin.

REFERENCES

Barr, W. 1985. The expeditions of the First International Polar Year, 1882-83. Arctic Institute of North America, Technical Paper No. 29.

Bruno, J.C.D. and T.O. Rockwell. 1984. The Greely Commemorative Expedition. Explorers Journal 62(2):50-53.

Greely, A.W. 1886. Three years of Arctic service: an account of the Lady Franklin Bay Expedition of 1881-1884. Scribner, New York.

_____. 1888. Report on the proceedings of the United States Expedition to Lady Franklin Bay, Grinnell Land. Government Printing Office, Washington, D.C.

Peary, R.E. 1920. The North Pole. Stokes, New York.

MacMillan, D.B. 1925. MacMillan Arctic Expedition returns. National Geographic 48:477-518.

MacMillan, M. 1951. Far North with 'Captain Mac'. National Geographic 100:465-513.

Rockwell, T. 1984A. Ross Gilmore Marvin (1880-1909): explorer and teacher. Fram: Journal of Polar Studies 1(2):375-378.

_____. 1984B. The 1983 Ellesmere Island Arctic Expedition. Fram: Journal of Polar Studies 1(2):447-460.

Schledermann, P. 1977. Eskimo trappers on Ellesmere Island, N.W.T. Western Canadian Journal of Anthropology 7(1):84-99.

Schledermann, P. 1978. Preliminary results of archaeological investigations in the Bache Peninsula region, Ellesmere Island, N.W.T. Arctic 31(4):459-474.

_____. 1980. Notes on Norse finds from the east coast of Ellesmere Island, N.W.T. Arctic 33(3):454-463.

Sverdrup, O. 1904. New land: four years in the Arctic region. Longmans, Green, London. 2 volumes.

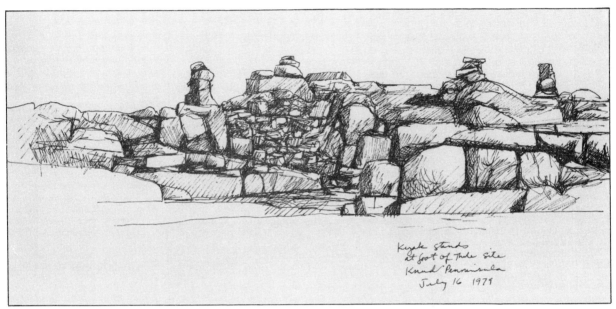

Illustrated by Brenda Carter

EXPLORATORY MOUNTAINEERING IN THE ARCTIC ISLANDS

G.V.B. Cochran[1]

Abstract: The superb mountain terrain that lines the eastern coasts of the Canadian Arctic Islands is little known outside Canada. In fact, although mapped by aerial photography, the interiors of these mountain ranges still harbour some of the last places on earth that have escaped human visitation. Tourist attention is being drawn to some of these areas by the establishment of National Parks on Baffin and Ellesmere islands, but elsewhere there still are vast areas that are seldom, if ever, visited that could offer a strong attraction to mountaineers around the world.

Since 1967, the author has organized 11 expeditions to explore and climb in virgin areas of these mountains. On Ellesmere Island, these expeditions have visited the mountains of Yelverton Bay and Mackinson Inlet. On Baffin Island, activities have been centred on Bylot Island, Erik Harbour, and two areas of the Cumberland Peninsula: one north of Kingnait Fiord and the other west of Cape Dyer. In addition to mountaineering, glacier studies have been conducted in cooperation with the Glacier Inventory of Canada, and strain-gauge studies, related to the stress analysis of sea ice, have been accomplished with logistical support from Polar Continental Shelf Project.

This paper reviews briefly the history of exploratory mountaineering in the Arctic Islands, comments on expedition logistics, and provides a synopsis of the author's experiences, highlighting the key role played by Inuit in the success of several of these undertakings.

Résumé: Les superbes montagnes qui bordent les côtes et des îles de l'Arctique canadien sont peu connues à l'extérieur du Canada. En fait, bien que cartographié par photographie aérienne, l'intérieur de ces chaînes de montagnes abrite certains des derniers endroits de la planète encore inexplorés par les humains. L'attention des touristes a été attirée sur certains de ces endroits par la création de parcs nationaux sur les îles de Baffin et d'Ellesmere, mais, ailleurs, il y a encore de vastes régions qui ne sont visitées que rarement, voire jamais, et qui pourraient fortement intéresser les alpinistes du monde entier.

Depuis 1967, l'auteur a organisé 11 expéditions d'exploration et d'alpinisme dans les régions vierges de ces montagnes. À Ellesmere, ces expéditions ont parcouru les montagnes de la baie Yelverton et de l'inlet Mackinson. Sur l'île de Baffin, elles ont porté sur l'île Bylot, Erik Harbour, et deux régions de la péninsule de Cumberland: une au nord du fjord Kingnait et l'autre à l'ouest de Cape Dyer. En plus d'y faire de l'alpinisme, on y a effectué des études de glaciers, en collaboration avec l'Inventaire des glaciers du Canada, et des études de tensiométrie, liées à l'analyse de stress de la glace de mer, avec le soutien logistique de l'Étude du plateau continental polaire.

Cette présentation fait un bref historique de l'alpinisme d'exploration dans les îles de l'Arctique, offre quelques commentaires sur la logistique des expéditions, et résume les expériences de l'auteur, soulignant le rôle essentiel des Inuit dans les succès de plusieurs de ces entreprises.

INTRODUCTION

Mountains, glaciers and ice caps are major features of the Arctic Islands. Aside from being of interest from a scientific standpoint, these mountainous areas have another intrinsic attraction: they represent one of the last frontiers for exploratory mountaineering - a discipline that might be described as mountaineering "not because it is there", but because one seeks to know what is there. It is mountaineering where curiosity is at least as important as challenge. Along with Antarctica, Greenland and the Himalayan Kingdom of Bhutan, the Arctic Islands offer a locale where there still are abundant unclimbed summits. Probably there are places where no one has ever been.

---

[1] Orthopaedic Engineering and Research Center, Helen Hayes Hospital, West Haverstraw, New York 19003, U.S.A.

The mountains of the Arctic Islands are part of a chain extending from Labrador up the east coast of Baffin, Devon and Ellesmere islands that continues west across northern Ellesmere Island. Most mountains are of Precambrian rock, but this changes to sedimentary formations as the range extends westward on Ellesmere Island. In general, the peaks range from 2,000-7,000 ft (610-2,130 m), not high as mountains go, but impressive in many locations because they rise from a base near sea level. A few higher summits such as Mount Barbeau (8,540 ft or 2,600 m) in northern Ellesmere Island exist, but they are nunataks that rise from high inland ice plateaus. Perhaps the best known mountains are those of Pangnirtung Pass on Baffin Island, now within Auyuittuq National Park. Here several impressive peaks such as Mount Queen Elizabeth rise to 7,000 ft (2,130 m). While this area attracts hundreds of visitors each year, few expeditions ever attempt to visit the thousands upon thousands of square miles of mountains that exist elsewhere in the Arctic Islands.

HISTORICAL ASPECTS

Development of exploratory mountaineering in the Arctic Islands is best understood in terms of the activities of several individuals, each of whom has organized a number of expeditions. On Baffin Island it began with the expedition led by J.M. Wordie (1935), a veteran of Shackleton's Antarctic expeditions. Arriving by boat, his group discovered the spectacular rock peaks in the region of Sam Ford Fiord, north of Clyde River. Longstaff and Hanham climbed Eglinton Tower, while Ritchie and Baird ascended Pioneer Peak.

Pat Baird, who became the true father of exploratory mountaineering on Baffin Island, thus began his career as a member of Wordie's expedition. After a dogsled exploration across part of Bylot Island (with several first ascents) in 1939, followed by important activities in the Arctic during the Second World War, Baird returned to the Clyde area with the joint Canadian-Swiss expedition in 1950 (Baird 1950). While this was mainly a government-sponsored scientific project based at Sam Ford Fiord, they managed to climb 17 peaks on the side! Later Baird was a prime-mover in the 1953 Arctic Institute Expedition that was based at Pangnirtung Pass and accounted for many first ascents in that area including Mount Asgard (6,598 ft or 2,010 m) (Baird 1953, 1954). Following this he organized two Alpine Club of Canada (ACC) expeditions in the early 1960s that made many more first ascents (Baird 1964, 1966).

Another important expedition to Pangnirtung Pass was made in 1961 by a group from Cambridge University led by R.E. Langford (1962). They completed the first crossing of the peninsula from North Pangnirtung Fiord to Pangnirtung Fiord in summer and achieved seven important new ascents.

In 1962, H.W. Tilman (1964A) sailed his schooner *Mischief* into Totnes Road near the Arctic Circle on Baffin Island. There he landed and climbed Mount Raleigh as well as a neighboring peak he named Mount Mischief. Typical of many of the prominent mountains of the Arctic coast, Mount Raleigh was named not by a mountaineer but by a seafarer (in this case John Davis in 1594). Tilman next sailed *Mischief* to the northern coast of Bylot Island in 1963 and from there made a complete crossing of the island, ending on the Sermilik Glacier opposite Pond Inlet. It was an extremely difficult trip due to deep, soft snow. Although he crossed a 5,700 ft (1,740 m) pass, he did not attempt any summits due to the snow conditions (Tilman 1964B). Two earlier ascents, including Mount Thule, had been made on the south coast of Bylot Island by two Americans in 1954 (Ferris 1955), whereas Baird had made others in the interior of that region in 1939.

Ted Whalley is another individual with a sustained dedication to Arctic mountains. Originally a member of two of the ACC expeditions to Pangnirtung (Baird 1964, 1966), he continued on his own with three major expeditions to the mountains north of Clyde River - an area of alpine terrain that rivals Pangnirtung Pass. In 1973 his expedition was based at Swiss Bay south of Sam Ford Fiord (Whalley 1974), in 1977 in Stewart Valley to the north (O'Connell and Whalley 1978), and in May 1979 among the virgin peaks of Ayr Lake, where they travelled overland by sleds from Clyde River (Whalley 1980). Whalley was co-leader with the author of two Canadian-American Expeditions to Makinson Inlet on Ellesmere Island in the 1970s (Cochran and Whalley 1977; Cochran 1979A).

I began my series of 11 expeditions in 1967 on Baffin Island when the days of the true pioneers drew to a close. As outlined below, these expeditions covered five areas ranging from Cumberland Peninsula to northern Ellesmere Island, and accounted for several dozen first-ascents, and exploration of a score of major glaciers from 1968 to 1987. In addition to the published accounts, complete reports of expeditions were submitted to appropriate agencies of the government of Canada and/or the Northwest Territories.

Laurie Dexter, an Anglican minister who lived for several years in Pond Inlet, is another dedicated exploratory mountaineer. He specialized in climbs along the southern coast of Bylot Island, and later completed an ambitious west-east traverse of Bylot Island on skis, making several first-ascents (Kelly 1978). He also made a number of first-ascents at Grise Fiord including Grise Tower.

Others who have made many trips to the Arctic include John Amatt, a Canadian with a special interest in student expeditions, typified by his 1974 expedition to Kingnait Fiord (Amatt 1975), and Dave McAdam, the famous lone-walker of Baffin. McAdam made a series of solo, summer expeditions through the Cumberland Peninsula and achieved many non-technical first-ascents as recorded frequently in the *Canadian Alpine Journal*. He also noted the lack of interest by outsiders in the more remote regions of Auyuittuq National Park (McAdam 1981). Aside from repeat visitors, a French ski-expedition explored the region southeast of Pond Inlet in the late 1970s, and several British schools sent expeditions to Baffin Island.

Ellesmere Island is extremely mountainous too: the northern part has summits exceeding 8,000 ft (2,440 m). Although many are nunataks, others, including Commonwealth Mountain, present a more alpine face and there are fine opportunities for ski-mountaineering. The first important summit climbed was named Mount Oxford by the Oxford University Ellesmere Land Expedition of 1935 - apparently the only group to visit the ice-cap before the 1950s (Moore 1936). Then after the Second World War, Geoff Hattersley-Smith led many scientific expeditions to northern Ellesmere Island under the auspices of the Defence Research Board (Hattersley-Smith 1974). Bases were established at Lake Hazen and later Tanquary Fiord. Although primarily concerned with science, he and members of his expeditions pioneered exploratory mountaineering on Ellesmere Island. They climbed many summits near Lake Hazen, including Mount Whistler (8,500 ft or 2,590 m)), seen and named by A.W. Greely in 1882. Later they discovered and climbed a slightly higher summit farther west (Mount Barbeau). This 8,540 ft (2,600 m) peak is the highest in North America east of the Rockies (Hattersley-Smith 1962, 1970).

The British armed services also climbed on northern Ellesmere Island. The Royal Air Force Ellesmere Island Expedition, led by Wing Commander Derek Bird, explored the northern mountains in 1967. From a base at Tanquary Fiord, his group crossed to McClintock Inlet and climbed Commonwealth Mountain and Mount Barbeau. Later, the

Royal Navy Ellesmere Island Expedition, led by Commander Angus Erskine, landed by air directly on the ice-cap near the head of Milne Glacier to explore the British Empire Range. After descending that glacier to the sea, they crossed the ice-cap back to Tanquary Fiord using skis and man-drawn sleds, climbing 13 peaks along the way (Erskine 1974). Expedition member Mike Banks probably described best the attraction of climbing north of latitude 80°: "These peaks ... were straight forward snow climbs. The attraction did not lie in their difficulty, but in the deep satisfaction in exploring and climbing lonely and shapely mountains in an exceptionally remote and inaccessible region of the Arctic" (Banks 1974). Not to be outdone, the British Army organized an extensive climbing expedition to the mountains of Axel Heiberg Island (Muston 1974). Also there was a primarily scientific, Joint Services Expedition to Princess Marie Bay on Ellesmere Island in 1980 (Williams 1980).

Steve Trafton and colleagues, mostly from the State of Washington, initiated two extensive ski-mountaineering expeditions across the high ice-plateaus of northern Ellesmere Island: one to the Victoria and Albert Mountains (Goodman 1982), and one to the Mount Barbeau area (Errington 1983). The same group had mounted an expedition to Broad Peak on Sam Ford Fiord, Baffin Island, in 1978 (Errington 1979).

Thus, only a few years ago, it was still possible for expeditions in the Arctic to reach vast, untouched terrain. Now the options are shrinking, and much unexplored mountain-eering country has been visited by helicopter-borne mapping and geological parties that have been active since the mid-1970s. Still, large areas of mountains remain unexplored by land-parties and there are hundreds, if not thousands, of virgin summits. Fortunately for exploratory mountaineers, most climbers seek the technical challenges among the peaks of Auyuittuq National Park. While many significant technical climbs from Pangnirtung Pass, such as those of Scott (1973), have been made since the 1960s, these activities are beyond the scope of this paper; details may be found in *The Canadian Alpine Journal*, and *The Alpine Journal*.

EXPEDITION ORGANIZATION AND LOGISTICS

Objectives

The first step in organizing an exploratory mountaineering expedition is to define an objective. Like any research project, finding unclimbed peaks requires knowledge of what is there and what has been done before. Knowledge of what exists stems from maps and aerial photographs, in particular the tri-camera coverage (from 20,000 ft or 6,100 m obtained about 1950) and the vertical coverage obtained from 30,000 ft (9,150 m) in the late 1950s (National Air Photo Library, Ottawa). The latter photographs are the basis for the excellent 1:250,000 maps first produced in the 1960s and 1970s by the Department of Energy Mines and Resources. Using these maps in conjunction with the original aerial photographs provides an excellent planning and navigation tool. Certain editions of the 1:500,000 National Topographic Series with aeronautical information also can be useful for spot altitudes. It is sometimes difficult to explain how one can reach an area where literally no one has ever been, and yet be standing there with an excellent map! Such is the advantage of photogrammetry.

Up to the mid-1960s the best maps of many remote areas of Canada were the older NTS 1:500,000 editions. Many of these included fascinatingly-vague areas marked "relief data incomplete", a sure clue to a possibly virgin area! Today relief data are good, but most features still lack names. Thus a cluster of named features on a map usually indicates that an expedition has been there. To find unclimbed peaks, one must locate a nameless area with map-contours indicating high relief, then research the mountaineering literature.

Organization

Once an objective is selected, the expedition must be organized, equipped and financed. My experience has been with small expeditions of four to 10 men and women. Six is probably the ideal, combining strength for safety with flexibility for simultaneous climbs on different objectives. Whatever the objective, it is important that all members agree on it beforehand. Misunderstandings about expectations for the expedition may cause problems that can be compounded by anxieties developing in the extreme isolation of the Arctic.

Financially, most small expeditions are best supported by dividing costs among the members. Although grants and commercial support are sometimes available, such support is ever more difficult and time-consuming to obtain. Surprisingly, while not cheap, most expeditions can be accomplished for no more than one might spend on a normal vacation. Once in the field, it costs little to remain because the expenses are mainly in air fare, charter costs, air-freight and major equipment such as boats, motors or snowmobiles. Usually such equipment can be sold at cost in the Arctic after a few weeks of expedition use. Firearms are necessary for protection from polar bears. But guns should be carried only in accordance with legal requirements and after consultation with the Royal Canadian Mounted Police. It is most efficient to prepack and send all backpacking food by air-freight. Although adequate food for local use is available in the settlements, an expedition can strain supplies. A week of extra rations is essential in an environment where weather rules transportation.

Communications today are easy using the SBX-11 single side-band radiotelephones made by Spillsbury and Tindall. This set, weighing less than 10 lbs. (4.5 kg) with batteries, usually provides excellent contact over several hundred miles (with a dipole antenna), but sunspot activity and problems due to geographical location can interfere.

Access

Reaching the mountains of the Arctic Islands first became feasible for small private expeditions in the 1960s when commercial flights began regular service to Frobisher Bay (Iqaluit) and Resolute at fares low enough to be competitive with those to mountains elsewhere. Even now it is amazing to think that one can fly to Resolute, within a thousand miles of the North Pole, for less than a full fare from Montreal to Vancouver!

From Iqaluit or Resolute, the next stage involves a flight to an Inuit settlement in a propeller-driven aircraft. Only a few years ago, scheduled service to the settlements was based more on imagination than reality, and flights were cancelled unless an adequate load was available; thus it was far safer to charter. Today, scheduled flights to the settlements along the coast of Baffin Island have greatly improved, although weather is always a critical factor. Also, direct flights from Iqaluit or Resolute to an expedition-base often are possible if suitable landing-site are available.

If an Inuit settlement is selected as the point of departure, the work begins in earnest from there, as the best mountain areas usually are 50-150 miles (80-240 km) distant. The method of reaching the mountains and the mode of travel among them depends on which of two seasonal "windows" has been selected.

The first is the *summer window*. This implies boat travel, but in most areas residual sea ice makes travel uncertain until August. While the water stays open into October, the weather tends to deteriorate in September, leaving August as the best compromise. A few places (e.g. Pangnirtung Pass) that require travel only on the inner reaches of fiords can be reached much earlier. Actually, August in the Arctic marks the beginning of fall with darkness (enough to see the stars, but light enough to climb) returning for a few hours at night. One advantage of August is that mosquitos are fewer.

Boats available range from diesel-driven "Peterhead"-type craft down to the ubiquitous 22-foot freighter canoe driven by a 20 h.p. outboard motor. In earlier years it was usually possible to reach an Inuit settlement and make arrangements for boat travel on the spot. Now with the advent of tourism, this has become more difficult and expensive. Except for visits to a tourist area such as Auyuittuq Park, expeditions today are best advised to bring their own inflatable craft.

Direct flights to a basecamp also are possible in the summer for Twin Otters with balloon tires, but landing-sites in the mountains are scarce, and are usually limited to beaches or flat gravel-beds along rivers. In summer, it is best to know of a landing-strip in advance lest the cost of a charter flight to and from the area be forfeit!

Once landed, whether by boat or air, expeditions must backpack anywhere from 5-20 miles (8-32 km) into the mountains. Probably two full loads per person will be required to support operations with climbing and emergency gear for 10 days or more. While trekking inland, rivers are a serious and dangerous obstacle in summer. Route planning must seek to avoid crossing rivers whenever possible. All but the smallest streams can be uncrossable without special gear, because a heavily-loaded climber who gets above the knees in a fast melt-stream can soon be in trouble. By August the diminution of glacier runoff at night may make early morning crossings easier.

Glacier valleys make the best highways, with the glaciers reaching to anywhere from tidewater to 10 miles (16 km) inland. The terminus usually is guarded by moraines which can make rough going. Once past the moraines, summer glacier travel in the zone of bare ice is easy, although one must be wary of crevasses. In this zone crevasses can be extremely deceptive because they may be covered by a residual and extremely fragile snow bridge that appears only as an innocent-looking band of dirty snow on the bare ice.

Moving up to more permanent snow (usually at an altitude of 1,500-2,500 ft or 460-760 m), a transition zone of glacier morasse or slush may appear. This can be extremely hard on the feet, and there seems to be no good way to deal with it, although modern plastic double boots help. Also it is convenient to carry a pair of wet-suit booties to use as an alternative to the regular inner boot, both for river crossings and morasses. Higher up the snow deepens, and may become impassable, because at each step one sinks unpredictably through successive layers of insubstantial crust. This condition usually does not improve much "at night", and firm snow seldom will be reached at altitudes below 4,000 ft (1,220 m). Thus small, lightweight snowshoes are essential items for summer travel. Substantial new snow also may be encountered in August. Temperatures in the summer window can range from -5° to 15°C.

The *spring window* for Arctic mountaineering is April through May or early June. Here an entirely different environment is encountered - the "spring weather" simulating January in Ottawa. On Ellesmere Island, snow covers much of the land down to sea level into June, and the sea ice is solid almost everywhere into July. Temperatures range from -35° to -15°C in late April and from -20° up to 0°C in May. Daylight lasts for 24 hours, and the sun's rapidly increasing ascension accounts for the rise in temperature leading to a major melt-off in June. On Baffin Island, conditions are similar, but with the season advanced by two weeks or more.

Under "spring" conditions, travel to the mountains from a coastal settlement can be accomplished over the sea ice by snowmobiles pulling komatiks. These Inuit sleds, 10-18 ft (3-5.5 m) long, can carry a load of 1,000 lbs (450 kg) including two riders. Under good snow conditions, overland travel to reach inland glaciers or to cross between fiords also can be accomplished, but with more difficulty. While the idea of dogs is attractive, it is rather impractical for a small, short-term mountaineering expedition to obtain and use dog-teams today.

Conditions during snowmobile sledding can be arduous. While the environment is different, it is difficult to say whether summer travel in an open boat (in a wind with wet snow or rain at temperatures around freezing) is more uncomfortable than riding into the wind on a speeding komatik at dry temperatures of -15°C. In both cases, the rule is put on *all* the clothes available *before* starting.

Komatik travel is a fascinating sport, best learned from Inuit by on-the-job training. For example, it is easy to drive a snowmobile on level sea ice at 20 mph (32 kph) while pulling a half-ton (.45 MT) komatik on a 20-ft (6-m) rope. But one's reflexes must be trained to drive the skidoo to the side when the brakes are applied: there are no brakes on the behemoth closing in from behind! On land, travelling with an overloaded komatik in soft snow can be backbreaking. Each time the skidoo tread "blows" traction, the riders jump off and haul the sledge up close behind the machine. Then the driver takes off at full speed to try a shock start while the riders push, then scramble to jump on before being stranded. Travelling downhill with the loaded komatik cinched up tight to the skidoo (which hopefully acts as the brake) can be terrifying, while travelling over rough sea ice in deep snow in the fog offers the opportunity for backbreaking work and terror simultaneously. The great flexibility of these sleds (held together by lashing) is the key to their superb performance on rough, hard terrain, but also makes securing the load a task of considerable art.

Flights by ski-equipped Twin Otter direct to an expedition base are far more feasible in spring than in summer, because landing sites on sea ice or snow covered glaciers are readily available. The main problem is that it is difficult to determine the weather at a remote site before departure. Even in good weather, local ground-fogs or an overcast sky can abort a landing in a spot where the white conditions make determination of ground-level difficult. Once a party is on the ground, tents or garbage-bag markers make it easier for incoming flights to discern ground-level. On-line satellite photos in Resolute now make it possible to detect cloud-cover over proposed landing-sites, so today this approach is more feasible than a few years ago.

Inland travel is relatively easy in the spring using skis equipped with synthetic "skins" for climbing and pulling fibreglass sleds (Mountainsmith, Boulder, Colorado). In this way, each expedition member can carry 100 lbs (45 kg) or more with ease: up to 40 lbs (18 kg) in a backpack and 60 lbs (27 kg) or more on the sled. This permits operation away from basecamp for two weeks on one load. Mountaineering skis with convertible bindings (such as Ramer or Silvretta) that are usable with plastic, double mountaineering boots are recommended. Insulated overboots or mukluks are useful as backup. While cross-country skis can be used by experts, they are less stable and provide less traction while pulling a sled uphill on difficult and icy terrain.

Other Mountaineering Aspects

On glaciers, at all seasons, extreme caution is required, because even relatively static Arctic glaciers can be heavily-crevassed and snowbridges tend to be fragile. On peaks, climbing routes range from simple walkups or ski ascents on rubbly ridges, to alpine-style ridges, to highly-technical faces, more or less at the option of the climber. Despite the low overall elevation, most climbs cover 2,000-4,000 ft (610-1,220 m) of altitude. Unfortunately, the rock usually is rotten. In the summer, new snow can bring frequent avalanches, and in the spring there can be *extreme* danger from heavy wind slab conditions.

Thus, it is well to remember that on almost any expedition to the Arctic mountains, the group must be entirely self-reliant and exercise utmost care. As the routes are unknown, full alpine gear, including crampons, should always be carried, even for an "easy" day, because many summits are covered by a thin capping of ice. For practical purposes any expedition can be cut off from effective outside aid for many days, and no expedition should get into any situation from which it cannot extricate itself.

Obligations and Rewards

Exploratory mountaineering implies a step beyond simple recreation, because there is an element of learning and an obligation to report one's findings and activities both in the literature and to government agencies. One reward is the fact that the first expedition to an area begins a local history which is extended by each successive foray. The opportunity to name important features in consultation with the Canadian Permanent Committee on Geographic Names is another attraction, as is the opportunity for undertaking even limited scientific observations. For example, I was pleased to be able to cooperate with the Glacier Inventory of Canada on several occasions and to conduct work on strain-measurements in sea ice (Cochran 1980).

Finally, the mountain explorer is a visitor to a land that is exceedingly fragile - one that must be treated with the utmost respect. Even the smallest wound on High Arctic tundra can take years to heal. The interests of the local people also deserve consideration. While the influx of tourists to the Arctic emphasises increasingly commercial relationships

816

with the Inuit, a more traditional interaction still can be sought. Expeditions that plan to operate through a settlement should remember that the simple diplomacy of formally requesting permission from the Town Council in advance can be of tremendous aid.

EXPEDITIONS 1967-1987: A PERSONAL ACCOUNT

Cape Dyer Region: 1967 and 1977

My interest in the Arctic began about 1965 with the revelation that Nordair ran scheduled flights to Frobisher Bay with monthly flights to the radar site at Cape Dyer on the Cumberland Peninsula of Baffin Island. Reading of expeditions to Pangnirtung Pass, I wondered what new mountains might be approached from Cape Dyer. Being familiar with the Canadian map and aerial-photo system from a prior expedition to the British Columbia Coast Range (Cochran 1958), I soon identified an objective lying north of Tilman's Mount Raleigh. Two Britishers had approached the area by walking from Cape Dyer and had named some topographic features (Gribbon 1961), but there were thousands of square miles of virgin territory left.

Getting there became a challenge. Then, it was particularly difficult for an outsider to find out how things were accomplished in the Arctic, but little by little, a plan emerged. Our *1967 Cape Dyer Arctic-Alpine Expedition* flew to Frobisher Bay and chartered a DC-3 to Broughton Island, the nearest settlement. On the way, we were treated to a spectacular, glacier-level flight directly through Pangnirtung Pass (Figure 1). On Broughton Island we were helped immensely by the then settlement manager Bob Pilot, who arranged for us to charter a 20-foot (6-m) whaleboat crewed by two highly-competent Inuit. They nursed the ancient, 6 hp Acadia make-and-break engine 70-80 miles (110-130 km) south to the head of an unnamed fiord. Once there, Mosesee Audlakiak and Ikalik Kokstak left with a promise to pick us up a month later, after we had crossed to the head of Sunneshine Fiord leading to Cape Dyer (named after one of John Davis's ships). We had no radio, and although we could have walked out to Cape Dyer in an emergency, we hailed the timely arrival of Mosesee after his 100-mile (160-km) journey through Davis Strait.

On this expedition we explored a large glacier system to its head, linking with the areas reached by our predecessors - Tillman (1963) to the south and Gribbon (1961) to the east.

FIGURE 1: Mt. Asgard (L) from DC-3 (wing on lower right) flying through Pangnirtung Pass, 1967.

Also, we achieved seven first-ascents and named such features as: Southwind Glacier, Southwind Peak, The Mitre, Delta Peak, and others later accepted by the Canadian Permanent Committee on Geographic Names (Figure 2) (Cochran and Ritterbush 1968; Cochran 1969). In addition, we obtained a series of glacier-survey photos for the Glacier Inventory of Canada.

In 1977 our five-man *Virginia Glacier Expedition* flew directly to Cape Dyer carrying inflatable boats, which we used to reach the head of Sunneshine Fiord (Cochran 1978A). From there, we retraced our steps inland (where bears had destroyed our cache), climbed several new peaks and once more carried out a photographic glacier-survey under a contract from the Glacier Inventory of Canada. Then we embarked on 100-mile (160-km) journey southward along the coast. The method of boat travel on this expedition was notable for its fuel-economy and portability. We carried ourselves, with all gear and fuel, in two 12-foot (3.6-m) Avon inflatable dinghies powered by 3 h.p. Seagull engines. Reaching the head of an unnamed fiord between Totnes Road and Clephane Bay, we worked inland to locate and climb two peaks whose summits we had photographed and triangulated from 40 miles (65 km) away while climbing in 1967.

Baffin-Kingnait Expeditions: 1972 and 1973

The first of these ventures involved a dramatic boat trip to Kingnait Fiord, this time with my wife as one of us. Originally our goal had been Clyde River. In fact, our one-man advance party with much of our gear, had reached Clyde on a "scheduled weekly" flight from Frobisher Bay (now Iqualuit). Trouble began when the rest of us arrived in Frobisher Bay for the next flight and were told we would be lucky if there were one in a month. Reluctantly, we borrowed gear, and flew to Pangnirtung and our secondary objective north of Kingnait Fiord. Inevitably it was again about a 90-mile (145-km) boat trip from the settlement.

With the help of Ross Peyton, owner of the first hotel in Pangnirtung, we chartered a freighter canoe. After a radiotelephone call to our friend in Clyde (who announced wistfully that he had begun to train local climbing-partners), we set off on an epic voyage to Kingnait with two Inuit. The first evening we hit a floating chunk of ice at full speed, knocking a hole in the bow and nearly upsetting. We struggled through heavy pack ice for two days. Then our last (and nearly terminal) accident occurred in open water, when

FIGURE 2: Heading inland toward The Mitre with Inuit companions. Cape Dyer, 1967.

820

following seas half-swamped us. Fortunately we were close to an hospitable shore, but we learned to respect localized, "wind tunnel" effects in northern fiords.

After landing we waved goodbye to our reckless boatmen, hoping that Ross would find someone else to pick us up. The next day we backpacked up the valley, but towards evening my wife and I became desperate to see what lay ahead. We dropped our loads and hurried excitedly to the top of an ancient moraine. There we saw the upper valley, choked by ice that was split by a symmetrically-beautiful pointed rock peak amid spectacular mountains rising from unexplored glaciers (Figure 3).

We returned to base, and the next day had started back up the valley when a Piper Cub zoomed overhead. An hour later our stranded friend appeared over a hill! He had hitchhiked (with all our gear) from Clyde with a bird-surveyor and found a landing-site nearby. Thus reinforced, we headed up-valley and after climbing two peaks, found a route onto the glacier. There we encountered a blizzard and our time ran out. Again our boat arrived on schedule, but recruits to retrieve us had been scarce after tales of our outward journey had circulated through Pangnirtung.

In 1973 our return coincided with the making of the film *Land of the Big Ice* by John and Janet Foster. Although rare in those days, a small helicopter was in Pangnirtung for the film, and we negotiated transport to Kingnait Fiord in return for supplying (somewhat tongue-in-cheek) film-footage on climbing. Thus we had plenty of time to engage in a celebration of mountaineering. Despite more than a foot of new snow, we achieved first-ascents of our main objective, Naulik Mountain (5,750 ft or 1,750 m) as well as Qilaut Mountain (6,600 ft or 2,010 m, the highest in the area), and several others (Cochran 1974; Figure 4). These and other names proposed by us were translated and finally accepted both by the local community and the Canadian Board on Geographic Names in 1980. Thus began an interesting history which was continued by a British school expedition (Harben and Barton 1974), a Canadian student expedition to the adjoining valley (Amatt 1975), a French expedition (Romain 1979), and another group in 1978 that completed most of the major technical climbs in the area (Cauthorn 1979).

North Baffin Expeditions: 1974 and 1981

By 1974, the urge to move northward resulted in our heading for Coutts Inlet in northern Baffin Island. With 12-foot (3.6-m) Zodiac boats powered by 15 h.p. outboard

FIGURE 3: Naulik Mountain and Aybinnamat Glacier, Kingnait Fiord, 1967. Valhalla Mountain in background.

FIGURE 4: Ascent of Naulik Mountain, 1973 via the west face (behind ridge on left in Figure 3).

engines, we flew to Pond Inlet via Resolute and established camp on the beach. Soon we met Laurie Dexter, the Anglican pastor and an ardent climber, and Hermann Steltner, already a local legend, in his Arctic Research Establishment. A preliminary Zodiac trip as far as Guys Bight convinced the advance party that our plan was overly ambitious for Baffin Bay, so we hitched a ride on a large boat that was laying caches for spring polar bear surveys. Eventually, heavy ice blocked us from Coutts Inlet, and we were landed instead in Erik Harbour where some prominent inland peaks were visible from sea (Figure 5). We followed a tidewater glacier inland for 6-7 miles (about 10 km) and once again entered virgin country, although not as alpine as Kingnait. After climbing several peaks, we returned to the sea and used our Zodiacs to follow a chain of moraine lakes to additional climbs.

The boat picked us up in late August, but a storm made the trip rough. On the way to Pond Inlet, we recalled that our *North Baffin-Bylot Expedition* had not yet reached Bylot Island. So my wife, Curt Saville and I decided to rectify this omission. We gathered our gear in the dark and heaving hold, and near midnight the ship's canoe left us on a beach below the Narsarsuk Glacier, chosen as our route because it never had been ascended. Moving inland, we climbed a glorious peak (5,064 ft or 1,545 m) under perfect snow conditions (Cochran 1975; Figure 6) and were back in Pond Inlet three days later.

In May 1981 we returned for a short ski-mountaineering expedition having gained "spring" experience on Ellesmere Island in 1978. With the aid of Hermann Steltner, we spent a week testing our strain-measuring gear in sea ice, then headed for to the Narsarsuk Glacier by komatik. This time my wife and I with two companions skied 10-miles (16 km) inland to the head of the glacier and climbed Peak 5332 and another 5,000-ft (1,520 m) summit, thus completing the first exploration of this neglected corner of Bylot Island (Cochran 1982A).

The Makinson Inlet Expeditions: 1976, 1978, 1980, 1987

A fascination with the High Arctic brought us to the southeast coast of Ellesmere Island in 1976. There our map-research had identified an 1,800-foot (550-m) rock tower (Bowman Island) near the middle of Makinson Inlet. The nearest settlement was Grise Fiord, where, in 1968, Explorers Club member Lewis Cotlow had made a documentary-film on this Inuit community just before houses were built by the government. We planned to

FIGURE 5: The peaks of Erik Harbour, North Baffin, as seen from the sea, 1974.

FIGURE 6: Van and Caroline Cochran on the summit of peak 5064, Bylot Island, 1974.

spend 10 days there recording the changes since Cotlow's visit, and then fly to a beach on Makinson Inlet whence we hoped to reach the island using inflatable Avon dinghies.

On this trip we brought our 16-month daughter. Once installed in our tent-camp outside town she became an immediate success and facilitated introductions, paving the way for many enduring friendships. With the aid of Laurie Dexter, we recorded many traditional Inuit songs. Curt Saville's sound-slide program on the community now is part of the permanent collections at the Haffenreffer Museum in Providence, Rhode Island.

We were then joined by Ted Whalley and his ACC contingent and flew on to Makinson Inlet, while my wife and daughter remained in Grise Fiord. We found the fiord choked with broken sea ice making the 7-mile (11-km) boat journey to the island impossible (Figure 7). Nevertheless, from our base we covered a large area, making many ascents (Cochran and Whalley 1977; Cochran 1978B).

In April 1978 we returned with our first ski-mountaineering venture in the "spring window". Our plan, arranged after months of communication with leaders of the Grise Fiord community, was to hire snowmobiles and komatiks for the trip. Our party was large, consisting of a four-man advance group followed by Ted Whalley's group of six, plus my wife a week later. This put a severe strain on the resources of Grise Fiord and required my formal appearance before a group meeting of the town hunters to negotiate their help. Then, the Grise Fiord Inuit made 14, 200-mile (320-km) round-trip sled journeys via the difficult overland route to Makinson Inlet; no more loyal or hardworking group of expedition members could ever have been found.

Riding on top of the komatiks was a wild and exhausting introduction to sled-travel. We drove at 30 mph (48 kph) into high winds at -15°C. Dragging the sleds out of deep snow, we struggled over a 1,000-foot (300-m) pass then rode downhill along boulder-strewn ravines in the dim midnight sun. After two days, we were dropped at a base-camp site in the loneliest terrain we had ever seen. We used a snowmobile to skijor (skiers drawn by a vehicle) about the inlet, enabling us to cover a wide area, and to climb the island as well as several other peaks (Cochran 1979A,B; Figure 8). Also we refined our techniques for strain-gauging sea ice (Cochran 1980). But, Makinson Inlet's peaks were no longer untouched! In 1977, officers of the Geological Survey of Canada had visited the island and other points by helicopter.

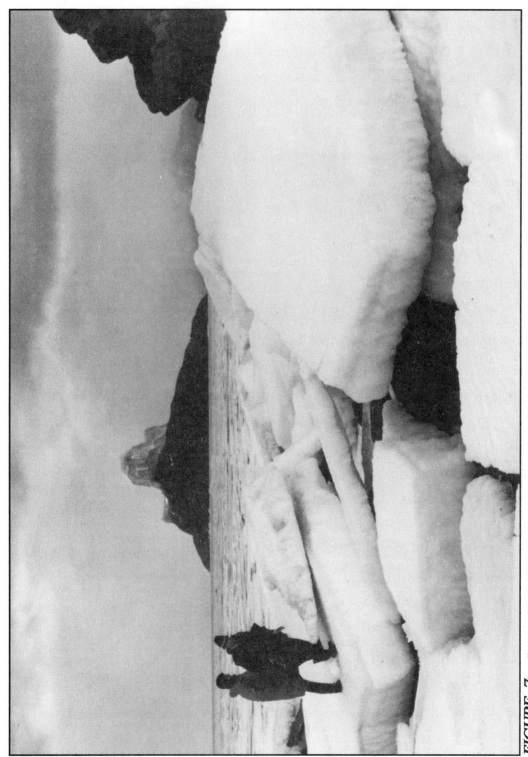

FIGURE 7: Bowman Island, Makinson Inlet, summer 1976.

828

FIGURE 8: Ski-mountaineering near Makinson Inlet, Ellesmere Island, 1978.

Lured by the Thorndike Peaks and Inglefield Mountains farther east along Makinson Inlet, I returned with another group, *The Inglefield Mountains Expedition*, in 1980 (Cochran 1983B). This time we brought two snowmobiles of our own and, using construction data acquired in 1978, built two komatiks in the South and air-freighted the lot to Grise Fiord. There our Inuit friends helped with the lashing, and in April we set off for Makinson Inlet, driving our own vehicles and komatiks with two supporting komatiks driven by our unforgettable coach Abraham Pijamini and a friend. If 1978 was difficult, 1980 was en eye-opener. The snow was so soft that four snowmobiles were needed to pull one load up the pass. Then we had to dig trails for hundreds of yards through the narrow ravines. Eventually, we arrived at Makinson Inlet only to find a jumbled nightmare of sea ice piled up by the fall winds and frozen in place. By now Pijamini's time off was over, and he left us with a comforting admonition: "You no watch out - you die!".

Now totally on our own, we tried route after route through the ice in fog and snow, winding back and forth, falling into holes and upending sledges. After a week we broke free near the Island (a two-hour trip on smooth ice), and later established base camp at the foot of a huge glacier leading north into the Inglefield Mountains. With barely a week left, all we could manage was an attempt on a 3,000-foot (910-m) peak at the gateway to Thorndike Peaks, and a three-day ski trip into the Inglefield Mountains, where we ascended one peak on skis and had a magnificent downhill run. On this trip we successfully used our combined sledge and backpack system for the first time.

In 1987, with satellite-photos available online at Resolute, we flew to Thorndike Peaks by Twin Otter. With limited time due to bad weather, our *Thorndike Peaks Expedition* managed a 25-mile (40-km) ski circuit of the range and made four first-ascents. So far, these four expeditions represent the only overland exploration of the peaks at Makinson Inlet (Cochran 1988).

Northern Ellesmere Island: 1982

Determined to climb north of Latitude 82°, we chose Yelverton Bay for our *Polar Mountains Expedition*. There we located several 6,000-foot (1,830-m) peaks in an area of the British Empire Range that had not been reached by earlier British expeditions. Flying direct from Resolute via Eureka, with the aid of Polar Continental Shelf Project, we had with us a snowmobile and one of our 1980 komatiks. Ambitiously, we planned climbs at several points around the bay as well as an extensive series of strain-gauge studies designed to use residual strain detection techniques to identify forces on the ice. Both plans were frustrated by yet another set of unforeseen circumstances. First, the ice was smooth but there was no wind in Yelverton Bay. This meant deep snow and difficult komatik travel. Second, the ice was the second-year variety: up to 14-ft (4.3-m) thick and not amenable to strain-gauge studies. We did manage to reach our major glacier objective, but ascending it on skis in deep snow, we encountered a maze of huge meltwater channels in the glacier - far more difficult to traverse than a crevasse-field. So, although we failed to climb the 6,000-ft (1,830-m) peaks, we did explore the glacier 16 miles (26 km) to its head, and there climbed a 5,000-ft (1,520-m) summit. Two other climbs also were made in this area (Cochran 1983).

SIGNIFICANCE

Over the years, great efforts have been expended on exploratory mountaineering in the Arctic Islands by many individuals. Aside from the personal rewards of these expeditions, they have been significant insofar as they have contributed to knowledge of the country and helped to open up new areas for recreational activities. National Parks exist on Baffin and Ellesmere islands today in places where scientists and exploratory mountaineers first walked. The Arctic has a seductive attraction that draws one back again and again. As such it constitutes a natural resource for Canada that should acquire increasing economic importance as the Arctic becomes more accessible - but hopefully never too accessible - to those who appreciate the wilderness of the unpredictable North.

ACKNOWLEDGEMENTS

I deeply appreciate the unfailing courtesy and assistance of individuals and agencies of the government of Canada and of the Northwest Territories, from senior officials to settlement managers and officers of the Royal Canadian Mounted Police. I am especially grateful to the Polar Continental Shelf Project for their logistical support on four expeditions.

Also, our Inuit friends of Grise Fiord and other settlements deserve special thanks, as do many other individuals including Jim Houston, Simon Ommanney, Hermann Steltner, Ross Peyton and Laurie Dexter. For financial aid, I thank George Wallace, The Albert Fried Foundation, The Harvey L. Karp Foundation, The Alpine Club of Canada and The Explorers Club. The expeditions were organized under the auspices of The Explorers Club and carried their traditional expedition flag.

REFERENCES

Amatt, J. 1975. Students in Baffin. Canadian Alpine Journal 58:54-55.

Baird, P.D. 1950. Baffin Island Expedition 1950: a preliminary report. Arctic 3(3):131-149.

_____. 1953. Baffin Island Expedition 1953: a preliminary report. Arctic 6(4):227-251.

_____. 1954. An ascent in Baffin Island. Canadian Alpine Journal 37:31-33.

_____. 1964. Alpine Club of Canada Baffin camp, 1963. Canadian Alpine Journal 47:1-15.

_____. 1966. Baffin Island 1965. Canadian Alpine Journal 49:28-42.

Banks, M. 1974. The uttermost North. Alpine Journal 79:174-177.

Cauthorn, D. 1979. The 1978 Northern Comfort Arctic Expedition. Canadian Alpine Journal 62:108.

Cochran, G.V.B. 1958. The mysterious plateau. Appalachia No. 126 (June):9-22.

_____. 1969. South to the Arctic Circle. Explorers Journal 47:214-225.

_____. 1974. Unexplored arctic mountains: 1972-73 Baffin Kingnait Expeditions. Canadian Alpine Journal 57:94-98.

_____. 1975. 1974 North Baffin-Bylot Expedition. Canadian Alpine Journal 58:95-98.

Cochran, G.V.B. 1978A. Virginia Glacier Expedition 1977. Canadian Alpine Journal 61:36-38.

_____. 1978B. Grise Fiord-Ellesmere Island Expedition. Explorers Journal 56:16-19.

_____. 1979A. Ellesmere-Bowman Island 1978. Canadian Alpine Journal 62:22-24.

Cochran, G.V.B. 1979B. Bowman Island Expedition. Explorers Journal 57:2-7.

_____. 1980. Field techniques for experimental stress analysis in arctic sea ice. Journal of Glaciology 25(91):175-182.

_____. 1982A. 1981 Bylot Island Expedition. Canadian Alpine Journal 65:97.

_____. 1982B. Ellesmere Island 1976-80: Makinson Inlet, Bowman Island and the Inglefield Mountains. Canadian Alpine Journal 65:38-41.

_____. 1983. Polar Mountains Expedition, Ellesmere Island,1982. Canadian Alpine Journal 66:28.

_____. 1988. Report of the Thorndike Peaks Expedition 1987 (Report submitted to Polar Continental Shelf Project).

Cochran, G.V.B. and P.C. Ritterbush. 1968. 1967 Cape Dyer Arctic-Alpine Expedition. Canadian Alpine Journal 51:185-198.

Cochran, G.V.B. and E. Whalley. 1977. 1976 Ellesmere-Makinson Expedition. Canadian Alpine Journal 60:11-12.

Errington, A. 1979. Broad Peak, Sam Ford Fiord, Baffin Island. American Alpine Journal 22:210-211.

_____. 1983. British Empire Range, Ellesmere Island. American Alpine Journal 25:175-178.

Erskine, A. 1974. A naval expedition to the shores of the Arctic Ocean 1972. Naval Review 62:18-21. (See also Expedition Report, privately published.)

Ferris, B.J. 1955. Arctic-Alpine ascents on Bylot Island. American Alpine Journal 9(2):168-169.

Goodman, D.J. 1982. Oh! Ellesmere. Canadian Alpine Journal 65:21-24.

Gribbon, P.W.F. 1961. Climbing in the Canadian northland. Irish Mountaineering 1961:31-37.

Harben, C. and R. Barton. 1974. Arctic Canada 74: the Clifton College Expedition to Baffin Island. Clifton College, Bristol. 72 pp. (Privately published report).

Hattersley-Smith, G. 1962. Ellesmere Island. Alpine Journal, 67:164-165.

_____. 1970. Barbeau Peak. Canadian Geographical Journal 80(3):86-91.

_____. 1974. North of Latitude Eighty. Defence Research Board, Canada, Ottawa. 121 pp.

Kelly, R. 1978. Bylot Island Expedition 1977. Canadian Alpine Journal 61:44-45.

Langford, R.E. 1962. The Cambridge Arctic Canada Expedition to Cumberland Peninsula, Baffin Island. Alpine Journal 67:97-110.

MacAdam, D.P. 1981. Island hopping at Padle Fiord, 1979. Canadian Alpine Journal 64:10-15.

Moore, A.W. 1936. The sledge journey to Grant Land. Oxford University Ellesmere Land Expedition III. Geographical Journal 87:419-427.

Muston, A.J. 1974. British Army Axel Heiberg Expedition, (Princess Margaret Range). Canadian Alpine Journal 57:93-94.

O'Connell, K. and E. Whalley. 1978. Baffin '77. Canadian Alpine Journal 61:50-52.

Romain, G. 1979. Expedition Dijonnaise à Kingnait Fiord 1978. Canadian Alpine Journal 62:104-105.

Scott, D. 1973. Mt. Asgard. Alpine Journal 78:85-88.

Tilman, H.W. 1964A. In: Mischief in Greenland. Hollis and Carter, London. pp. 160-167.

_____. 1964B. A crossing of Bylot Island. American Alpine Journal 14(1):205. (See also pp. 47-62 in Mostly Mischief. Hollis and Carter, London. 1966.)

Whalley, E. 1974. Baffin Island 1973. Canadian Alpine Journal 57:22-30.

_____. 1980. Baffin Island ACC climbing camp 1979. Canadian Alpine Journal 63:29-32.

Williams, S. 1980. Report of the Joint Services Expedition to Princess Marie Bay, Ellesmere Island, 1980. Directorate of Naval Physical Training and Sport, U.K. (Privately published).

Wordie, J.M. 1935. An expedition to Melville Bay and N.E. Baffinland. Geographical Journal 86:297-316.

Illustrated by Brenda Carter

INDEX

A

---

* *To gather all references to plant and animal species, please refer to both their common and scientific names.*

D

G

Galathée, 769
galeaspids, 69
Garrett Island, 610
Garrow Lake, 188, 189, 190, 198, 199, 200
Garry Island, 143
Gateshead Island, 593, 615
Gaul, 744
Gavia stellata, 519
Gaviidae, 519, 531
geese, 30, 283, 546, 564
genetic adaptations (insects), 457
Geochelone, 98
geographical exploration, 744
Geographical Society (London), 756
geography, 42, 44, 747, 760, 762
Geological Survey of Canada, 10, 37, 58, 106, 271, 763, 824
geology, 45, 758, 763, 764
Geomagnetic Pole, 44
geomagnetics, 37
geomorphology, 48
geophysics, 44, 754, 759
geopolitics, 46
Georyssus, 122
Gesellschaft für Erdkunde (Berlin), 756
Gilbert, William, 751
Gjøa, 26
Gjøa Expedition, 387
Gjøa Haven, 387, 614
Glacier Inventory of Canada, 816, 819
glaciers, 6, 265
Glaucous Gull, 526, 553
Glenelg Bay, 592
Glenn Highway, 34
Gleysols, 355
Glyptostrobus, 93, 115
gnathostomes (fish), 55, 63, 68, 75
gnats (fungus), 451
Godfrey, W.E., 572
Godthåb (Nuuk), 771
Good Friday Bay, 390
Government of Canada, 16, 344
government research stations, 582
Government of Canada, 763, 808
Government of Northwest Territories, 808
Government of Northwest Territories regional biologists, 583
graminoid-moss meadows, 367
Grant Land, 386
Granville, Earl, 771
graptolites, 59
grass-moss tundra, 356
grasses, 354, 480, 639, 647, 654
Gray, D.R., 571
Great Britain, 445, 754
Great Plain of the Koukdjuak, 728
Great Plains, 273
Great Whale River, 212
Greater White-fronted Goose, 522
Greece, 744
Greely Expedition (1881-1883), 386, 569, 793, 797, 799, 803
Greely, A.W., 570, 575, 799, 801, 809
green alder, 432
green algae, 375
Green Bay, 107, 116, 117, 119, 120, 123
Greenaway, K., 9
Greene, M.T., 22
Greenhithe, 768
"Greenhouse" effect, 46, 269, 271, 285, 286, 603

Greenland, 7, 14, 28, 29, 32, 33, 34, 42, 93, 188, 267, 269, 283, 284, 297, 353, 385, 386, 387, 472, 487, 518, 522, 527, 544, 546, 548, 549, 550, 573, 600, 602, 603, 610, 623, 667, 670, 672, 673, 675, 678, 688, 696, 699, 706, 738, 744, 746, 747, 752, 753, 754, 757, 761, 762, 763, 771, 797, 799, 806
Greenland Ice Cap, 761
Greenlanders, 30
Greenlandic Norse, 672
Greenpeace, 25, 28
Greenwich, 756
Grenfell, Lady, 797
Grenfell, Sir Wilfred, 794, 797
Griffith Island, 146, 773
Griffith, Captain, 773
Griffiths, F., 30
Grinnell Land, 386
Griper, 385, 572, 758
Grise Fiord, 613, 641, 794, 809, 824, 830
Grise Tower, 809
ground sloth, 162
ground squirrel (carcasses), 163
ground stone tools, 686
groundwater, 189
Growing Degree-Days, 422
growing-season, 451
Gruidae, 525, 531
Grus canadensis, 525
Gulf, 321
Gulf of Alaska, 353
gulls, 481
Gunn, A., 617
Guys Bight, 824
Gvozdev, Mikhail, 754
Gymnusa, 122
Gynaephora groenlandica, 456, 486, 487, 488, 489, 499, 500, 501, 502, 503, 504, 505, 506
Gynaephora rossii, 487, 501
Gynaephora, 455
gypsy moth, 500, 501, 503
Gyrfalcon, 522, 572, 574

H

Hadley Bay, 592
Hadley, John, 754
hadrosaur (juvenile), 88
Haffenreffer Museum (Providence, Rhode Island), 824
Halagoland, 746
Hale, Mason E., 389
half-buried (semi-subterranean) dwellings, 672, 688, 712, 717, 734, 771, 802
Haliaetus albicilla, 522
Hall Land, 761
Hall, Charles Francis, 761
halocline, 198, 247
Hamelin, L.-E., 23
Hamilton Island, 610, 619
Hamilton, Lieutenant, 771, 785
Hampson, C.G., 644
Hans Island, 390
Hantzch, B., 734
Hare, F.K., 337
hares, 575, 576, 648, 650, 657, 660, 661, 662, 778
Harington, C.R., 390, 570, 633
Harlequin Duck, 522
harpoons, 669, 672, 686, 688, 699, 704
Harrison, J., 9
Harrison, John, 754
Hart, H.C., 386

844

N

T

taeniodont, 94
Taimyr, 66
Talbot, 787
"talik", 189, 192, 200
Tamir, 763
Tanquary Fiord, 345, 390, 809, 810
taphonomy, 123
Taxodium, 115
Taylor Island, 574
Taylor, W.E., 705
technology, 50
Tedrow, J.C.F., 350
Tegethoff, 762
Teloschistes arcticus ("*Bonera* aurantiaca"), 390
temperature, 45, 311
Tener, John S., 1, 373, 390, 582, 616
tent rings, 712
terrestrial arthropods, 444, 445
territorial activities, 548, 563
Terror, 760, 769
Tertiary, 45, 91, 93, 101, 105, 117, 118, 124, 125
Tetraoninae, 524, 531
Thames River, 771
Thamnolia subuliformis, 357, 396
The Alpine Journal, 810
"The Birds of Canada", 517, 572
The Canadian Alpine Journal, 809, 810
The Dinosaur Project, 85
The Inglefield Mountains Expedition (1980), 830
The Mitre, 819
The Wash, 549
thelodont (fossils), 62, 63, 64, 67, 69, 75
thermocline, 198, 199
theropod (dinosaurs) - Alaskan, 86
Thick-billed Murre, 527
Thomson, J.W., 389, 390
Thorndike Peaks, 830
Thorndike Peaks Expedition (1987), 830
Thorne, Robert, 752
Thorsteinsson, R., 11, 58, 63, 65, 390
Thraupinae, 530
Thuidium abietinum, 120
Thuja occidentalis, 114
Thuja, 117
Thule (dog skull), 172
Thule (houses), 168, 174, 175, 178, 670, 673, 686, 688, 704
Thule (snow knife), 178
Thule Air Base, 27
Thule culture, 591, 672, 673, 675, 677, 678, 679, 680, 681, 685, 686, 687, 691, 693, 695, 697, 702, 705, 706, 707, 708, 711, 712, 718, 733, 734, 738, 740, 802
"Thule" (land), 744
Thule sites, 699, 702, 703, 704, 706, 716, 733
Thule whaling, 709
Thumb Mountain Formation, 192
tidal mixing, 216
tides, 214, 215, 219, 224
Tikera Bay, 734
Tilman, H.W., 808
Timmia, 119
Tipula (Arctotipula) besselsi, 474, 475, 477, 478
Tipula (Arctotipula), 477, 478
Tipula (Vestiplex) arctica, 475, 476
Tipula carinifrons, 456
Tipula hewitti, 475
Tipula sacra, 476
Tipula suttoni, 477
Tipula tribulator, 477

Tipulidae, 459, 471, 472, 474, 476, 477, 478, 480, 481
Titanic, 27
Todds Island, 614
Toll, E., 763
Tomenthypnum nitens, 119
Tomenthypnum, 120
toothed birds (hesperornithiforms), 86
Tortella fragillis, 119
tortoise, 98
Tortula ruralis, 357
Totnes Road, 808, 819
Toulon, 769
tourism, 48, 569, 813, 816
toxicology, 48, 291
Tozer, E.T., 11, 82, 111
trading posts, 593, 594, 596, 598
Trafton, Steve, 810
Transpolar Current, 759
Transport Canada, 298
transportation, 48
trapping, 593, 599, 601, 753
traquairaspids, 69, 74
Treaty of Tordesillas, 751
treeline, 124, 304, 423, 430, 437, 438, 516, 517, 519, 522, 524, 667
Trent, 758
Triassic, 82, 85
Trichocera columbiana, 460
trilophosaur, 82
Trochilidae, 530
Tromsö, 761
trout, 101
Truelove Inlet, 571
Truelove Lowland, 167, 341, 367, 489, 633, 635, 639, 640, 641
Truelove Valley, 635, 640
Tsar Alexander I, 754
Tsar Peter the Great, 754
Tsuga, 101
Tuckerman, Edward, 386
Tuktoyaktuk, 11, 19
tundra, 350, 355
Tundra Swan, 522
tunnit, 672, 673
turnstones, 548, 549, 550, 553, 555, 556, 559, 560, 562, 563, 564, 565
turtles, 86, 94, 99
twin flower, 430
Twin Otter aircraft, 619, 797, 813, 815, 830
Tyrannidae, 530

U

U.S. Academy of Sciences, 285
U.S. Defense Meteorological Satellite Program, 322
Ulmus, 115
umiaks, 672, 680, 699, 704
Ungava, 332, 333, 335, 387, 390, 434, 671
Union Bay, 772
United Kingdom, 550
United States, 32, 85, 304, 308, 322, 757, 801, 802, 803
University of Bristol, 71
University of Colorado, 390
University of Ottawa, 58, 71
University of Windsor, 340
University of Wisconsin, 390, 393
university students, 583
Upernavik, 771
Uria aalge, 527
Ursus arctos, 612
Ursus maritimus, 754
Uummannaq (Greenland), 163

V

W

Y

Z